SO YOU WANT TO SING MUSIC BY WOMEN

So You Want to Sing

Guides for Performers and Professionals

A Project of the National Association of Teachers of Singing

So You Want to Sing: Guides for Performers and Professionals is a series of works devoted to providing a complete survey of what it means to sing within a particular genre. Each contribution functions as a touchstone work not only for professional singers but also for students and teachers of singing. Titles in the series offer a common set of topics so readers can navigate easily the various genres addressed in each volume. This series is produced under the direction of the National Association of Teachers of Singing, the leading professional organization devoted to the science and art of singing.

So You Want to Sing Music Theater: A Guide for Professionals, by Karen S. Hall, 2013
So You Want to Sing Rock 'n' Roll: A Guide for Professionals, by Matthew Edwards, 2014
So You Want to Sing Jazz: A Guide for Professionals, by Jan Shapiro, 2015
So You Want to Sing Country: A Guide for Performers, by Kelly K. Garner, 2016
So You Want to Sing Gospel: A Guide for Performers, by Trineice Robinson-Martin, 2016
So You Want to Sing Sacred Music: A Guide for Performers, edited by Matthew Hoch, 2017
So You Want to Sing Folk Music: A Guide for Performers, by Valerie Mindel, 2017
So You Want to Sing Barbershop: A Guide for Performers, by Diane M. Clarke & Billy J. Biffle, 2017
So You Want to Sing A Cappella: A Guide for Performers, by Deke Sharon, 2017
So You Want to Sing Light Opera: A Guide for Performers, by Linda Lister, 2018
So You Want to Sing CCM (Contemporary Commercial Music): A Guide for Performers, edited by Matthew Hoch, 2018
So You Want to Sing for a Lifetime: A Guide for Performers, by Brenda Smith, 2018
So You Want to Sing the Blues: A Guide for Performers, by Eli Yamin, 2018
So You Want to Sing Chamber Music: A Guide for Performers by Susan Hochmiller, 2019
So You Want to Sing Early Music: A Guide for Performers, by Martha Elliot, 2019
So You Want to Sing Music by Women: A Guide for Performers, by Matthew Hoch and Linda Lister, 2019

SO YOU WANT TO SING MUSIC BY WOMEN

A Guide for Performers

Matthew Hoch
Linda Lister

Allen Henderson
Executive Editor, NATS

Matthew Hoch
Series Editor

A Project of the National Association of
Teachers of Singing

ROWMAN & LITTLEFIELD
Lanham • Boulder • New York • London

Published by Rowman & Littlefield
An imprint of The Rowman & Littlefield Publishing Group, Inc.
4501 Forbes Boulevard, Suite 200, Lanham, Maryland 20706
www.rowman.com

6 Tinworth Street, London, SE11 5AL, United Kingdom

British Library Cataloguing in Publication Information Available

Library of Congress Cataloging-in-Publication Data

Names: Hoch, Matthew, 1975– author. | Lister, Linda, 1969– author.
Title: So you want to sing music by women : a guide for performers / Matthew Hoch, Linda Lister.
Description: Lanham : Rowman & Littlefield, [2019] | Series: So you want to sing | Includes bibliographical references and index.
Identifiers: LCCN 2018047732 (print) | LCCN 2018048455 (ebook) | ISBN 9781538116074 (Electronic) | ISBN 9781538116050 (cloth : alk. paper) | ISBN 9781538116067 (pbk. : alk. paper)
Subjects: LCSH: Singing—Instruction and study. | Music by women composers—History and criticism.
Classification: LCC MT820 (ebook) | LCC MT820 .H696 2019 (print) | DDC 783/.043082—dc23
LC record available at https://lccn.loc.gov/2018047732

♾TM The paper used in this publication meets the minimum requirements of American National Standard for Information Sciences—Permanence of Paper for Printed Library Materials, ANSI/NISO Z39.48-1992.

Printed in the United States of America

To the female composers who blazed the trail,
and to those who continue to forge new paths for music by women.

CONTENTS

FIGURES

EXECUTIVE EDITOR'S FOREWORD

With this volume in the So You Want to Sing series, we have deviated from the traditional genre construct of this series and have chosen to emphasize and highlight the important contributions women composers have made and continue to make to the vocal art. It is a fact that compositions by women, although plentiful and of the highest quality, remain woefully underrepresented on every type of ensemble program, solo recital program, contemporary commercial music concert, and music theater and opera season in the world.

Why is that? We can place fault on the Western musical canon, male-dominated culture, well-documented historical attitudes within the composition world, the constraints of academic degree programs, the content of textbooks that blatantly omitted or ignorantly diminished the contributions of women composers, the historic lack of readily available editions of music by women, and a host of other factors. However, we must be realistic and honest with ourselves that the real reason lies within our own individual lack of initiative. Many of us have fallen under the influence of one or more of the "faults" listed above and taken the easy way out by programming recitals and concerts with the usual chestnuts found in published anthologies that grace our shelves, which are also dominated by male composers. Despite the voices in our field that have long supported and raised awareness of music by women, we remain somewhat complacent in our efforts.

In preparing this foreword, I recalled three important instances in my own career that have influenced me on this subject. When I was a doctoral student at the University of Cincinnati College-Conservatory of Music in the late 1980s and early 1990s, music history professor Karin Pendle was teaching a course on women in music at the same time that she published the first edition of her landmark textbook *Women in Music: A History* in 1991. While I am not sure that course was actually an option for me in meeting degree requirements, regretfully I did not register for it. However, the buzz around the conservatory at the time was that this was an important book, and indeed that has proven to be so. An opportunity was lost.

In 1994, I had the good fortune as a young academic to join the faculty of Austin Peay State University. There, I became a colleague of Sharon Mabry. For reasons that will become clear upon reading her introduction to this volume, I was the beneficiary of her wisdom, knowledge, and advocacy for music by women and—more broadly—contemporary composers. Her many columns in the *Journal of Singing* were of great service to the cause, advocating ardently for the programming of music by women.

Shortly after joining the faculty at Austin Peay, I was selected as an intern in one of the early classes of the NATS Intern Program, a selective professional mentoring program for voice teachers. The master teacher I was fortunate to be paired with was none other than Carol Kimball. She was feverishly working that summer on the completion of her book *Song: A Guide to Style and Literature*. Every morning—and at most meals together—we were treated to her revisions from the night before; most of her efforts involved adding more works by women and underrepresented composers to the manuscript.

These three women are among the many who have been championing music by women for decades. You may have similar stories of opportunities lost or enriching relationships that have influenced your thinking, performing, or teaching regarding this important topic. If not, perhaps this volume of collected wisdom will be that for you. With the publication of this book, it is our hope that our melting pot of lovers of singing will continue to build upon the efforts of these pioneering advocates, and that we will see a day when programming music by women becomes equitable—not because these are fine works of art by women, but because they are fine works of art . . . period.

Allen Henderson
Executive Editor, So You Want to Sing Series
Executive Director, National Association of Teachers of Singing

FOREWORD

Music written by women composers is all around us, and we may not know it. We hear it on the radio, on television, over earbuds, on the Internet, and on whatever platform we listen to music. It also appears in concert halls, but not nearly often enough. For too long, it has been a much-neglected repertoire in the teaching studio and on the concert stage.

When we are listening to music, do we consciously think, "That sounds like it was written by a woman"? I rather doubt it. No one has been able to define a concrete signal that would alert the musical mind to a particular sound that is "women's music" as opposed to that written by men. Yet, it seems that performers, teachers, and conductors most often choose music that was written by men for their own performances or those of their students. Why is that? Is it simply easier to rely on what we know and eschew curiosity, or do we assume that anything written by a woman might not be as good or popular as music written by a man? Whatever the reason, music written by men continues to be studied and programmed more than music by women. We must make a concerted effort to change that dynamic.

I had excellent training in voice and piano from the age of six, attended two outstanding music schools for undergraduate and graduate degrees, and studied voice with well-established, much-respected voice teachers. But it never occurred to me until 1982—when I was asked to present a recital at the Women in Music Festival at the University of Michigan—that I had never performed or even studied a piece of music by a female composer. When I looked back over all of my vocal repertoire, I was stunned. I immediately set out to alter that oversight, initially because I had to sing that recital at the University of Michigan. But later, I continued to add music by women to my repertoire because I discovered there is a wealth of great music out there to choose from. And because it was the right thing to do.

Over the past forty years, I have made it a point to include music by women equally with that of men in my recitals and those of my students. I have found that most of the singers who come to my studio as graduate students have done no music by women or perhaps only a piece or two, still to this day. We have to remember that women composers do not want to be segregated or thought of as better or different than their counterparts. They just want to be noticed and judged equally. It is the performers and programmers who have the greatest responsibility to respond to this need. So I encourage you, as singers and teachers of singing, to investigate this vast, untapped repertoire and bring something fresh to your audience.

Now that women have won all of the major composition prizes—from the Pulitzer Prize to the Prix de Rome to the Grawemeyer Award—plus a multitude of Grammy and Tony Awards, we can say that they are being judged on an equal basis with men for the first time in history. Therefore, we must provide a platform for the performance and criticism of music by women. Though women are making some strides, the programming of music by women is still at the single percentage level among all music programmed by ensembles and soloists. These appalling statistics concerning performance opportunities for the music and the lack of knowledge and recognition of major and lesser-known female composers stand for themselves.

It is obvious that music by women is still receiving too little attention by symphony orchestras, university curricula, performers, and teachers, as well as major arts organizations and awards entities such as the Academy and Tony Awards, where few women have won the award for Best Original Score. The current thinking is that concerts of only music by women are useful, but the music of women must be made more mainstream and included on a regular basis—alongside that of men—in order for it to be thought of as a normal thing to do. Much more has to be done to make this repertoire inclusive. As teachers, performers, conductors, music critics, and listeners, today's students will be the future for women in music. It is up to us, the educators and performers of today, to introduce this exciting new music to our students and the general public.

I am delighted to see this important volume, *So You Want to Sing Music by Women*, added to the So You Want to Sing series. It should be in the hands of anyone who wants to expand their repertoire, unearth hidden musical gems, and bring the music of women into the spotlight where it belongs.

Sharon Mabry
Professor of Voice
Austin Peay State University

ACKNOWLEDGMENTS

Many people were involved in the creation of this book, and the authors would like to thank several individuals in particular. First, we would like to thank the staff of Rowman & Littlefield, especially Natalie Mandziuk, Lara Hahn, Michael Tan, and the entire editing and production team for the opportunity to contribute to this series and for their help throughout the entire process. We would also like to thank Allen Henderson, executive director of NATS, for his support of this project and the entire NATS organization for their affirmation of women composers. The authors are indebted to Erin Guinup and Amanda Wansa Morgen for their expertise on music theater, CCM, and advocacy, as well as Sharon Mabry for her eager willingness to write the foreword. We are honored that such accomplished composers—Lori Laitman, Leanna Kirchoff, Rosephanye Powell, Meredith Monk, Georgia Stitt, and Martha Bassett—consented to being interviewed for the six profiles in the genre chapters. Linda would like to thank her coauthor, husband, and grandson Kyren for reminding her to take ballet dance breaks during the writing process. Matthew would like to thank his wife, Theresa, for her patience throughout the writing and editing process—for months, the dining room table was transformed into a writing workspace—and especially Linda for being everything he could hope for in a coauthor.

Last, but certainly not least, the authors would like to thank all of the women composers who inspired this book. *So You Want to Sing Music by Women* was written out of our deep conviction to advocate for them and celebrate their music, and the opportunity to publish this volume is one of the most worthwhile projects we have ever undertaken.

INTRODUCTION

Ithaca College, 1996. Dr. Edward Swenson, our music history professor, asked our class of about thirty music majors: "How many of you can name a woman composer?" Silence ensued.

True, this was more than twenty years ago, but my experience as a college professor over the past fourteen years has brought to my attention the problems of musical culture as it relates to gender. My students, now all millennials, also have trouble naming even one woman composer, and even the more erudite ones who have taken a music appreciation class tend to get stuck after "Clara Schumann" and "Fanny Mendelssohn (Hensel)." And who am I to judge? A look back at my seven degree-required recitals—from my BM through my DMA—reveals that all of the music I sang, 100 percent, was written by men. I am not proud of this, but no one at the time brought it to my attention. I was oblivious. And I sang these recitals in Ithaca, West Hartford, and Boston, three of the most progressive cities in the Northeast.

This culture, fostered in the shadow of the Western musical canon—or, in other words, white, male-dominated European culture—is precisely the reason why *So You Want to Sing Music by Women* is necessary. In addition to being a survey of the repertoire across all genres, it is also—and perhaps first and foremost—an advocacy book, encouraging singers and teachers of singing across all genres to program and perform music by women composers. While most of the books in the So You Want to Sing series have focused on a particular genre—music theater, rock 'n' roll, jazz, gospel, country, folk, barbershop, light opera, blues, and others—*So You Want to Sing Music by Women* is one of only three books that assumes another angle for the purpose of addressing an important issue with pedagogues and performers.[1]

From the moment of conception, I thought it was important for this project to be a coauthored book by a woman and a man. The feminine perspective is obvious and necessary, but culture cannot change unless everyone is on board. Since the musical world is still male-dominant, men have to be fully engaged as feminists and fighters for equality. Linda Lister—my friend, colleague, and *Voice Secrets* coauthor—instantly came to mind. A composer herself, Linda has long been an advocate for women composers. As colleagues at Shorter College from 2006 through 2010, I watched her engage in numerous projects championing women, including writing the libretto and music for an original opera about the Brontë sisters entitled *How Clear She Shines!* and writing the libretto for a show entitled *Your True Calling: Composing in the Shadow of Schumann, Mendelssohn, and Mahler* that featured the songs of Clara Schumann, Fanny Hensel, and Alma Mahler. During this time, I also founded the Shorter College New Music series, and our first composer-in-residence was a woman: Jocelyn Hagen of Minneapolis. Linda premiered her song cycle *The Time of Singing Has Come* in the fall of 2009.[2] These are just two of many examples of Linda's untiring support for women in our profession. Plus, we are a great writing team and were eager to follow up *Voice Secrets* with a "sequel" of sorts.

Since advocacy for women composers is an issue that transcends all genres, it was also important for us to include chapters devoted to music theater and CCM. Erin Guinup is a Seattle-based performer, teacher of singing, and director of the Tacoma Refugee Choir. She has toured internationally with her one-woman show *The Ladies of Lyric and Song: Female Composers and Lyricists of the American Musical Theatre*, in which she is both singer and narrator of a script she wrote herself. Upon watching her perform this piece in Stockholm, Sweden, at the 2017 International Congress of Voice Teachers (ICVT), I invited Erin to contribute the chapter on women in music theater. She also contributes an additional chapter on advocacy. Amanda Wansa Morgan, assistant professor and coordinator of musical theater at Kennesaw State University, was the perfect choice for the chapter on women in CCM. Also a composer herself—in addition to being a successful singer, pianist, music director, director, sound designer, dialect coach, and music arranger—Amanda is one of the most engaged younger members of our profession. These chapters both enrich the book and broaden its perspective.

We are also grateful to Sharon Mabry for writing the foreword to *So You Want to Sing Music by Women*. Not only is Dr. Mabry a longtime member of NATS, but she has also been a keen advocate for women composers for more than four decades. She was the perfect choice, and we are grateful for her eager and willing contribution. Like all books in the So You Want to Sing series, there are also several "common chapters." Scott McCoy contributes a chapter on voice production, Wendy LeBorge offers recommendations for maintaining vocal health, and Matthew Edwards addresses the basics of audio enhancement technology.

We hope this book will educate, inspire, and serve as a beacon of hope for the future, when the works of women composers will be heard as frequently as their male counterparts. The following passage—from Willa Cather's *O Pioneers!*—captures the essence of the woman composer's soul:

> Her lantern, held firmly, made a moving point of light along the highway, going deeper and deeper into the dark country. . . . She had never known how much the country meant to her. The chirping of the insects down in the long grass had been like the sweetest music. She had felt as if her heart were hiding down there, somewhere, with the quail and the plover and all the little wild things that crooned or buzzed in the sun. Under the long shaggy ridges, she felt the future stirring.[3]

NOTES

1. The other two are *So You Want to Sing for a Lifetime* (2018) by Brenda Smith and the forthcoming *So You Want to Sing with Awareness* (2020), edited by Matthew Hoch.

2. The premiere, which took place on September 14, 2009, also featured Chuck Chandler (b. 1979), tenor, and Ben Harris (b. 1978), piano.

3. The author first encountered this quotation in the introduction to James Briscoe's *Contemporary Anthology of Music by Women* (Bloomington: Indiana University Press, 1997).

ONLINE SUPPLEMENT NOTE

So You Want to Sing Music by Women features an online supplement courtesy of the National Association of Teachers of Singing. Visit the link below to discover additional exercises and examples, as well as links to recordings of the songs referenced in this book.

http://www.nats.org/So_You_Want_To_Sing_Book_Series.html

A musical note symbol ♪ in this book will mark every instance of corresponding online supplement material.

1

MUSIC BY WOMEN

A Brief History

Over the past four decades, there has been increased interest in exploring the contributions of women to the canon of Western classical music. This long-overdue appearance of "women in music" as an academic subject has resulted in the publication of textbooks and the creation of courses devoted to the topic at many colleges and universities across the United States and abroad. This opening chapter will present a broad historical overview of women in music, outlining the most important topics that one might study in an undergraduate survey course. In the following pages, the music of all eras, instruments, and genres will be considered before proceeding to the rest of the book, which will focus exclusively on vocal music composed by women.

REEXAMINING HISTORY

Throughout most of history, women who wished to compose worked in the shadows, requiring the modern musicologist to engage in some detective work when seeking to rediscover their music. While occasional publications by women did occur prior to the nineteenth century, these instances were rare, and most compositions by women were never published. Many other manuscripts have been lost. The convents were one venue through which women had the opportunity to both compose and preserve their work, and many of the earliest examples of music by women were sacred works written by abbesses and nuns.

As history moved along, women composed secular music for performance in the home; their works were mostly songs and piano music and occasional chamber works. Women generally did not attempt larger genres such as symphonies and operas, as these performances were public endeavors that were difficult to organize and expensive to mount. In other words, they were the province of men. The few women who were given these opportunities were almost always related—by blood or by marriage—to famous male composers, were extremely wealthy, or both. These historical challenges that women composers faced will be discussed in greater detail in chapter 2 of this book.

Studying the history of women in music is also multifaceted, exploring their music from all angles. Many textbooks examine women performers and patronesses of music alongside composers, painting a fuller and more complete portrait of contributions of women to each era. Although this book focuses primarily on the composers—advocating that we actively study, program, and perform the literature created by women—this survey will also mention several of the patronesses and performers who made a significant impact on history, especially during the medieval and Renaissance eras, when very few women were afforded opportunities to perform and publish works.

WOMEN COMPOSERS: A TIMELINE

The following pages will provide a walkthrough of some of the most important women composers in Western music, as well as some of the most important events. Due to the confines of this single chapter, many composers—even important ones—will unfortunately be omitted, but the names listed here are likely to be the ones most commonly encountered when first exploring the topic of women in music. This portion of the chapter, by convention, is organized according to broad historical epochs, but the dates indicated are for the convenience of oversimplification. There is considerable overlap between eras; the seeds of the future are almost always planted before the era begins, just as conservative composers tend to cling to past traditions. While this overview is devoted exclusively to composers of the Western classical canon, this is by no means the only tradition in which women created music. Chapters 7 and 8 of this book will be devoted to exploring the history of women's contributions to music theater and contemporary commercial music (CCM) styles.

The Medieval Era (ca. 800–1400)

Women have been creating music ever since ancient times. Sappho (ca. 612 BCE), for example, was renowned as a poet-musician in ancient Greece. It is also almost certain that women in convents participated in sung liturgy from the early Christian era. We know in particular that the psalms were intended to be sung. The Greek word ψαλμοι or *psalmoi* literally means "songs accompanied by string instruments." Kassia (ca. 810–865) was an important composer of Byzantine chant, and there is also evidence that women were active as troubadours and trouvères. Beatriz de Dia (ca. 1160–1212)—also called "La Comtessa de Dia"—was a famous example of a female troubadour, or *trobairitz*, and Maria de Ventadorn (1165–1221) and Eleanor of Aquitaine (1122–1204) were important patrons of troubadours. Dame Maroie de Diergnau and Dame Margot (both fl. ca. 1250) were trouvères from Arras. Together, they wrote a *jeu-parti* (debate song) that has been preserved in two manuscripts.[1]

By far the most important woman composer of the medieval era—and one of the most important names in the history of women in music—is the Benedictine abbess Hildegard von Bingen (1098–1179). Hildegard was born in Bermersheim, near Alzey in Rhine-Hesse. One of the great thinkers of her day, her achievements went well beyond musical and poetic endeavors and encompassed many other disciplines, including theology, hagiography, medicine, and science. Among musicians, she is best known for her dramatic play, *Ordo virtutum* (*Play of Virtues*), and for her collection of nearly eighty chants, all gathered under the title *Symphonia armoniae celestium revelationum* (*Symphony of the Harmony of Celestial Revelations*). Hildegard wrote many antiphons for the Virgin Mary, including "O frondens virga." The melismatic text setting and wide vocal range in comparison to other twelfth-century chants

Figure 1.1. Hildegard von Bingen (line engraving by W. Marshall). *Creative Commons (CCBY-SA 4.0)*

typifies her sophisticated compositional style. Hildegard lived until the age of eighty-one, dying in her convent at Rupertsberg. ♪

The Renaissance Era (1400–1600)

While the Renaissance era does not seem to have a woman whose stature looms as largely as Hildegard's, women actively made music during this period—although their work was not acknowledged in most music history books until recently. One of the most frequently cited figures from the Renaissance is Margaret of Austria (1480–1530), who was also one of the most important political figures in Europe. Margaret's principal contribution to music history was her curation of an extensive library, which contained many volumes of music. Some of the manuscripts preserved are believed to have been composed—in whole or part—by Margaret herself. The motet "Se je souspire / Ecce itrum novus dolor" is one such piece. The Italian composer Maddalena Casulana (ca. 1544–ca. 1590) was also an accomplished composer of madrigals and the first woman who successfully published volumes of her own music.[2] ♪

During the Renaissance, it is much easier to identify patronesses of music than composers. In addition to Margaret of Austria, Queen Elizabeth I (1533–1603) of England and Isabella d'Este (1474–1539) at the court of Mantua are other examples of political figures who did much to encourage and support composers. The reality is, however, that the Renaissance represents a very bleak era in the history of women in music. Musically inclined women by and large gave up their studies when they became wives or entered the convent. It is possible that we have not yet uncovered the full story of the role that women composers played during this fruitful age of artistic creativity and intellectual thought. Karin Pendle (b. 1939) wisely writes, "Perhaps with more time and research we can someday claim that women of early modern Europe had a Renaissance."[3]

The Baroque Era (1600–1750)

The birth of opera signaled the dawn of the baroque era, characterized musically by the invention of monody, instrumental writing, and an explosion of secular compositions. Claudio Monteverdi (1567–1643) is often credited with the conscious shift from the prima prattica—or Renaissance style of composition—to the seconda prattica, or baroque style, in his *Fifth Book of Madrigals* (1605). In the middle of this work, Monteverdi shifts from the imitative, unaccompanied Renaissance style of composition in the style of Giovanni Pierluigi da Palestrina (ca. 1525–1594) to a baroque, monodic style with basso continuo and figured bass.

The Florentine Camerata also championed monody, and the earliest operas were all written in this new baroque style. Opera composers began to write roles intended to be sung by women. Claudio Monteverdi wrote his opera *Arianna* as a vehicle for the famous soprano Caterina Martinelli (ca. 1589–1608).[4]

By the early 1600s, publications by women composers began to occur more frequently. The Benedictine nun Caterina Assandra (ca. 1590–after 1618) published her *Motetti*, Op. 2, in 1609, and Lucia Quinciani (ca. 1566–fl. ca. 1611) and Francesca Caccini (1587–after 1641) published monodies in 1611 and 1618, respectively. A most significant event in the early Italian baroque period occurred on February 3, 1625, when Francesca Caccini's opera, *La liberazione di Ruggiero dall'isola d'Alcina*, was performed in Florence as part of the Carnaval festival and celebration. This work is the earliest example of a complete opera written by a woman; the score has also survived in its entirety, and the work is still programmed today. Caccini's opera is discussed in greater detail in chapter 4 of this book. Other important secular music that was published in the following years included a 1629 book of arias by Francesca Campana (ca. 1615–1655), and Barbara Strozzi (1619–1677) published her first book of solo madrigals in 1644. Strozzi's secular songs—which will be covered in chapter 3—were important forerunners of the romantic art song.

Sacred music published during this time included *Sacri concerti* (1630) by the Milanese nun Claudia Rusca (1593–1676), the *Primavera de fiori musicali* (1640) by Chiara Margarita Cozzolani (1602–1678), and a 1665 book of motets by Isabella Leonarda (1620–1704). Cozzolani published several collections of works, many of which are now lost. Sophie Elisabeth, Duchess of Brunswick-Lüneberg (1613–1676) also published several collections of hymn melodies. Maria Margherita Grimani (fl. ca. 1713–1718) is a rare example of a late baroque woman composer who wrote oratorios and dramatic works, the most important of which are *Pallade e Marte* (1713), *La visitazione di Santa Elisabetta* (1713), and *La decollazione di Santa Giovanni Battista* (1715).

The most important figure from the French baroque is Élisabeth Jacquet de la Guerre (1665–1729). Jacquet de la Guerre was a child prodigy and harpsichord virtuoso who attracted the attention of Louis XIV (1638–1715), who served as her patron until his death.[5] At Louis XIV's court, she was introduced to and heavily influenced by the *tra-*

Figure 1.2. Élisabeth Jacquet de la Guerre (portrait by François de Troy). *Creative Commons (CCBY-SA 3.0)*

gédies en musique of Jean-Baptiste Lully (1632–1687) and his librettist, Jean-Philippe Quinault (1635–1688). Jacquet de la Guerre's accomplishment cannot be understated; she prolifically wrote and published in virtually every genre popular in France at the time and is credited with introducing the Italian style to Lully and his contemporaries. Although she composed a wide variety of vocal and instrumental works, Jacquet de la Guerre is perhaps best known for her many works for harpsichord (or cembalo). She published a total of six cembalo suites: four in 1687 and two in 1707. These virtuosic works feature improvisatory preludes that are considered to be an important influence on the works of her contemporary François Couperin (1668–1733) and essential precursors to the keyboard suites of George Frideric Handel (1685–1759). ♪

The Classical Era (1750–1820)

The triumvirate of Joseph Haydn (1732–1809), Wolfgang Amadeus Mozart (1756–1791), and Ludwig van Beethoven (1770–1827) looms large over the classical era, eclipsing most other male composers let alone female ones. Most students of music—even those who have completed their undergraduate history sequence—have difficulty naming composers in addition to these three.[6] Nevertheless, several names of women composers (some of whom were also performers) during this period are remembered, including Maria Teresa Agnesi (1720–1795), Princess Anna Amalia of Prussia (1723–1787), Anna Bon (1739–1767), Elisabeth Olin (1740–1828), Maddalena Laura Lombardini Sirmen (1745–1818), Henriette Adélaïde Villard de Beaumesnil (1748–1813), Corona Schröter (1751–1802), Maria Hester Park (1760–1813), and Maria Theresia von Paradis (1759–1824), all minor figures in the shadows of Haydn, Mozart, and Beethoven.

The most accomplished woman composer of the classical era is Marianna von Martines (1744–1812). Martines was born into a wealthy musical family in Vienna, where her father served as *maestro di camera* (master of ceremonies) at the papal embassy. Thus, from an early age, Martines had the opportunity through her father to meet many of Vienna's most accomplished composers and hear their music.[7] A child of great privilege, Martines studied singing with Nicola Porpora (1686–

1768) and harpsichord with Haydn. Over the course of her long life, she composed more than two hundred works, nearly seventy of which are extant today. Her most well-known pieces are the orchestral work *Overture in C* (1770), the motet *Dixit Dominus* (1774), and her many keyboard works. Martines's keyboard works exemplify the rococo style that was in vogue in Vienna during the eighteenth century.[5] ♪

The Romantic Era (1820–1900)

By the close of the classical era, pianos began to become common-place in private residences, a phenomenon that opened numerous doors to homebound wives with compositional aspirations. In the early eighteenth century, several important collections of lieder by women composers were published, most notably the *Zwölf Gesänge* of Louise Reichardt (1779–1826) in 1811 and the *Sechs Lieder*, Op. 6, of Emilie Zumsteeg (1796–1857) in 1842. In between these two publications, the French composer and musicologist Sophie Bawr (1773–1860) published the first history of women in music—the *Histoire de la musique*—which was part of a larger multivolume work entitled *Encyclopédie des Dames* (1823). The Polish composer Maria Szymanowska (1789–1831) also published two important works in 1820: the *Divertimento* for violin and piano and *Sérénade* for cello and piano. The most prominent women composers who were active during the first half of the nineteenth century were the wife and sister of two of the most famous composers in Europe: Clara Wieck Schumann (1818–1896), the wife of Robert Schumann (1810–1856), and Fanny Mendelssohn Hensel (1805–1847), the older sister of Felix Mendelssohn (1809–1847). Clara's *Piano Trio in G Minor*, Op. 17 (1846), is a rare example of nineteenth-century work composed by a woman that is part of the standard chamber music reper-tory. The achievements of these two female titans of classical music will be discussed at greater length later in this book. ♪

The most important women composers of the second half of the cen-tury included giants such as Louise Farrenc (1804–1875), Pauline Viar-dot (1821–1910), and Cécile Chaminade (1857–1944) of France; Amy Beach (1867–1944) and Teresa Carreño (1853–1917) of the United States; and Ethel Smyth (1858–1944) of England. European schools began to admit women into their composition programs. Smyth studied at the Leipzig Conservatory in 1877, and in 1879, Maude Valérie White (1855–1937) became the first woman to win the Mendelssohn Prize while at the Royal Academy of Music in London. That same year, Alma Mahler (1879–1964) was born, a woman who would write some of the most important lieder by a female composer. The last two decades of the nineteenth century saw the birth of Rebecca Clarke (1886–1979), Germaine Tailleferre (1892–1983), and Lili Boulanger (1893–1918), three women composers who would each, in her own way, usher in the modern era.

The Modern Era (1900–present)

The twentieth century—perhaps the most transformational century in the history of the world due to the technological revolution—witnessed an explosion of activity by women composers, with literally thousands of works written, published, and performed. The century witnessed numerous "firsts," including the founding of the Society of Women Musicians (1911), the first woman to win the Prix de Rome (1913), the first knighting of a woman composer (1922), the first performance of a work by an African American woman composer by a major symphony orchestra (1933), the first opera by an American woman to be produced at a major European opera house (1962), the first female president of the American Musicological Society (1975), the first woman to win the Pulitzer Prize in Music (1983), and the founding of the International Alliance for Women in Music (1995).[9] Clearly, some progress was being made.

Because of this intense flowering of compositional activity, much of this book will focus on women composers born in the twentieth century and their works. Ruth Crawford Seeger (1901–1953) is perhaps the first major woman composer who was born in the twentieth century; her posttonal, modernist style can be heard in her 1926 work *Music for Small Orchestra*. There are too many additional important female composers to list adequately here, but some of the most frequently studied in survey courses include Miriam Gideon (1906–1996), Elizabeth Maconchy (1907–1994), Vivian Fine (1913–2000), Violet Archer (1913–2000), Thea Musgrave (b. 1928), Sofia Gubaidulina (b. 1931), Pauline Oliveros (1932–2016), Ellen Taaffe Zwilich (b. 1939), Meredith Monk (b. 1942), and Augusta Read Thomas (b. 1964). This book will discuss the vocal works of some of these composers in chapters 3 through 6, which examine the achievements of women in the genres of art song, opera, choral music, and experimental works. ♪

WOMEN IN POPULAR AND WORLD MUSIC

If the history of classical music revolves around composers, performers emerge as the central figures of popular music, and over the course of the twentieth century—when popular music became a worldwide phenomenon through recordings and radio airplay—many women emerged as icons of the genre. Although this book focuses on composers, most courses on women in music include the study of popular music, which examines the social impact of women performers. In the United States, some of the most important singers of the twentieth century included Broadway's Ethel Merman (1908–1984), gospel's Mahalia Jackson (1911–1972), the jazz singer Ella Fitzgerald (1917–1996), rock's Janis Joplin (1943–1970), the folk singer Joni Mitchell (b. 1943), and R&B/hip-hop icon Lauryn Hill (b. 1975). Still other women became so synonymous with their genre that they earned sobriquets: Kitty Wells (1919–2012) was known as the "Queen of Country," Irma Thomas (b. 1941) as the "Soul Queen of New Orleans," and Madonna (b. 1958) as the "Queen of Pop." These are just a few historical examples of the many women performers who shaped the history of popular music. ♪

Female performers have also had significant impact in the arena of world music, serving as cultural ambassadors of their nations and introducing audiences across the globe to new genres and vocal styles. Some of the most famous examples include Egypt's Umm Kulthum (1904–1975), who introduced Arabic music to listeners outside of the Middle East; Édith Piaf (1915–1963), a French cabaret singer of chansons; Chavela Vargas (1919–2012), a Mexican *ranchera* singer; Portugal's Amália Rodrigues (1920–1990), known as the "Rainho do Fado" ("Queen of Fado"); and Celia Cruz (1925–2003) of Cuba, who specialized in salsa. Asha Bhosle (b. 1933) has performed as a playback singer for more than one thousand Bollywood films, cementing her status as the most recognized voice in India. Other important women in

Figure I.3. Joni Mitchell, 1974. *Creative Commons (CCBY-SA 1.0)*

world music include the Romani singer Esma Redžepova (1943–2016) of Macedonia, bossa nova singer Elis Regina (1945–1982) of Brazil, flamenco artist Concha Buika (b. 1972) of Spain, and Radmilla Cody (b. 1975), who actively works to preserve the traditional Navajo music of North America. "As the world's axes of population, power, and commerce shift from North to South and from East to West, the old Eurocentric model of culture is giving way to a new global paradigm."[10] The study of women in world music is certain to be an essential part of twenty-first-century studies devoted to music by women. ♪

PRIZE-WINNING WOMEN COMPOSERS

Since the early twentieth century, several awards and prizes have become important beacons of recognition for composers. Some of the

Figure 1.4.   Radmilla Cody, 2002. *Creative Commons (CCBY-SA 1.0)*

most significant for classical composers have been the Prix de Rome, the Pulitzer Prize, and the Grawemeyer Award. The Academy Awards—the annual awards ceremony of the Academy of Motion Picture Arts and Sciences—offer two "Oscars" for Best Original Score and Best Original Song, and the Antoinette Perry or "Tony" Awards of the American Theatre Wing recognize the Best Original Score of the Broadway season. Perhaps not surprisingly, these awards have been overwhelmingly won by men over the years, with only a few women breaking the glass ceiling in each category. These trailblazers are discussed below.

The Prix de Rome

The Prix de Rome was an annual prize offered by the French Académie des Beaux-Arts in Paris. The award was established in 1663 during the reign of Louis XIV, but prizes were only awarded to painters and sculptors. The category for music composition was established in 1803, suspended only during the two world wars. Winners of the Prix de Rome were awarded with a funded period of study in Rome. The last Prix de Rome awards were given in 1968, when the program was abolished by French minister of culture André Malraux (1901–1976). Lili Boulanger (1893–1918) became famous throughout Europe in 1913, when she became the first woman to win the Prix de Rome for her cantata *Faust et Hélène*.[11] Boulanger was the first of ten women who were Prix de Rome winners. The other nine were Margarite Canal (1890–1978) in 1920, Jeanne Leleu (1898–1979) in 1923, Elsa Barraine (1910–1999) in 1929, Yvonne Desportes (1907–1993) in 1932, Odette Gartenlaub (1922–2014) in 1948, Adrienne Clostre (1921–2006) in 1949, Éveline Plicque-Andreani (fl. ca. 1960) in 1950, Thérèse Brenet (b. 1935) in 1965, and Monic Cecconi-Botella (b. 1936) in 1966. Although most of these women went on to have successful careers as musicians, none of the composers who followed Boulanger have come close to matching her legacy.[12]

The Pulitzer Prize

The Pulitzer Prize is an award given to honor outstanding achievements in American journalism, literature, and music composition. Administered by Columbia University in New York City, the prizes were first awarded in 1917, and the first Pulitzer Prize for Music was given in 1943. At the time of the writing of this book, seven women have won the Pulitzer Prize for Music, four of them since the year 2010. In 1983, Ellen Taaffe Zwilich became the first woman in history to win the Pulitzer Prize for her *Three Movements for Orchestra*. Zwilich, also the first woman to receive the DMA from the Juilliard School, has had a long career as professor of composition at Florida State University. The other six women composers who have won the Pulitzer Prize include Shulamit Ran (b. 1949) in 1991 for her *Symphony*; Melinda Wagner (b. 1956) in 1999 for her *Concerto for Flute, Strings, and Percussion*; Jennifer Higdon (b. 1962) in 2010 for her *Violin Concerto*; Caroline Shaw (b. 1982) in 2013 for her choral work *Partita for 8 Voices*; Julia Wolfe (b. 1958) in 2015 for her secular oratorio *Anthracite Fields*; and Du Yun (b. 1977) in 2017 for her opera *Angel's Bone*. The trend of the past decade—with women winning every other year (the same frequency as men)—represents an important shift and a sign of progress that hopefully will continue. ♪

The Grawemeyer Award

The Grawemeyer Awards are five awards that are given annually by the University of Louisville.[13] One of these prizes is the Grawemeyer Award for Music Composition. The award is one of the most substantial in the composition world, ranging from $100,000 to $150,000 over the course of the award's history. Unlike the Pulitzer Prize, which only honors American citizens, the Grawemeyer Foundation accepts nominations from all over the world. Since 1985—the prize's inaugural year—only two women have won the Grawemeyer Award for Music Composition: Finnish composer Kaija Saariaho (b. 1952) in 2003 for her opera *L'amour de loin* and South Korean composer Unsuk Chin (b. 1961) in 2004 for her *Concerto for Violin and Orchestra*. ♪

The Academy Awards

The annual Academy Awards—or "Oscars" as they are called in American culture—are Hollywood's biggest event of the year, and there are two categories in which the Oscars honor composers: Best Original Score and Best Original Song. The first Academy Awards ceremony was held on May 16, 1929, and the Oscars for these two categories were first awarded in 1935. Since that time, only three women have won in the scoring categories—two of them for music and one for lyrics. Composers Rachel Portman (b. 1960) and Anne Dudley (b. 1956) won Oscars for *Emma* (1996) and *The Full Monty* (1997), respectively, and lyricist Marilyn Bergman (b. 1929) won an Oscar in the Best Original Score category for *Yentl* (1983). Only three other woman—Angela Morley (1924–2009), Lynn Ahrens (b. 1948), and Mica Levi (b. 1987)—have ever been nominated in the category of Best Original Score.[14] ♪

Fortunately, women have fared a bit better in Best Original Song category, with ten women winning twelve Academy Awards since 1936, when Dorothy Fields (1904–1974) took home an Oscar as lyricist for "The Way You Look Tonight" from *Swing Time*. Five of these women songwriters wrote both the music and the lyrics: Carly Simon (b. 1945), Carole Bayer Sager (b. 1947), Melissa Etheridge (b. 1961), Adele (b. 1988), and Kristen Anderson-Lopez (b. 1972). Two of them—Buffy Sainte-Marie (b. 1941) and Barbra Streisand (b. 1942)—were composers only, and the remaining three were lyricists: Fields, Bergman, and Irene Cara (b. 1959). Bergman and Lopez are the only two women who have won multiple times in this category, each winning the award twice. As of 2018, women have received a collective total of seventy nominations for Best Original Song at the Academy Awards.[15]

The Tony Awards

The Antoinette Perry Awards—commonly known as the "Tony" Awards—are given each June by the American Theatre Wing to honor excellence in Broadway theater. The first Tony Awards ceremony was held on April 6, 1947, and the Tony for Best Original Score has been awarded every year since then. In spite of this long history, only three women have won the Tony for Best Original Score without male writing partners and for only two musicals: Cyndi Lauper (b. 1953) won her Tony for the music and lyrics to *Kinky Boots* in 2013, and Jeanine Tesori (b. 1961) and Lisa Kron (b. 1961) each took home a Tony for the music and lyrics (respectively) for *Fun Home* in 2015. As of 2018, Lauper and

Tesori are the only composers who have won the Tony for Best Original Score, but three others have won as lyricists: Betty Comden (1917–2006), Lynn Ahrens, and Lisa Lambert (b. 1962). These three women have won a total of five Tonys but all with the assistance of male writing partners. Comden's three Tonys were for the musicals *Hallelujah, Baby!* (1968), *On the Twentieth Century* (1978), and *The Will Rogers Follies* (1991); Lynn Ahrens won in 1998 for *Ragtime*; and Lisa Lambert took home a Tony in 2006 as the co-composer and lyricist of *The Drowsy Chaperone*.[16] These dismal numbers—particularly in the lack of women composers represented—are indicative of the challenges women writers face in the music theater industry and on Broadway in particular. These issues will be examined in greater detail in chapter 7.

ALL-WOMEN ORCHESTRAS

Beginning in the late nineteenth century, an interesting phenomenon began to emerge: the first appearance of all-women orchestras. Shut out of the many all-male orchestras on both sides of the Atlantic, women simply decided to form their own ensembles in the early 1870s. Some of the earliest all-women orchestras were the Vienna Damen Orchester and Berlin Damen Orchester in Europe and, in the United States, the Ladies Philharmony and the Women's String Orchestra of New York. In 1888, the Boston Fadette Orchestra was formed; this ensemble would tour the United States for the next thirty years, performing more than six thousand concerts. By the end of the second decade of the twentieth century, male orchestras began admitting women. The first orchestra to do so was the Queens Hall Orchestra of London in 1919. But the tradition of all-female ensembles was by then well established, and the tradition continued.[17]

The oldest continuously running women's orchestra in the world that is still active is the Cleveland Women's Orchestra, which was founded in 1935; the current conductor is Robert Cronquist (b. 1929). During World War II, two notable ensembles were formed by prisoners of war: the Women's Orchestra of Auschwitz in the spring of 1943 and the Women's Vocal Orchestra of Sumatra (1943–1944), which was technically a choral group, not an orchestra.[18] Women's ensembles that are

Figure 1.5. Vienna Damen Orchester. *Creative Commons (CCBY-SA 1.0)*

no longer active include the Montreal Women's Symphony Orchestra (1940–1965), Orchestrette Classique of New York (1832–1943), and the Women's Philharmonic of San Francisco (1981–2004).

THE EMERGENCE OF PROFESSIONAL ORGANIZATIONS

In the early twentieth century, women composers began to organize, and the first professional organizations for women composers were created. In 1911, the Society of Women Musicians was founded in London with composer and soprano Liza Lehmann (1862–1918) as its first president. At its opening meeting, pianist and composer Katharine Emily Eggar (1874–1951) proclaimed: "The conventions of music must be challenged. Women are already challenging conventions in all kinds of ways. Everywhere we see them refusing to accept artificialities for realities. We believe in a great future for women composers."[19] The Society of Women Musicians ran for sixty-one years and with many prominent composers assuming the presidency, including Cécile Chaminade and Elizabeth Poston (1905–1987). The society disbanded in 1972, and its archives were given to the Royal College of Music in London.

The most visible organization for women composers that is active today is the International Alliance for Women in Music (IAWM). The IAWM was formed in 1995 from the merger of three organizations that "arose during the women's rights movements of the 1970s to combat inequitable treatment of women in music": the International League of Women Composers (ILWC), the International Congress on Women in Music (ICWM), and American Women Composers (AWC), Inc.[20] According to the IAWM website, the organization comprises "women and men dedicated to fostering and encouraging the activities of women in music, particularly in the areas of musical activity such as composing, performing, and research in which gender discrimination is an historic and ongoing concern."[21] The IAWM hosts international congresses and annual competitions and publishes two journals: *Women and Music: A Journal of Gender and Culture* and the *Journal of the International Alliance for Women in Music*.

Although IAWM is the most well-known far-reaching organization for women composers, there are also many other organizations, mostly regional in scope, that have emerged over the past several decades. These include the Asian Women Composers Association New York City, Association of Canadian Women Composers (ACWC), the Boulanger Initiative, the Chinese Woman Composers Association (CWCA), Clara Schumann Society, Frau und Musik, Luna Composition Lab, Nadia and Lili Boulanger International Centre, New York Women Composers, Inc. (NYWC), the Rebecca Clarke Society, the Sorel Organization, Women in Music (WiM), and Women in Music Los Angeles. More information about these organizations is available in the appendix of this book.

ACCEPTANCE IN ACADEMIA

Women in music was not taken seriously as a musicological discipline until the 1980s. Over the course of this decade, several seminal books emerged that introduced women in music survey and graduate courses to American colleges and universities for the first time. The first of these was *Women in Music: An Anthology of Source Readings* (1982) by Carol Neuls-Bates (b. 1939). The most important year of the decade for women in music studies was 1987, which saw the release of the first true textbook—*Women Making Music: The Western Art Tradition: 1150–1950* by Jane Bowers (b. 1936) and Judith Tick (b. 1943)—and, perhaps even more important, the first anthology: the *Historical Anthology of Music by Women* (HAMW) by James Briscoe (b. 1949). These two volumes became standard resources in collegiate classrooms across the country. In 1991, *Women and Music: A History* by Karin Pendle (b. 1939) was released, and in 1995 Rhian Samuel (b. 1944) and Julie Anne Sadie (b. 1948) edited and published *The Norton/Grove Dictionary of Women Composers*, the first concise reference work of its kind. Although they are now more than twenty years old, these books are still a great place to start if you are a newcomer to the discipline.[22]

What began as a reexamination of the white European women who played "minor" characters in Western classical music has now become an intersectional discipline that explores the impact of sexism, racism, classism, ableism, sizeism, homophobia, and transphobia on twenty-first-century women composers and their works. It is likely that these discussions will continue to play out over the next several decades.

FINAL THOUGHTS

Although progress has been made in recent decades, much work remains. Concert programs across the United States and abroad are still overwhelmingly dominated by male composers. Catherine Roma (b. 1948) muses on this phenomenon when she writes:

> Women's voices—where can they be found? How can they be defined? How have they been muted, silenced, adapted to the dominant male culture of their times and places? These are questions being asked of the artistic products of women that have been recovered, rediscovered, and reread since the resurgence of feminism in recent years drew to our attention the messages and lesson that needed to be reclaimed as part of our heritage. It seems ironic, then, that the field of music scholarship, dealing with an art in which the voice is often literally present, has been slow to take up the challenge of finding and defining the contributions and roles of women. Yet it can no longer be denied that women at all times and in all places have both created and performed music. Their voices need to

be heard if we are to comprehend the score and variety of the musical experience throughout history.[23]

This brief chapter is nothing more than a thumbnail sketch of some of the biggest names and most important events in the history of music by women, with an emphasis on Western music, and a description of where we are today. It is intended as a primer for readers who have not had the privilege of taking an undergraduate survey course devoted to women in music. The chapters that follow will flesh out this backdrop, first examining historical challenges faced by women and then moving on to explore vocal music composed by women across a variety of genres, periods, and styles.

NOTES

1. Maria V. Coldwell, "Dame Margot and Dame Maroie," *The Norton/ Grove Dictionary of Women Composers*, ed. Julie Anne Sadie and Rhian Samuel (New York: W.W. Norton, 1995), 313.

2. Casulana's three books of madrigals were published in 1568, 1570, and 1583, respectively.

3. Karin Pendle, *Women and Music: A History*, 2nd ed. (Bloomington: Indiana University Press, 2001), 91.

4. When she died shortly before the premiere, Monteverdi composed his well-known *Lagrime d'amante al sepolcro dell'amata*, a lament dedicated to her memory.

5. Louis XIV's death in 1715 is likely related to Jacquet de la Guerre's retirement two years later in 1717.

6. The classical era is actually rife with hundreds of composers who made an impact on the era. Readers who wish to explore a fleshed-out view of the classical era are encouraged to explore the following two excellent volumes: John Rice's *Music in the Eighteenth Century* (New York: W.W. Norton, 2013) is a recent volume that gives a thorough overview of classical Viennese style, beginning with its roots in the late baroque era. Also, Leonard G. Ratner's *Classic Music: Expression, Form, and Style* (New York: Schirmer, 1985), although published more than thirty years ago, still remains one of the best resources.

7. Some of the composers whom Martines knew as a child and young woman included Carl Ditters von Dittersdorf (1739–1799), Luigi Boccherini (1743–1805), Domenico Cimarosa (1749–1801), Antonio Salieri (1750–1825), and Johann Anton André (1774–1842).

8. Rococo was an eighteenth-century reaction to the formal and grandiose structure of baroque music. Rococo music—most often associated with the keyboard works of François Couperin (1668–1733)—is characterized as graceful and free flowing and often features ornaments or embellishments called *agréments*. Rococo is one of the signals of a late-baroque shift toward the dawning classical era.

9. The composers alluded to here are as follows: Lili Boulanger (1913), Ethel Smyth (1922), Florence Price (1933), Louise Talma (1962), Janet Knapp (1975), and Ellen Taaffe Zwilich (1983).

10. Kwame Anthony Appiah and Henry Louis Gates Jr., *The Dictionary of Global Culture* (New York: Vintage Books, 1996), xi.

11. Lili's older sister, Nadia Boulanger (1887–1979) was a finalist for the award in 1907, as will be described in greater detail in chapter 2.

12. Since the Prix de Rome honors a student work, most of the pieces that won the award quickly fell into obscurity. Even Boulanger's *Faust et Hélène* is not regarded as one of Boulanger's more notable works and rarely receives performances in the present day. Many Prix de Rome winners do not even acknowledge their prize-winning work as part of their oeuvre. Some of the Prix de Rome–winning pieces by women composers that are still known include Canal's opera *Don Juan*, Leleu's cantata *Béatrix*, Barraine's *La vierge guerrière* (a "sacred trilogy" for Joan of Arc), and a work by Brenet entitled *Les visions prophétiques de Cassandre*.

13. Music Composition was the original Grawemeyer Award, first given in 1985. The other four categories instituted since then are as follows: Ideas Improving World Order (1988), Education (1989), Religion (1990), and Psychology (2000).

14. Morley was nominated twice—for *The Little Prince* (1974) and *The Slipper and the Rose* (1976)—but never won. Levi—who is known by her stage name Micahu—was also nominated for *Jackie* (2008). Ahrens, a lyricist, received a nomination for *Anastasia* (1997). Portman went on to receive two additional nominations for Best Original Score for *The Cider House Rules* (1999) and *Chocolat* (2000).

15. The other eleven songs—in addition to Fields's—that have won in this category are as follows: "All His Children" from *Sometimes a Great Notion* (Bergman, 1971); "The Way We Were" from *The Way We Were* (Bergman, 1973); "Evergreen" from *A Star Is Born* (Streisand, 1976); "Arthur's Theme" from *Arthur* (Sager, 1981); "Up Where We Belong" from *An Officer and a Gentleman* (Sainte-Marie, 1982); "Flashdance . . . What a Feeling" from *Flashdance* (Cara, 1983); "Let the River Run" from *Working Girl* (Simon, 1988); "I Need to Wake Up" from *An Inconvenient Truth* (Etheridge, 2006); "Skyfall"

from *Skyfall* (Adele, 2012); "Let It Go" from *Frozen* (Anderson-Lopez, 2013); and "Remember Me" from *Coco* (Anderson-Lopez, 2017).

16. Comden shared all three of her Tonys with her longtime lyric-writing partner, Adolph Green (1914–2002).

17. Maureen Buja, "Playing Together: Women's Orchestras and Women in Orchestras," www.interlude.hk/front/playing-together-womens-orchestras-women-orchestras/ (February 27, 2018).

18. Auschwitz was a German concentration camp that was active from 1940 to 1945; Sumatra is an Indonesian island in Southeast Asia that was home to a Japanese prisoner of war camp from 1942 to 1945.

19. Marianne Reissinger, "Katharine Emily Eggar," *The Norton/Grove Dictionary of Women Composers*, ed. Julie Anne Sadie and Rhian Samuel (New York: W.W. Norton, 1995), 157.

20. iawm.org/about-us, accessed September 1, 2018. The ILWC was founded in 1975 by Nancy Van de Vate (b. 1930) to create and expand opportunities for women composers of music; the organization published the *ILWC Journal* and supervised various projects, including the publication of a directory of music by women, several radio series, an association with Arsis Press (which specializes in the publication of music by women), and a competition for student composers. The ICWM was founded in 1979 by Jeannie Pool (b. 1951) to form an organizational basis for women-in-music conferences and meetings; ICWM congresses consisted of concerts, workshops, and academic papers all aimed at an international exchange of information about music by women. The AWC was founded in 1976 by Tommie Ewart Carl (b. 1921) to promote music by women composers; the AWC created a library of music scores at George Washington University; published a journal, the *AWC News/Forum*; and produced concerts and recordings of music by American women.

21. iawm.org/about-us, accessed September 1, 2018.

22. Carol Neuls-Bates, *Women in Music: An Anthology of Source Readings* (New York: Harper & Row, 1982); Jane Bowers and Judith Tick, eds., *Women Making Music: The Western Art Tradition: 1150–1950* (Champaign: University of Illinois Press, 1987); James Briscoe, *Historical Anthology of Music by Women* (Bloomington: Indiana University Press, 1987); Karin Pendle, *Women and Music: A History* (Bloomington: Indiana University Press, 1991); and Julie Anne Sadie and Rhian Samuel, The *Norton/Grove Dictionary of Women Composers* (New York: W.W. Norton, 1995). Neuls-Bates's, Briscoe's, and Pendle's books are available in revised editions (1995, 2004, and 2001, respectively).

23. Catherine Roma, *The Choral Music of Twentieth-Century Women Composers: Elisabeth Lutyens, Elizabeth Maconchy, and Thea Musgrave* (Lanham, MD: Scarecrow Press, 2006), xiii.

2

WOMEN COMPOSERS

Historical and Contemporary Challenges

Throughout history, women composers have routinely encountered societal issues that hindered their creative endeavors. Long-held traditional gender roles kept them relegated to the home and domestic duties. Women did not have equal access to education (something that remains an issue today on a global scale). It wasn't until the nineteenth century that the creation of women's colleges expanded educational opportunities. The Seven Sisters colleges in the United States (starting with the founding of Mount Holyoke in 1837) and women's colleges in England (including Cambridge's Girton and Newnham, the latter which remains all-female to this day) provided new avenues for female students.[1] Despite these advances, many women still had more of a finishing school education. A cultivated young lady in the nineteenth and early twentieth century often took piano lessons and might be expected to play in the parlor or salon for family and friends.

Fanny Mendelssohn Hensel (1805–1847) was born into an affluent German banking family. Her first piano teacher was her mother, Lea, who actually had trained with a former student of Johann Sebastian Bach (1685–1750). Both Fanny and her younger brother Felix Mendelssohn (1809–1847) took composition lessons with Carl Zelter (1758–1832),

Figure 2.1. Fanny Mendelssohn Hensel (portrait by her husband, Wilhelm Hensel). *Creative Commons (CCBY-SA 3.0)*

but different paths emerged for them as dictated by societal expectations. Fanny's father, Abraham, told her that "music will perhaps become his [Felix's] profession, while for *you* it can only be an ornament, never the root of your being," advising her on her twenty-third birthday: "You must prepare more earnestly and eagerly for your real calling, the *only* calling of a young woman—I mean the state of a housewife."[2]

In 1827, Felix was attending the University of Berlin. In that same year, he published *Zwölf Gesänge*, Op. 8, in his name, which consisted of two volumes of six songs each. But three of the songs were actually composed by Fanny: "Das Heimweh," "Italien," and "Suleika und Hatem." In what could be viewed as an entertaining or disheartening anecdote, Queen Victoria decided to sing "Italien" for Felix during a palace visit, calling it one of her favorite songs. Then Felix was forced to admit its actual authorship: "I was obliged to confess that Fanny had written the song (which I found very hard, but pride must have a fall)."[3] Felix also published three of Fanny's songs in his *Zwölf Lieder*, Op. 9, in 1830: "Sehnsucht," "Verlust," and "Die Nonne." It wasn't until the final year of her life that Felix finally supported her publishing in her own name. Due to years of misattribution and squelched publication, it remains unclear how many works she actually composed and some manuscripts remain undiscovered and unpublished. While Felix's endorsement was long delayed, Fanny's husband, the painter Wilhelm Hensel (1784–1861), supported his wife's compositional ambitions, unlike many other husbands of the era. ♪

COMPOSING IN THE SHADOW OF SPOUSES

Numerous books have idealized the romance between composer Robert Schumann (1810–1856) and Clara Wieck Schumann (1819–1896) as the inspiration for his prolific *Liederjahr* of 1840. But the romance brought profound struggles for Clara due to Robert's suicide attempt and severe mental illness. Clara had been a piano prodigy, touring Europe under the tutelage of her father, Friedrich Wieck (1785–1873). Wieck opposed their marriage but the young lovers took their case to court and won the right to wed. Anna Beer (b. 1964) explores the inconsistency of Robert's vision of their union as spouses and composers, supposedly based on equality but eventually undermined by ego: "Is it any surprise that Clara could not sustain her joy in composition, when she had a husband who, on a regular basis, reminded her of his superior status as artist?"[4] ♪

Alma Schindler Mahler (1879–1964) faced similar challenges in her marriage to Viennese composer and conductor Gustav Mahler (1860–1911). After a secret romance with her composition teacher, Alexander von Zemlinsky (1871–1942), Alma began a whirlwind courtship that led to her engagement to Gustav just a few weeks after their first meeting. But in a letter he wrote to Alma on December 19, 1901, Gustav said their lives would be ridiculous unless she gave up composing. He asked, "How do you imagine both husband and wife as composers?" and demanded she give up her own music.[5] Nearly twenty years her senior, he seemed ruled by the notion of the predominance of the husband and his career, not to mention the concept of a wife being a possession. Still, Alma did marry him in 1902. It is hard to say whether the creative sub- jugation or her inherent passionate nature led to her affair with architect Walter Gropius (who later became her second husband after Gustav's death). But after this marital drama, Mahler became more accepting of her continuing to compose, even editing and helping to orchestrate some of her songs and facilitating their release by his own publisher.

Luckily, contemporary examples of composer couples reveal a more egalitarian environment. Jocelyn Hagen (b. 1980) and Timothy C. Takach (b. 1978) share a marriage as well as active careers as composers. Hagen won the 2018 American Prize in Composition for her dance opera *Test Pilot* (2014), and Takach has had his works performed by the Boston Pops and on *A Prairie Home Companion*. Hagen and Takach have also collaborated in ways big and small, performing as Nation (a vocal band specializing in finely crafted covers of pop songs and original tunes) and as composers through a joint commission from the Esoterics, a choir in Seattle. In 2017 they co-composed a thirty-five-minute a cappella choral work called *This Is How You Love*, which focuses on the ups and downs of being in a long relationship. Together they are also cofounders of Graphite Publishing, what their website calls "an online vocal music pub- lisher of digital scores." Both Hagen and Takach are well-reviewed and award-winning composers who share a mission of helping other compos- ers disseminate their work. Hagen shared: "We are cheerleaders for each other's work. We also understand the demands and responsibilities each of us has as a full-time composer. We are constantly evaluating and striv- ing for balance in our work and personal lives."[6] ♪

Broadway composer and three-time Tony Award winner Jason Rob- ert Brown (b. 1970) is married to composer and musical director Geor- gia Stitt (b. 1972). A graduate of the New York University MFA music theater writing program, Stitt has written musicals such as *Samantha Spade – Ace Detective* (2014), *Snow Child* (2018), and *Big Red Sun* (2018), as well as numerous stand-alone songs. Brown is a supportive spouse who wrote "Caravan of Angels" in honor of their ten-year anni- versary. Still, Stitt notes, "I get asked about my husband all of the time and he never gets asked about me. Like, 'What's it like to be married to a composer?'—I don't know if he's *ever* been asked that question."[7] In the realm of popular music, Jay-Z (b. 1969)—otherwise known as

Sean Carter—has recently demonstrated he is a husband unthreatened by his wife's huge success, even when Beyoncé (b. 1981)—whose full name is Beyoncé Knowles-Carter—released her blockbuster *Lemonade* (2016), which openly addressed issues in their own marriage. The rapper also appeared in the videos for "Sandcastles" and "All Night" on her groundbreaking visual album. In a magazine interview, Jay-Z shared that he was "really proud of the music she made" and that "we have a healthy respect for one another's craft. I think she's amazing."[8] The power couple collaborated on a joint album, *Everything Is Love* (2018), listing the artists' names as the Carters. ♪

SISTERS IN SONG

Nadia Boulanger (1887–1979) proved to be a much more supportive sibling than Felix Mendelssohn was. The Boulanger family had a strong musical reputation, with her father, Ernest Boulanger (1815–1900), winning the Prix de Rome for composition in 1835. Nadia was a finalist for the prestigious prize in 1907, but after experiencing frustrations with the competition, she turned her focus to teaching and conducting. In fact, she was the first female conductor at several major symphonies including the New York Philharmonic and the Philadelphia Orchestra. She also worked actively to mentor her sister, Lili Boulanger (1893–1918). As her reputation grew, Nadia "did her best for her little sister, using her prestige as a teacher and conductor to draw attention to Lili's work" and exploiting Lili's "status as a *femme fragile* to win the Prix de Rome."[9] The prodigy of the family, Lili managed to win the Prix de Rome in 1913 at age nineteen for her cantata *Faust et Hélène*; she was the first woman to win the award. But her life was cut short by various chronic illnesses (pneumonia, gastrointestinal tuberculosis), which eventually caused her death at age twenty-four. Nadia established a memorial fund in 1939 to foster continued interest in Lili's work. The legacy of both Nadia and Lili is celebrated by the Nadia and Lili Boulanger International Centre, which supports talented young French musicians through scholarships and a voice-piano competition. Nadia's impact resonates throughout the music world. She became the premier composition teacher. The composers she instructed often became famous and influential figures themselves: Walter Piston (1894–1976), Virgil Thomson (1896–1989), Roy Harris (1898–1979), Aaron Copland (1900–1990), Marc Blitzstein (1905–1964), Elliott Carter (1908–2012), David Diamond (1915–2005), Philip Glass (b. 1937), and Quincy Jones (b. 1933). Americans in particular flocked to Paris to train under her tutelage. Besides assisting her younger sister, Nadia also instructed many notable female composers including Mary Howe (1882–1974), Louise Talma (1906–1996), Evelyn

Figure 2.2.   Nadia and Lili Boulanger, 1913. *Creative Commons (CCBY-SA 3.0)*

Pittman (1910–1992), Peggy Glanville-Hicks (1912–1990), Julia Perry (1924–1979), Thea Musgrave (b. 1928), and Elizabeth R. Austin (b. 1938).

Another noteworthy trio of sisters is Joanna Simon (b. 1940), Lucy Simon (b. 1943), and Carly Simon (b. 1945). Joanna had a successful career as an opera singer, performing roles such as Cherubino in Mozart's *Le nozze di Figaro* with New York City Opera and Brangäne in Wagner's *Tristan und Isolde* with the New York Philharmonic. In the 1960s, Lucy and Carly performed as the folk duo the Simon Sisters and released three albums aimed at children. When Lucy got married, Carly Simon took the spotlight as a singer-songwriter in the 1970s with a number of hit records including "You're So Vain" and "Nobody Does It Better." In 1988, she went on to win a Golden Globe, a Grammy, and an Academy Award for "Let the River Run" from the film *Working Girl*. Meanwhile Lucy made a name for herself composing the score for the Broadway musical *The Secret Garden* (1991) as well as songs for Off-Broadway shows like *A . . . My Name is Alice* (1983) and *Mama and Her Boys* (2011). In an interview with the *New York Times*, Lucy shared, "We've been able to protect ourselves, as sisters, from anger and ferocious jealousy by putting ourselves in different areas of music. Joanna was an opera singer. And after a try at folk rock, I placed myself in musical theater. We're not in competition with each other."[10]

Some people don't realize that country artists Loretta Lynn (b. 1932) and Crystal Gayle (b. 1951) are sisters. Loretta gained fame as the singer-songwriter of the now iconic "Coal Miner's Daughter" (1970). Loretta also wrote Crystal Gayle's debut single "I've Cried (the Blue Right out of My Eyes)" (1970). After being inducted into the Nashville Songwriters Hall of Fame in 1983, the Country Music Hall of Fame in 1988, and the Songwriters Hall of Fame in 2008, Loretta Lynn seems to have achieved her goal of being remembered more as a songwriter than as a singer. Most people also don't realize that the Pointer Sisters came to fame via a country single. Originally comprising June Pointer (1953–2006), Bonnie Pointer (b. 1950), and Anita Pointer (b. 1948), the R&B trio had more than a dozen top hits. Anita and Bonnie cowrote "Fairytale" (1974), which was nominated for Best Country Song at the Grammys. It also led to the Pointer Sisters being the first African American female group to perform at the Grand Ole Opry. Along with

Trevor Lawrence, the three sisters cowrote the hit song "I'm So Excited" (1982), and they also collaborated on the aptly titled "Only Sisters Can Do That" (1993). ♪

A more recent sister act is the country duo Court Yard Hounds. Fiddler Martie Maguire (b. 1969) and guitarist/banjo player Emily Strayer (b. 1972), formerly Emily Robison, initially won fame and twelve Grammy Awards as the Dixie Chicks, along with singer Natalie Maines (b. 1974); but the Court Yard Hounds side project gave the Erwin sisters an opportunity to write more songs on their own. Sisters Beyoncé and Solange Knowles (b. 1986) collaborated with others to write the song "Get Me Bodied" (2007) for Beyoncé's album *B-Day*; at the 2018 Coachella festival, they had a good laugh after falling onstage together while performing the song. Although Beyoncé may have won twenty Grammy Awards while Solange won her first for *Cranes in the Sky* (2017), the older sister touts her younger sister's talent: "She's just an incredible songwriter—so creative."[11] From the Boulangers to the Simons, Erwin to Knowles, with a supportive sister, female composers and songwriters can soar to great heights. As the title of the hit Eurythmics song says, "Sisters Are Doin' It for Themselves," writing their own music and championing their female siblings in their composing endeavors. ♪

NO LADY COMPOSERS

In their fight for women's right to vote, late nineteenth- and early twentieth-century suffragettes drew attention to their status as women who were not being treated equally by society. In the 1970s, supporters of the Equal Rights Amendment lobbied and protested, hoping to have the Constitution ratified to ensure equal rights for women. Despite these public demonstrations of women's diminished opportunities, some women composers have resisted gender designations. For example, British composer Elisabeth Lutyens (1906–1983) "notoriously opposed being labelled as a woman composer" despite conceding: "I am fifteen years behind any man. If Britten wrote a bad score they'd say 'He's had a bad day.' If I'd written one it was because I was a woman."[12] Understandably, most female composers just want to have their works recognized on their own merits. Some may fear embracing the "female composer" label because it might relegate them to a concert of female composers rather than a standard performance without labels. It is an issue faced by different minorities as well. An African American conductor friend wondered why orchestras only asked him to conduct *Porgy and Bess* and overlooked him when Beethoven was on the program. Labels can put people in a box and inadvertently limit opportunities instead of opening new doors. Or sometimes, labels can carry a derogatory undertone.

Pioneering composer Pauline Oliveros (1934–2016) was a key figure in experimental and electronic music. She was a unique thinker, playing the accordion, exploring the concept of "deep listening" and "sonic awareness," and incorporating taped sounds into her compositions. Oliveros shared her strong opinions about the subjugation of women in society and as composers, bemoaning the "cute" and "condescending" label of "lady composer" and arguing, "What critic today speaks of a 'gentleman composer'?"[13] These thoughts, shared in a 1970 article in the *New York Times*, reflect what is considered second-wave feminism with its emphasis on gender equity. Oliveros displays both anger and frustration but also appeals to men to help make the societal shift toward equality possible:

> Men do not have to commit sexual suicide in order to encourage their sisters in music. Since they have been on top for so long, they could seek out women and encourage them. . . . Women need to know they can achieve. . . . Certainly the greatest problems in society will never be solved until an egalitarian atmosphere utilizing the total creative energies exists among all men and women.[14]

The egalitarian environment she envisioned has not yet been achieved. The Metropolitan Opera has still only produced two operas composed by women: *Der Wald* by Ethel Smyth (1858–1944) in 1903 and *L'amour de loin* by Kaija Saariaho (b. 1952) in 2016.[15] A survey of major American orchestras revealed that the work of women composers constituted only 1.8 percent of concert programs and only 14.3 percent of works programmed by living composers.[16] These rather discouraging statistics show that we as a society have a long way to go in giving female composers an equal playing field. Female opera composers will be discussed at greater length in chapter 4.

Especially in the operatic and symphonic realms, women seem to come up short. There is a long-standing and misguided concept that female composers can only write in "small forms." In the nineteenth and early twentieth century, proper young ladies played piano and occasionally sang parlor pieces to entertain guests. Yes, Fanny Hensel and Clara Wieck Schumann did write songs and piano pieces, as did Amy Beach (1867–1944). But Beach also wrote her *Gaelic Symphony* (1896), the first symphony published by an American woman, and a number of works for orchestra and voice. And Francesca Caccini (1587–after 1641) is evidence that women have been composing opera since the seventeenth century. Still, the notion of women writing small, delicate pieces persisted. Composer Joan Tower (b. 1938) recalls Aaron Copland saying in the 1940s that women "couldn't think in long forms" and that he had no reply in 1980 when she asked him, "Do you have a different opinion now?"[17] But Tower revealed her opinion by composing *Fanfare for the Uncommon Woman* (1987–1993). Written in response to Copland's *Fanfare for the Common Man* (1942) and dedicated to female conductor Marin Alsop (b. 1956), the first fanfare of this orchestral work was commissioned by the Houston Symphony, the second by Absolut Vodka, the third by Carnegie Hall, the fourth by the Kansas City Symphony, and the fifth by the Aspen Music Festival. Tower's significant support from major symphony orchestras, concert halls and music festivals, and even corporate sponsors attests that many believe that a woman composer can compose a "large form" work even if Aaron Copland does not. "Lady" composers are no longer limited in the scale and scope of their creativity.

CHALLENGES OF GENDER AND RACE

Sometimes women composers have faced not just issues of gender but also those of race. Florence Price (1887–1953) worked hard to promote herself and seek out performances of her work, but her efforts often went unacknowledged. Price wrote in a letter to conductor Serge Koussevitzky (1874–1951) that she had "two handicaps—those of sex and race. I am a woman; and I have some Negro blood in my veins."[18] He never replied. Eventually Frederick Stock (1872–1942) began to support Price, conducting the Chicago Symphony at the 1933 World's Fair in a performance of her *Symphony No. 1 in E Minor*. Today, her compositions are still being rediscovered, with manuscripts and recordings emerging in the past ten years. But her works remain underperformed,

Figure 2.3. Margaret Bonds. *Creative Commons (CCBY-SA 3.0)*

although she has gained name recognition as the first African American woman to have a symphony performed by a major American orchestra. Besides her orchestral works, Price also wrote a number of art songs including "The Glory of the Day Was in Her Face" (1949) and "Sympathy" in addition to her settings of the Langston Hughes poems "Bewilderment," "Fantasy in Purple," and "Hold Fast to Dreams" (1945). Sometimes Price set her own poetry, as in "Trouble Done Come My Way" and "Resignation." Most of Price's songs are undated. ♪

Price was actually living with the family of her student Margaret Bonds (1913–1972) in 1932 when Price's symphony won the Wanamaker Foundation's symphonic competition. Bonds won the song category that year for "Sea Ghost." Also a gifted concert pianist, Bonds became the first African American soloist with the Chicago Symphony when she played piano concerti by John Alden Carpenter (1876–1951) and Florence Price in 1933. After completing both her BM and MM degrees at Northwestern University, Bonds moved to New York City for composition studies at the Juilliard School.

> When in New York Bonds met Nadia Boulanger and hoped to study composition with her, but the French teacher turned her down flat. Boulanger admired the composition Bonds showed her—it was [the song] "The Negro Speaks of Rivers"—but told her she should go on as she was and not study with anyone. No doubt Boulanger realized that Bonds had grasped European compositional techniques but her style combined these with . . . the influence of the blues and jazz she heard so much during her youth in Chicago.[19]

Bonds formed a fruitful collaboration and friendship with the Harlem Renaissance poet Langston Hughes (1902–1967), setting his poems to song including "The Negro Speaks of Rivers" (1942), the cantata *The Ballad of the Brown King* (1954), and *Three Dream Portraits* (1959). Bonds and Hughes also wrote a music-theater work called *Shakespeare in Harlem* (1957). Zubin Mehta (b. 1936) conducted the Los Angeles Philharmonic in the premiere of her last major work—*Credo* (1972) for baritone, chorus, and orchestra—just a few months before her death at the age of fifty-nine. In addition to these compositions, Bonds also created a number of spiritual arrangements for soprano Leontyne Price (b. 1927). The music of Margaret Bonds has recently been championed by American soprano Louise Toppin (b. ca. 1961). Her Albany Records release *Ah! Love, but a Day: Songs and Spirituals of American Women* (2000) showcases songs by Bonds including "Song of the Season" and "The Pasture." Toppin also highlights the work of other African American female composers on the recording: Florence Price, Undine Smith Moore (1904–1989), Betsy Jackson King (1928–1994), and Jacqueline Hairston (b. 1938). As Toppin writes in the CD liner notes:

> Although frequently neglected, art songs have consistently appeared in the output of women composers. From the parlor songs of Amy Beach to the jazzy accompaniments and lush tunes of Margaret Bonds, American and African American women have created well-written and interesting compositions and made exciting contributions to the art song repertoire. . . . These unsung (and in some instances unpublished) art songs . . . are replete with charm and dignity, and worthy to be heard.[20]

Hopefully neither gender nor race will prevent singers from exploring the rich repertoire of vocal music by composers such as Price and Bonds and programming their songs on concerts and recitals. ♪

FEMALE COMPOSERS ON BROADWAY

Broadway has been a fairly fertile creative space for female composers. Mary Rodgers (1931–2014), daughter of famed Broadway composer Richard Rodgers (1902–1979), made a name for herself with *Once upon a Mattress* (1959). The show's song "Shy"—sung by Winnifred aka Fred, from the Princess and the Pea—was a great comic vehicle for Carol Burnett (b. 1933). Elizabeth Swados (1951–2016) garnered attention and a Tony nomination for Best Score for *Runaways* (1978), but then it wasn't until 1991 that Lucy Simon scored the same nomination for *The Secret Garden*. And then it wasn't until 2006 that a woman finally won a Tony for Best Score for *The Drowsy Chaperone*: Lisa Lambert (b. 1962) shared the win with her collaborator, Greg Morrison (b. 1965). Other Tony-nominated female composers include Anna Duquesnay—who cowrote *Bring in 'da Noise, Bring in 'da Funk* (1996)—and Brenda Russell (b. 1949) and Allee Willis (b. 1947), who teamed up for *The Color Purple* (2006); Nell Benjamin (b. ca.1972), who cowrote *Legally Blonde*

(2007); and the legendary Dolly Parton (b. 1946), who wrote the songs for the musical *9 to 5* (2009).

Certainly the female Broadway composer with the most awards and productions to her credit is Jeanine Tesori (b. 1961). A graduate of Barnard College and a classically trained pianist, Tesori has enumerated her musical influences: Carole King (b. 1942), Karen Carpenter (1950–1983), and Joni Mitchell (b. 1943). Her highly successful musicals include *Thoroughly Modern Millie* (2000), *Caroline, or Change* (2004), and *Shrek the Musical* (2008), all earning Tony nominations for Best Score. Finally, Tesori won the Tony in 2015 for *Fun Home*, which was the first Broadway musical to feature a lesbian as its heroine. When asked about how to improve gender parity in the theater world, she says that female composers need to be actively mentored and supported: "So ask someone to go see that piece by a woman. Bring ten people."[21] ♪

Certainly more than ten people have seen the Broadway smash hit *Waitress* (2016). Pop star Sara Bareilles (b. 1979) wrote the score for the musical adaptation of the 2007 indie film, which was written and directed by Adrienne Shelly (1966–2006) and starred Keri Russell (b. 1976). The production made Broadway history with the first-ever all-female creative team: Bareilles as songwriter, Jessie Nelson as bookwriter, Diane Paulus (b. 1966) as director, and Lorin Latarro (b. 1977) as choreographer.[22] After Jessie Mueller (b. 1983) created the role and played it for nearly a year, Sara Bareilles herself portrayed the leading role in *Waitress* on Broadway for ten weeks in 2017 and another ten weeks in 2018. And certainly in almost any other year, one that did not include *Hamilton* (2015) by Lin-Manuel Miranda (b. 1980), *Waitress* might have won the Tony. Among Bareilles's fellow nominees that year were Andrew Lloyd Webber (b. 1948) and Edie Brickell (b. 1966), a folk-rock songwriter (and wife of Paul Simon) who wrote the score for *Bright Star*, a 2014 musical by Steve Martin (b. 1945). ♪

Pop and rock music have become commonplace on Broadway since the rise of "jukebox musicals," or shows built around existing popular music. Examples of jukebox musicals include *Mamma Mia!* (1999), *Movin' Out* (2002), *Jersey Boys* (2005), and *American Idiot* (2010). *Beautiful: The Carole King Musical* (2014) won Jessie Mueller a Tony Award for Best Actress for her portrayal of Carole King. And the highly anticipated musical *Jagged Little Pill* premiered at the American Repertory Theatre in 2018; it is based on the 1996 Grammy Album of the Year winner by Alanis Morissette (b. 1974) and staged by *Waitress* director Diane Paulus. Its positive initial reviews will hopefully ensure a Broadway debut for the production. *The Cher Show* (2018) premiered in Chicago and is headed to Broadway, while other jukebox musicals using music by Britney Spears (b. 1981) and Pat Benatar (b. 1953) are reportedly in the works. A 1980s icon, Cyndi Lauper (b. 1953) collaborated with Harvey Fierstein (b. 1954) on *Kinky Boots* (2013), a more traditional book musical about a less traditional subject; this musical earned Lauper a Tony Award for Best Score. Well known for her pop hits "Girls Just Wanna Have Fun" and "True Colors," Lauper admits she was challenged by writing songs not for herself to sing but for other characters, such as a drag queen. She talked to the *Kansas City Star* about the cathartic nature of portraying different types of people in her music: "I had a lot of 'Aha!' moments writing for the great characters that inhabit the *Kinky Boots* world. It honestly made me a better person, and a much better songwriter."[23]

Both Lauper and Bareilles contributed songs to the Tony-nominated score of *SpongeBob SquarePants: The Broadway Musical* (2018), as did Yolanda Adams (b. 1961). In 2018, Lauper also announced she is working with her "Time after Time" cowriter Rob Hyman (b. 1950) on a Broadway adaptation of the movie *Working Girl* (supposedly minus its signature Carly Simon song), while Sara Bareilles is teaming with Duncan Sheik (b. 1969) on an *Alice in Wonderland* musical. Kristen Anderson-Lopez (b. 1972) received a 2018 Tony nomination for best score for *Frozen* (2017) with her cowriter and husband, Robert Lopez (b. 1975). Based on the 2013 animated Disney movie, which won her an Academy Award for Best Song ("Let It Go") and two Grammy Awards, *Frozen* and its celebration of sisterhood will continue in the film sequel *Frozen 2* (2019) and—who knows—maybe a second *Frozen* Broadway musical. And the ever-prolific Jeanine Tesori premiered her new show *Soft Power* (2018) in Los Angeles. With a book by David Henry Hwang (b. 1957), who wrote *M. Butterfly* (1988), the musical examines 2016 American politics from an Asian viewpoint and takes an interesting twist on *The King and I* (1951): instead of a British schoolteacher falling in love with a king, a Chinese executive falls in love with Hillary Clinton (b. 1947). With creative ideas such as these, the future is bright. Female

composers are finding their voice on Broadway, bringing to life a multitude of characters from waitress to working girl and from drag queen to
female presidential candidate. Female songwriters in music theater will
be covered extensively in chapter 7 of this volume.

FEMALE SONGWRITERS IN POPULAR MUSIC

The 1960s and 1970s saw the rise of the female singer-songwriter. A
number of talented women became successful recording artists including Joan Baez (b. 1941), Carole King, Joni Mitchell, and Carly Simon.
With the creation of MTV in 1981, popular music in the 1980s took a
new angle, favoring choreography and fancy visuals over the "girl with
a guitar" look. But female singer-songwriters emerged throughout the
1990s. Still, there seemed to be less radio time and fewer touring opportunities for women artists. Canadian singer, pianist, and guitarist Sarah
McLachlan (b. 1968) took note and decided to create the first all-female
touring music festival, Lilith Fair. She named the festival after Lilith,
Adam's first wife from the Bible. McLachlan recognized that "she was
the world's first feminist. Now we're restoring her to her proper position in society."[24] The original 1997 festival featured McLachlan and
Suzanne Vega (b. 1959)—of "Tom's Diner" fame—on all of the tour
dates, but Lilith Fair had an innovative three-stage format. Headliners
such as Emmylou Harris (b. 1947), Sheryl Crow (b. 1962), Tracy Chapman (b. 1964), Paula Cole (b. 1968), Jewel (b. 1974), and India Arie (b.
1975) played the main stage while the second stage and village stage
offered opportunities for other artists. Sometimes the secondary stages
featured established stars like Pat Benatar (b. 1953) and Cassandra Wilson (b. 1955), but mostly they showcased up-and-comers. By the second
Lilith Fair in 1998, the main stage stars included Bonnie Raitt (b. 1949),
Diana Krall (b. 1964), Sinéad O'Connor (b. 1966), Liz Phair (b. 1967),
Queen Latifah (b. 1970), Erykah Badu (b. 1971), Lauryn Hill (b. 1975),
and Missy Elliott (b. 1971); among the second and village stage artists
were Martina McBride (b. 1966), Idina Menzel (b. 1971), and *Saturday
Night Live*'s Ana Gasteyer (b. 1967). Besides its all-female lineup, the
festival was unique in its mix of genres, encompassing pop, rock, indie,
folk, country, jazz, blues, R&B, and rap. Lilith Fair toured North Amer-

ica again in 1999 but then went dormant for a decade. It was revived in 2010, featuring some familiar faces (McLachlan, Crow, Harris, Badu) and bands old and new (the Bangles, Court Yard Hounds), but this time Lilith Fair highlighted a whole new generation of female singer-songwriters: Sara Bareilles, Ingrid Michaelson (b. 1979), Miranda Lambert (b. 1983), Colbie Caillat (b. 1985), and Janelle Monáe (b. 1985). ♪

Figure 2.4. Sarah McLachlan at the 2017 Invictus Games (photo by E. J. Hersom). *Creative Commons (CCBY-SA 2.0)*

From this proliferation of talent, one would think that women were finding equal ground in the recording industry. But 2018 proved there were still road blocks for female songwriters: on January 25, a shocking study was released about gender, race, and inclusion in the recording studio. Across six hundred songs from 2012 to 2017, the study reported that "few females work as songwriters" (12.3 percent) and that "the gender gap at the Grammys is real" with only 9.3 percent of Grammy nominees being female.[25] The 2018 Grammy Awards were held January 28, three days after the release of this study by the University of Southern California's Annenberg Inclusion Initiative, and the broadcast only reinforced its findings. New Zealand singer-songwriter Lorde (b. 1996) was the only female nominee for Album of the Year, yet she was the only nominee not invited to perform an excerpt from her album on the awards show. Lorde had actually won the Grammy for Song of the Year in 2014, but this accolade apparently didn't help her four years later. And in 2012, the Grammys eliminated the separate Male and Female Pop Solo Performance categories, combining them into one Pop Solo category. Since then it has been won by Lorde in 2014 and Adele (b. 1988) in 2012, 2013, and 2017; but the 2018 winner was Ed Sheeran (b. 1991), who beat out four female nominees: Kelly Clarkson (b. 1982), Kesha (b. 1987), Lady Gaga (b. 1986), and Pink (b. 1979). Finally, to top it all off, Recording Academy president Neil Portnow (b. 1948) said that women need to "step up" if they want to win Grammys and succeed in the recording industry. This tone-deaf comment, especially in the so-called Year of the Woman and in the birth of the Me Too and Time's Up movements, angered many and resulted in considerable backlash. By February 1, a group of six female music executives sent him an open letter demanding his resignation. Then, on February 2, a group of thirty-eight male music executives called on Portnow to end gender disparity. Portnow has announced he will retire as president of the Recording Academy when his contract expires in 2019. Perhaps three-time Grammy Award winner and singer-songwriter Alecia Moore (aka Pink) said it best in her tweet to Portnow on January 29:

> Women in music do not need to "step up"—women have been stepping since the beginning of time. Stepping up, and also stepping aside, women OWNED music this year. They've been KILLING IT. And every year before this. When we celebrate and honor the talent and accomplishments of women, and how much women STEP UP every year, against all odds, we show the next generation of women and girls and boys and men, what it means to be equal.[26]

Female songwriters in CCM will be covered extensively in chapter 8 of this volume.

FINAL THOUGHTS

Opportunities for female composers have come a long way, but challenges still remain despite recent accomplishments. The media took note when Kaija Saariaho saw her opera *L'amour de loin* (2000) produced by the Metropolitan Opera in 2016, primarily because it was only the second time the Met had done an opera by a woman. Du Yun (b. 1977) won the 2017 Pulitzer Prize for Music for her haunting opera *Angel's Bone* (2016). Both of these steps are progress for women composers. In June 2018, Alicia Keys (b. 1981) stepped up to launch the initiative She Is the Music, dedicated to equality, inclusivity, and opportunity for women in the music industry. The Grammy events of 2018 seem to show a path of the proverbial "two steps forward, one step back." In the words of Joan Tower: "It's true that over the last fifteen years more women composers have been included in books and there have been a few more recordings and publications of their work, but we still have a long way to go."[27] ♪

NOTES

1. The Seven Sisters are Barnard College, Bryn Mawr College, Mount Holyoke, Wellesley College, Vassar College, Smith College, and Radcliffe College. Vassar College became coeducational in 1969.
2. Abraham to Fanny, *The Letters of Fanny Hensel to Felix Mendelssohn*, ed. Marcia Citron (Hillsdale, NY: Pendragon Press, 1987), xl.
3. *24 Songs: Felix Mendelssohn and Fanny Mendelssohn Hensel*, ed. John Glenn Paton (Van Nuys, CA: Alfred Publishing, 1992), 15.
4. Anna Beer, *Sounds and Sweet Airs: The Forgotten Women of Classical Music* (London: Oneworld Publications, 2016), 227.
5. www.alma-mahler.at/engl/almas_life/almas_life1.html, accessed June 7, 2018.
6. Personal correspondence with Jocelyn Hagen, June 19, 2018.
7. Georgia Stitt, interview with Victoria Myers, *The Interval*, www.theintervalny.com/interviews/2014/08/an-interview-with-georgia-stitt/, accessed August 11, 2018.
8. Jay-Z, "Jay-Z Talks Infidelity, Music as Therapy in New Interview," *Rolling Stone*, www.rollingstone.com/music/news/jay-z-talks-infidelity-music-as-therapy-in-new-interview-w512910, accessed June 7, 2018.

9. Beer, *Sounds and Sweet Airs*, 282–83.

10. Lucy Simon, interview by Philip Galanes, "Carly and Lucy Simon on Music, Fame, Sibling Rivalry and, Yes, James Taylor," *New York Times*, www.nytimes.com/2015/04/26/fashion/carly-and-lucy-simon-on-sibling-rivlary-and-yes-james-taylor.html, accessed June 8, 2018.

11. Beyoncé, "7 Times Beyoncé and Solange Were Sister Goals," *Vibe*, www.vibe.com/2018/04/beyonce-solange-best-sister-love-moments/, accessed June 8, 2018.

12. Jill Halstead, *The Woman Composer: Creativity and the Gendered Politics of Musical Composition* (Aldershot, UK: Ashgate, 1997), 162.

13. Pauline Oliveros, "And Don't Call Them Lady Composers," *New York Times*, www.nytimes.com/1970/09/13/archives/and-dont-call-them-lady-composers-and-dont-call-them-lady-composers.html, accessed June 7, 2018.

14. Ibid.

15. Priscilla Frank, "In Just over One Hundred Years, the Met Has Only Staged Two Operas by Women," *Huffington Post*, www.huffingtonpost.com/entry/met-opera-woman-composer_us_58583f7ae4b03904470a19d6, accessed August 12, 2018.

16. Ricky O'Bannon, "By the Numbers: Female Composers," Baltimore Symphony Orchestra website, www.bscomusic.org/stories/by-the-numbers-female-composers/, accessed June 9, 2018.

17. Joan Tower, interview by Ann McCutchan, *The Muse that Sings: Composers Speak about the Creative Process* (New York: Oxford University Press, 1999), 60.

18. Florence Price, letter to Serge Koussevitzsky, "The Rediscovery of Florence Price: How an African American Composer's Works Were Saved from Destruction," *The New Yorker*, newyorker.com/magazine/2018/02/05/the-rediscovery-of-florence-price, accessed June 9, 2018.

19. Christine Ammer, *Unsung: A History of Women in American Music* (Portland: Amadeus Press, 2001), 175–76.

20. Louise Toppin, *Ah! Love, but a Day: Songs and Spirituals of American Women*, Albany Records, 2000.

21. Jeanine Tesori, interview by Victoria Myers, "Composer Jeanine Tesori on Her Artistic Process and Rewarding Female Ambition," *IndieWire*, www.indiewire.com/2015/03/composer-jeanine-tesori-on-her-artistic-process-and-rewarding-female-ambition-204160/, accessed June 9, 2018.

22. In 1991, *The Secret Garden* had a female team with composer Lucy Simon, bookwriter Marsha Norman, director Susan Schulman, and set designer Heidi Ettinger. Jessie Nelson's age is a mystery—she refuses to disclose this information in interviews.

23. Cyndi Lauper, interview by Robert Trussell, "Cyndi Lauper Got a Kick Out of Writing 'Kinky Boots' Songs," *Kansas City Star*, www.kansascity.com/entertainment/performing-arts/article69217662.html, accessed June 9, 2018.

24. Sarah McLachlan, interview by Lucy O'Brien, *She Bop: The Definitive History of Women in Popular Music*, revised 3rd edition (London: Jawbone Press, 2012), 375–76.

25. Stacy Smith, Marc Choueiti, and Katherine Pieper, "Inclusion in the Recording Studio? Gender and Race/Ethnicity of Artists, Songwriters, and Producers across Six Hundred Songs from 2012–2017," Annenberg Inclusion Initiative, assets.uscannenberg.org/docs/inclusion-in-the-recording-studio.pdf, accessed June 10, 2018.

26. Pink, Twitter Post, January 29, 2018, 4:35 p.m., https://twitter.com/Pink/status/958121509540761600.

27. Tower, *The Muse That Sings*, 60.

3

ART SONGS BY WOMEN

Throughout the history of Western music, women have had a strong affinity with the art song genre. This is not surprising, as women composers were usually considered to be "amateur" composers—not full-time, professional ones—who were often confined to the home. If they wrote any music at all, it would be "music for the parlor": songs, piano pieces, and occasional pieces of chamber music. Even if women had the ambition to compose larger works (and were privileged enough to receive the requisite training in orchestration), they rarely were given the opportunity and funding to actually program their works and hear their pieces performed, particularly before the twentieth century. Thus, many of the works we find that were written by women during the nineteenth century are art songs. This robust body of literature provides substantive repertoire for the recitalist. This chapter will offer a survey of art songs written by women from the early romantic era to the present day.

PRECURSORS TO THE ART SONG

An art song—as we have accepted the term in the modern era—is defined as the following:

A composition for voice and piano intended for private or concert performance. Art songs are usually short in length and are settings of poems. More than any other genre, the art song is the place where a composer attempts to synthesize the poet's words with music through vivid text painting in both the vocal line and the piano accompaniment.[1]

Songs without piano accompaniment were written as early as the troubadours and trouvères of medieval France. These monophonic secular songs were later followed by the Minnesingers and Meistersingers of Germany, and "lute songs"—which were accompanied, of course, by a lutenist—became a fixture in England during the late Renaissance era. Although John Dowland (1563–1626) is widely recognized as the master of the lute song, musicologists believe that Anne Boleyn (ca. 1501–1536)—the second wife of King Henry VIII who was also a poet and composer—contributed to this genre.[2] In the early baroque era, songs were composed for intimate music making in court or private settings. These pieces were usually accompanied by a lute, continuo (such as a viola da gamba and harpsichord), or a small consort of instruments (such as the theorbo, harp, or *veille*).

The songs of Barbara Strozzi (1619–1677) were written in this vein. Strozzi's compositions, which were published during her lifetime in eight opus numbers, are a rich body of songs that are worthy of exploration and programming. Although most modern recordings observe historically informed performance (HIP) practice through the use of period instruments, there are many published piano realizations of Strozzi's songs. Although these piano arrangements are often unapologetically romanticized—similar to the famous *Twenty-Four Italian Songs and Arias* published by Schirmer—they provide ideal fodder for studio use and recital programming. Strozzi is perhaps the most important woman song composer prior to the invention of the piano. "Spesso per entro al petto" comes from her Op. 2 (1651), which was published under the title *Cantate, ariette e duette.* ♪

The genre of the art song was not truly born until the invention of the fortepiano during the eighteenth century. Although the earliest instruments were built by Bartolomeo Cristofori (1655–1731) as early as 1700, the modern piano—as we recognize it—did not come into regular use until the late eighteenth and early nineteenth centuries. The first art

Figure 3.1.   Anna Amalia (painting by Johann Ernst Heinsius, ca. 1769). *Creative Commons (CCBY-SA 1.0)*

songs—settings of German Romantic poetry—were written during the late classical era by composers like Johann Friedrich Reichardt (1752–1814), Carl Friedrich Zelter (1758–1832), and Johann Rudolf Zumsteeg (1760–1802). The piano offered new expressive possibilities for text setting, but the accompaniments tended to be just that—an accompaniment; harmonies that supported the singer. The piano was not yet an equal partner or part of the storytelling. Words and music were not yet truly synthesized with one another. These works were still precursors to the mature German lieder of Franz Schubert (1797–1828) and Robert Schumann (1810–1856).

There were several women who contributed to the art song genre during this time. Anna Amalia (1739–1807) was the Duchess of Saxe-Weimar and an amateur musician and composer. She played the organ, violin, and flute and established a renowned music library. This collection—now known as the Amalia-Bibliotek—is housed at the Royal Library in Berlin. While not a prolific composer of her own works, she did write several songs that appeared in singspiels and did much to encourage the art form through her archival work and patronage. Amalia wrote "her own compositions to texts of Goethe" and played "a significant role in joining the poetry and music of the time."[3] Corona Schröter (1751–1802) was one of the most prolific of the early art song writers. She composed approximately four hundred vocal works, including two collections of lieder. Schröter is often remembered as the composer of the earliest known setting of Goethe's "Erlkönig," the poem later immortalized through Schubert's famous setting. In addition to being a composer, Schröter was also a virtuosic singer and actress. Louise Reichardt (1779–1826), daughter of Friedrich Reichardt, also wrote more than ninety songs. She was "a composer of memorable melodies" whose songs share similarities with "Schubert's gifts for melodic lyricism."[4] ♪

Maria Theresia von Paradis (1759–1824) holds a special place in late nineteenth-century musical life. She was known as the "Blind Enchantress" due to the fact that she lost her eyesight at the age of three. A musical prodigy, von Paradis performed as a singer and keyboard player throughout Europe as a young child and teenager, becoming famous in Viennese musical society. In 1786, she published the *Zwölf Lieder auf ihrer Reise in Musik gesetzt* (*Twelve Songs Set to Music upon Her*

Journey). The title of this collection references a three-year European concert tour that von Paradis undertook from 1783 to 1786. Her most famous song is "Morgenlied eines armen Mannes," the eighth song from this collection. The poem and musical setting exemplify the Sturm und Drang characteristics that were in vogue in Vienna during the late eighteenth century. ♪

GERMAN LIEDER

Fanny Mendelssohn Hensel (1805–1847) and Clara Wieck Schumann (1819–1896) emerged as the most important women composers of the mature German lied. Coincidentally, both women had close relationships to two of the most important male composers of the romantic era: Fanny was the older sister of Felix Mendelssohn (1809–1849), and Clara was the wife of Robert Schumann. These relationships had different effects on their careers. While Clara benefited from Robert's efforts to champion her music—both through his encouragement and promotion in his journal, the *Neue Zeitschrift für Musik*—Fanny's compositional ambitions were hampered by her family's lack of support. The Mendelssohns felt that composition was an inappropriate career for a woman and lavished all of their musical attention on her younger brother Felix. Anna Beer recounts the famous story of a gift Fanny received from her father when she was fourteen years old—a necklace of Scottish jewels—while her brother received writing implements so that he might compose his first opera.[5] Fortunately, she soon found an affirming advocate in her husband, the painter Wilhelm Hensel (1794–1861), who encouraged and nurtured her compositional ambitions.

Although Fanny Hensel focused mostly on smaller-scale works—songs and piano music—she composed regularly and prolifically. Few works were published during her lifetime, but recently she has gained considerable attention by performers and scholars as a genius in her own right, worthy of study alongside her brother. In total, she composed more than three hundred lieder. Hensel's "choice of German romantic poets and her setting of the texts is more similar to [Robert] Schumann style than to the simplistic style . . . of her predecessors, Louise Reichardt and the Berlin School."[6] "Nachtwanderer," Op. 7, No. 1 (1846) a setting of a poem by the great German romantic poet Joseph Freiherr von Eichendorff (1788–1857), exemplifies Hensel's skill as a composer of lieder. Although this poem was set to music eight times by various composers, Hensel's setting is by far the most famous. ♪

In addition to being a composer, Clara Schumann was primarily known during her lifetime as a piano virtuoso, attracting attention all over Europe while still in her teens. After her marriage to Robert Schumann (her piano teacher), she settled into a domestic life and performed and composed less frequently. Nevertheless, many of her works—particularly songs, piano music, and chamber music—have become part of the standard repertory. Schumann composed twenty-eight lieder, eighteen of which were published during her lifetime. "Lorelei" (1843) is a setting of a poem by Heinrich Heine (1797–1856), who—along with Eichendorff—is one of the most important poets of German romanticism. Schumann's is one of six settings of this poem, the most famous of which is by another nineteenth-century piano virtuoso, Franz Liszt (1811–1886). ♪

Josephine Lang (1815–1880) was a contemporary of the Hensels and (Clara) Schumann and also a close friend of the Schumann family. A mother of six children, she composed in her spare time, and over half her song output dates from the 1830s. After Lang was widowed in 1856 (the same year as Clara), she pursued publication of her songs, hoping to earn some money for her family. More than 150 of her songs were ultimately printed, making Lang one of the most published women composers of the nineteenth century. Besides setting classic German romantic poets such as Heine, Johann Wolfgang von Goethe (1749–1832), and Friedrich Schiller (1759–1805), she composed more than forty songs based on poems by her husband, Christian Reinhold Köstlin (1813–1856).[7] Her style was strongly influenced by Schubert, (Robert) Schumann, and Mendelssohn, as evidenced in "Im Frühling," Op. 10, No. 4, which dates from 1841. ♪

Alma Schindler Mahler (1879–1964) is best known to musicians as the wife of the Austrian composer Gustav Mahler (1860–1911), but he was only the first of her three husbands. The daughter of the painter Emil Jakob Schindler (1842–1892), she first fell in love with the composer and conductor (and her private composition teacher) Alexander von Zemlinsky (1871–1942) but married Mahler in 1902. After Gustav's death in 1911, she married the architect Walter Gropius (1883–1969) in 1915. After they divorced in 1920, she married her third husband, the poet and writer Franz Werfel (1890–1945). Although they did not marry until 1929, their relationship actually began as early as 1917, during her marriage to Gropius.[8] Most of Alma's compositions were destroyed during World War II—a period of time during which she lived in France and the United States. Her only surviving works are three volumes of lieder. These fourteen songs in total constitute approximately one hour of music. ♪

PAULINE VIARDOT: A COSMOPOLITAN FIGURE

Pauline Viardot (1821–1910) is a fascinating figure in the history of women in music. She was born into one of the most famous musical families in Europe: the Garcías. Her father, Manuel (1775–1832), was a renowned tenor and voice teacher, and her mother, Joaquina (1780–1864), was also an actress and singer. The second of three children, her older brother, Manuel García II (1805–1906), was a baritone who later made significant contributions to the field of voice pedagogy, and her younger sister was the mezzo-soprano Maria Malibran (1808–1836), one of the most famous singers of the nineteenth century. Viardot too began her career as one of Europe's most celebrated opera singers. Her many roles included Fidès in *Le prophète* (1849) of Giacomo Meyerbeer (1791–1864), which was written for her. Viardot was considered to be one of the best actresses of her era. Also a composer, Viardot traveled extensively across Europe, and this is reflected in her compositional style and choice of song texts. In addition to French, she also composed settings of German, Russian, and Italian texts. Her compositional style is overtly theatrical, channeling her life on the operatic stage. The exoticism of "Havanaise" exemplifies Viardot's cosmopolitan style. ♪

FRENCH *MÉLODIES*

The French *mélodie* developed somewhat later than the German lied, reaching its maturity with the songs of Gabriel Fauré (1845–1924),

Henri Duparc (1848–1933), and Claude Debussy (1862–1918). The first important female composer of *mélodies*, Cécile Chaminade (1857–1944), was a contemporary of these three composers. Chaminade was born into a musical family in Paris, and her first piano teacher was her mother. As a teenager, her talent caught the attention of Georges Bizet, who recommended that Chaminade study at the Paris Conservatoire. Her father refused, uttering the famous quotation, "Girls of the Bourgeoisie were intended to become wives and mothers."[9] In spite of this, Chaminade managed to secure a solid music education, studying piano and composition privately. She eventually settled into a career as a concert pianist, and her programs regularly included her own compositions. Her vast catalog consists of approximately four hundred works, including over one hundred songs. Nearly all of her works are published. The song "Mignonne" (1894) is typical of the style of Chaminade's songs, which are firmly rooted in nineteenth-century French romanticism and feature pianistic accompaniments. ♪

One of the most important musical families in Europe were the Boulangers, who lived in Paris at the turn of the twentieth century. The patriarch of the family was the pianist and composer Ernest Boulanger (1815–1900), but the two most famous members were his daughters, Nadia Boulanger (1887–1979) and Lili Boulanger (1893–1918). Lili, who was six years younger than Nadia, was the more celebrated composer. Her very short life was plagued by chronic illness. Her poor health prevented her from enrolling at the Paris Conservatoire, and she was taught privately by Nadia until her premature death at the age of twenty-four. Her most famous composition is *Clarières dans le ciel* (1914), a visionary setting of thirteen poems by Francis Jammes (1868–1938). "Reflets" (1911) is a setting of a poem by the French symbolist Maurice Maeterlinck (1862–1949), the same poet-playwright who provided the libretto for the opera *Pelléas et Mélisande* (1902) by Claude Debussy. Nadia Boulanger is widely regarded as the most important composition teacher of the early twentieth century. During this time, many American composers journeyed to Paris to be in her studio. Like many female composers of her era, she moved into teaching in part because her compositional activity was discouraged. Although her output was small, she wrote some pieces of exceptional quality, including the cantata *La sirène*, which was the runner-up for the Prix de Rome in 1908. "Le couteau" (1910) is a setting of the lesser-known French symbolist poet Camille Mauclair (1872–1944). ♪

Germaine Tailleferre (1892–1983) is perhaps best known as the only female member of Les Six, the group of Parisian composers whose music was reactionary against both the music dramas of Richard Wagner (1813–1883) and the impressionism of Claude Debussy.[10] Tailleferre was a child prodigy as a pianist and studied composition with Charles Koechlin (1867–1950) from 1916 to 1923. During World War II, she moved to the United States, returning to France in 1946, the year after the war ended. Although Tailleferre is best known for her piano pieces and instrumental chamber music, she also composed several dozen songs, including three song cycles: *Six chansons françaises* (1929), *Paris sentimental* (1949), and *Pancarte pour une porte d'entrée* (1961). *Six chansons françaises* are Tailleferre's most frequently performed songs. They are settings of distinctly feminist texts from the fifteenth, seventeenth, and eighteenth centuries. Each poem revolves around love, and each song is dedicated to one of Tailleferre's close friends. ♪

ENGLISH AND AMERICAN SONG

During the second half of the nineteenth century, several important women composers of art song in English were born. In this section, we will discuss five of these figures—two who hail from England and three who are from the United States.

Ethel Smyth (1858–1944) is often described as a Victorian-Edwardian composer, as her life evenly saddled both eras. She was born in Sidcup, Kent, as the fourth of eight children. Against her father's wishes, she studied composition at the Leipzig Conservatory, which began admitting women in the 1870s. This education connected her with composers all over Europe. When she returned to England, she found success with the *Mass in D*, and she went on to write six operas, including *The Wreckers* (1906).[11] Smyth was an extremely prolific composer with hundreds of works in her catalog, including several dozen songs in both English and German. "The Clown" is the first of her *Three Songs* (1913). It is typical of Smyth's mature style, which effectively combines elements from both the English and German schools of composition. ♪

Figure 3.2. Amy Beach.
Creative Commons (CCBY-SA 1.0)

Amy Beach (1867–1944), an American composer, is one of the most frequently cited names in the history of women in music. During her lifetime, she published her songs under the name "Mrs. H. H. A. Beach," reflecting her marriage to Dr. Henry Harris Aubrey Beach (1843–1910), a prominent Boston physician who was twenty-five years older than she. Her wealth and social status introduced her to some of the most important musical figures in New England, and she was recognized as the only female member of the Second New England School or "Boston Six."[12] Almost all of her compositions were published during her lifetime. After her husband's death, Beach lived for another thirty-six years, concertizing as a pianist and serving as the head of several national organizations, including the Music Educators National Conference (MENC) and Music Teachers National Association (MTNA). She composed prolifically across all genres. Her 115 songs are written in the somewhat conservative style of American romanticism championed by Edward MacDowell (1861–1944). Her *Three Browning Songs* (1900) are frequently programmed on recitals. Setting a poem by her husband, "Twilight," Op. 2, No. 1, dates from 1891; the song also inspired the third movement of her *Piano Concerto in C-sharp Minor*, Op. 45 (1900). ♪

Mary Howe (1882–1964) was a younger contemporary of Beach and a prominent American composer and pianist. At the age of forty—and as a mother of three children—she completed a degree in composition at the Peabody Institute in Baltimore. She was also one of many prominent American composers (mostly men) who studied in Paris under the tutelage of Nadia Boulanger. Howe composed across all genres, including large orchestral works, chamber music, and piano pieces. During her lifetime, she published seven volumes of songs with texts in English, French, and German. In 1925, with the help of Amy Beach, she organized the Society of Women Composers. Her style is very much in the romantic vein of the Second New England School, as evidenced in the song "The Lake Isle of Innisfree," a setting of a poem by William Butler Yeats (1865–1939). ♪

Rebecca Clarke (1886–1979), an English composer, was born in Harrow, a suburb of London. She was educated at the Royal Academy of Music and the Royal College of Music, where she studied with Charles Villiers Stanford (1852–1924), one of the most important composition teachers in Europe. She was a contemporary of and personal friends with several prominent turn-of-the-century composers, including Ralph Vaughan Williams (1872–1958), Gustav Holst (1874–1934), and Maurice Ravel (1875–1937). Ravel in particular—along with Debussy—had a tremendous influence on Clarke's compositional style, which often features chromatic, octatonic, and modal writing. Although primarily known as an instrumental composer—her most famous pieces are her works for viola—she wrote several dozen songs. "The Cloths of Heaven" also features a text by Yeats. ♪

One other little-known American composer who was born in the nineteenth century should also be mentioned. Katherine Kennicott Davis (1892–1980) was born in St. Joseph, Missouri, but moved to Boston after high school to study at the New England Conservatory. After graduation, she studied with Nadia Boulanger in Paris. Over the course of her long life, she composed dozens of works across all genres, including many secular and sacred songs. Although she is most famous for composing the popular Christmas song "The Little Drummer Boy," most of her songs are more neo-romantic and contemplative in style. "Nancy Hanks" is a particularly touching art song that sets a poem by Rosemary Benét (1900–1962) about Nancy Hanks Lincoln (1784–1818), the mother of Abraham Lincoln (1809–1865).

BREAKING BARRIERS

Florence Price (1888–1953) broke barriers as one of the first female African American composers to gain national prominence. Price was very accomplished in the orchestral idiom, but her art songs prove worthy of study and performance. Price's student Margaret Bonds (1913–1972) also made a significant contribution to the art song repertoire. In the songs of Price and Bonds, "we find gripping, effective settings that fuse their music with the compelling images and words of the African American poet Langston Hughes (1902–1967), thereby creating unified, lyric structures."[13] Perhaps Price's most famous vocal work is "Songs to the Dark Virgin" (1941). Often sung by Marian Anderson (1897–1993), it has a sweeping melodic line and flowing accompaniment. Its soaring sentiment is echoed in other Price/Hughes songs such as "My Dream" (1935) and "Hold Fast to Dreams" (1946). In her settings of "The Negro Speaks of Rivers" (1941) and *Three Dream Portraits* (1959), Bonds explores more of the anguish of Hughes's poetry and "incorporates the blues harmonies of African American performers and melodic characteristics borrowed from plantation songs" in a "fusion of her formal training and her musical heritage."[14] Bonds takes a more somber turn in the haunting Countee Cullen (1903–1946) setting "To a Brown Girl Dead" (1933), while Price maintains a more optimistic outlook in "Sympathy" (from *Five Art Songs*) with a lyrical realization of the text by Paul Laurence Dunbar (1872–1906), which ends with the famous line, "I know why the caged bird sings!"[15] ♪

Undine Smith Moore (1904–1989) is revered as "the Dean of Black Women Composers." A graduate of Fisk University, the Juilliard School, and Columbia University, she returned to her native Virginia to become a professor at Virginia State University. She received a Pulitzer Prize nomination for *Scenes from the Life of a Martyr* (1981), her oratorio about Dr. Martin Luther King Jr. Her art songs seem to favor poems by women, including "I Am in Doubt" (1975) and "Lyric for Truelove" (1975) by Florence Hynes Willette (1901–1982) as well as "I Want You to Die While You Love Me" (1975) by Georgia Douglas Johnson (1880–1966). But her signature song is "Love, Let the Wind Cry" (1961), an effusive translation of the Greek poet Sappho (630 BCE–580 BCE). With its operatic phrasing and high notes, it is a suitable soprano showcase and apt recital set ending. ♪

Sharing a similar pedigree from Juilliard and Columbia, Jacqueline Hairston (b. 1938) is a graduate of Howard University whose compositions have been recorded and performed by the London Symphony Orchestra and the San Francisco Women's Philharmonic. Cousin of the well-known composer and spiritual arranger Jester Hairston (1901–2000), she gained notoriety for her own spiritual arrangements for famous singers such as Kathleen Battle (b. 1948) and Denyce Graves (b. 1964). She follows the example of Margaret Bonds in setting the poetry of Cullen with her song cycle for bass-baritone, the *Countee Cullen Trilogy* (2016). It opens with the song "Pagan Prayer," in which "Hairston uses rhythm in the voice and piano line in various ways to further illuminate the idea of a struggle between how one is expected to feel and the reality of how one may truly feel," creating "a very unsettling rhythm" reflecting the meaning of the poem.[16]

Dorothy Rudd Moore (b. 1940) is also a Howard alumna. She was a student of Nadia Boulanger who went on to write commissions for the Buffalo Philharmonic, Opera Ebony, and the National Symphony Orchestra. She lists Johann Sebastion Bach (1685–1750) and Duke Ellington (1899–1974) among her early influences. Pondering the labels of race and gender, she said: "If it so happens that someone finds inspiration from the fact I'm a female and that I'm black, that's wonderful."[17] Her work celebrates African American historical figures—such as her 1985 opera *Frederick Douglass*—and poets. Written for Hilda Harris (b. ca. 1936), *From The Dark Tower* (1970) joins the mezzo-soprano voice with cello and piano in dramatic fashion in settings of Hughes ("Dream Variation") and Cullen ("For a Poet" and the climactic "From the Dark Tower"). The soprano cycle *Sonnets on Love, Rosebuds, and Death* (1976) also celebrates Cullen (in "Youth Sings a Song of Rosebuds") and Hughes ("Song for a Dark Girl") but features female poets Alice Dunbar Nelson (1875–1935), Gwendolyn B. Bennett (1903–1981), and Helene Johnson (1906–1995) in "I Had No Thoughts of Violets of Late" (Nelson), "Some Things Are Very Dear to Me" (Bennett), and "Invocation" (Johnson). For tenor and piano, Rudd Moore's later song cycle *Flowers of Darkness* (1990) highlights texts by Leslie Morgan Col-

Figure 3.3. Tania León. *Creative Commons (CCBY-SA 3.0)*

lins (1914–2014) and Hughes in "Creole Girl" and "Harlem Sweeties," respectively. ♪

Harlem served as a creative venue for Cuban-born composer and conductor Tania León (b. 1943); she was the first musical director of the Dance Theatre of Harlem. After her early conservatory training in Havana, she moved to New York City and completed several degrees at New York University. In addition to her international symphonic conducting appearances, she has composed commissions for the Los Angeles Philharmonic, the International Contemporary Ensemble, Orpheus Chamber Orchestra, and the New World Symphony. Drawing on her diverse experience encompassing dance, orchestral music, and opera, León conducted *The Wiz* on Broadway, served as the Latin American advisor to the American Composers Orchestra, and is writing an opera about desegregation entitled *Little Rock Nine*. Her art songs explore a variety of approaches and authors, from the complex and moody *To and Fro* (1990) for mezzo-soprano with poetry by avant-garde Alison Knowles (b. 1933) to the elegiac *Mi amor es* (2015) for baritone set to the poetry of Cuban-American Carlos Pintado (b. 1974). In her *Atwood Songs* (2007), rhythmic vibrancy and unpredictability ably portray the pointed writing style of Canadian Margaret Atwood (b. 1939).

Breaking barriers and boundaries, her compositions "join contemporary techniques with numerous stylistic elements of Latin American, jazz, and gospel music. This pluralistic approach to composition results in an individual style that defies categorization."[18] ♪

BRITISH VOICES

London-born composer and actress Madeleine Dring (1923–1977) studied with Herbert Howells (1892–1983) and Vaughan Williams at the Royal College of Music. Her songs display both lyricism and wit, and though they "might remind one of the works of Roger Quilter, Dring thought of herself as having a musical personality similar to Francis Poulenc."[19] Certainly "Song of a Nightclub Proprietress" from *Five Betjeman Songs* (1976) is more like Poulenc than Quilter, with its jazzy jocularity; but her *Seven Shakespeare Songs* (published posthumously in 1992) exhibit a more typically British understated lyricism. ♪

On her website, Welsh composer Rhian Samuel (b. 1944) states that she "identifies with her female colleagues in a profession still dominated by males, seeing her position, somewhat outside the male tradition, as an exciting one with many challenges and opportunities, not one, as in former times for many woman composers, that must be denied."[20] Samuel's songs show a fondness for American-British poet Anne Stevenson (b. 1933), setting her texts in *Nantcol Songs* (2003) for medium/high voice, *Wildflower Songbook* (2014) for mezzo-soprano, and *Spring Diary* (2010) for baritone. Samuel also seems to have a fondness for baritones, providing a showcase in the song cycle *A Swift Radiant Morning* (2015). The texts of the five songs are by Charles Sorley (1895–1915), who wrote them shortly before his death during World War I at age twenty. Baritones can also enjoy singing her setting of Samuel Beckett (1906–1989) in the cycle *The Flowing Sand* (2006). A particularly interesting work is *Yr Alarch* or *The Swan* (2009), an unaccompanied work for solo baritone. *Yr Alarch* is a setting of an anonymous fourteenth-century Welsh text that requires some unique articulatory effects from the singer.[21] ♪

The songs of Emily Hall (b. 1978) also call for some unique effects, combining electronica, folk, and popular music with her more traditional training at the Royal College of Music. (British composer Emily Hall is not to be confused with Canadian composer Emily Hall [b. 1976].) Currently teaching at the Guildhall School of Music and Drama, Hall is a founding member of C3, the Camberwell Composers Collective. A participant in the Hear Her Song initiative, she has composed a trilogy of song cycles about the cycle of life: *Befalling* (2007), *Life Cycle* (2011)—which was staged at the WOW Festival (which stands for "Women of the World")— and *Rest* (2013). In addition, Hall payed homage to Robert Schumann by writing three new songs (2012) for baritone after *Dichterliebe* (1840). Cambridge-based composer Jenni Pinnock (b. 1988) has also explored new parameters of the song cycle, most notably with *Cracked Voices* (2018). This sixty-minute, twelve-song cycle "gives voice to forgotten characters from the borderlands of Hertfordshire and Cambridgeshire" with "an attached educational project in which . . . students were given the opportunity to write art songs."[22] Therefore, young composers like Pinnock are truly cultivating British voices and the future of British art song.

AMERICAN ART SONG ADVOCATES

Judith Lang Zaimont (b. 1945) received her musical education at the Juilliard Preparatory School, Queens College, and Columbia University, studying with Hugo Weisgall (1912–1997), Otto Luening (1900–1996), and Jack Beeson (1921–2010). She won the BMI prize at age eighteen for her settings of e. e. cummings (1894–1962) in *Four Songs for Mezzo-Soprano* (1965), and most of her art song compositions come from this early period of her career. Her song cycles *The Ages of Love* (1971) for baritone, *Chansons nobles et sentimentales* (1974) for high voice, and *New-Fashioned Songs* (1983) for low voice show a predilection for mainstream poets: Lord Byron (1788–1824), Charles Baudelaire (1821–1867), Paul Verlaine (1844–1896), Lord Tennyson (1809–1892), William Wordsworth (1770–1850), and William Butler Yeats. She sets female poets—Edna St. Vincent Millay (1892–1950), Sara Teasdale (1884–1933), Christina Rossetti (1830–1894)—in *Greyed Sonnets: Five Serious Songs* (1975) for soprano and piano. Zaimont received rave reviews for the cycle *From the Great Land: Women's Songs* (1982) for mezzo-soprano, Eskimo drum, and piano. Besides her substantial art song output, Zaimont has also served as an advocate for fellow female composers. She authored the book *Contemporary Concert Music by Women: A Directory of the Composers and Their Works* (1981) and edited the three-volume series *The Musical Woman: An International Perspective* (1984–1991). Both her artistry and advocacy are aligned with the title of a piece she wrote in 1977 for mezzo-soprano and string quartet: *A Woman of Valor.*

The leading female American art song composers of our time are Libby Larsen (b. 1950) and Lori Laitman (b. 1955). Larsen's art songs are a mainstay of the current recital repertory, especially for female singers. "Not only are many of Larsen's subjects female, but the majority of her solo vocal repertoire is composed for the female voice, and she primarily selects texts written by female writers, including Elizabeth Barrett Browning, Emily Dickinson, and Brenda Ueland."[23] Her soprano song cycles *Cowboy Songs* (1979) and *Songs from Letters* (1989) vividly portray American frontier characters including Calamity Jane (1852–1903). Another soprano cycle, *Margaret Songs: Three Songs of Willa Cather* (1996), conjures Americana with the train-like accompaniment of "Bright Rails" while *Sonnets from the Portuguese* (1991) is imbued with literary Britishism as in "I once thought how Theocritus had sung." The earnest, bluesy *Love after 1950* (2000) for mezzo-soprano shows great humor: its third song "Big Sister Says, 1967" begins with the honest outburst: "Beauty hurts!" The apogee of her art songs can be found in the masterful cycle *Try Me, Good King: Last Words of the Wives of Henry VIII* (2000), in which the soprano gets to portray five different queens. Luckily Larsen is still writing songs, including some with male singers in mind: *Wolf Song in Los Angeles* (2017) for tenor and *Recuerdo* (2017) for baritone. ♪

It is no coincidence that the very fitting address for Lori Laitman's website is www.artsongs.com. Laitman is also a champion of other composers, serving as a benefactor for the NATS Art Song Composition Award. But her greatest contribution is as a prolific composer of more than 250 art songs. Likened to Ned Rorem (b. 1923), Laitman possesses "an innate ability to capture the essence of textual meaning, a keen perception of vocal nuance, and a lavish intellectual and musical vocabulary that she uses with a facile ease."[24] Her songs are so numerous

Figure 3.4. Lori Laitman (photo by Christian Steiner). *Creative Commons (CCBY-SA 2.0)*

that it is hard to select a few to discuss. For those unfamiliar with her work, the Albany album *Within These Spaces: Songs of Lori Laitman* (2009) provides a thorough overview. Perhaps some of her best-known pieces are two sets for soprano: the Holocaust-themed cycle with clarinet or alto saxophone *I Never Saw Another Butterfly* (1996) and *Two Dickinson Songs* (2002). Some of my personal favorites include another Emily Dickinson (1830–1886) setting, the Rorem-esque "An Amethyst Remembrance" from *The Perfected Life* (2006), and the sexy "Second Date" from *Five Lovers* (2004), commissioned by its poet, soprano Jāma Jandroković (fl. ca. 2005). Laitman is a giving and active presence in the singing community and online. By inviting inquiries and conversation between singer and composer, she continues to nurture the well-being and sustainability of the art song genre. ♪

PROFILE: LORI LAITMAN

Describe your musical background and what led you to become a composer.

I was born into a musical family—my mother was a pianist, violinist, and singer, and my sisters were both musicians. I began studying piano at age five and flute at age seven. During the summers, I attended music camps and met young composers, but composing seemed "magical" and beyond my reach. It wasn't until I attended Yale, where many of my friends were composers, that I realized composition might be something I could also try. I began studying composition my sophomore year, with the wonderful teacher Jonathan Kramer. However, it wasn't until I started writing for the voice, in 1991, at the urging of soprano Lauren Wagner, that I felt I had finally discovered my compositional voice. And I haven't stopped writing for the voice since then.

Describe your compositional style and what it says about who you are.

My music is very lyrical. I always begin with the vocal line and custom-craft my melodies to best fit the words, hoping to create a beautiful and singable vocal line that will allow the singer to effectively communicate the words to the audience. My melodies emphasize what I consider important and also aim to comment on the meaning of the text. I feel that the "DNA" of my music is contained in the melody. After I have completed the vocal line, I proceed to the accompaniment—where all other musical aspects are additional layers of commentary on the text. I always hope to do justice to the words and hope to please the poet (if alive) with my musical interpretation. I also hope I am adding beauty to the world.

What hurdles have you encountered as a woman composer? How did you overcome them? Are there any you have yet to overcome?

I have no way of knowing whether my gender has affected my career in a negative way. I do know of instances where gender has worked in my favor. The hurdles I have had to overcome have derived more from a prejudice against melody than anything else, and that is something that I find ongoing. I try to ignore anything negative and keep writing music.

Who are your greatest inspirations, musically and artistically?
I am drawn to composers that are melodic and dramatic. Of course, I love Schubert, Schumann, Puccini, Verdi, Monteverdi, Bach, Mozart, Beethoven, Prokofiev, Tchaikovsky, Stravinsky, Barber, Bernstein, and so many other composers. I admire musicians who bring music to life with a wealth of color and imagination. My greatest inspirations are my three children, who are all wonderful musicians. My favorite composer is my daughter, Diana Rosenblum, who is currently finishing a PhD in composition at the Eastman School of Music. Her works shine with intellect, drama, and humor, and I stand in awe.

Juliana Hall (b. 1958) and Judith Cloud (b. 1954) are both active art song composers. Hall is a graduate of the Yale School of Music and a former student of Dominick Argento (b. 1927). In the words of Katherine Eberle (b. 1954), "What sets Hall's songs apart from others of her generation is that she gives great attention to detail, chooses emotionally charged texts, and . . . uses constantly changing rhythmic motives that highlight her text settings, so that no two songs sound alike."[25] Like Larsen and Laitman, she has been drawn to Emily Dickinson and Elizabeth Barrett Browning (1806–1861), composing *Syllables of Velvet: Seven Songs for Soprano and Piano on Letters of Emily Dickinson* (1989) and *How Do I Love Thee? Five Songs for Soprano and Piano* (2015). Of special interest is Hall's Shakespearean song cycle *O Mistress Mine: Twelve Songs for Countertenor and Piano* (2015), which is sung by Darryl Taylor (b. 1969) on the MSR Classics CD *Love's Signature* (2016) with Hall herself at the piano. Cloud is a mezzo-soprano and professor of voice at Northern Arizona University. Not surprisingly, her writing shows great sensitivity to the voice. In a review of her album *Letting Escape a Song: Art Songs of Judith Cloud* (2011), she was praised for her "dual excellence as both composer and singer" as well as her *Four Sonnets by Pablo Neruda, Set 2* (2008), which reveal "some of her richest and most moving music."[26] The set opens with "If Your Eyes Were Not the Color of the Moon" and its effusive triplet melismas. Some of her most popular song cycles are *Botany of the Gods* (2016) for soprano, *Five Edgar Allen Poe Songs* (2014) for bass-baritone, *Cowboy Dreams* (2013) for tenor or high baritone, and the Margaret Atwood settings of *Night Dreams* (2006) for soprano or mezzo-soprano. Eberle, a fellow mezzo-soprano, has recorded several of Cloud's songs including another Neruda sonnet, "I Do Not Love You as If You Were Salt-Rose, or Topaz," "The Death of the Tango" from *The Secret History of Water* (2003), and "The Shape of Laughter" from *Awake on a Spring Night* (1994). Cloud and Hall—along with Laitman and Larsen—are featured on Eberle's album *In This Moment: Women and Their Songs* (2013), a celebration of these accomplished art song composers and advocates. ♪

THE NEXT GENERATION

Fortunately, the art song continues to be championed by the next generation of female composers. Sarah Kirkland Snider (b. 1973) is a graduate of Wesleyan University and the Yale School of Music whose works have been commissioned and performed by the New York Philharmonic, the San Francisco Symphony, and the St. Paul Chamber Orchestra, among others. Her song cycle *Penelope* (2009) revisits Homer's *Odyssey* from the viewpoint of his wife who waits for his return. Snider describes it as "suspended somewhere between art song, indie rock, and chamber folk."[27] She is also part of the collaborative evening-length song cycle *The Blue Hour* (2017) composed along with Rachel Grimes (b. 1970), Shara Nova (b. 1974), Angélica Negrón (b. 1981), and Caroline Shaw (b. 1982). In her individual songs, Snider has set the poetry of William Blake (1757–1827), William Butler Yeats, and Anne Sexton (1928–1974) in "Mad Song" (1998) for tenor and "The Heart of the Woman" (1998) and "Just Once" (1997), both for soprano. In 2006, she was the pianist at the premiere of her song for countertenor, "Passenger Seat."

Another pianist-composer is Jocelyn Hagen (b. 1980). A former student of Judith Lang Zaimont, Hagen holds music degrees from St.

Olaf College and the University of Minnesota. She has more than a dozen songs and song cycles to her credit.[28] One of the pioneering approaches Hagen brings to the field is her advocacy of a commissioning consortium. She encourages performers or donors to come together as a group to share the benefits and the cost of the commission. This crowd-commissioning is what led to the creation of her song cycle *Kiss* (2013) for soprano and piano with texts by Julia Klatt Singer (b. 1963). Another group, the North Dakota Music Teachers' Association, commissioned her soprano cycle *Songs of Fields and Prairies* (2004), which won the San Francisco Song Festival Composition Competition as well as honorable mention in the Lotte Lehmann Foundation Song Cycle Competition. Abbie Betinis (b. 1980) has also won a number of awards including the Craig and Janet Swan Composer Prize and the Polyphonos Young Composer Prize, and like Hagen, she is also a graduate of St. Olaf College and the University of Minnesota. The Linden Duo commissioned her cycle *The Clan of the Lichens* (2004) for high voice using poetry by American nature writer Opal Whiteley (1897–1992). Betinis set Norwegian texts in the cycle *Nattsanger* or *Night Songs* (2008) for soprano, commissioned by the Schubert Club. Also of interest is her song for tenor, piano, and snare drum entitled *Abraham Lincoln Walks at Moonlight* (2014). Betinis worked briefly as an assistant to Larsen but her primary mentor is Zaimont. On her website, she writes: "Professor Zaimont, who praised my vocal music most highly, still worries that my affinity toward texted music could develop into a 'crutch.'"[29] It is hard to imagine that this "crutch" wouldn't be a great gift for an art song composer.

The University of Nevada, Las Vegas, boasts two talented female composers on its faculty: Juilliard graduate Cynthia Lee Wong (b. 1982) and Eastman graduate Jennifer Bellor (b. 1983). In 2013, Wong was selected as the second composer of the New Voices project, which has Boosey and Hawkes, the San Francisco Symphony, and the New World Symphony partner in mentoring emerging composers. And in 2017, she received an Opera America Discovery Grant for Female Composers for her work-in-progress android comedy *No Guarantees*. Like Sarah Kirkland Snider, Wong set Anne Sexton in her soprano song "Just Once" (2002). The New York State Music Teachers Association (NYSMTA) and the Music Teachers National Association (MTNA) commissioned her *Six Gupta Songs* (2013). The very earnest and contemporary poetry by Deepali Gupta brings out Wong's playful wit in "Howling" and "A Vision." Her humor is not surprising since she is also a cartoonist, but Wong can also be vulnerable and heartfelt, as in "Ends and Beginnings" and "The Only One." Bellor has also won a number of awards, including the 2016 American Prize for Orchestral Composition, the Judith Lang Zaimont Prize, and a Downbeat Award. Also a vocalist, she often performs her own works. Her cycle *Songs in the Dark* (2016) highlights the gothic, atmospheric quality of the poetry of Emily Brontë (1818–1848). With pop and jazz influences inflecting her works, Bellor almost evokes a post-millennial Kate Bush (b. 1958). Her music always has a mesmerizing mood. This is demonstrated in *My Doleful Prison* (2017), her setting of a letter to Henry VIII from the imprisoned Anne Boleyn awaiting her execution. It is written for soprano and piano with optional electronics and projected imagery. Bellor says:

> When I first read the letter, I knew I wanted to create a mad scene. . . . In addition to the soprano and piano parts, I used Logic samples to create a present-day atmosphere that one might experience sitting in a jail cell. One would hear footsteps of prison guards approaching on a regular basis, along with clanging of the metal bars, people yelling, and even abstract sounds that one might experience in electrocution chambers.[30]

This immersive effect creates an engrossing soundscape, only heightened by the visual impact of the projected images. The art song as a multimedia experience is a twenty-first-century trend gaining traction at song recitals across the country, and Bellor illuminates this movement toward an immersive art song environment. ♪

A graduate of Yale and Northwestern, Alex Temple (b. 1983) also strives to create a specific mood by distorting "iconic sounds to create new meanings" and "reclaiming socially disapproved-of ('cheesy') sounds, playing with the boundary between funny and frightening, and investigating lost memories and secret histories."[31] She studied under Tania León at the University of Michigan, another bit of the lineage of female composers of American art song. Her two-song set of *Whitman Songs* (2006) was inspired by dream pop singer Julee Cruise (b. 1956), who performed the theme song of the early 1990s television show *Twin Peaks*. Part of a commission of fifteen different composers to write a

Figure 3.5. Alex Temple. *Creative Commons (CCBY-SA 3.0)*

response to Arnold Schoenberg's *Das Buch der hängenden Gärten*, "Second Moon" brings a jazzy feel with its bossa nova style marking. In more reverence to Schoenberg, "The White-Walled Room" (2012) combines *Pierrot lunaire* sprechstimme and trip-hop techniques with electronica to create something both familiar and entirely new. With works like "The White-Walled Room," Temple seems to suggest the next step in the evolution of art song could be voice and electronica. ♪

FINAL THOUGHTS

The contributions of women to the art song canon cannot be overstated. There is perhaps no genre with a richer history of literature by women composers. The composers listed in this chapter deserve to be performed as often as their male colleagues who constitute the majority of most recital programs. Women are no longer confined to smaller forms, but some choose to excel at it. It is our hope that this chapter introduces the reader to fresh ideas, new names, and exquisite repertoire to program and celebrate.

NOTES

1. Matthew Hoch, *A Dictionary for the Modern Singer* (Lanham, MD: Rowman & Littlefield, 2014), 15.
2. James R. Briscoe, *New Historical Anthology of Music by Women* (Bloomington: Indiana University Press, 2004), 39–41.
3. Christine A. Colin, "Exceptions to the Rule: German Women in Music in the Eighteenth Century," *UCLA Historical Journal* 14 (1994): 242.
4. Diane Peacock Jezic, *Women Composers: The Lost Tradition Found*, 2nd edition (New York: The Feminist Press, 1988), 66.
5. Anna Beer, *Sounds and Sweet Airs: The Forgotten Women of Classical Music* (London: Oneworld, 2016), 160.
6. Jezic, *Women Composers*, 76.
7. Ibid., 85.
8. Alma Mahler's turbulent love life was dramatized in the 2001 film *Bride of the Wind*, although the adaptation is considered to be only loosely based on facts. Nevertheless, it is an entertaining film that effectively captures Alma's romantic (and feisty) spirit.
9. Carol Kimball, *Song: A Guide to Art Song Style and Literature*, rev. ed. (New York: Hal Leonard, 2006), 201.
10. The six members of Les Six were Georges Auric (1899–1983), Louis Durey (1888–1979), Arthur Honegger (1892–1955), Darius Milhaud (1892–1974), Francis Poulenc (1899–1963), and Germaine Tailleferre (1892–1983). The name derives from a 1920 article written by the French music critic Henri Collet (1885–1951).
11. For more on Ethel Smyth's operas, see chapter 4.
12. The members of the "Boston Six" were John Knowles Paine (1839–1906), Arthur Foote (1853–1937), George Chadwick (1854–1931), Amy Beach (1867–1944), Edward MacDowell (1861–1908), and Horatio Parker (1863–1919). The "Second New England School" contrasts with the "First New England School" of the previous century, a designation for the style of William Billings (1746–1800) and his contemporaries. The name is also a spinoff of the "Second Viennese School" represented by Arnold Schoenberg (1874–1951), Alban Berg (1885–1935), and Anton Webern (1883–1945).
13. Penelope Peters, "Deep Rivers: Selected Songs of Florence Price and Margaret Bonds," *Canadian University Music Review* 16, no. 1 (1995): 74.
14. Ibid., 83, 86.
15. For more on Florence Price and Margaret Bonds, see chapter 2.
16. Phillip Harris, "Spiritual Roots and Classical Fruits: A Stylistic Analysis and Performance Guide of Selected Spirituals and Art Songs by Jacqueline Hairston" (DMA dissertation, University of Nevada, Las Vegas, 2018), 48.

17. Dorothy Rudd Moore, interview with Bruce Duffie, February 10, 1990, www.bruceduffie.com/moore.html, accessed July 27, 2018.

18. James Spinazzola, "A Conversation with Tania León," *Women of Influence in Contemporary Music: Nine American Composers*, ed. Michael K. Slayton (Lanham, MD: Scarecrow Press, 2011), 256.

19. Wanda Brister, "The Songs of Madeleine Dring," *Journal of Singing* 64, no. 5 (2008): 568.

20. www.rhiansamuel.com/p/about.html, accessed July 28, 2018.

21. Matthew Hoch (b. 1975), coauthor of this book, sang the American premiere of *Yr Alarch* at the 2018 Music by Women Festival at Mississippi University for Women.

22. www.jennipinnock.com, accessed July 28, 2018.

23. Tina Milhorn Stallard, "A Conversation with Libby Larsen," *Women of Influence in Contemporary Music: Nine American Composers*, 212. The poets' birth and death dates are as follows: Elizabeth Barrett Browning (1806–1861), Emily Dickinson (1830–1886), and Brenda Ueland (1891–1985).

24. Sharon Mabry, "The Masterful Lori Laitman," *Journal of Singing* 64, no. 1 (2007): 95.

25. Katherine Eberle, "From Words to Music: Three Song Cycles of Juliana Hall," *Journal of Singing* 71, no. 5 (2015): 573.

26. Gregory Berg, "The Listener's Gallery," *Journal of Singing* 68, no. 2 (2011): 239–40.

27. www.penelope-music.com, accessed July 29, 2018.

28. Linda Lister (b. 1969), coauthor of this book, sang the world premiere of Jocelyn Hagen's *The Time of Singing Has Come* at the Shorter College New Music Series on September 14, 2009.

29. www.abbiebetinis.com, accessed July 29, 2018.

30. www.jenniferbellor.com, accessed July 29, 2018.

31. www.alextemple.com, accessed July 29, 2018.

4

OPERAS BY WOMEN

As mentioned in previous chapters, a glance at the repertory of major opera companies gives the impression that there are very few women composing operas. Since its founding in 1880, the Metropolitan Opera has performed only two operas by female composers. Dame Ethel Smyth (1858–1944) saw her Wagner-inspired one-act opera *Der Wald* (1901) play in Berlin and Covent Garden prior to its presentation at the Met in 1903. Paired alternately with *Il trovatore* (1853) and *La fille du régiment* (1839), *Der Wald* has not found the success of these counterparts, to some extent due to gender-based criticism questioning how "a well-bred (and unmarried) English lady could comprehend the difference between sacred and profane love."[1] It is doubtful that reviews of Giuseppe Verdi (1813–1901) and Gaetano Donizetti (1797–1848) included discussion of their marital status and its impact on their compositions. Smyth's other operas, mostly comic in nature, were performed throughout Germany and England. They include *Fantasio* (1894), *The Wreckers* (1904), *The Boatswain's Mate* (1914), *Fête galante* (1922), and *Entente cordiale* (1924). Besides breaking ground at the opera house, Smyth paved the way for women in other ways, composing the suffragette anthem "The March of the Women" (1910) and going to jail in the fight for women's right to vote. ♪

Figure 4.1.   Ethel Smyth (portrait by John Singer Sargent, 1901). *Creative Commons (CCBY-SA-1.0)*

It would be 113 years before the Met staged another opera by a woman. In 2016, Finnish composer Kaija Saariaho (b. 1952) witnessed the Metropolitan Opera production and Met HD Live broadcast of her opera *L'amour de loin* (2000). This luminous work evokes both the medieval and the modern and has been produced multiple times across Europe (premiering at the Salzburg Festival) and North America (Canadian Opera

Company and Santa Fe Opera). Saariaho's other operas include *Adriana Mater* (2006), which addresses contemporary issues of war and rape, and the soprano monodrama *Émilie* (2010) about mathematician, philosopher, and physicist Émilie du Châtelet (1706–1749). While she was initially reluctant to discuss the label of woman composer, an NPR interview led Saariaho to acknowledge the gender barrier, "even if it seems so unbelievable. You know, half of humanity has something to say, also."[2] ♪

WOMEN COMPOSING OPERA: A BRIEF OVERVIEW FROM CACCINI TO TALMA

Despite the limited representation of female composers at the Met, women have been composing operas for centuries. Francesca Caccini (1587–after 1641) was the daughter of Giulio Caccini (1551–1618), familiar to many as the composer of the song "Amarilli, mia bella." A musician in the Medici court in Florence, he was instrumental in the development of *stile recitativo* through his compositions in *Le nuove musiche* (1602). No doubt his work, along with that of the Florentine Camerata, influenced the monodic writings of his daughter. Francesca Caccini participated in the birth of opera as a genre. She sang in Jacopo Peri's *Euridice* (1600), which remains the earliest extant opera. (Peri's earlier opera, *Dafne*, was written in 1597; it is considered to be the first opera written, but no manuscript has survived.) The inception of both opera and the baroque era provided the inspiration, and the Medici court provided the outlet for Caccini to compose. Although it was labeled a *balletto*, her theatrical work *La liberazione di Ruggiero dall'isola d'Alcina* (1625) is often named as the first opera written by a woman. Performed at court during Carnaval "for the visit of Polish Prince Sigismund," the premiere "was so lavishly staged that it even included Spanish riding horses!"[3] Recently, *La liberazione* has enjoyed renewed interest, with recordings and performances by the Warsaw Chamber Opera, Ensemble Renaissance, the Toronto Consort, and the Brighton Early Music Festival. Opera Ithaca, a strong proponent of female composers, programmed a double bill for their 2018–2019 season comprising Caccini's *La liberazione* and the world premiere of *Enchantress* by Kamala Sankaram (b. ca. 1979). ♪

Francesca Caccini's operatic trailblazing led to a blossoming of female opera composers in France. For instance, seven works by three women are known during the first fifty years of French opera (1670–1720), while the next fifty years (1720–1770) had twelve operas by seven women, increasing to fifty-four operas by twenty-three women leading into the nineteenth century (1770–1820).[4] Despite this burst of creative activity, these female French composers remain mostly unknown today. Amélie-Julie Candeille (1767–1834) saw multiple performances of her opera *Catherine, ou la belle fermière* (1792), while none of the nine operas by Isabelle de Charrière (1740–1805) ever reached the stage. With famous opera singers as her father—tenor Manuel García I (1775–1832)—and sister—mezzo-soprano Maria Malibran (1808–1836)—it is not surprising that Pauline Viardot (1821–1910) ventured into the genre as performer and then composer. After performing a number of leading mezzo-soprano roles, including originating the title role in *Sapho* (1850) by Charles Gounod (1818–1893), she was encouraged to compose by Franz Liszt (1811–1886). Of Viardot's five operas, the best known today is *Cendrillon*, which premiered in 1904 when she was eighty-three. Her version of the Cinderella story has been seeing more performances particularly at American universities such as Cornell, Ithaca College, and Southeastern Louisiana University, due in part to a new English translation by Rachel M. Harris (b. 1963).

By the twentieth century, North American women were writing operas, but they too encountered challenges in bringing their works to the stage. Known primarily for her art songs, Amy Beach (1867–1944) did compose one chamber opera, *Cabildo*, although she did not live to see its premiere in 1947. Nadia Boulanger (1887–1978) disciple and Sibelius Medal winner Louise Talma (1906–1996) collaborated with famed playwright Thornton Wilder (1897–1975) on the opera *The Alcestiad* (1962). Sung in German at its premiere in Frankfurt, the opera "was the first work by an American woman to be produced by a major European opera house. Despite the warm reception, it was not performed again"[5] until Phyllis Curtin (1921–2016) sang excerpts in English at the Yale School of Music in 1976. Australian-born composer Peggy Glanville-Hicks (1912–1990) became an American citizen in 1948. A pupil of both Boulanger and Ralph Vaughan Williams (1872–1958), she received a commission to write *The Transposed Heads* for Kentucky Opera and the Louisville Philharmonic Society in 1953. It was "apparently the first opera commission awarded to a woman composer."[6] This led to a commission from San Francisco Opera in 1963; written as a star vehicle for Maria Callas (1923–1977), Glanville-Hicks's *Sappho* went unperformed.[7] Thus even when female opera composers began to receive commissions, getting operas produced remained a challenge.

OPERAS BY AFRICAN AMERICAN WOMEN

One of the first African American female opera composers to gain notice was Evelyn LaRue Pittman (1910–1992). Following studies at Spelman College and the University of Oklahoma, she attended the Juilliard School, where she worked with Robert Ward (1917–2013). After perusing an early draft of Pittman's biblical folk opera *Cousin Esther* (1954), Nadia Boulanger invited Pittman to study with her in Paris, writing in a letter: "I comprehend what you are doing, and it's charming, charming, charming. . . . Let me help you. You have the spark."[8] Pittman finished *Cousin Esther* under Boulanger and saw portions of the opera premiere in Paris before it was performed at Carnegie Hall and presented at the WNYC American Music Festival in 1963. Her opera about Martin Luther King Jr. (1929–1968) entitled *Freedom Child* (1972) seems ready for rediscovery and worthy of a twenty-first-century production. More recently, jazz composer and cellist Diedre Murray (b. 1951) collaborated with librettist Carl Hancock Rux (b. 1975) on an opera about another historically significant figure. Premiering at the Bard College SummerScape festival, Murray's *The Blackamoor Angel* (2007) explores the life of Angelo Soliman (1721–1796), the first African freemason. With a remarkable ascendancy from slave to royal tutor to friend of Mozart, Soliman possibly inspired characters in Mozart's operas, namely Selim in *Die Entführung aus dem Serail* (1782) and Monastatos in *Die Zauberflöte* (1791). Soliman's Mozartean interaction is explored in Murray's opera along with the macabre taxidermic exhibition of his body in the Viennese Imperial Library. Winner of an Obie Award and a finalist for the 1999 Pulitzer Prize in Drama, the "roots" opera *Running Man* deals more with the plight of the common man, specifically a middle-class family and their son's struggle with drug addiction. From Boulanger-trained

Figure 4.2.   Evelyn LaRue Pittman (photo by Carl Van Vechten, 1962). *Creative Commons (CCBY-SA 2.0)*

Evelyn Pittman to jazz-inspired Diedre Murray, African American female composers have made important contributions by synthesizing elements of American music with the European operatic tradition. ♪

BRITISH OPERA BY WOMEN

Dame Elizabeth Maconchy (1907–1994) is an important figure among female composers of British opera. She trained with Ralph Vaughan

Williams at the Royal College of Music, where female students were initially separated from male students and even forced to use a separate entrance. But her music did not fit the traditional mode. In fact, Maconchy was sometimes "described as a 'quasi-masculine' composer who uses her intellect to compose rather than being guided by her 'feminine' emotions (as, by implication, most other women composers were)."[9] Her five operas include *The Sofa* (1957) and *The Departure* (1961), which have regained public attention thanks to the Independent Opera 2009 production and recording.

As we move to an examination of living female composers, it is important to note that there would be no Musgrave without Maconchy. Scottish-born Thea Musgrave (b. 1928) is part of the Boulanger lineage but she was also a student of Aaron Copland (1900–1990). Her operatic output is prolific, with ten theatrical works. The heroines of her operas are often famous female historical figures. They include the aptly Scottish subject *Mary, Queen of Scots* (1977); *Harriet, the Woman Called Moses* (1983), about Harriet Tubman (ca. 1822–1913); and *Pontalba* (2003), based on the nineteenth-century New Orleans heiress the Baroness de Pontalba (1795–1874). Musgrave has been fortunate in that a number of her works have been commissioned and/or produced by companies all over the world, such as Scottish Opera, the Royal Opera House, Virginia Opera, and New Orleans Opera. When she conducted the New York City Opera production of *The Voice of Ariadne* in 1977, it was "the first opera by a woman performed by a major New York company since the Met put on Ethyl Smyth's *Der Wald* in 1903."[10] In May 2018, her ninetieth birthday was celebrated on social media with the hashtag #Musgrave90. ♪

After training at Cambridge and Tanglewood with John Tavener (1944–2013), Robin Holloway (b. 1943), and Gunther Schuller (1925–2015), Judith Weir (b. 1954) followed in Musgrave's footsteps to become a highly successful British composer. While Musgrave's musical language often explores expanding tonalities bordering on expressionism, Weir cultivates a more traditionally tonal landscape. She has ten operas ranging from the ten-minute tour de force *King Harald's Saga* (1979), in which the solitary soprano sings all eight roles, to the full-length work *A Night at the Chinese Opera* (1987). *Miss Fortune* (2011), her most recent opera, has been staged at Covent Garden as well as at the prestigious Bregenzer Festspiele. In 2014, Weir was named the first female Master of the Queen's Music.

A new generation of female composers continues to bring British opera to life. Emily Hall (b. 1978) has written five operas. *Sante* (2006), her first, was premiered by the London Sinfonietta. She explored the boundaries of genre with her film-opera *The Nightingale and the Rose* (2010), her concept album/opera *Folie à deux* (2015), and her site-specific operatic installation *Found and Lost* (2016) performed at the Corinthia Hotel London. London-born Hannah Kendall (b. 1984) gained notice for her baritone monodrama *The Knife of Dawn* (2016) portraying the Guyanese poet and activist Martin Carter (1927–1997). The opera was inspired by her mother's Afro-Caribbean roots. Recognizing issues of gender and race, Kendall has noted that the music world is "generally run by men; by white middle-class, middle-aged men" and that she wanted to write an operatic role "for a person of African/Caribbean descent. I think it's really important."[11] Both Hall and Kendall represent the evolving cultural creativity of British opera by women.

WOMEN WRITING AMERICAN OPERA

If there were the title of female "Master of American Opera," it would have to be bestowed on Libby Larsen (b. 1950). With eleven operas to her credit, her output is substantial. Opera Theater of Arkansas premiered her *Clair de lune* in 1985. It features a refreshingly nontraditional leading lady, a fifty-year-old soprano aviatrix, whose aria is a striking reenvisioning of Debussy's "Clair de lune" from *Suite bergamasque* (1905). *Eric Hermannson's Soul* (1998) was commissioned by Opera Omaha, while Minnesota Opera commissioned the ambitious *Frankenstein, the Modern Prometheus* (1990). The original multimedia elements did not fully realize Larsen's vision of the Mary Shelley (1797–1851) character, most likely due to the era's limited technical capabilities. But the 2017 West Edge Opera production in Berkeley, California, more successfully implemented the high-tech special effects and projections to support the composer's concept. The young adult science-fiction novel by Madeline L'Engle (1918–2007) was the inspiration for the Opera Delaware commission of *A Wrinkle in Time*. Act I was produced in 1992, but then the opera was put on hold for more than twenty years. Imagining another elaborate staging, Fort Worth Opera scheduled its full world premiere for 2015 as part of their Opera of the Americas festival; but when company fund-raising fell short of the million dollars needed to mount the production, *A Wrinkle in Time* was abruptly cut from the season in early 2014. Larsen has also premiered some of her works in university settings. Based on the novel by Virginia Woolf (1882–1941), *Mrs. Dalloway* (1993) was first staged at the Cleveland Institute of Music. *Every Man Jack* (2006) took its first bow at Sonoma State University, and I (Linda) had the pleasure of singing Madge in the world premiere of Larsen's *Picnic* (2009) at the University of North Carolina at Greensboro. With its six soprano roles, *Picnic* is ideal for many collegiate opera forces, and the jazz-inspired portions and all-American subject add to its audience appeal. ♪

Like Larsen, Lori Laitman (b. 1955) is well regarded for her art song compositions. Her first operatic endeavor was *Come to Me in My Dreams* (2004), a chamber opera that repurposed some of her songs. A children's opera featuring a cast of three princesses, a frog prince, and a frog king, *The Three Feathers* (2014) was commissioned by Virginia Tech in cooperation with Opera Roanoke and the Blacksburg Children's Chorale. But Laitman's most notable operatic achievement is her realization of the familiar novel *The Scarlet Letter* by Nathaniel Hawthorne (1804–1864). Collaborating with librettist David Mason (b. 1954), she initially composed the work in 2008 but revised it in 2015 for its 2016 premiere with Opera Colorado. The opera showcases a vibrant portrayal of the character of Hester Prynne:

> That Laitman might be attracted to a strong woman who defies convention and devotes her life to motherhood comes as no surprise. Laitman has defied the traditional conventions of a life in opera. During her twenties, when most composers devote their primary attention to hustling for performances, Laitman devoted her life to raising three children in suburban Washington, D.C. It was, she says, a conscientious plan: children before career, carpools before commissions.[12]

Laitman may have made conscious choices to prioritize motherhood earlier in her life, but the deferred success may be even sweeter. She was patient and persistent through the delays in the genesis and eventual premiere of *The Scarlet Letter*, using the time to continue revising and refining the opera. Its positive reception has heightened expectation for the completion of her works in progress: *Ludlow* and *Uncovered*. ♪

Composer, singer, choreographer, and filmmaker Meredith Monk (b. 1942) has been a pioneer in the American arts scene since she began writing vocal music in the 1960s. Many of her compositions do not fit standard genre labels, leading to descriptions such as music-theater works. She calls *Vessel* (1972) an opera epic for seventy-five voices, electronic organ, dulcimer, and accordion. Monk sang the role of Joan of Arc at the opera's premiere. Portraying a woman aging in reverse à la Benjamin Button, she also performed her monodrama *Education of the Girlchild* (1973) in its first incarnation before the revised *Education of the Girlchild Revisited* (2010), which incorporated more singers. Her theater piece *Quarry* (1976), an opera in three movements, played Off-Broadway at La MaMa. When Houston Grand Opera commissioned Monk's opera *Atlas* (1991), it was actually her first work for an opera company instead of her own ensemble. In the words of composer William Albright (1944–1998):

> Monk has been calling her larger theater works "operas" since 1971. But they have little in common with the "museum pieces" that are the backbone of opera seasons around the world. To her, an opera is not a play set to music but "a multi-perceptual form combining music, movement, theater and visual images. I'm a fan of the *idea* of opera but not the way it has been done," she said a couple of days after the premiere [of *Atlas*].[13]

Monk's multidisciplinary method and label-averse approach paved the way for many contemporary female composers to follow her.

MORE OPERA COMMISSIONS FOR FEMALE COMPOSERS

Houston Grand Opera commissioned a more traditional work in Rachel Portman's *The Little Prince* (2003). Portman (b. 1960) is a prolific film composer, winning an Academy Award for *Emma* (1996) as well as receiving Oscar nominations for Best Original Score for *The Cider House Rules* (1999) and *Chocolat* (2000). Befitting her British heritage (and its choirboy tradition), she made the Little Prince a boy soprano. The highly appealing children's opera was considered enjoyable but not revolutionary: "Ms. Portman's music . . . tells us nothing we haven't known for 110 years, offering Vaughan Williams-like declamation and impressionistic gesture as synthesized for Broadway. Yet . . . it is unfailingly graceful and acutely responsive to the mood of the stage."[14] Portman's *Prince* has since been produced by San Francisco Opera, Santa Fe Opera, New York City Opera, and Tulsa Opera, as well as on a special BBC broadcast. ♪

Jennifer Higdon (b. 1962) made a name for herself via her highly regarded concerti, winning the Pulitzer Prize and two Grammy Awards among other accolades. Once a student at the Curtis Institute of Music, she now serves as their Rock Chair of Composition. With a seemingly halcyon ascent to success, Higdon acknowledges her female forebearers: "I actually think that there are a lot of composers who have ahead of me, like Joan Tower and Libby Larsen, who helped kick the doors down. . . . Those ladies did pave the way for us."[15] Her first opera came to be through a prestigious commission based on the popular Oprah's Book Club selection *Cold Mountain* (1997) by Charles Frazier (b. 1950). After an abandoned commitment from San Francisco Opera, four companies were involved in the opera's commission, leading to a four-year schedule of performances at Santa Fe Opera (2015), Opera Philadelphia (2016), North Carolina Opera (2017), and Minnesota Opera (2018). Although Minnesota Opera ultimately did not produce the opera as scheduled, *Cold Mountain* has received mostly positive reviews, especially for its orchestral writing, and garnered more Grammy nominations for Higdon. It also won the International Opera Award for Best World Premiere in 2016. In 2018, Higdon won an Opera America Female Composer Grant for her first chamber opera—with a working title of *Ashes*—which will premiere in 2020 at Opera Philadelphia's Festival O20. ♪

Besides commissioning operas by Larsen and Higdon, Minnesota Opera has also supported female composers Susan Kander (b. 1957) and Paola Prestini (b. 1975). Minnesota Opera worked with Lyric Opera of Kansas City to commission Kander's chamber opera *The Giver* (2012), based on the Newbery Medal–winning young adult novel by Lois Lowry (b. 1937). Kander's work seems greatly inspired by young people and often involves them directly in the production. Her one-act *One False Move* (2004) is described as an opera for girls and young women, written for a cast of elementary and high school age singers. And her youth opera *Somebody's Children* (2001) calls for three professional singers and a children's chorus. Kander also shows an interest in African American issues relating to the Civil War, as portrayed in *Somebody's Children* and *She Never Lost a Passenger: Harriet Tubman and the Underground Railroad* (1995). In addition, she wrote the libretto for Adolphus Hailstork's opera *Joshua's Boots* (1999) about African American cowboys in Dodge City, Kansas. The visceral impact of the civil rights and social issues explored in her operas has led to many productions at companies such as Shreveport Opera, Opera Memphis, Central City Opera, Amarillo Opera, Baltimore Lyric Opera, and Cape Town Opera, among others.

Another recent Minnesota Opera commission is Paola Prestini's *The Miraculous Journey of Edward Tulane*. Still in progress, this work is another realization of a young adult novel, this time the tale of a toy rabbit by Kate DiCamillo (b. 1964). Prestini's website envisions that the opera will involve "advanced puppetry and state-of-the-art projection design in its storytelling."[16] Her multimedia opera *Oceanic Verses* (2009), commissioned by Carnegie Hall, features an eclectic cast pairing opera singers with a folk singer and improviser. An ongoing intriguing project called *Film Stills* is a series of monodramas by various composers including Prestini and Missy Mazzoli (b. 1980), inspired by the photography of Cindy Sherman (b. 1954) and designed to be performed in museum and gallery settings. Prestini actively supports other artists through collaborations such as this through her work as creative director of National Sawdust, cultivating interdisciplinary arts activities in Brooklyn and touring works with social and ecological themes. Younger Internet-savvy composers such as Prestini and Mazzoli have learned to reach a worldwide audience with their web presence, sharing and marketing their works via Vimeo, YouTube, Twitter, and Instagram.

Fellow Brooklynite Missy Mazzoli has been called "Brooklyn's postmillennial Mozart" by *Time Out New York* magazine. With a fascinating female lead, her opera *Song from the Uproar* (2012) tells the story of Isabelle Eberhardt (1877–1904), a nineteenth-century Swiss adventurer who dressed in male attire and became a Sufi. The opera utilizes electronics to help create Mazzoli's unique soundscape. Opera Philadelphia commissioned her next major work, *Breaking the Waves* (2016), which won Best New Opera of the year from the Music Critics Association of North America. Mazzoli breaks new ground with her controversial subject matter; it is not often that an opera comes with a content warning such as this one from the Opera Philadelphia website: "This production includes explicit language, nudity, and sexual content, some of a violent nature. Recommended for mature audiences only."[17] Even Mazzoli's promotional photos have a dynamic edge evoking her indie-rock influences. Aptly, she leads an all-female band named Victoire that combines classical music with electronica. But she has taken her rock-infused opera all the way to the Kennedy Center, where her latest work, *Proving Up* (2018), premiered. And soon she will take an opera to the Met: in September 2018, the Metropolitan Opera announced its first commissions by female composers, Jeanine Tesori (b.1961) and Mazzoli. ♪

Figure 4.3. Missy Mazzoli (photo by Marylene May). *Creative Commons (CCBY-SA 2.0)*

CANADIAN WOMEN IN OPERA

Canadian women are also composing interesting and exciting new works exploring topics previously untouched on the operatic stage. Juliet Palmer (b. 1967) has an idiosyncratic output including an atomic cartoon opera entitled *Shelter* (2012) and *Sweat* (2014), an a cappella opera about female factory workers. Palmer broke boundaries with *Voice-Box* (2010), an interdisciplinary work fusing boxing, dance, and opera and featuring an all-female cast. Women couldn't legally box in Canada until 1991, so both the opera's subject and its action shape it into a vehicle of female empowerment. Librettist-performer Anna Chatterton (b. 1975) says that with its ballerinas and boxers, "the production often juxtaposes stereotypes of masculine and feminine. . . . We get to play off the diva against the fighter."[18] Palmer plays with gender roles as well as electronic and alternative sounds to bring her distinctive ethos to life.

Another up-and-coming Canadian opera composer is Monica Pearce (b. 1984). Both executive director of the Music Gallery and co-artistic director of the Toy Piano Composers, Pearce has said: "What I love about writing contemporary opera especially is that you can take experiences from everyday life and really give them the dramatic framework they deserve."[19] Pearce's female-centered works have been performed by a number of cutting-edge festivals and workshops such as New Fangled Opera, Opera from Scratch, and the Bicycle Opera Project ("the only opera company that tours by bicycle"). Her opera *April* (2016) is about a woman's experience on a biking trail, while the soprano monodrama *Aunt Helen* (2012) is one side of an interview with a folk-song collector. Commissioned by Essential Opera, Pearce's *Etiquette* (2014) features three famous women who would all be fascinating dinner guests: Emily Post (1872–1960), Dorothy Parker (1893–1967), and Lady Nancy Astor (1879–1964).

WOMEN WRITING OPERAS FOR WOMEN

While women composers are often underrepresented on concert programs, female singers most often outnumber male singers in collegiate opera programs. For instance, I (Linda) had twenty-four students in my most recent opera workshop course and nineteen were women; thus, women constituted three-quarters of the class. Colleagues across the country concur that this is a common scenario. Considering the predominance of female singers, some composers have wisely written works for all-female casts.

A graduate of the University of Minnesota, Leanna Kirchoff (b. 1969) studied with both Dominick Argento (b. 1927) and Judith Lang Zaimont (b. 1945). She completed her DMA at the University of Colorado, where her composition teachers included Richard Toensing (1940–2014), Carter Pann (b. 1972), and Daniel Kellogg (b. 1976). Kirchoff serves on the composition faculties of both the University of Denver and Metropolitan State University of Denver. In 2015, she won the National Opera Association Chamber Opera Competition for *The Clever Artifice of Harriet and Margaret* (2013). Based on the play *Overtones* (1913) by Alice Gerstenberg (1885–1972), Kirchoff's chamber opera has a cast of

Figure 4.4.   Leanna Kirchoff. *Courtesy of the artist*

four women: dignified Harriet and her "flapper-girl" inner self Hetty, along with overbearing Margaret and her melodramatic inner self Maggie; Kirchoff notes on the opera's website that the staging of the characters' "outer and inner selves (Harriet/Hetty and Margaret/Maggie) as a construct . . . mirrors Freud's concept of the struggle between the ego and the id."[20] The opera is an insightful exploration of the psyches of its female characters, as exemplified in the quartet "The Ballad of Good Women." Kirchoff has also written a mini-operetta for two sopranos called *Scrapbookers* (2015). ♪

PROFILE: LEANNA KIRCHOFF

Describe your musical background and what led you to be a composer.
I grew up on a farm in eastern Colorado. In our rural community, there were not many opportunities to participate in music other than in church or in the small school band. I took piano lessons from age seven and was proficient enough to begin playing the piano and organ for services at my local church by the time I was in high school. This was my primary exposure to hymns, choral music, and classical music. Otherwise, what was playing on the stereo at home was the soundtrack to *Saturday Night Fever* or Elton John's latest album.

Shortly after beginning piano lessons, my parents brought home a guitar one day after they had been shopping in one of the surrounding larger towns. I learned to play chords, and soon I was making up songs that I could sing and accompany myself with on the guitar. Songwriting was an early impulse as my first songs were written down by my mom. Otherwise, penciling lyrics was a really slow task for an eight-year-old.

I pursued an undergraduate degree in music at the University of Denver. My piano professor assigned me Bartók, Crumb, and Messiaen instead of more standard piano repertoire, which really inspired my love for contemporary music. I also decided to get a degree in commercial music instead of music education, which involved courses in jazz and commercial music theory, recording technology, and electronic music. I think this opened up creative channels for me, and I began taking composition lessons toward the end of my time at DU.

At that time I didn't think of composing as a career path. Up until that point, writing music was just something I knew how to do. During my master's degree at the University of Minnesota, I was around fellow students who were composing music for other student performers, for school ensembles, and for other music groups in the Twin Cities. Basically, they were creating new opportunities for themselves to write music. Also, the Minnesota Composers Forum (later the American Composers Forum) was a prominent organization in the area. There were so many important influences surrounding me, and step by step I found myself on the pathway toward being a composer.

Describe your compositional style and what it says about who you are.

I love words and really wish I could have been a poet. I don't quite have that gift, so for me, I do the next best thing, which is to use words and music fused together to ruminate on a thought or tell a story that interests me. When I begin a new piece, I tend to work conceptually at first, thinking about the main ideas that are emerging and what kind of musical design I can give to these ideas. My primary works all involve text; for example, I have written extensively in the genres of vocal chamber music, song cycles, choral music, and also dramatic works such as operas and musicals.

What hurdles have you encountered as a woman composer? How did you overcome them? Are there any you have yet to overcome?

Growing up in a small community, there were few musical opportunities and role models during my childhood and teenage years. I was supported by friends and family, but most of them didn't know too much about making a career in music. In retrospect, I can see what I missed, and I may have developed more quickly as a musician if there had been mentors around to open my mind to what was possible. However, there were some advantages as well. I created and performed music without much criticism or competition but mostly enthusiasm and praise. This may have been better for developing my musicianship than had I been in more musically advanced environments.

My biggest hurdle in succeeding as a female composer has been dealing with my own self-doubt. I think a part of this is related to personality, but also overcoming self-imposed limitations seems a common dilemma for women. Feeling inadequate pushes me to work hard at the music I am writing and also to be a worthy collaborator and a good colleague.

I've often been the only woman in the room in a variety of circumstances as a composer. For example, I was the only female doctoral student when I began my DMA work at the University of Colorado. The only other female composer in the department was a freshman undergraduate student. All of the composition professors were male. I noticed the gender imbalance but embraced it as a positive distinction, and I think that *not* looking for instances of discrimination has led to many affirming experiences.

My most influential role is working with the student composers as faculty at the University of Denver. In my composition seminar class, roughly one-third to one-half of the composers are female. As a routine part of the course, we study music by women and frequently host guest female composers. The students are also aware of my own activities as a composer. I hope that being in this teaching and mentorship role may have a positive impact on all of the composers, but in particular cultivate in the female composers the idea that their music is important and that there is a place for them in the world of composition.

Who are your greatest inspirations, musically and artistically?
I continually discover new composers that inspire me, but I do find myself returning again and again to the music of Luciano Berio and Kaija Saariaho when I need to spark some new thoughts. I have also

spent quite a bit of time studying the operas of Dutch composer Michel van der Aa, who incorporates film into his operas.

Others who have inspired me are those I have collaborated with, those who perform my music, and those who have supported my work as a composer. I really didn't appreciate the value of collaborating with other people until I began writing opera. Seeing a team of writers, composers, and musicians work together toward a common artistic goal is a thing of beauty and one of the greatest rewards for me as a composer. In fact, I think creative collaboration is one of the most important gifts that artists routinely cultivate and offer to the world.

NEW TRENDS IN CONTEMPORARY OPERA BY WOMEN

Three notable twenty-first-century operas by women have won awards and received productions across the country. Their range of subjects—from a transgender woman to Alice in Wonderland to fallen angels—has brought new perspectives to the operatic genre. Laura Kaminsky (b. 1956) has garnered attention for her socially progressive chamber opera *As One* (2014), which depicts a transgender protagonist named Hannah sung by two voices, a mezzo-soprano and a baritone. The timely and topical opera has reached a wide audience through multiple stagings across America. It breaks new ground with an operatic exploration of LGBTQ+ themes, leading the *Denver Post* to call it a game-changing work: "*As One* is the hottest opera title right now, at least among the titles written in the last 100 years."[21] In addition to writing an issue-specific work, Kaminsky has also composed a site-specific opera. Houston Grand Opera's HGOco opera initiative commissioned *Some Light Emerges* (2017) celebrating the art and spirituality of Houston's famous Rothko Chapel. By embracing modern trends and community concerns, Kaminsky has given her operas a powerful relevance and platform. In its annual survey of operatic performances, Opera America found that Kaminsky's *As One* was the most frequently produced North American opera of the 2017–2018 season, ahead of the familiar works *Candide*

(1956) by Leonard Bernstein (1918–1990) and *The Consul* (1950) by Gian Carlo Menotti (1911–2007). ♪

While Kaminsky's transgender lead is an operatic first, Unsuk Chin (b. 1961) reexamines a familiar heroine in the title character of *Alice in Wonderland* (2007). Born in South Korea, Chin settled in Germany, where she studied with György Ligeti (1923–2006). Her only opera, *Alice in Wonderland* premiered at the Bavarian State Opera as part of the Munich Opera Festival. Dramatic soprano Dame Gwyneth Jones (b. 1936) created the role of the Queen of Hearts. Fittingly, Alice is a coloratura soprano, but Chin has countertenors as the White Rabbit and March Hare. When asked why she chose the Lewis Carroll (1832–1898) classic for her first operatic endeavor, she said: "Because the book corresponds to my thoughts on contemporary opera. The stories in the book are nonlinear, labyrinthine and crazy dream stories, but at the same time it contains a very strong dramatic aspect."[22] *Alice in Wonderland* had originally been commissioned by Los Angeles Opera but was thwarted by the recession; it finally had its West Coast debut in 2015, appropriately at Walt Disney Hall. Distinctly un-Disney-like, her orchestration gives the opera an idiosyncratic sound, calling for trash cans with kitchenalia and pop bottles, not to mention accordion, harpsichord, Javanese gongs, Jew's harp, and wind machine. ♪

As with Alice and *As One*'s Hannah, Chinese-born composer and performance artist Du Yun (b. 1977) creates two pairs of juicy roles in her Pulitzer Prize–winning opera *Angel's Bone* (2016). While the Boy Angel is a tenor—originally sung by classical/pop crossover artist Kyle Bielfield (b. ca. 1987)—the Girl Angel is to be sung by what she calls "a female voice who can do punk rock." The two angels fall to earth and an evil (and more operatically sung) suburban couple forces them into sexual slavery to regain their wings. The pioneering subject matter and innovative musical style almost defy description and categorization; if you watch the YouTube video inspired by the opera that was produced by National Sawdust and directed by Spa Theory, you can get a taste of its heterogeneous Gestalt. At its premiere at the Prototype Festival, the *New York Times* praised "Du Yun's audacious and searing *Angel's Bone*. It's an appallingly good work when you consider that it takes on the subject of child trafficking and mixes in . . . a musical cocktail of Renaissance polyphony, electronica, modernism, punk rock, and cabaret."[23] Yun's other operas also seem quite captivating in their focus on female subjects. The chamber opera *Zolle* (2005) is about a dead woman wandering between the afterlife and earth, while *Women: The War Within* (2013) features among its leading characters both Cleopatra (69 BCE–30 BCE) and Hillary Clinton (b. 1947). ♪

Figure 4.5.   Du Yun (photo by Matthew Jelacic). *Creative Commons (CCBY-SA 3.0)*

Speaking of Hillary Clinton, or female presidential candidates, Victoria Bond (b. 1945) composed an opera about Victoria Woodhull (1838–1927), who in 1872 was the first woman to run for president of the United States. Rochester Lyric Opera premiered *Mrs. President* (2002) on November 18, 2017, marking the one-hundred-year anniversary of women gaining the right to vote in the state of New York. In the final scene of the opera, Woodhull makes an impassioned prediction: "From my ashes a thousand more will rise. They will seize what I've begun, hold it high and carry it on. Arise!"[24] Female operatic composers are definitely on the rise in the United States and throughout the world. Bond had to wait until she was seventy-two to see the premiere of her opera. But British prodigy Alma Deutscher (b. 2005) wrote her *Cinderella* opera when she was only ten years old and saw its premiere in Vienna in 2016 when she was eleven. Changing the familiar detail of Cinderella's glass slipper, Deutscher says: "In my opera, I don't have a shoe, because I think the shoe is a little bit silly. The prince doesn't find Cinderella with a shoe, but he finds her with a melody. So you see now she isn't just a pretty girl who cleans and keeps quiet; she's actually clever. She's a composer."[25] So in the operas of Bond and Deutscher, a woman could be president and Cinderella can be a composer. Thus, female composers of all ages are writing operas, breaking societal barriers for their characters, and bit by bit removing barriers that prevented their operas from reaching their audiences.

FINAL THOUGHTS

Many operatic works by women are still waiting to receive the platform they deserve; it is up to us to give them an equal opportunity to be seen and heard. Thus, the authors invite you to produce an opera by a female composer. Explore underperformed but historically important options such as Francesca Caccini's *La liberazione* and Evelyn LaRue Pittman's *Freedom Child*. Or support a living female composer by programming her work. Consider Judith Cloud's monodrama *Beethoven's Slippers* (2016), Leanna Kirchoff's micro-opera *Scrapbookers* (2015), or chamber operas such as *Shaman* (1987) by Alice Shields (b. 1943), *Wonderglass* (1993) by Susan Botti (b. 1962), and *Marie Curie Learns to Swim* (2018) by Jessica Rudman (b. 1982). Or commission a new opera by a female composer and become part of the history of women in opera.

NOTES

1. John Yohalem, "A Woman's Opera at the Met: Ethel Smyth's *Der Wald* in New York," archives.metoperafamily.org/imgs/DerWald.htm, accessed May 28, 2018.
2. Kaija Saariaho, "Half of Humanity Has Something to Say: Composer Kaija Saariaho on Her Met Debut," www.npr.org/sections/deceptivecadence

/2016/12/03/503986298/half-of-humanity-has-something-to-say-composer
-kaija-saariaho-on-her-met-debut, accessed May 28, 2018.

3. Diane Peacock Jezic, *Women Composers: The Lost Tradition Found*, 2nd ed. (New York: The Feminist Press at The City University of New York, 1994), 18, 20.

4. Jacqueline Letzter and Robert Adelson, *Women Writing Opera: Creativity and Controversy in the Age of the French Revolution* (Berkeley: University of California Press, 2001), 4, 219–37.

5. Christine Ammer, *Unsung: A History of Women in American Music*, century edition (Portland: Amadeus Press, 1991), 159–60.

6. Ibid., 206.

7. In 2013, Toccata Classics released a recording with soprano Deborah Polaski.

8. Mildred Enby Green, *Black Women Composers: A Genesis* (Boston: Twayne Publishers, 1983), 101.

9. Jill Halstead, *The Woman Composer: Creativity and the Gendered Politics of Musical Composition* (Aldershot, UK: Ashgate, 1997), 146.

10. Ammer, *Unsung*, 207.

11. Hannah Kendall, interview with Charlotte Bibby, *Ghost*, www.ghosttt.com/music-interview-classical-composer-hannah-kendall/, accessed August 6, 2018.

12. Matthew Sigman, "Scarlet Fever," *Opera News* 80, no. 11, www.operanews.com/Opera_News_Magazine/2016/5/Features/Scarlet_Fever.html, accessed May 28, 2018.

13. William Albright, "The Wordless Libretto: There's an Absence of Text in Avant-Garde Composer Meredith Monk's 'Atlas' but No Absence of Adventure," *Los Angeles Times*, articles.latimes.com/1991-03-03/entertainment/ca-108_1_composer-meredith-monk-s-atlas, accessed May 31, 2018.

14. Bernard Holland, "Review: Taking Off on a Wing and a Balancing Act," *New York Times*, www.nytimes.com/2003/06/05/arts/opera-review-taking-off-on-a-wing-and-a-balancing-act.html, accessed May 31, 2018.

15. Jennifer Higdon, interview with Donald McKinney, *Women of Influence in Contemporary Music: Nine American Composers* (Lanham, MD: Scarecrow Press, 2011), 161.

16. paolaprestini.com/projects/edwardtulane/, accessed May 31, 2018.

17. www.operaphila.org/whats-on-stage-2016-2017/breaking-the-waves/, accessed May 31, 2018.

18. Anna Chatterton, interview with Jon Kaplan, "Punching Out the High Notes," *Now Magazine*, nowtoronto.com/culture/stage/punching-out-the-high-notes/, accessed June 3, 2018.

19. Monica Pearce, "Travelogue Composer Q&A," The Bicycle Opera Project, bicycleopera.com/travelogue-composer-qa-monica-pearce-2/, accessed June 3, 2018.

20. www.cleverartifice.com/about/background/, accessed August 26, 2018.

21. Ray Mark Rinaldi, "Looking to Get into Opera? Now Is the Time When 'As One' Swings through Denver," *Denver Post*, theknow.denverposter .com/2017/02/25/as-one-opera-denver/137227/, accessed May 31, 2018.

22. Unsuk Chin, interview with Justine Nguyen, "Unsuk Chin: Composer with an Independent Mind," *Limelight Magazine*, www.limelightmagazine.com .au/features/unsuk-chin-composer-with-an-independent-mind/, accessed May 31, 2018.

23. Corinna de Fonesca-Wollheim, "Review: In Angel's Bone, Terrified Seraphim at the Mercy of Mere Mortals," *New York Times*, www.nytimes.com /2016/01/08/arts/music/review-in-angels-bone-terrified-seraphim-at-the -mercy-of-mere-mortals.html, accessed May 31, 2018.

24. www.victoriabond.com/artist.php?view=prog&rid=1971, accessed May 31, 2018.

25. Alma Deutscher, interview in *Finding Cinderella*, www.youtube.com/ watch?v=b0mb0F8fjqQ, accessed August 6, 2018.

5

CHORAL MUSIC BY WOMEN

Although women composers are now a formidable force in the choral world, this has largely been a twentieth-century development. Ever since biblical times—and perhaps before that—men and women have sung together as a part of sacred worship. Beginning with the development of Gregorian chant during the eighth century, this music began to be notated in preserved manuscripts. This means that vocal works are the oldest form of Western music, comprising most of the repertoire of the medieval and Renaissance eras. But because women assumed such a marginal role in the Catholic church, forbidden from entering the priesthood or leading any kind of liturgy (except within the all-female convents), virtually all of the polyphonic vocal reper-toire composed before 1600 was written by men. The story of female composers of choral music begins just before the dawn of the baroque era, when a lone madrigalist and a handful of ambitious nuns began creating the first polyphonic secular and sacred music written by women.

WOMEN COMPOSERS OF CHORAL
MUSIC BEFORE 1800

Although there is evidence of compositional activity by women in the genres of plainchant and monophonic secular song during the medieval era, the earliest known female composer of polyphonic choral music was the sixteenth-century madrigalist Maddalena Casulana (ca. 1544–ca. 1590). Casulana, an Italian, was a lutenist and singer in addition to being a composer. She is best known for her three books of madrigals, all of which were published during her lifetime—in 1568, 1570, and 1583, respectively. This publication record was an extraordinary feat for a Renaissance woman composer. "Morir non può il mio core"—a four-voice madrigal from *Il primo libro di magrigali* (the first collection)—is a work firmly rooted in the Italian madrigal style of the sixteenth century, and its counterpoint and text painting are representative of Casulana's mature compositional style. ♪

In the early baroque era, there was also a flurry of sacred music composition by women that emanated from Italian convents. The earliest known works were penned by the Aleotti sisters: Rafaella Aleotti (ca. 1570–1646) and her younger sister, Vittoria Aleotti (ca. 1573–1620). Rafaella took her vows at the San Vito convent in Ferrara in 1590 and soon became the musical director of an ensemble of twenty-three singers and instrumentalists. As a result of this position, she had the opportunity to write not only for voices but also "harpsichord, lutes, viols, flutes, cornetts, and trombones"—foreshadowing the emerging baroque ensembles of the turn of the century.[1] In 1593, she published a book of motets for five, seven, eight, and nine voices with instrumental accompaniment. Her motets "show a thorough mastery of contrapuntal technique, rhythmic vitality, and sensitivity to the meaning of the texts."[2] Although the younger Aleotti, Vittoria, was also a nun in the same convent as her sister, she focused more on secular works, publishing several madrigals during her lifetime.

The two most significant women composers of the Italian baroque were Chiara Margarita Cozzolani (1602–1678) and Isabella Leonarda (1620–1704). Margarita Cozzolani was born into a wealthy family in Milan. She took her vows in 1620 at the age of eighteen, at which time she took "Chiara" as her religious name. All of her works were published

Figure 5.1. Chiara Margarita Cozzolani. *Creative Commons (CCBY-SA 1.0)*

between 1640 and 1650, although many have been lost. Today, Cozzolani is best known for her *Concerti sacri* (1642) and *Salmi à otto voci concertati* (1650). Her two settings of the Magnificat canticle are from this latter collection. Like Cozzolani, Isabella Leonarda was also a nun. Leonarda lived in Novara, a city in the Piedmont region in the far north of Italy. She published an astonishing twenty volumes of music during her lifetime, including three mass settings and various motets, litanies, Magnificats, Marian antiphons, and psalm settings. Most of her works are settings for one to four voices with continuo. Leonarda's entire oeuvre is sacred. ♪

THE LONG ROMANTIC ERA: 1800–1930

The Viennese classical era afforded few opportunities for women to compose, and those that did seemed to avoid choral genres. The lone exception seems to be Marianna von Martines (1744–1812), whose masterpiece is her 1774 motet *Dixit Dominus*. This major work is scored for chorus, soloists, and full orchestra. But Martines was a composer of great privilege; she was born into a wealthy family, and her father was *maestro di cappella* to the papal embassy in Vienna. Most choral music was written for the church, and church music was a man's profession. As a result, very few women composed choral works during the eighteenth century.

As the romantic era dawned, more names of women composers began to emerge, but the works they produced were overwhelmingly songs and piano music. There were, however, some women who tackled the choral genre, and they did so in a major way, producing a collection of major choral-orchestral works. Between 1800 and 1925, four names stand out as the most important women composers of choral music. These individuals also—perhaps not surprisingly—occupied positions of privilege not afforded to most women from this time period: they all came from prominent musical families or enormous wealth, which opened doors that were closed to most nineteenth-century and early twentieth-century women. Their names are familiar ones to anyone who studies the history of women in music: Fanny Hensel (1805–1847) of Germany, Ethel Smyth (1858–1944) of England, Amy Beach (1867–1944) of the United States, and Lili Boulanger (1893–1918) of France.

Fanny Hensel, the older sister of Felix Mendelssohn (1809–1847), is well known for her songs and piano music, but many people do not realize that she also composed twenty-eight choral works. Three of these are major choral-orchestral works—an oratorio entitled *Oratorium nach den Bildern der Bible* and two cantatas, *Hiob* (*Job*) and *Lobgesang*—the only such pieces by a woman composer during the first half of the nineteenth century. All three of these compositions were written in 1831. Other choral works include pieces for SATB chorus and piano, two vocal quartets (one for SATB and one for TTBB), and several a cappella works.[3] Her most popular and often-performed choral works are her six partsongs for SATB voices a cappella, which were published together as a collection entitled *Gartenlieder*, Op. 3, in 1846. In nineteenth-century Germany and Austria, partsongs were usually four-part lieder that set German romantic poetry. The *Gartenlieder* set three poems by Joseph Freiherr von Eichendorff (1788–1857) and one poem each by Ludwig Uhland (1787–1862), Emanuel von Geibel (1815–1884), and her husband, Wilhelm Hensel (1794–1861).[4] ♪

Figure 5.2. Partsong Performance at a Nineteenth-Century *Liederabend*. *Creative Commons (CCBY-SA 1.0)*

In England, Ethel Smyth is remembered by the choral world for her colossal one-hour choral-orchestral work: the *Mass in D*. Smyth composed the work during the summer of 1891, while she was a guest of the Empress Eugénie (1826–1920) at Cape Martin.[5] The mass was orchestrated over the next eighteen months, and the premiere took place at Royal Albert Hall in London on January 18, 1893, in a performance by the Royal Choral Society conducted by Joseph Barnby (1838–1896). The *Mass in D* is unique because of its unconventional six-movement structure and reordering of the five texts of the mass ordinary; Smyth splits the Sanctus-Benedictus into two separate movements and—more significantly—stations the Gloria last instead of second. Although the *Mass in D* is by far Smyth's most famous choral work, she also composed *Five Sacred Part-Songs Based on Chorale Tunes* (1884), *Wedding Anthem* (1900), and a cantata entitled *The Song of Love* (1888). She also composed several secular works for choir and orchestra, including a cantata entitled *The Prison* (1930), which was one of her final works.[6] ♪

American composer Amy Beach was a prolific composer of choral music. Her dozens of works include "one mass, one Anglican service, approximately ten canticle and related service settings, twenty-four anthems and motets, and thirty-four secular works (twenty for female chorus, four for children, four for male chorus, and six for mixed voices)."[7] Her four most important sacred works are the *Mass in E-flat*, Op. 5 (1890); *Festival Jubilate*, Op. 17 (1893); *Service in A*, Op. 63 (1905); and the *Canticle of the Sun*, Op. 123 (1924). Some of the most prominent ensembles in the Northeast premiered these works: the *Mass in E-flat* was performed by the Handel and Haydn Society in Boston on February 2, 1892, and the *Service in A* was performed by Emmanuel Church in Boston and St. Bartholomew's Episcopal Church in New York City in 1906. *Festival Jubilate* is believed to be the first work commissioned of an American woman composer; it was performed at the dedication ceremonies of the Women's Building at the Chicago World's Columbian Exposition in 1893. *Canticle of the Sun*, which also premiered at St. Bartholomew's Episcopal Church, sets an English translation by Matthew Arnold (1822–1888) of the *Canticum Solis* of St. Francis of Assisi (1181/1182–1226). Beach's most well-known secular works include *Three Shakespeare Choruses*, Op. 39 (1897); *The Sea-Fairies*, Op. 59 (1904); and *The Chambered Nautilus*, Op. 66 (1907). ♪

Although she died at the young age of twenty-four, Lili Boulanger nevertheless produced an extensive catalog of works, and her oeuvre includes fifteen choral pieces: eight for chorus and orchestra, three for chorus and orchestra or piano, and four for chorus and piano.[8] Her best-known and most often-performed choral works are her three psalm settings for chorus, soloists, and orchestra: *Psalm CXXX* ("Du fond l'abîme"), *Psalm XXIV* ("La terre appartient à l'Éternel"), and *Psalm CXXIX* ("Ils m'ont assez opprimé).[9] Other notable choral pieces include four works for a single soloist with chorus: *Les sirènes* and *Hymne au soleil*, both for an alto (or mezzo-soprano) soloist; *Pour les funérailles d'un soldat* for bass; and *Vieille prière bouddhique*, a Buddhist prayer with a text from the *Visuddhimagga*. *Psalm CXXX* is Boulanger's most adventurous work, featuring complex rhythms and impressionistic harmonies that mark a turning point away from romanticism and toward the new era of modernism. ♪

THE MODERN ERA: 1930–PRESENT

The United Kingdom

Ethel Smyth may have been the matriarch of women composers in Great Britain, but for most of her career she was very much a lone woman in a man's profession, having few female colleagues throughout most of her long career. The generations that followed Smyth introduced a surge of women who began contributing hundreds of new works to the repertory. In the choral world, Elizabeth Poston (1905–1987) emerged as the first important composer of the post-Smyth generation. Poston studied at the Royal Academy of Music, where she met Peter Warlock (1894–1930) and Ralph Vaughan Williams (1872–1958), who both encouraged her work.[10] Over the next several decades, she wrote several dozen choral works, including *Laudate Dominum* (1955)—a setting of Psalm 117 for mixed voices and organ—and a Magnificat for treble voices and organ (1961). Her most frequently performed piece is the a cappella "Jesus Christ the Apple Tree," often presented as a carol during the Christmas season. An advocate for women composers, Poston served as president of the Society of Women Musicians from 1955 to 1961.

But Poston's conservative compositional style—very much in the post-Victorian mold of Vaughan Williams, Gustav Holst (1874–1934), and Herbert Howells (1892–1983)—was not to last for long. An emerging generation of English modernists also began to compose works during this time, with three women in particular contributing to the choral genre. Musicologist and conductor Catherine Roma (b. 1948) writes:

> The importance of the English Musical Renaissance and the revitalization of the British choral tradition cannot be overestimated. Musicologists have looked back, sometimes with disdain, on the provincialism and resistant shores of England's green and pleasant land. In addition, the various British institutions and individuals dedicated to the performance and promotion of new music of native composers laid the groundwork for the development of a recognizably national school. The increased compositional activity, coupled with quality and confidence, generated strength and at the same time established something against which to rebel. It is in this context that the successful compositional careers of Elisabeth Lutyens, Elizabeth Maconchy, and Thea Musgrave were allowed to flourish.[11]

Elisabeth Lutyens (1906–1983) studied at the École Normale in Paris and at the Royal College of Music in London, where she excelled as a violist. Her earliest works were twelve-tone and serial, but she soon adopted a free chromaticism that characterizes her mature compositions. One of Lutyens's earliest choral works was a full-length secular oratorio entitled *Requiem for the Living*, Op. 16 (1948), a piece she later withdrew from her canon. Her most famous choral works include the motet *Excerpta tractatus logicophilosophici*, Op. 27 (1953), for mixed chorus; the cantata *De amore*, Op. 39 (1957), for soprano and tenor soloists, mixed chorus, and orchestra; and *The Essence of Our Happiness*, Op. 69 (1968), for tenor soloist, mixed chorus, and orchestra. Elizabeth Maconchy (1907–1994) was an astonishingly prolific composer across all genres. At the age of sixteen, she enrolled at Royal College of Music, where she studied with Vaughan Williams and Charles Wood (1866–1926). Although Maconchy is primarily known for her symphonic works and string quartets, she also composed dozens of choral works. These pieces—both a cappella and orchestrated—are mostly secular, setting texts written by prominent British poets. Thea Musgrave (b. 1928) is a Scottish composer who studied at the University of Edinburgh and with Nadia Boulanger (1887–1979) in France. She moved to London in 1954 and ultimately settled in the United States in 1970. Mostly known for her operas, Musgrave also composed twenty choral works, most of which are scored for a cappella chorus. *Rorate coeli* is one of her most interesting choral pieces, combining two texts: the sacred Latin text "Rorate coeli desuper" and the medieval poem "Done Is a Battle on the Dragon Black" by the Scottish poet William Dunbar (1459–1520). ♪

Figure 5.3. Thea Musgrave. *Creative Commons (CCBY-SA 3.0)*

The next generation of British women choral composers were all born in the 1940s. Rhian Samuel (b. 1944) was born in Aberdare, Wales, into a Welsh-speaking family. Although she studied at the University of Reading in England and at Washington University in St. Louis, she has kept strong ties to her native Wales. Samuel's vocal and choral compositions sometimes set Welsh texts, and her 120 published pieces include twenty-one choral works. Nicola LeFanu (b. 1947), the daughter of Elizabeth Maconchy, studied at Oxford University, the Royal College of Music, and Harvard University. She later taught composition at Kings College, London, and the University of York, retiring in 2008. She has published more than one hundred compositions, including eighteen choral works. Her most well-known choral pieces are three cantatas published by Novello: *The Valleys Shall Sing* (1973), *Like a Wave of the Sea* (1981), and *Stranded on My Heart* (1984). Hilary Tann (b. 1947), another Welsh composer, holds degrees from the University of Wales, Cardiff, and Princeton University. Although primarily an instrumental composer, she has composed approximately one dozen choral works, including several psalm settings.

Three additional seasoned women composers of choral music, all of whom are English, must also be mentioned. Cecilia McDowall (b. 1951) studied at the Trinity Laban Conservatoire of Music and Dance before proceeding to a marvelous career as a prolific and prize-winning composer. Although she has composed across all genres, she is best known for her many choral works and was the recipient of the British Composer Award for Choral Music in 2014. McDowall's commissions include works for the BBC Singers, Westminster Cathedral Choir, and the Choir of King's College, Cambridge. Judith Bingham (b. 1952) studied voice and composition at the Royal Academy of Music, winning the BBC Young Composer Award in 1977. After her schooling, Bingham sang full-time with the BBC Singers for thirteen years (1983–1996); this experience as a performer of choral music was essential to the formation of her mature compositional style. Many of her works have been recorded by professional choral ensembles. *Water Lilies* (1999) is a seven-minute work that is typical of Bingham's compositional approach to choral music. She writes:

> The idea was to create a tapestry of sound, multi-dividing the choir and having lots of tiny solos which would further thin out the texture. This was something akin to dots of impressionistic paint. The work opens in a dream-like way where the word "nympheas" rises from the texture like sirens calling. The sound is warm and dreamy but gradually becomes more worrying. In the middle section all is ice with tiny staccato chords and long high melodic lines. Finally the summer returns, ecstatically, and the water lilies flower.[12] ♪

Roxana Panufnik (b. 1968) is an English composer of Polish heritage. The daughter of Polish conductor Andrzej Panufnik (1914–1991), she studied at the Royal Academy of Music before embarking on her compositional career. Her most famous choral works include *West-minster Mass*, commissioned in 1997 by the Westminster Cathedral Choir to celebrate the seventy-fifth birthday of Cardinal Basil Hume (1923–1999); *Dance of Life*, an oratorio commissioned in 2011 by the Tallinn Philharmonic Society in Tallinn, Estonia; and *Magnificat* and *Nunc Dimittis*, canticle settings written in 2012 for the London Festival of Contemporary Church Music.

Canada

Several Canadian women have also made important contributions to the choral repertory. Ruth Watson Henderson (b. 1932) is a composer and pianist who accompanied the Festival Singers of Canada and the Toronto Children's Chorus until her retirement in 2007. Over the course of her long career, Henderson wrote more than two hundred choral works. In 1992, *Voices of Earth*—scored for double SATB choir and children's choir—won the Canadian National Choral Award for Outstanding Choral Composition. Eleanor Daley (b. 1955) was educated at Queen's University in Kingston, Ontario, and the Royal Conservatory of Music in Toronto. Since 1982, she has served as director of music at Fairlawn Avenue United Church of Christ in Toronto. Daley has written more than one hundred choral works, including commissions from the Toronto Children's Chorus, Vancouver Men's Chorus, and the American Choral Directors Association (ACDA). She has won the Canadian National Choral Award for Outstanding Choral Composition twice: for *Requiem* in 1994 and *Rose Trilogy* in 2004. Her requiem setting is Daley's most frequently heard work and perhaps the most famous requiem written by a woman composer. Ramona Luengen (b. 1960) and Veronika Krausas (b. 1963) are two other Canadian women composers who have made important contributions to the choral repertoire.

The United States

As the twentieth century proceeded, choral music by American women composers began to flourish. Louise Talma (1906–1996) studied with Nadia Boulanger in Paris before settling into a long career teaching at Hunter College in New York, a position she held from 1928 to

1979. Her seventeen choral works are mostly composed in what can be described as an "advanced tonal idiom."[13] *Let's Touch the Sky* (1952)—a setting of three poems by e. e. cummings (1894–1962)—is her most recognized choral composition.[14] Alice Parker (b. 1925) was born in Boston, Massachusetts, and educated at Smith College and the Juilliard School, where she studied conducting with Robert Shaw (1916–1999). During this time, she began making choral arrangements of folk songs, hymns, and spirituals that were performed and recorded by the Robert Shaw Chorale. It is these arrangements for which Parker is most famous; they have become staples of the repertoire and have cemented her legacy in the choral world. Many people do not realize, however, that Parker also composed more than 250 original choral works. "You Can Tell the World" is an excellent example of Parker's contribution to the choral canon.[15] ♪

Although often overlooked in the music history books, the contribution of women to church music should be mentioned. Three women in particular—Jane Marshall (b. 1924), Emma Lou Diemer (b. 1927), and Natalie Sleeth (1930–1992)—have had enormous impact on the music programs of small parishes across the United States, writing accessible anthems that can be sung successfully by volunteers in amateur church choirs. Marshall, who spent her long career as a member of the sacred music faculty at Southern Methodist University, has written many choral octavos, perhaps none more famous than "My Eternal King" (1954). Emma Lou Diemer was born in Kansas City, studied at Yale University and the Eastman School of Music, and eventually settled into a career as a composition professor at the University of California, Santa Barbara. Although she composed across all genres, Diemer is particularly recognized for contributions to church music in the form of organ and choral works. Natalie Sleeth majored in music at Wellesley College before moving to Dallas, where she became the director of children's choirs at Highland Park Methodist Church. At the time of her death, she had published more than 180 choral pieces. She is especially known for her children's choir anthems, many of which were written for her very own children's choir at Highland Park.

Needless to say, the avant-garde music scene of the mid-century—which found its home in major metropolitan areas such as New York, Boston, San Francisco, and San Diego—turned out a very different kind

of choral music. Pauline Oliveros (1932–2016), one of the most important forces in new music of the twentieth century, employs extended
techniques in her most famous choral work, *Sound Patterns*, written in
1961. Pozzi Escot (b. 1933) was born in New York City, educated at the
Juilliard School, and joined the faculty of the New England Conservatory in Boston in 1964. Her most notable choral work, the *Missa Triste*
of 1981, is a setting of four parts of the mass ordinary in an atypical
order—Agnus Dei, Credo, Kyrie, and Gloria—"as a representation of
peace, belief, mercy, and glory."[16] Escot's other choral works include
the a cappella works *Ainu I* (1970) and *Visione 97* (1997). Judith Lang
Zaimont (b. 1945) studied at Queens College and Columbia University,
eventually becoming a professor of composition at the University of
Minnesota. Her many choral works include *Sacred Service for the Sab-
bath Evening* (1976), *Serenade: To Music* (1981), and *Parable: A Tale
of Abraham and Isaac* (1985). Gwyneth Walker (b. 1947)—educated at
Brown University and the Hartt School—enjoys a full-time career as a
composer. She has written dozens of choral works, including *Harlem
Songs* (2000), *An Hour to Dance* (1998), *Appalachian Carols* (1998),
and *The Great Trees* (2009). Carol Barnett (b. 1949) studied with Dominick Argento (b. 1927) at the University of Minnesota. A Minneapolis-
based composer, she was composer-in-residence for the Dale Warland
Singers from 1992 until the ensemble's disbanding in 2004. Barnett's
most important works include *Cinco poemas de Bécquer* (1979), *Requiem* (1981), *Epitaphs* (1986), and *The Last Invocation* (1992). ♪

Two foreign-born women composers of this generation have made a
significant impact on American choral music. Tania León (b. 1943) was
born in Havana, Cuba, where she studied music at the Carlos Alfredo
Peyrellade Conservatory and the National Conservatory. In 1967, she
moved to New York City to attend New York University and has based
her career there ever since. A professor at Brooklyn College, her works
across all genres have been performed by prominent ensembles glob-
ally. León's choral works are often written for unique combinations of
voices and instruments. *Inura* is scored for SATB voices, strings, and
percussion; the work sets texts from the Yoruban Candomblé religion.
Chen Yi (b. 1953) was born and raised in Guangzhou, China, and was
the first Chinese woman to receive a master's degree in composition
from the Central Conservatory of Music in Beijing. She later moved to

New York City, where she studied composition with Chou Wen-chung (b. 1923) and Mario Davidovsky (b. 1934) at Columbia University, earning her DMA in 1993. She has composed dozens of choral works, many of which set Chinese texts.[17] Theodore Presser notes that Chen Yi is a "cultural ambassador" and a "strong advocate of new music, Asian composers, and women in music."[18] ♪

Figure 5.4. Chen Yi. *Creative Commons (CCBY-SA 3.0)*

Over the course of the second half of the twentieth century and into the new millennium, numerous women composers have contributed to the American choral canon. Libby Larsen (b. 1950)—who earned all of her degrees (BM, MM, and DMA) under the tutelage of Dominick Argento at the University of Minnesota—has composed more than one hundred choral works. Several of her best large-scale works include *Dance Set* (1980), *Ringeltanze* (1983), *A Creeley Collection* (1984), and *The Settling Years* (1988). Janika Vandervelde (b. 1955), another Minneapolis-based Argento protégée, is primarily known for her choral music, with commissions and performances from ensembles such as Chanticleer and the Dale Warland Singers. In 2015, Julia Wolfe (b. 1958) won the Pulitzer Prize for *Anthracite Fields*, a modern secular oratorio about Pennsylvania coal miners. Edie Hill (b. 1962) attended Bennington College and the University of Minnesota. Her principal composition teachers were Vivian Fine (1913–2013), Lloyd Ultan (1929–1988), and Libby Larsen. Hill's style is more conservative than her Minnesota colleagues Larsen and Vandervelde, as can be heard in the five-minute *Alma beata et bella* (1999), a setting of a fifteenth-century Italian text commissioned by the Rose Ensemble.

African American Voices

African American women composers have made an important impact on the choral world, bringing their heritage, traditions, and stories to an important body of works. Undine Smith Moore (1904–1989) was one of the most important African American women composers of the twentieth century. Although she wrote more than one hundred compositions, only twenty-six of these works were published during her lifetime. Many of these pieces were choral works, including the oratorio *Scenes from the Life of a Martyr* (1982) and two cantatas: *Sir Olaf and the Erl King's Daughter* (1925) and *Glory to God* (1976). She is also known for her many arrangements of spirituals. Moore spent most of her career as a professor at Virginia State University, where she taught for forty-five years (1927–1972). Bernice Johnson Reagon (b. 1942) enjoys a multifaceted career as a song leader, composer, scholar, and social activist. "Perhaps no individual today better illustrates the transformative power and instruction of traditional African American music and cultural history. . . . [Reagon] has excelled equally in the realms of scholarship, composition, and performance."[19] Her choral works include a series of octavos and the *Liberty or Death Suite* (2004), which was commissioned by the MUSE, Cincinnati Women's Choir conducted by Catherine Roma (b. 1948).[20]

In recent decades, Rosephanye Powell (b. 1962) has emerged as an extraordinary force in the choral world. Powell was born in Lanett, Alabama, and studied music throughout her childhood, eventually earning degrees from Alabama State University, Westminster Choir College, and Florida State University. An accomplished singer, Powell has done extensive research on the African American spiritual, and her compositional style "utilizes techniques that reflect her African American heritage, including layering songs with multiple lines, syncopation, and strong rhythmic emphasis."[21] She has received commissions from organizations such as the American Guild of Organists (AGO) and American Choral Directors Association (ACDA) as well as numerous ensembles, including Chanticleer, Cantus, and the St. Olaf Choir. One of the best-selling choral composers in the United States, her works are published by Hal Leonard, Oxford University Press, Alliance Music Publications, and Shawnee Press. Since 2001, she has served on the music faculty of Auburn University, where she is a Charles Barkley Endowed Professor and professor of voice. Her dozens of choral works include "The Word Was God" (1996), "Still I Rise" (2005), *Gospel Trilogy* (2015), and *The Cry of Jeremiah* (2012), a four-movement work for chorus, organ, and orchestra with narration. ♪

Figure 5.5. Rosephanye Powell. *Courtesy of the artist*

PROFILE: ROSEPHANYE POWELL

Describe your musical background and what led you to become a composer.

I began taking piano lessons in elementary school. As a preteen, I served as secondary pianist for my church choir when the primary pianist was not available. In junior high and high school, I played saxophone in the concert and marching bands. Also in high school, I sang soprano and sang solos in the school choir and was a member of the girls' trio in solo and ensemble competitions. In high school, I enjoyed writing poems when not playing sports such as basketball and softball and I ran on the track team. In addition, I sang in a girls' gospel quartet, composing and arranging songs for the group. All of these early experiences guided me to a career in music.

I became a composer by accident when I composed "The Word Was God" for the Philander Smith Collegiate Choir in Little Rock, Arkansas. This choir, conducted by my husband, Dr. William C. Powell, and for which I served as associate conductor, needed original songs to be recorded on CD and sold during our concert tours to raise funds. "The Word Was God" was one of these songs. I submitted the work to ten publishers and, to my amazement, received ten acceptance letters. Unfortunately, I received letters of reprimand from the companies that I didn't choose. I learned an important lesson from that experience that I share with young composers: submit your work to only one publisher at a time!

Describe your compositional style and what it says about who you are.

My style of composition has been characterized as lyrical (singable melodies); strong rhythmic emphasis, including much use of syncopation; rich harmonies often derived from African American popular styles; and varied vocal textures including layering, interweaving melodies, and counterpoint. I am grateful for a diverse musical background that includes classical music, spirituals, gospel, rhythm and blues, jazz, African folk music, Caribbean music, traditional hymns, and lined hymns. Although they are not always identifiable in my works, I am often calling upon each of these genres as part of my musical vocabulary for composition.

When I compose, the music grows out of the text. This includes the mood, tempo, harmonic vocabulary, rhythm, and form. I endeavor to compose melodies that are healthy for the voice, avoiding overuse of the extremes of the range. As a singer, I prefer to employ lyrical melodies that use the practical parts of the range, saving the extreme highs and lows for climaxes, color, or emphasis. I am compelled by rhythm. As a high schooler, I wanted to play drums in the band, but my mother felt (at the time) that "girls don't play drums." So I followed in my older brother's footsteps and played saxophone. But rhythmic energy has always been an important part of my musical impetus.

What hurdles have you encountered as an African American woman composer? How did you overcome them? Are there any you have yet to overcome?
The majority of my experiences as a composer have been very positive. However, one hurdle that I have encountered is the assumption made by many in the choral world that since I am African American, my sacred works should be categorized as "spirituals" or "gospel" even when it is most apparent that they are not. I have composed numerous anthems and psalms. As a matter of fact, my first published work, "The Word Was God" is composed in the style of an a cappella motet or anthem. When it was first released, the work was categorized as an anthem; however, as my reputation grew and the choral community became aware that I was African American, the work began to be labeled a spiritual, despite the fact that it does not follow the form, style, rhythm, or harmonies of a spiritual. Moreover, I found it puzzling and quite humorous that a professional, European-focused chorale sang the work at a nationally sponsored gospel competition and won. Imagine that!

As I travel, perform, and work with choirs and choral directors, I explain and distinguish the differences between the spiritual, gospel music, and anthems. Of the African American sacred choral music styles, the anthem is more aligned with European classical music in form, harmonies, text underlay, tone quality, and diction.

A second hurdle that I have encountered is not being addressed as Dr. Powell. In professional settings, often enough, people will introduce or address me by my first name (often mispronouncing it), Ms. Rosephanye, Ms. Powell, or Mrs. Powell, rather than Dr. Powell. At these times, the males with titles are addressed with their title. It occurs especially when my husband and I perform or serve together. I rarely, if ever, have heard anyone address him as Mr. Powell. I have yet to overcome this hurdle. Sometimes I will make the correction politely. At other times, I am inclined to overlook the matter.

Who are your greatest inspirations, musically and artistically?
Within the European classical tradition, strong influences include the contrapuntal choral works of J. S. Bach and Handel; the structured, classical form of Haydn and Mozart; the text setting found in the art songs of Schubert, Schumann, Debussy, Obradors, and others; and the romantic vocal lines and harmonies heard in the operas of Puccini and Verdi. I grew up on the spiritual arrangements of H. T. Burleigh, J. Rosamond Johnson, William Dawson, Hall Johnson, Lena McLin, and Roland Carter. And I was truly inspired as a singer by contemporary African American classical composers such as William Grant Still, Adolphus Hailstork, and David N. Baker. Especially influential were the African American women composers to whom I was first introduced in college: Undine Smith Moore, Margaret Bonds, Betty Jackson King, Julia Perry, and Florence Price.

THE NEXT GENERATION:
WOMEN IN THE NEW MILLENNIUM

A vibrant generation of female choral composers who were born after 1975 have emerged over the past several decades, ushering in the next millennium with a burgeoning oeuvre of evocative choral works. Anna

Thorvaldsdottir (b. 1977), an Icelandic composer, has had enormous international success as a writer of choral pieces.[22] According to the composer's website, Thorvaldsdottir "works with large sonic structures that tend to reveal the presence of a vast variety of sustained sound materials, reflecting her sense of imaginative listening to landscapes and nature. Her music tends to portray a flowing world of sounds with an enigmatic lyrical atmosphere."[23] Thorvaldsdottir's success has transcended the new music community to reach many of the world's major orchestras; the New York Philharmonic, Los Angeles Philharmonic, and London Philharmonia Orchestra are three that have performed and premiered her works.[24] Santa Ratneice (b. 1977), a Latvian composer, is another example of an adventurous young woman who is transforming the choral landscape with adventurous works that challenge singers to explore nontraditional sounds and embrace post–bel canto vocal technique. According to Ratneice's blog: "Words are not enough to describe her music and illuminate the process of creation. . . . It is the abundant, plentiful imagination that charms and even bewitches listeners."[25] "Horo horo hata hata" is an example of a choral work that is representative of Ratneice's idiosyncratic sonic palette. ♪

The United States continues to be a fruitful haven for aspiring choral composers, and perhaps no city is more supportive of the genre than Minneapolis, Minnesota.[26] Abbie Betinis (b. 1980) and Jocelyn Hagen (b. 1980), both graduates of the University of Minnesota, are two of the nation's most accomplished young choral composers. Betinis's works have achieved positive reviews in the *New York Times* and *Boston Globe*, and she has received commissions from many prominent choral groups, including the Dale Warland Singers and the Rose Ensemble. Hagen likewise enjoys a regular stream of commissions and awards from organizations like the American Composers Forum and prominent ensembles such as VocalEssence, Conspirare, and the Minnesota Choral Artists. In 2018, Hagen premiered a major work for choir, orchestra, and multimedia video projections entitled *The Notebooks of Leonardo da Vinci*, which has since received performances on both sides of the Atlantic.[27]

Caroline Shaw (b. 1982) is another American composer who needs little introduction after bursting into fame on April 15, 2013—the day she became the youngest composer in history to win the Pulitzer Prize for Music. The prize-winning work was *Partita for 8 Voices*, which was written for Roomful of Teeth, a new music ensemble with which Shaw performs. Another prominent choral work of hers is *Ad manus* ("To the Hands"), a "response cantata" that was commissioned by the Crossing for their 2016 major work, *Seven Responses*—a twenty-first-century reimagining of *Membra Jesu nostri* (1680) by Dietrich Buxtehude (1737/1739–1797).[28] One of the youngest choral composers who has emerged nationally is Dale Trumbore (b. 1987), who has been praised by the *New York Times* for her "soaring melodies and beguiling harmonies."[29] Her impressively extensive catalog of choral works has been performed by the American Contemporary Music Ensemble (ACME), Minnesota Choral Artists, and the Los Angeles Master Chorale. Trumbore is a graduate of the University of Southern California's composition program, where she studied with Morten Lauridsen (b. 1943). "Threads of Joy" (2007) is one of her best-known choral compositions. ♪

FINAL THOUGHTS

Over the past several decades, professional organizations like the American Choral Directors Association (ACDA) and International Federation of Choral Music (IFCM) have had significant impact on promoting choral music in universities, colleges, and public schools. The explosion of professional choral ensembles and extensive discography of recordings that these elite groups produce has exponentially raised the bar of choral excellence. As a result, choral culture—in both the United States and abroad—is thriving in the twenty-first century. The rich catalog of works produced by the women composers introduced in this chapter deserves to be explored, programed, sung, and celebrated on a regular basis. If we do not actively engage in this effort, think of the magnificent choral repertoire that we, and future generations, will never have the privilege of hearing or singing.

NOTES

1. Adriano Cavicchi and Suzanne G. Cusick, "Rafaella Aleotti," *The Norton/Grove Dictionary of Women Composers*, ed. Julie Anne Sadie and Rhian Samuel (New York: Macmillan, 1995), 7.

2. Ibid.

3. The works for SATB chorus and piano include *Zum Fest der heiligen Cäcilia* (1833) and *Enleitung zu lebenden Bilder* (1841). A cappella choral works include *Nachtreigen* (1829) and *Schweigend sinkt die Nacht* (1846), both scored for SATB/SATB double choir; Fanny's husband, Wilhelm Hensel, wrote the text for the *Nachtreigen*. The two vocal quartets include the SATB *Dämmernd liegt der Sommerabend* and the TTBB *Laß fahren hin*, both composed in 1840. The SAB partsongs include *Wer will mir wehren zu singen*, *O Herbst*, and *Schweigt der Menschen laute Lust*, all composed in 1846.

4. The specific poems set in *Gartenlieder* are as follows: "Hörst du nicht die Bäume rauschen," "Schöne Fremde," and "Abendlich schon rauscht der Wald" (Eichendorff); "Morgengruß" (Hensel); "Im Herbst" (Uhland); and "Im Wald" (Geibel).

5. Cape Martin is a Mediterranean headland in the south of France, between Monaco and Menton.

6. Smyth's secular choral-orchestral works include *We Watched Her Breathing through the Night* (1876), *A Spring Canticle* (1903), *Hey Nonny No* (1910), *Sleepless Dreams* (1910), and *Songs of Sunrise* (1910).

7. Dennis Shrock, *Choral Repertoire* (New York: Oxford University Press, 2009), 556.

8. Ibid., 577.

9. *Psalm XXIV* (Psalm 24) and *Psalm CXXIX* (Psalm 129) were both composed in 1916. *Psalm CXXX* (Psalm 130) was written one year later in 1917.

10. Poston's *Two Carols in Memory of Peter Warlock* were written in 1956.

11. Catherine Roma, *The Choral Music of Twentieth-Century Women Composers: Elisabeth Lutyens, Elizabeth Maconchy, and Thea Musgrave* (Lanham, MD: Scarecrow Press, 2006), 7.

12. Judith Bingham, *Remoter Worlds: The Choral Music of Judith Bingham*, Hyperion, 2008, CD liner notes.

13. Dennis Shrock, *Choral Repertoire* (New York: Oxford University Press, 2009), 723.

14. The three cummings poems are "anyone lived in a pretty how town," "love is more thicker than forget," and "if up's the word."

15. At the time of this writing (2018), Alice Parker is ninety-two years old and still keeping an extremely active schedule traveling the country, headlining conferences, and leading community hymn sings. In 1984, Parker founded the organization Melodious Accord with the mission of presenting concerts, making recordings, and providing opportunities for advanced study under her tutelage. In the summer of 2007, I (Matthew) was fortunate enough to be selected as a Melodious Accord Fellow, which gave me the opportunity to study

with Alice as part of a small group at her home in Hawley, Massachusetts. Living in the same quarters and cooking meals together over the course of three days fostered a unique and unforgettable seminar experience and revealed the endearing personal touch that Parker brings to all of her endeavors.

16. Dennis Shrock, *Choral Repertoire* (New York: Oxford University Press, 2009), 747.

17. I (Matthew) had the privilege of working with Chen Yi when the Ithaca College Choir premiered her choral work *Spring Dreams* in 1998. Her excitement, elation, and kindness endeared her to the entire choir. I earned my BM in vocal performance, music education, and music theory from Ithaca College in 1999.

18. www.presser.com/composer/chen-yi/, accessed August 25, 2018.

19. www.bernicejohnsonreagon.com/about/, accessed August 24, 2018.

20. Some of Reagon's most well-known octavos include *Ella's Song* (1991); *Seven Principles* (1994); *Greed* (1995); *We Are the Ones We Been Waiting For* (1995); *I Remember, I Believe* (1995); and *Come Unto Me* (1999).

21. blogs.jwpepper.com/index.php/19-groundbreaking-women-composers-part-2/, accessed August 25, 2018.

22. Thorvaldsdottir's last name is technically spelled "Þorvaldsdóttir," but most American publications transcribe the first character—which exists in Icelandic but not English—as *Th*.

23. www.annathorvalds.com/bio/, accessed August 24, 2018.

24. In April of 2018, Esa-Pekka Salonen (b. 1958) led the New York Philharmonic in the premiere of Thorvaldsdottir's *Metacosmos*, which was commissioned by the orchestra. The work received its European premiere with the Berlin Philharmonic, conducted by Alan Gilbert (b. 1967), in January of 2019.

25. santaratniece.blogspot.com, accessed August 24, 2018.

26. The Minneapolis–St. Paul metropolitan area is nestled in the heart of "Luther Land"—a regional sobriquet reflecting the deeply rooted choral culture of the upper Midwest. Lutheran liberal arts colleges such as St. Olaf, Luther, Concordia, and Gustavus Adolphus all boast rich and storied choral programs and are home to some of the United States' best choral ensembles.

27. *The Notebooks of Leonardo da Vinci* received its European premiere on July 9, 2019, as part of the Leonardo da Vinci International Choral Festival. The festival honors the five hundredth anniversary of the death of Leonardo da Vinci (1452–1519).

28. Anna Thorvaldsdottir also contributed a movement to *Seven Responses* entitled *Ad genua* ("To the Knees").

29. www.daletrumbore.com/about, accessed August 24, 2018.

6

EXPERIMENTAL MUSIC AND EXTENDED TECHNIQUES

Women have had extraordinary impact on the field of new music, both as performers and composers. Although new and experimental music is not a gender-specific genre, the female singer's range and flexibility have made her an ideal executant of extended vocal techniques. Many avant-garde composers have found their muse in specific singers as well, resulting in a stunning body of evocative musical works. This chapter will provide an overview of some of this repertoire, the techniques necessary to perform it, and representative performers and composers who have made a significant mark in the field of new music for voice.[1]

AVANT-GARDE MUSIC FOR VOICE

In the twentieth century, the world of classical music took a turn toward a host of revolutionary new styles, and new schools of composition emerged. The rules and traditions of Western harmony and form—from Johann Sebastian Bach (1685–1750) through Johannes Brahms (1833–1897)—no longer seemed to apply to a new generation of avant-garde composers. For vocalists, one of the most pioneering and groundbreaking works was *Pierrot lunaire*, Op. 21, an infamous 1912 composition by Arnold Schoenberg (1874–1951). This dark piece of chamber music, which sets the expressionist poetry of Albert Giraud (1860–1929), introduced sprechstimme—a style of "singing" that falls somewhere in between traditional singing and human speech—to a wide audience for the first time.

Sprechstimme challenged everything that classical audiences thought they knew about singing. Over the next several decades, other composers would continue to explore these new vocal possibilities, most famously Alban Berg (1885–1935)—Schoenberg's pupil—in his 1925 opera *Wozzeck*. Other prominent composers who explored new possibilities for the voice—usually called "extended techniques"—included John Cage (1912–1992), György Ligeti (1923–2006), Luciano Berio (1925–2003), Hans Werner Henze (1926–2012), Karlheinz Stockhausen (1928–2007), George Crumb (b. 1929), Pauline Oliveros (1932–2016), and Peter Maxwell Davies (1934–2016). Most of these composers worked directly with a new generation of singers who were eager to stretch their voices. Notable singers who specialized in these extended techniques are discussed below.

SINGER-COMPOSERS

The first group of three singers that we will discuss are notable not only as avant-garde singers but as composers as well. All three of these women—Cathy Berberian (1925–1983), Meredith Monk (b. 1942), and Joan La Barbara (b. 1947)—have created many works for themselves and their colleagues, often exploring the unique qualities of their own extraordinary voices.

Cathy Berberian was an American mezzo-soprano who based her career out of Rome, Italy. She was born in Massachusetts and received a broad education at Columbia University and New York University, simultaneously studying mime, writing, costuming, Spanish dancing, Hinduism, and opera.[2] She was renowned for her extraordinary vocal range, which spanned three octaves; one critic noted that she had the notes required "to sing both Tristan and Isolde."[3] Over the course of her long career, many well-known contemporary composers wrote pieces for her, including Darius Milhaud (1892–1974), Igor Stravinsky (1882–1971), Hans Werner Henze, John Cage, Sylvano Bussotti

Figure 6.1. Cathy Berberian. *Creative Commons (CCBY-SA 3.0)*

(b. 1931), and Luciano Berio (1925–2003), to whom she was married. She became renowned as an interpreter of Berio's works. The most famous Berio compositions that were written for her include *Circles* (1960), *Visage* (1961), *Sequenza III* (1965), and *Recital I* (1972). Berberian also sang the world premiere of Cage's *Aria with Fontana Mix* (1958), which made her a household name within the new music community. In addition to being an interpreter, Berberian also composed. Her most famous vocal work is entitled *Stripsody* (1966), the score of which consists of only hand-drawn cartoons. Berberian also recorded prolifically; most of the works that were written for her have been preserved in her extensive discography. Interestingly, not all of her recordings were of new music. A famous example is the twelve-track album *Beatles Arias* (1967)—twelve humorous baroque covers of Beatles songs. Berberian died suddenly of a heart attack in Rome on March 3, 1983. ♪

Meredith Monk is a multifaceted American vocalist and composer. A lifelong New Yorker, Monk graduated from Sarah Lawrence College in 1964 and soon became a part of an avant-garde circle of New York experimental composers, the most famous of whom was Cage. Her works are eclectic in nature and scope and often interdisciplinary, combining music, theater, dance, and even film in innovative and creative

ways. Monk is probably best known for her singing and vocal compositions, most of which she has performed and recorded herself with the
collaboration of other vocal artists. She is a pioneer of extended vocal
techniques, and her prolific output of new music for the voice is one of
the most unusual and intriguing oeuvres in contemporary music. Her
three operas—*Education of the Girlchild* (1973), *Quarry* (1976), and
Atlas (1991)—stretch our understanding of the genre and its possibilities. Her films include *Turtle Dreams* (1983) and *Book of Days* (1989).
While Monk does not altogether depart from traditional musical nota-
tion, the score only offers a starting point for the interpretation of her
works. Her compositions and vocals can be heard on more than a dozen
CDs, most of them recorded for the ECM label. At the writing of this
book, Monk is seventy-six years old and still maintains a full-time touring and performance schedule.

Joan La Barbara, another American, is the third great composer-
performer who specializes in extended techniques for voice. In some
ways, La Barbara is the most virtuosic, boasting a panoramic palette of
vocal sounds while inventing and championing new ones, such as circular singing and multiphonics. Born in Philadelphia, La Barbara studied
with Helen Boatwright (1919–2010) at Syracuse University and Marion
Freschl (1896–1984) at the Juilliard School. Beginning in the mid-1970s,
she became a part of the New York City new music community, creating
her first works and experimenting with new vocal sounds. Many of the
important avant-garde composers of the twentieth century—including
Cage, Morton Feldman (1926–1987), Robert Ashley (1930–2014), Al-
vin Lucier (b. 1931), Philip Glass (b. 1937), and her husband, Morton
Subotnik (b. 1933)—wrote music especially for La Barbara's voice,
most of which she recorded in a vast discography of almost fifty albums.
Twelvesong (*Zwölfgesang*), commissioned by Radio Bremen in 1977, is
a work for voice and multi-track tape that is a representative example of
La Barbara's creative work. ♪

OTHER NOTABLE PERFORMERS

The four women discussed in this section are not composers but
champions of new music with many important works written for their

voices. Bethany Beardslee (b. 1925) is an American soprano who gained substantial fame in the new music world through her collaborations with four high-profile twentieth-century composers: Igor Stravinsky, George Perle (1915–2009), Pierre Boulez (1925–2016), and especially Milton Babbitt (1916–2011), with whom she sustained a legendary collaboration. Beardslee was born in Lansing, Michigan, and educated at Michigan State College (now Michigan State University) and the Juilliard School. In 1951, she married the French conductor Jacques-Louis Monod (b. 1927), who introduced her to the repertoire of the Second Viennese School and set her on a path to a career in new music. Her second husband, composer Godfrey Winham (1934–1975), introduced her to avant-garde music with computer. Babbitt's *Philomel* (1964) is one of Beardslee's signature pieces. The three-movement work—recitative/arioso/aria—combines live soprano with recorded soprano and synthesizer. The libretto is based on Ovid's myth of Philomela, a speechless maiden who is turned into a nightingale. ♪

Of all the interpretative artists discussed in this chapter, Jan De-Gaetani (1933–1989) has recorded the most widely. DeGaetani was born in Massillon, Ohio, and educated at the Juilliard School, where she studied with Sergius Kagen (1909–1964). Her repertoire encompassed much of the traditional classical art song canon in addition to avant-garde music. Nevertheless, her contributions to new music were considerable. Although many composers wrote works for DeGaetani, her collaboration with George Crumb was perhaps the most fruitful. Crumb wrote both *Ancient Voices of Children* (1970) and *Apparition* (1979) specifically for DeGaetani's voice. She recorded more than two dozen albums and performed with some of the world's leading orchestras. During the last two decades of her career, she taught on the voice faculty of the Eastman School of Music and at the Aspen Music Festival in Aspen, Colorado.

Phyllis Bryn-Julson (b. 1945) was born in Bowdon, North Dakota, and trained as a pianist at Concordia College in Moorhead, Minnesota. Like La Barbara, Bryn-Julson studied at Syracuse University with Boatwright. In 1966 she made an acclaimed debut with the Boston Symphony Orchestra in Berg's *Lulu Suite*. This success was followed by engagements with major orchestras throughout the United States, including the New York Philharmonic under Boulez, with whom she became a regular collaborator. Although Bryn-Julson has sung a wide repertoire, her perfect pitch and three-octave vocal range have made her internationally renowned as an interpreter of avant-garde music, particularly the twelve-tone works of the Second Viennese School. One of her signature pieces is Schoenberg's *Pierrot lunaire*, Op. 21, a work which she has performed hundreds of times, even coauthoring a book on how to sing the work's sprechstimme.[4] Since 1984, Bryn-Julson has been on the voice faculty of the Peabody Institute in Baltimore.

American mezzo-soprano Sharon Mabry (b. 1945) was educated at Florida State University and George Peabody College/Vanderbilt University before settling into a long career as a professor of voice at Austin Peay State University, where she has taught for more than four decades. Mabry first received national recognition as a featured recitalist in the 1980 National Public Radio "Art of Song" series. Her repertoire consists largely of contemporary works and works by women composers. Mabry has premiered compositions by more than thirty composers and continues to have new works written for her. Her album entitled *Music by Women: A Celebration* (2003) features selections by Lili Boulanger (1893–1918), Rhian Samuel (b. 1944), Elizabeth Vercoe (b. 1941), and Mary Howe (1884–1964). Mabry is especially important to the national pedagogy community through her writings devoted to the performance of avant-garde music. Between 1985 and 2009, she wrote the "New Directions" column in the *Journal of Singing*; these articles are devoted to discussions of trends in contemporary music. Mabry is also the author of the 2002 book *Exploring Twentieth-Century Vocal Music*. Now in its second edition, this book introduces the literature and pedagogy of this era.[5] She has championed new music by women composers and has made several recordings including *Irreveries from Sappho* (1982) by Vercoe, a composer whom Mabry has championed.[6] ♪

ENSEMBLES

Some choral repertoire also calls for the use of extended techniques. In recent years, several professional choral groups have emerged that are devoted almost exclusively to performing new music. Roomful of Teeth is one such ensemble. Founded in 2009 by Brad Wells (b. 1962), its stated mission is to "mine the expressive potential of the human voice."[7] The ensemble's eponymous debut album, *Roomful of Teeth* (2012), was nominated for three Grammy Awards and won one: the Grammy Award for Best Chamber Music/Small Ensemble Performance. Roomful of Teeth achieved further national acclaim the following year, when Caroline Shaw (b. 1982)—a member of the ensemble—won the 2013 Pulitzer Prize in Music for *Partita for 8 Voices*, a work written expressly for Roomful of Teeth. According to the Pulitzer Board, *Partita for 8 Voices* is "a highly polished and inventive a cappella work uniquely embracing speech, whispers, sighs, murmurs, wordless melodies, and novel vocal effects."[8] Roomful of Teeth also specializes in a wide variety of additional extended techniques, including "Tuvan throat singing, yodeling, Broadway belting, Inuit throat singing, Korean *pansori*, Georgian singing, Sardinian *cantu a tenore*, Hindustani music, Persian classical singing, and death metal singing."[9] ♪

Figure 6.2. Caroline Shaw (photo by Kait Moreno). *Creative Commons (CCBY-SA 2.0)*

The Crossing is a Philadelphia-based chamber ensemble founded in 2005 and directed by Donald Nally (b. 1960). The ensemble focuses exclusively on new music, with commissioning and premiering new works a top artistic priority. In 2009, the ensemble started an annual summer festival called the Month of Moderns, during which several concerts were devoted to a common theme, such as the texts of a single poet. At the time of the writing of this book, more than fifty new works have been commissioned and premiered by the Crossing. The Crossing also records many of the works they commission. As of 2018, they have recorded fourteen albums, one of which—*Gavin Bryars: The Fifth Century*—won the Grammy Award for Best Choral Performance in 2018. One of the Crossing's most ambitious projects was entitled *Seven Responses* (2016). For this work, seven of the world's most accomplished composers wrote a fifteen-minute musical response to one of the seven cantatas that constitute *Membra Jesu nostri* (1680), a seventeenth-century sacred work by Dietrich Buxtehude (ca. 1638–1707).[10] The composers came from five different countries—Denmark, Latvia, Germany, Iceland, and the United States—and featured two Pulitzer Prize winners, Louis Spratlan (b. 1940) and Caroline Shaw. Another woman composer, Anna Thorvaldsdottir (b. 1977), contributed the response entitled *Ad genua* ("To the Knees"). Much of the Crossing's repertoire requires the use of extended techniques, and listening to their discography is a good way to understand how they can be used in a choral ensemble setting. ♪

EXTENDED VOCAL TECHNIQUES

To perform new music well, you need to possess excellent musicianship, a voice that is flexible, an attitude that is open-minded, a thirst for adventure, and a willingness to step out of your comfort zone. In order to realize the composer's intentions, a wide variety of extended techniques must be practiced and mastered. Some of these techniques are listed below.

Buccal Speech

Buccal speech is an alternative way of speaking that does not utilize the lungs or larynx. In buccal speech, air is stored in the oral cavity (usually the cheek), which acts as an alternate lung. The air is then sent into the mouth, where speech is created without the engagement of the vocal folds. Buccal speech is also widely known as "Donald Duck talk," as the famous Disney character is the quintessential example of buccal speech in the mass media.

Circular Singing

Circular singing is the vocal equivalent of the circular breathing practiced by instrumentalists. The term was coined by Joan La Barbara, who utilized the technique in her 1974 work *Circular Singing*.

Glottal Fry

Glottal fry is phonation at the lowest pitches of the voice, either male or female. It produces an imprecise phonation reminiscent of "clicking." Minimal airflow is needed to produce glottal fry.

Growling

Growling is exactly what it sounds like—a low, guttural vocalization. In addition to new music, growling is also applied in some types of heavy metal music.

Inhaled Singing

Inhaled singing is a technique that involves singing while inhaling as opposed to exhaling. The result is a sound rooted in glottal fry. While some pitch variation is possible, the technique is limited in scope compared to traditional singing.

Multiphonics

Multiphonics refers to more than one pitch produced at the same time. While traditionally an instrumental technique, vocalists can also produce multiphonics, typically in one of two ways: through either throat singing or whistling while phonating.

Screaming

This technique is self-explanatory, although there is a technique to screaming in a nondamaging way. Consultation with a knowledgeable acting voice teacher is highly recommended.

Sprechstimme

Sprechstimme is a vocal quality or style that lies somewhere in between speech and singing. Although exact pitches are notated—with an x over each note stem—and are expected to be performed with accuracy, it is also incumbent on the performer to give the vocal line a speech-like quality.

Throat Singing

Throat singing is an eccentric singing technique that involves specific manipulation of the singer's jaw, lips, mouth, and sinuses to produce several overtones simultaneously. The fundamental note that produces these overtones is always a specific pitch in the TA/mode 1 register.

Ululation

Ululation is a long, wavering, high-pitched vocal sound produced by the deliberate and rapid manipulation of the tongue. Ululation is a distinct and idiomatic sound heard in certain types of world music.

Yodeling

Yodeling is a style of singing often associated with folk music of the Swiss Alps. Yodeling features the singing of leaps and a rapid alternation between the two principal vocal registers (TA and CT).[11] A "yodel" can also be a short section of yodeling, sung on a single breath. Derived from the (middle-high) German verb "jôlen," meaning "to call," yodeling is thought to have originated as a call between mountain peoples. Whether there was a practical use for yodeling is unclear, but its popularity as an interesting and engaging folk music endures. Due to the use of both registers, yodelers often have an extensive range of three octaves or more. A singer who practices yodeling is called a yodeler.

PERFORMING NEW MUSIC

The best way to enter the new music world is to first attend institutions with strong composition programs that are devoted to new music. Making friends with composers and working collaboratively with them as

Figure 6.3. Meredith Monk performing *On Behalf of Nature* at the Brooklyn Academy of Music, 2014 (photo by Steven Pisano). *Creative Commons (CCBY-SA 2.0)*

you work to premiere new works is the ultimate education in developing your skills as a new music singer. Finding a knowledgeable and supportive teacher is also key. There are many wonderful singing teachers who are not comfortable singing or teaching sounds that fall outside of the traditional bel canto or "classical" sound ideal. However, with the explosion of CCM pedagogy and the proliferation of courses and programs that are devoted to function-based voice pedagogy, an ever-increasing number of singing teachers are feeling more comfortable teaching a wide variety of styles in a healthy way. Jeannette LoVetri (b. 1949), a New York–based singing teacher and founder of Somatic Voicework, is an example of a high-profile pedagogue who has cultivated a reputation as a teacher of extended vocal techniques; Meredith Monk has studied with her for decades. Some notable performers are also affiliated with academic institutions: Sharon Mabry is a professor at Austin Peay State University, and Phyllis Bryn-Julson has taught for many years at the Peabody Institute at Johns Hopkins University.

PROFILE: MEREDITH MONK

Describe your musical background and what led you to become a composer.
I come from a musical family and am a fourth-generation singer. My mother sang popular music and jingles on the radio, my maternal grandfather was a bass-baritone and founded a music conservatory with my grandmother, and my great-grandfather was a cantor in Russia. I studied piano throughout my childhood and learned to read music before I could read words. I was also enrolled in Dalcroze eurhythmics classes. Early on, I realized that I wanted to create my own work, rather than follow in my family's footsteps of being interpreters of music.

While at Sarah Lawrence College, I studied voice but also dance and theater, creating my own combined performing arts major. After moving to New York in the mid-1960s, I had a revelation that the voice could be an instrument and that the voice itself was a language. Within it are myriad characters, landscapes, colors, textures, and ways of producing sound. I intuitively sensed the ancient power of the voice as the first human instrument. It changed my whole work from that point on. I knew then what the heart of my work would be.

Describe your compositional process and what it says about who you are.

I work with the voice as a kinetic, embodied instrument, and I think of the voice and body as one thing; our voices dance and our bodies sing. Early on, I worked with my own voice to explore its possibilities and what it could evoke, delineate, and uncover. I trusted the voice's ability to communicate nonverbally, to be universal, and to connect directly to the heart. It could uncover subtle shades of feeling that exist between what we think of as emotions. Right from the beginning, I was interested in primordial utterance: what were the first human sounds? I began playing with what a vocal gesture would be. How would the voice jump, spin, spiral, fall? How would I abstract the sound of a laugh, of sobbing, of shouting, into a musical phrase?

For the first ten years, I created work for solo voice and voice and keyboard, using organ or piano as a ground base for my voice to either blend with or leap from. I then formed Meredith Monk & Vocal Ensemble to enrich the textures, counterpoint, and color in my music, while honoring the uniqueness of each voice. This inspired me to compose intricate, rhythmically complex, and shimmering forms.

My method was and continues to be one of exploring the possibilities, qualities, and mysteries of the voice; of listening and trusting what it reveals. I consider each piece its own world, and I try to start from zero to discover what the laws of that world are. From intuitive moments of uncovering material, to the rigorous intellectual process of refining and sculpting the material into forms, I've continued to expand my approach in an effort to discover and learn something new. Within the last fifteen years or so, I have extended this exploration to my writing for instruments. Whereas I have always thought of voices as instruments, I have begun thinking about instruments as voices.

Working with principles of layering and weaving have always been interesting to me. I continually think about a balance of elements. While individual strands of material are pared down to their essence, each is an essential part of the whole. When they are put together, a complex and multidimensional mosaic of sound is created. In much of my music, I aim for directness, asymmetry, and above all transparency, which allows for implied space and silence to underlie my compositions. Because my focus has been on composing music for the voice, melodic invention, variety of timbre, and spontaneity within a rigorous form are aspects I try for. Spaciousness, interdependence, playfulness, clarity, honesty, and fluidity are some principles that I have tried to reflect in my work. I believe that these qualities relate directly to my values as a human being and as an artist.

What hurdles have you encountered as a woman composer? How did you overcome them? Are there any you have yet to overcome?
Since I began working in the 1960s, things have shifted somewhat, but in retrospect I will say that there have been times when I felt I had not been given the same opportunity as some of my male colleagues and that some critics of my work had written about me in a sexist manner. I have done my best just to stay the course, to focus on my work and inner vision. That rigor and sense of trust have been what has guided me.

I don't think of myself as a female composer but as a composer who happens to be a woman. I've always worked with gender fluidity in the music itself. I'll have men sing in falsetto and women sing in a very low range, for example. I'm not someone who likes to work with a sense of limitation or being categorized in a specific way. To me the work comes first, and other people's notions of gender can be a way of not allowing for the scope and power that each of us have as human beings. I have tried hard to transcend

_135

this. I have been privileged to live a life in music and very fortunate
to have fulfilled most of my artistic aspirations.

Who are your greatest inspirations, musically and artistically?
From an early age I was drawn to composers such as Béla Bartók,
Erik Satie, and Federico Mompou, but I also love all kinds of
music. Mildred Bailey and Caetano Veloso are among some of my
favorite singers for the ways that they have allowed their voices to
convey a purity of feeling. Other singers like Janis Joplin, Peggy
Seeger, and Joni Mitchell inspired me with their honesty and
authenticity. I was also lucky to have wonderful mentors like Bes-
sie Schoenberg and Ruth Lloyd while at Sarah Lawrence, who
encouraged me to find my own way.

I'm a great admirer of film and such film directors as Maya
Deren, Robert Bresson, Yasujirō Ozu, Carl Theodor Dreyer, Laurent Cantet, Deepa Mehta, and Roberto Rossellini, among many
others. There have been numerous writers and visual artists who
have also inspired me. I admire anyone who has followed their
own path, asked questions, and found places that fall between the
cracks of genres or categories.

While not numerous (in comparison to programs devoted to opera,
art song, and CCM), there are also workshops and training programs
that are devoted to new music. When I (Matthew) was a much younger
singer, I had the great privilege of being selected for the Meredith Monk
Young Artist Program, which was offered through the Weill Institute at
Carnegie Hall. It was an intense but magnificent weeklong workshop
that gave me the opportunity to work directly with Monk and members
of her ensemble on her compositions. The eighteen young artists—all
selected by Monk herself—rehearsed long days in a loft studio on the far
west side of Manhattan. The week concluded with a sold-out recital in
Carnegie's Zankel Hall. It was truly an unforgettable formative week—
still one of the most memorable of my career. The chamber music we
worked on under her close supervision was some of the most challenging
I had encountered in my career, stretching me as a musician and taking

me completely out of my comfort zone. In addition, Monk was not only knowledgeable but also a generous spirit—she was truly invested in us as musicians and people. Monk continues to offer workshops and is devoted to educating the next generation of new music performers.

Certain cities in the United States—such as New York, Boston, and Minneapolis—are a haven for avant-garde composers who can offer interesting opportunities for singers. Being in the right place to perform new music is key, as smaller cities are more likely to program traditional repertoire and are less likely to "branch out" to avant-garde composers and composers of new music simply due to the limited box office.

FINAL THOUGHTS

Although only a small segment of the singing population engages in the regular performance of new music, the singer with the right skillset and vocal flexibility might find a comfortable niche in this genre. Opportunities are especially ripe for women—especially excellent musicians with flexible, three-octave ranges. New music is a genre in which female singers have had extraordinary impact.

NOTES

1. Several passages in this chapter were previously published in the authors' book *Voice Secrets: 100 Performance Strategies for the Advanced Singer* (Lanham, MD: Rowman & Littlefield, 2016).

2. Tim Page, "Cathy Berberian, Mezzo-Soprano," *New York Times*, March 8, 1983.

3. Ibid.

4. Phyllis Bryn-Julson and Paul Matthews, *Inside Pierrot Lunaire: Performing the Sprechstimme in Schoenberg's Masterpiece* (Lanham, MD: Scarecrow Press, 2008).

5. Sharon Mabry, *Exploring Twentieth-Century Vocal Music: A Practical Guide to Innovations in Performance and Repertoire* (New York: Oxford University Press, 2002).

6. In 1986, Mabry also recorded Vercoe's *Herstory III: Jeanne de Lorraine*, a twenty-five-minute melodrama about Joan of Arc. The *American Record*

Guide noted that this work was one of the best pieces by a female composer of the twentieth century. Mabry responded to this somewhat sexist remark that it is "one of the best by *anybody* in the twentieth century" (personal correspondence with Matthew Hoch, August 16, 2018).

7. www.roomfulofteeth.org, accessed July 30, 2018.

8. www.pulitzer.org/winners/caroline-shaw, accessed July 30, 2018.

9. www.roomfulofteeth.org, accessed July 30, 2018.

10. Each of the seven cantatas in *Membra Jesu nostri* is dedicated to one of the parts of the body of the crucified Jesus Christ. The seven movements are as follows: I. *Ad pedes* ("To the Feet"); II. *Ad genua* ("To the Knees"); III. *Ad manus* ("To the Hands"); IV. *Ad latus* ("To the Sides"); V. *Ad pectus* ("To the Breast"); VI. *Ad cor* ("To the Heart"); and VII. *Ad faciem* ("To the Face").

11. TA stands for "thyroarytenoid" or mode 1/chest voice, whereas CT stands for "cricothyroid" or mode 2/head voice.

7

MUSIC THEATER BY WOMEN

Erin Guinup

During a rehearsal for the original Broadway production of *South Pacific* (1950), music theater star Mary Martin (1913–1990) cartwheeled herself right off of the stage and into the orchestra pit. When everyone rushed to the famous performer's aid, Martin triumphantly arose, climbed out of the pit, and continued with the show. Several minutes passed before Oscar Hammerstein II (1895–1960) noticed the production's arranger and music coordinator, Trude Rittman (1908–2005), unconscious and slumped across the piano keys.[1] During her death-defying acrobatic stunt, Martin had fallen directly on top of Rittman and knocked her out cold. The fact that it took several minutes for anyone to notice the arranger's collapse provides a fitting, if grim, parallel to her career in music theater. Rittman played a pivotal role in the development of many of the most beloved musicals of the twentieth century, yet many readers will likely not recognize her name. Even when injured, she was virtually invisible to those around her, and this lack of proper recognition has dimmed our historical memory of her as well.

INTRODUCTION: THERE IS NOTHIN' LIKE A DAME

Jill Halstead (b. 1968), in her book *The Woman Composer: Creativity and the Gendered Politics of Musical Composition*, writes that "the most obvious way of suppressing awareness and encouragement of female creativity is by denying its existence. Although it is now clear that women have participated in music as composers throughout history and across cultures, the term composer has usually been understood to denote a male creator."[2] Perhaps in no area has this been more true than music theater, one of the most male-dominated of all musical genres. This chapter is devoted to some of the unsung female heroes of the Great White Way.

When prompted to think of the great music theater creators of the twentieth century, our minds almost immediately leap to household names such as Irving Berlin (1888–1989), Richard Rodgers (1902–1979) and Oscar Hammerstein II, John Kander (b. 1927) and Fred Ebb (1928–2004), Stephen Sondheim (b. 1930), Stephen Schwartz (b. 1948), and countless others. These revered composers and lyricists have certainly earned their notoriety. It seems strange, however, that when asked to name even one of their female contemporaries, many of us invariably draw a blank. As you may guess, the disparity is not for a lack of talented female writers to choose from. Women have contributed actively to the music theater canon since its beginnings. This chapter offers insight into the lives and careers of exceptional women who have written for the music theater stage and persisted in overcoming barriers to make their voices heard. The women discussed here by no means constitute an exhaustive list of notable female creators; rather, their stories will hopefully provide signposts by which we can begin building a counternarrative to the idea that music theater was solely created by white men.

Since the writing process for music theater is so collaborative, I have chosen to include lyricists with composers in this discussion. Unlike in art song, text for music theater is often created simultaneously with music. Composers and lyricists often play on each other's strengths to create shows, and the early music theater industry was more hospitable to women who wrote lyrics rather than music. Ignoring the work of lyricists would diminish the contributions of many women who first paved the path for those who would later achieve prominence in all aspects of the creative process.

The purpose of sharing these women's stories is to encourage contemporary theater artists to rediscover their work and become inspired by their exceptional tenacity and grit. Modern creators can find encouragement in the legacy these women built, and collectively, we can improve efforts to promote and perform work created by women, people of color, and other underrepresented groups. By remembering our predecessors, we can begin to reclaim the history of music theater and strive for a more inclusive future.

ANYTHING YOU CAN DO: THE FIRST GENERATION

Even before the Nineteenth Amendment gave women the right to vote in 1920, a number of women courageously stepped into traditionally male occupations and made an impact. In this early era of music theater, the music scene was dominated by male publishers and songwriters working on one street in Manhattan dubbed Tin Pan Alley. Female librettists, dramatists, and composers contributed to this early music theater period, but their employers often denied them credit for their work, and they remain largely anonymous today. Their obscurity contrasts starkly with their male contemporaries' enduring legacies. Despite history's best efforts at silencing and erasing these early female creators, several success stories stand out as noteworthy.

Rida Johnson Young (1875–1926) was an enormously successful lyricist and songwriter credited with more than thirty Broadway shows and five hundred songs. Her first Broadway show, *Brown of Harvard*, opened in 1906 and featured the song "When Love Is Young." Johnson Young subsequently collaborated with composer Victor Herbert (1859–1923), writing the book and lyrics for the hit show *Naughty Marietta* (1910). The musical's success led to a popular film adaptation, which starred famous duo Jeanette MacDonald (1903–1965) and Nelson Eddy (1901–1967) and earned an Academy Award nomination for Best Picture.

Johnson Young was immensely prolific; she made over a million dollars in royalties and often had multiple shows running on Broadway in the same year. One article stated, "She earns her triumphs by hard work. . . . She says she doesn't know what a real vacation is. She never

Figure 7.1.   Rida Johnson Young, 1910. *Creative Commons (CCBY-SA 3.0)*

goes anywhere without taking her work with her."[3] Some of her most enduring songs include "Italian Street Song," "I'm Falling in Love with Someone," and "Ah, Sweet Mystery of Life" from *Naughty Marietta*; "Will You Remember" from *Maytime* (1917); and the Irish ballad "Mother Machree" from *Barry of Ballymore* (1910). ♪

Despite her success, Johnson Young still found herself up against a society that valued traditional female roles over accomplishment. One article written in 1917 describes her gardening and hobbies in great detail while also adding that she was "uncommonly 'easy to look at.'" The article continues, "She wears her beautiful clothes so well that one cannot envy her the riotous royalties which enable her to buy them. She is quite unspoiled by her successes too and she is so willing to share with others the credit for her achievements."[4] Modern readers may feel a familiar sting at the article's tone, given that a century later, many women in entertainment still find their physical appearances brought into conversations apropos of nothing. We should also note that the article considered it a mark of virtue that Johnson Young often credited others for her achievements. While the best artists respect their collaborators, it seems worth questioning that Johnson Young should be expected to deflect her own success, especially after working so hard for it.

Dorothy Donnelly (1880–1928) was an actor, playwright, librettist, producer, and director. She wrote more than a dozen Broadway hits, with her most famous work being *The Student Prince*, written in collaboration with Sigmund Romberg (1887–1951) in 1924. *The Student Prince* was the biggest Broadway hit of the 1920s, running for an impressive 608 performances. Despite this success, Donnelly was sometimes not even credited in reviews, and one journalist simply referred to the creative duo behind the show as "Mr. Romberg and his lyricist."[5] Donnelly's work was often topical, and her lyrics for the "Drinking Song" in *The Student Prince* were particularly appealing to Prohibition-era audiences. Her first success on Broadway was the operetta *Blossom Time* (1921), a biography of Franz Schubert (1797–1828) that used his music as the foundation for her lyrics. She also wrote and directed *Poppy* (1923), an original musical that would eventually be adapted for film and launch performer W. C. Fields (1880–1946) into stardom.

Anne Caldwell (1867–1936) was a singing and dancing comedian until she tripped on stage and broke her leg. Not easily discouraged, she turned to writing after this setback and launched a successful career. Caldwell is now credited with more than thirty shows as a lyricist, dramatist, or composer, and she frequently collaborated with composers Jerome Kern (1885–1945), Vincent Youmans (1898–1946), and Victor Herbert. Her songs include "Whose Baby Are You?" (1920), "Once in a Blue Moon" (1923), and "I Know That You Know" (1926), which have been covered by dozens of notable artists, including Nat King Cole (1919–1965) and Leslie Odom Jr. (b. 1981).[6] ♪

Doug Reside, curator for New York Public Library for the Performing Arts, writes: "Along with Rida Johnson Young and Dorothy

Donnelly, Anne Caldwell's work and career helped to establish the fact that writing American musical comedy was not solely a male domain and that a female writer could create works for the stage that were equally as satirical, witty, timely, and simply as comical as the work of any man."[7] Caldwell also cofounded the American Society of Composers, Authors, and Publishers (ASCAP) and the Songwriters Hall of Fame and worked in Hollywood as a script doctor. But for all her success, she could not escape critics and their remarks on her unattractiveness. After enduring years of scrutiny, she became so insecure about her looks that she published her daughter's picture as her own.

THE GERSHWIN GALS: CAN'T WE BE FRIENDS?

Nora Bayes (1880–1928) was a popular singing comedian who rose to fame after being discovered by the mother of George M. Cohan (1878–1942) and became one of the industry's first mega-celebrities.[8] Bill Edwards notes that "a typical advertisement for her that stressed her clothing as much as her talent read: 'The World's Greatest Singing Single Comedienne, NORA BAYES. New Hits, Funny Lyrics, Live Topics, Diamond-Decked Gowns.'"[9] Bayes is credited as composer or songwriter in eleven shows. She is most famous for the song "Shine On, Harvest Moon" (1908), which was featured in the *Ziegfeld Follies of 1908*. However, the authorship of this popular song—cowritten with Jack Norworth (1879–1959), the second of her five husbands—has been questioned. Her one-woman show, *Songs as Is and Songs as Was*, employed then-nineteen-year-old pianist George Gershwin (1898–1937), whom she later fired for not changing one of his songs to suit her tastes. A busy recording artist, she had a rendition of Cohan's "Over There" (1917) that became an international hit and rallied troops during World War I. Many of her own songs have withered to obscurity, but a 1944 movie that fictionalized her life story repopularized "Shine On, Harvest Moon."

Kay Swift (1897–1993), originally named Katherine, holds the distinction of being the first woman to score a complete Broadway musical. Her career began with songs penned for Broadway revues, with one of her biggest and most enduring hits, "Can't We Be Friends," debuting

This quotation about Bayes's choice to not move to Los Angeles and become a film star gives a glimpse of her humor:

> Why don't I become a screen star? Because there is too much money in the picture business. Moving-picture actors, authors, directors and everybody identified with the industry receive altogether too much money for their own good. I know, because everybody tells me so. You understand English, don't you? What do you suppose I would do with all the money I would make in the movies? It would worry my young life away picking out good, reliable banks where my stupendous earnings would be secure. I'd probably deposit my savings in a dozen or more banks and then I would have to hire a couple of dozen detectives to watch each institution and report to me daily as to their solvency. The mental anguish I would suffer would make me unfit to enjoy life. No, siree. No movie work for me! I am quite content with my little two thousand dollars per in vaudeville and nothing to worry about. Say, I wouldn't be Charlie Chaplin with six hundred and seventy million dollars a year or Mary Pickford getting five hundred decillion dollars every time a promoter with a lead pencil comes in contact with a scrap of paper for anything in the world. I would have so much business on my brain that it would interfere with my art and I wouldn't be worth the money I get from my managers. Please don't take my delirium seriously. While it is true that I am now receiving eight thousand dollars a week I will shortly raise myself to ten thousand dollars. I will begin to throw about with careless abandon conversational dollar marks with zeros without end trailing along behind, unaccompanied by decimal points. You know my time is worth two hundred dollars a minute, and I figure I have now consumed six thousand dollars' worth of my time just to give a measly little interview.[10]

in *The Little Show* in 1929. Swift's Broadway musical, *Fine and Dandy*, premiered the next year in 1930 and featured humor, political satire, and songs meant to uplift and entertain. The score is full of hits, including "Can This Be Love?," "I'll Hit a New High," "Let's Go Eat Worms in the Garden," and the title song, which became popular as a jazz standard recorded by Bing Crosby (1903–1977) and Barbra Streisand (b.

Figure 7.2.   Kay Swift, 1959. *Creative Commons (CCBY-SA 3.0)*

1942) and served as theme music for magician Art Metrano (b. 1936) and New York City television weatherman Tex Antoine (1923–1983). That first musical, written by Swift and her husband James Warburg (1896–1969), who wrote under the pseudonym Paul James, was a smash hit, and the pair seemed well-positioned for a long and successful career had the Depression not devastated the fortunes of most Broadway investors. James ultimately returned his focus to banking amid the economic crisis, and Kay became more focused on her romance with George Gershwin. ♪

Gershwin and Swift had first bonded over the piano at a dinner party at her home in 1925, and they developed a deep musical and romantic relationship. Despite the success of *Fine and Dandy* and several bona fide hit songs, Kay Swift took several years off from writing original music beginning in 1931 and instead dedicated herself to assisting Gershwin with his work. When the love of her life died unexpectedly in 1937 at the early age of thirty-eight, she was devastated. However, her keen memory proved instrumental to preserving his works. She was able to play from memory the complete uncut score of *Porgy and Bess* (1935) into her eighties and worked with Gershwin's brother Ira and scholars to provide critical notes.[11] She also arranged and reconstructed more than fifty of his songs from his sketchbooks and her memory.[12] Swift also wrote extensively for the Rockettes at Radio City Music Hall as a staff composer, churning out songs monthly. In 1943, Swift published a memoir, *Who Could Ask for Anything More?*, which focused on her second marriage to a cowboy.[13] That book was later made into the film *Never a Dull Moment*, starring Irene Dunne as Kay Swift and featuring a few of Swift's songs, including "Once You Find Your Guy."

Another female composer romantically linked to George Gershwin was Ann Ronnell (1905–1993). Her most famous song was "Willow Weep for Me" (1932), which she dedicated to Gershwin and wrote while she was romantically involved with him. There was some speculation in the New York composer community that Gershwin actually wrote the song and gave her the copyright as a gift—as if to suggest that a woman could not be this competent—but those rumors were never proven.[14] With the fall of fortunes during the Depression, Ronnell was part of the mass exodus of Broadway to Hollywood, where she created a number of huge hits including "Who's Afraid of the Big Bad Wolf" from the Disney cartoon *Three Little Pigs* (1933), cowritten with Frank Churchill (1901–1942). She wrote songs and background music for films, received two Oscar nominations, and was the first woman in Hollywood to conduct a film score.[15] Ronnell returned to Broadway in 1942 with *Count Me In* and earned the distinction of being the first woman credited with writing both lyrics and music for a Broadway show. Though it flopped, Cole Porter (1891–1964) praised her work as "the most singable score to be heard in years."[16] Ronnell wrote, "It was not so easy to get a hearing. There were many other people with tunes at their fingertips, most of them boys. Girls were few in this keenly competitive field and most of those in it at that time dropped out later."[17]

Dana Suesse (1909–1987) was nicknamed "the girl Gershwin" by the press but was *not* romantically involved with Gershwin. A prolific talent, some of her best songs were written for musicals, including Fanny Brice's song "I Knew Him Before He Was Spanish" in *Sweet and Low* (1930). Other hit songs include "Whistling in the Dark" and "Ho Hum!," both published in 1931. Suesse's lyricist, Edward Heyman (1907–1981), bragged that she could write a hit song in under twenty minutes. "You Oughta Be in Pictures" (1934)—called "Hollywood's Anthem" by the *New York Times* and featured in more than forty movies—was written in a mere eighteen minutes.[18]

Mexican American composer María Grever (1885–1951) was one of the first successful Hispanic composers in the United States but "never enjoyed widespread name recognition, despite the fact that her songs achieved 'an immensely deserved run of popularity.'"[19] Grever wrote more than eight hundred songs, many of which remain popular in Mexico and South America, and she is best known for the Grammy Award–winning "What a Difference a Day Makes" (1934), originally written as "Cuando vuelva a tu lado," recorded by artists including Dinah Washington (1924–1963) and Aretha Franklin (1942–2018). Grever frequently collaborated with American lyricists to translate her Spanish songs to make them more accessible to American audiences. She was best known for her film scores and popular songs but composed for several Broadway shows, including the 1941 musical *Viva O'Brien*. The musical featured the songs "El Matador Terrifico," "Broken Hearted Romeo," and "Wrap Me in Your Serape."[20] "Often based on the folk rhythms and styles of Latin American music, particularly Mexican or Spanish tangos, the lyrics are lushly romantic, full of meaning, and easy to recall."[21] She became an advocate for the blind after a dangerous eye infection and used her music to raise funds benefiting Spanish blind programs. Her multifaceted career also included singing opera internationally, producing concerts, and teaching voice. ♪

I COULD WRITE A BOOK: LYRICISTS
OF THE MID-CENTURY

Dorothy Fields (1904–1974) was a librettist and lyricist with a prolific career spanning before and into the Golden Age of music theater. Her father, Broadway impresario Lew Fields (1867–1941), tried to keep Fields and her siblings out of show business and crushed her acting ambitions, but she found her voice as a writer. Fields cowrote more than four hundred songs and worked on fifteen musicals and at least twenty-six movies, collaborating with composers including Arthur Schwartz (1900–1964), Irving Berlin, Cy Coleman (1929–2004), and Jerome Kern.

Fields began her career as a collaborator with Jimmy McHugh (1894–1969), writing songs for *Blackbirds of 1928* (1928), a musical revue featuring an all-black cast including artists such as Duke Ellington (1899–1974). Songs from this revue include "I Can't Give You Anything but Love" and "I Must Have That Man." Other important songs by Fields include "On the Sunny Side of the Street" (1930), "Don't Blame Me" (1932), "I'm in the Mood for Love" (1935), and "The Way You Look Tonight" (1936), for which she and Jerome Kern won an Oscar.[22] She created the concept and book for *Annie Get Your Gun* (1946) and was set to collaborate with Kern on the musical before his untimely death, but Irving Berlin subsequently picked up the project and completed it on his own. Her musical *Redhead*, written with Albert Hague (1920–2001) in 1959, received five Tony Awards including one for Best Musical.

In his 2004 documentary *Broadway: The American Musical*, Michael Kantor writes: "Fields' work habits were highly disciplined. Typically, she would spend eight weeks researching, discussing, and making notes on a project before settling into an 8:30 a.m. to 4:00 p.m. daily work routine. She worked at a bridge table in her apartment on the Upper West Side of Manhattan, and preferred to write with pencil on a yellow legal pad. She kept notebooks in which she copied passages from Dryden, Shaw, and Thoreau; unusual synonyms for commonly used words; humorous proverbs; rhyming phrases; odd-sounding words; and anything else that might come in handy in writing a lyric."[23]

Fields was known for her ability to adapt to the times and continue producing relevant work throughout her lengthy forty-eight-year career. She began collaborating with Cy Coleman in the 1960s and wrote

Sweet Charity (1966), which was nominated for nine Tony Awards and featured such memorable songs as "If My Friends Could See Me Now" and "Big Spender." Her final Broadway show was the Coleman musical *Seesaw* (1973), featuring the song "It's Not Where You Start, It's Where You Finish." In 1971, Dorothy Fields became the first woman inducted into the Songwriters Hall of Fame. ♪

Another collaborator of Cy Coleman's, Carolyn Leigh (1926–1983) is perhaps best known for penning "The Best Is Yet to Come."[24] Her Broadway shows include *Peter Pan* (1954); *Little Me* (1962) with Sid Caesar (1922–2014) and Bob Fosse (1927–1987), featuring the song "I've Got Your Number"; *Wildcat* (1960), which starred Lucille Ball; and *How Now, Dow Jones* (1967).[25] Leigh said, "I've never felt that gender was important to the writing of lyrics or the writing of anything else for that matter . . . but a woman writing about and for a woman has the advantage of a constant intimacy, to say nothing of fascination with the subject."[26] ♪

Betty Comden (1917–2006) and her comedic partner, Adolph Green (1915–2002), made up the longest-running creative partnership in Broadway history with a sixty-year working relationship. Together, they wrote lyrics and scripts for many beloved and successful musicals of the mid-twentieth century, and Comden is one of the most prolific and renowned lyricists in music theater. Over the course of their career, Comden and Green were nominated for twelve Tony Awards, winning seven, and received two Academy Award nominations for their shows, which included *Singin' in the Rain* (1952), *Wonderful Town* (1953), *Bells Are Ringing* (1956), and *On the Twentieth Century* (1978).[27] Leonard Bernstein (1918–1990) was one of their first collaborators, and he helped to launch their storied career with *On the Town* (1944), featuring the memorable song "New York, New York." Among Comden and Green's many songs are classics like "Lonely Town" and "Lucky to Be Me" from *On the Town* (1944), "One Hundred Easy Ways" from *Wonderful Town*, "Never Never Land" from *Peter Pan*, "Just in Time" and "The Party's Over" from *Bells Are Ringing*, and "Make Someone Happy" from *Do Re Mi* (1960).[28] ♪

Comden said in a 1977 interview with the *New York Times* about her collaboration process with Green, "We stare at each other. We meet, whether or not we have a project, just to keep up a continuity of working. There are long periods when nothing happens, and it's just boring and disheartening. But we have a theory that nothing's wasted, even those long days of staring at one another. You sort of have to believe that, don't you? That you had to go through all that to get to the day when something did happen."[29]

EVERYBODY SAYS DON'T: MARY RODGERS

Following World War II, there were very few female composers, with Mary Rodgers (1931–2014) being one of the few success stories. Her father, Richard Rodgers, was perhaps the king of the Golden Age of music theater, but this did not necessarily make her path as a composer easy. "As a famous man's daughter," Rodgers explained, "I always had an urgent, rebellious desire to retain my own identity at any cost."[30] She was apparently delighted when one reviewer said her music was "nothing like dad's."[31] "They obviously didn't think women should or could write music."[32]

Rodgers worked with Leonard Bernstein on the Young People's Concert Series, and his encouragement and support led to the opportunity to write her first and most well-known musical, *Once upon a Mattress*, in 1959. Rodgers's popular spin on the Princess and the Pea, written in just three weeks, is musically complex and features three female leads, none of whom are quite what you would expect from the traditional musical heroine. Princess Fred defies all princess stereotypes, swims moats, and sings the bold classic "Shy," while Queen Aggravain and Lady Larken flout tradition with subplots that address female power and premarital pregnancy. These unique subversions of female archetypes are full of depth and provide a clear example of how female writers often have an advantage in creating complex and relevant female characters. ♪

Mary Rodgers wrote six more Broadway musicals that received mixed reviews, with the negative reviews often commenting on her gender. "My music was called feminine when they didn't like it," Rodgers commented. "I had a pleasant talent but not an incredible talent. I was not my father or my son. And you have to abandon all kinds of things."[33] It was a difficult environment for a female writer, and Rodgers ultimately abandoned her music theater career to focus on novel-writing, philanthropy, and her family of five children, which included Adam Guettel (b. 1964), the Tony Award–winning composer of *The Light in the Piazza* (2003).

THE INVISIBLE AND FORGOTTEN

Trude Rittman was a promising young composer in Germany when she fled the Nazis as a Jewish refugee and arrived in the United States in 1937. Over the next forty years, she would play a pivotal but largely invisible role in the composition of more than forty Broadway shows, including *My Fair Lady* (1956), *South Pacific* (1949), *Peter Pan*, *Brigadoon* (1947), *Camelot* (1960), and *Gentlemen Prefer Blondes* (1949). Some of her most memorable contributions include the entire eighteen-minute score for the "Small House of Uncle Thomas" ballet in *The King and I* (1951) and vocal arrangements for *The Sound of Music* (1959), including the opening Nuns' chorus and the iconic countermelodies in "Do, Re, Mi." Rittman, however, often went without credit for her contributions to these beloved musicals, and the anecdote at the beginning of this chapter is just one example of how little regard she was given. According to Rittman, "Women were not welcome—we were appreciated because we got things done—but Agnes [de Mille] and I had a very tough time doing what men thought was their job. We had to battle our way through troubles, but Agnes was a very strong and resourceful woman; I guess in our own ways we were both strong women."[34]

Figure 7.3. Trude Rittman.
Creative Commons (CCBY-SA 3.0)

Rittman was a chief collaborator with Richard Rodgers, but the relationship was often difficult. She said of her colleague, "Rodgers was very appreciative of my work but he wouldn't let it out—wouldn't do anything to let it slip from his, what is the word . . . glory."[35] Choreographer Agnes de Mille (1905–1993) added, "If you're going to talk to Trude Rittman you'd better have something to say to her because Rodgers stole her soul."[36] Her working relationship with Frederick Loewe (1901–1988) was more positive, but her income still did not provide her the financial independence to pursue her own compositions freely. Arrangers were not protected by the musicians' union, and the pay was substantially less than that offered to the men she worked with. "I would like to have continued my own compositions, but I had to support myself," Rittman asserted.[37] One wonders what musicals she would have written if she had been more fairly compensated earlier in her career.

In 1976, late in Rittman's career, her musical *Rip Van Winkle* was performed at the Kennedy Center. Like the time-trapped titular character, this musical echoes the challenges she faced while living in a time that did not recognize what she had to offer. The unpublished scores for songs like the hauntingly beautiful "Lop-Sided House" remain hidden in library archives[38] and largely forgotten, much like she was during her career. After Richard Rodgers's death in 1979, Mary Rodgers convinced the Rodgers and Hammerstein Organization to credit Rittman for the music she had composed and arranged and provide much-deserved royalties. "Agnes de Mille once said that Rittman would fight for everyone but herself. It is telling that those who have championed Trude Rittman are other women, many of whom also struggled to succeed in a male dominated profession."[39]

STRONG WOMAN NUMBER:
THE FEMINISTS AND CHANGE MAKERS

With the wave of feminism that began in the early 1960s came shifts in the arts that reflected and influenced the era. These changing attitudes and perspectives once again emboldened women to pursue unique and self-defined creative careers and share their own perspectives through their work.

After meeting in a music class in college, Gretchen Cryer (b. 1935) and Nancy Ford (b. 1935) began writing together and are notable as Broadway's first female composer-lyricist team. Their work was socially conscious and controversial, addressing Vietnam War pacifism, sex, self-delusion, and feminism. *The Last Sweet Days of Isaac*, a two-person show about the negative impact of technology, was described by New York critics as "the freshest musical since *Hair*"[40] when it opened in 1970. It was later revived in 1997 in a remix with *Shelter* (1973), another one of their musicals on a similar topic. However, their work frequently received critical denigration because reviewers seemed to expect "certain things of their shows because they were women."[41]

Cryer and Ford's most notable success came with the Off-Broadway production of *I'm Getting My Act Together and Taking It on the Road* (1978). This feminist folk rock musical based on Cryer's life and starring her in the lead role ran for 1,165 performances and featured such joyous songs as "Natural High," "Miss America," "Old Friend," and "Strong Woman Number." This show often sparked passionate responses from the audience. Women credited the show for major life and perspective changes, and the musical sparked lively conversations about the role of women in society. Not all responses were positive, though. One man threatened to kill Cryer at a performance, saying: "Don't you realize that you women are causing a lot of problems in the world? You're trying to change things too fast."[42] Cryer said, "We were not prepared for how inflammatory the show would be or for the kind of hostile reviews it got because it was treated as though 'we women' were making a very hostile statement. It was a funny show, laughing at male chauvinism, but that was intolerable at that time."[43] ♪

Elizabeth Swados (1951–2016) had an unstable upbringing that caused her to run away from home at age sixteen. Her personal experiences provided some of the source material for her most well-known musical, *Runaways* (1978). This hard-hitting show, for which she wrote the book, lyrics, and music—and also directed and choreographed—was nominated for five Tony Awards. It featured young actors addressing difficult issues faced by the marginalized, such as homelessness, human trafficking, and neglect and abuse. Swados hired a diverse cast for the project and also sought to feature amateur students who understood the pain associated with the conditions addressed in the show. The musical's songs are equally diverse and influenced by reggae, soul, punk, rock, and hip-hop. "Enterprise" and the haunting "Lullaby from Baby to Baby" exemplify the show's innovative sound. ♪

Swados's follow-up efforts were not nearly as successful. Political satire *Doonesbury* (1983) with Garry Trudeau (b. 1948) was a major flop, and *Rap Master Ronnie* (1984), her revue attacking then-president Ronald Reagan, received mixed reviews. She also created five musicals on religious themes including *Esther: A Vaudeville Megillah* (1988) and *Job: A Circus* (1991).

Swados had strong opinions about the challenges of being a female composer:

> I'm not one to wait around for a male music director to choose my chamber piece for performance. I do what I can to initiate performances even if they have a budget one-eighth as large as a funded institutional production. I know I have to be aggressive and that, at times, I threaten my male peers. I don't like feeling harsh and being the object of condescension and mockery. I want to work with men and share music with them because music is a mirror of our chemistry, mood, attractions, repulsions, and mutual discomfort—such feelings feed the compositional fire. But a portion of almost every day of my working life is also devoted to some struggle with sexism, and every woman composer I know has to cope with anxiety and depression because the jobs and funding, already so scarce, are almost unavailable to them.[44]

A multitalented African American artist, Micki Grant (b. 1941) made her mark as a notable singer, actress, composer, and writer. Grant began her career as an actor, appearing on Broadway and breaking boundaries in 1965 as the first African American woman to appear on a daytime soap opera on NBC's *Another World*. She had a long creative partnership with Vinnette Carroll (1922–2002), the first African American woman to direct on Broadway, and together they created works including the critically acclaimed and long-running *Don't Bother Me, I Can't Cope* (1971). Regarding the writing of this musical, Grant writes, "There was a lot of angry theater out there at the time, especially in the black community. I wanted to come at it with a soft fist. I wanted to open eyes but not turn eyes away."[45] In another interview, Grant said,

> The last line is "you gotta cope, I gotta cope, all God's children gotta cope," and that's essentially the message. The song tells a story, too—you got to cope. At the end of the show when I was in it, a couple of us come down the aisle and take the hands of the audience, and everyone is holding hands with each other and it was such a thrill. I used to get letters when I was part of the production. I'll never forget this line from a white person's letter. She said, "You made me bleed, but your incision was so clean." This was the kind of piece that was trying to enlighten people. It wasn't putting a fist in anybody's face. Even though the piece is part of history, it is filled with history. That's what I wanted to do. I wanted to tell our story. . . . This musical was written to give recognition of things that are ignored.[46]

Time Square Chronicles wrote of a recent Off-Broadway revival, "In seeing this you know without Micki Grant there could be no Lin-Manuel Miranda (b. 1980) or *Hamilton* (2015). This show broke new grounds both politically and musically."[47] ♪

Together, Carroll and Grant created nine productions including the Broadway hit *Your Arms Too Short to Box with God* (1976) and a number of Off-Broadway and youth productions including a musical about

Figure 7.4. **Micki Grant.** *Creative Commons (CCBY-SA 3.0)*

George Washington Carver (1864–1943) titled *Don't Underestimate a Nut* (1994). Grant also contributed several songs to the musical *Working* (1977) including "Cleanin' Women" and "If I Could've Been." Of her musical *It's So Nice to Be Civilized* (1980), Grant recalled, "What arrived on Broadway was a different show. I had written book, music, and lyrics, but I used to walk into the theatre and hear lines I'd never heard before and characters I didn't know anything about. The director got rid of the main character. It became a work by committee. He would not have done that to a man's show."[48]

I CAN DO BETTER THAN THAT: WOMEN TAKING THE LEAD

The Secret Garden's debut in 1991 made news for being helmed by four women: composer Lucy Simon (b. 1943), lyricist and bookwriter Marsha Norman (b. 1947), director Susan Schulman (b. 1947), and producer and set designer Heidi Ettinger (b. 1951). The show received seven Tony nominations and won in three categories, including Best Performance by a Featured Actress in a Musical for Daisy Egan (b. 1979) for her portrayal of Mary Lennox. With Egan's victory, *The Secret Garden* made more history by casting the youngest winner of a Tony Award. The show is often credited with reshaping child roles on Broadway and cracking the door open for future female composers. *The Secret Garden* remains one of the most produced musicals due to its memorable score and touching story that appeals to children and adults. "Lily's Eyes," a duet between the character of Archibald and his brother Neville, exemplifies Simon's gift for vocal writing. The musical was revived during the 2018–2019 Broadway season. ♪

Simon's musical *Doctor Zhivago* (2011) had a short Broadway run, but it contains lovely songs for legit singers including "Now" and "On the Edge of Time." In an interview, Simon said, "These days what you hear is, 'We need more women, we need more minorities,' . . . so now it's significantly easier twenty-five years on for a female team to come forward with something, but back then that was real trailblazing." Norman added, "We began to feel at the time, though, that it was distracting people from the show itself. That it's this, 'Oh it's odd. These girls.'

Figure 7.5. Lucy Simon. *Creative Commons (CCBY-SA 3.0)*

However, we believed that we were opening the door, and that all the other musicals written by women would come storming in—but no. Not until this year, with Lisa and Jeanine [the *Fun Home* writing team]. It is a struggle that requires to be won again and again. I'm happy that we're talking about it, but I'm sorry that we haven't just been flooded by women." Lucy concluded with, "I may be wrong, I may just be a little paranoid, but it seems to me women have made a lot of progress in everything but composers. It's much harder for composers."[49] Marsha Norman contributed to several other shows including the libretto for the Jule Styne musical *Red Shoes* (1993) and the book for Jason Robert Brown's *The Bridges of Madison County* (2014). Norman lamented, "I find it odd that people still don't think of me as a person who makes musicals, even though *The Secret Garden* is one of the most performed musicals in America. When people need work on musical books, they don't call me, despite the fact that's what my Tony is for."[50]

Arguably the most successful female stage composer to date, Jeanine Tesori (b. 1961) is the composer of five Broadway musicals including *Violet* (1997), *Thoroughly Modern Millie* (2002), *Caroline, or Change* (2004), *Shrek the Musical* (2008), and *Fun Home* (2015). She has been nominated for five Tony awards and made history with Lisa Kron (b. 1961) for being the first all-female team to win the Tony Award for Best Score of a Musical (*Fun Home*). Her shows often feature strong women with unconventional journeys and backgrounds and memorable songs such as "Gimme, Gimme" from *Thoroughly Modern Millie*, "I Know It's Today" from *Shrek the Musical*, and "Ring of Keys" from *Fun Home*. In their Tony Award acceptance speech—which was not aired on prime-time television and was instead relegated to a recap after the commercial break—Tesori said, "For girls, you have to see it to be it. We stand on the shoulders of other women who have come before us."[51] This has certainly been true for Tesori. ♪

Tesori began her career as an associate conductor for *The Secret Garden* and was inspired by Simon and Norman, as well as (Mary) Rodgers and (Trude) Rittman. She writes: "We need to uncover the lives of women who have been lost to us, women like Trude, the early writers. These women were taught not to break a code but out came their talent

Figure 7.6. Jeanine Tesori. *Creative Commons (CCBY-SA 3.0)*

anyway! They didn't get to claim it for their own, it was in the service of a male composer, that's what's so painful."[52]

Tony Award–winning power duo Lynn Ahrens (b. 1948) and Stephen Flaherty (b. 1960) created their first show, *Lucky Stiff*, in 1988 and have gone on to an impressive run of Broadway hits in the modern era. Their thirteen Broadway shows as of this writing include *Once on This Island* (1990), *A Christmas Carol* (1994), *Ragtime* (1998), *Seussical* (2000), *Rocky the Musical* (2012), and *Anastasia* (2016). Ahrens and Flaherty also wrote for film and television with songs for *Schoolhouse Rock!* and the original film score for *Anastasia* (1997). *New York Times* critic Charles Isherwood (b. 1964/1965) wrote, "A few composers and lyricists continue to risk irrelevance by pursuing their own lonely paths. Stephen Flaherty and Lynn Ahrens are among them. Mr. Flaherty and Ms. Ahrens, best known for their score for *Ragtime*, continue to see the humanist potential in the medium. They insist on writing musicals that explore the struggles of men and women, as opposed to the synthetic creatures razzle-dazzling Broadway audiences with their preening vulgarity and self-devouring jokes."[53] Ahrens said, "Women bring a certain sensibility to a collaboration. In 'Ragtime,' I wrote for the Mother, 'Each day the maids trudge up the hill. The hired help arrives. I never stopped to think they might have lives beyond our lives.' That's not in Doctorow. I created, 'She was nothing to them, she was a woman, nothing and no one to them, so they beat her and beat her and beat her.' Sections like that aren't in the novel. Most of *Ragtime*'s lyrics are mine. I don't think a man would have written those lyrics."[54] ♪

I'M HERE: CONTEMPORARY WOMEN MAKING THEIR MARK

In the past decade, an increasing number of female composers and lyricists have had successful Broadway runs, including Mindi Dickstein (b. ca. 1960) with *Little Women* (2005), Nell Benjamin (b. ca. 1972) with *Legally Blonde* (2007), Dolly Parton (b. 1946) with *9 to 5* (2009), Markéta Irglová (b. 1988) with *Once* (2011), and Edie Brickell (b. 1966) with *Bright Star* (2016). Some of the prominent women making their mark in the last fifteen years include Barbara Anselmi (fl. ca. 2015), Brenda Russell (b. 1949), Allee Willis (b. 1947), Cyndi Lauper (b. 1953), Amanda Green (b. 1963), Sara Bareilles (b. 1979), and Kristen Anderson-Lopez (b. 1972).

Brenda Russell and Allee Willis were among the first women to foray into Broadway after successful careers in pop music. Russell was a successful singer and songwriter best known for the hit "Piano in the Dark" (1988), while Willis was well known for the song "You're the Best" from *The Karate Kid* (1984) and the *Friends* theme song "I'll Be There for You" (1994).[55] With bookwriter Marsha Norman and songwriter Stephen Bray (b. 1956), Russell and Willis created *The Color Purple* (2005). The Oprah Winfrey–produced musical based on the 1982 book by Alice Walker (b. 1944) and 1985 film directed by Steven Spielberg (b. 1946) addresses racism and women's rights through a moving score of songs including "Hell No" and "I'm Here." ♪

Canadian composer Lisa Lambert (b. 1962) initially created the musical *The Drowsy Chaperone* for a friend's bachelor party.[56] The madcap plot was so well-received that it was further developed into a full show that debuted on Broadway in 2006. The 1920s-themed jazz-inspired musical includes the memorable songs "Show Off" and "I am Aldolpho." ♪

As the daughter of Broadway icons Adolph Green (Betty Comden's collaborator) and actress Phyllis Newman (b. 1933), Amanda Green grew up with prominent composers such as Leonard Bernstein, Cy Coleman, and Jule Styne (1905–1994) coming regularly to their home. She began her career in Nashville writing country songs and then attended a music theater workshop and had the epiphany, "What have I been wasting my time for? This is where I belong. I was so happy to be writing for characters and situations."[57] Green has continued the family legacy with three Broadway shows thus far: *High Fidelity* (2006), *Bring It On: The Musical* (2012), and *Hands on a Hardbody* (2012) with Phish front man Trey Anastasio (b. 1964).

Iconic 1980s singer Cyndi Lauper made Broadway history as the first woman to win a Tony Award for Best Musical and Best Score with *Kinky Boots* (2013). The show, centered on a drag queen who saves a shoe factory, has a contagious score of high-energy numbers and ballads about the challenges of parental expectations. This was Lauper's first Broadway show, but she joked, "How much of a stretch is it for me to write songs about fashion, funny relationships, people changing their minds and shoes?"[58]

Barbara Anselmi is an unassuming and hardworking music director and orchestrator who was finally given the chance to create her own show: *It Shoulda Been You* (2015). The wedding-themed comedy directed by David Hyde Pierce (b. 1959) features songs that range from jazz to contemporary music theater. Regarding the challenges of being a woman writing for music theater, Anselmi writes, "I would love to work on a show one day when the women on the creative side are equal in numbers to the men. . . . Perspective and point of view are the difference between women and men when it comes to working on drama."[59] Like Lauper, Parton, and the duo team of Russell and Willis, Sara Bareilles had a successful career in pop music before creating the musical *Waitress* in 2016. Bareilles told an interviewer, "I had left Los Angeles, my home of fourteen years, I had just moved to New York City, I didn't really know many people, and I was having a mini midlife crisis. Everything about my life was in major flux. I said yes to this project almost as an experiment. I didn't really even think I could do it."[60] The show was helmed by an all-female team and Bareilles said, "It's really fun to be an example of the way it can look. We're a bunch of women who are deeply committed to finding a way to build a unified vision."[61] Bareilles recorded the concept album in 2015 and starred in the show on Broadway for limited runs in 2017 and 2018. "She Used to Be Mine" from *Waitress* typifies her songwriting style. Bareilles also contributed to the 2018 musical *SpongeBob SquarePants*. ♪

Kristen Anderson-Lopez shot to stardom with the blockbuster Disney animated movie *Frozen* (2013), cowritten with her husband, Robert Lopez (b. 1975). The film became the highest-grossing animated movie and the twelfth-highest-grossing film of all time, with the empowerment anthem "Let It Go" and whimsical songs like "Do You Want to Build a Snowman?" and "Love Is an Open Door." Anderson-Lopez explained, "For us, 'Let It Go' was just solving a problem for a story. And then it became something far different than that. It almost doesn't feel like it belongs to us anymore. It feels like it belongs to the singing little girls and all of the people who have taken it and made it part of their lives."[62] The Broadway musical of *Frozen* debuted in 2018 and doubled the number of songs with memorable numbers including "Monster." Anderson-Lopez also wrote the Disney World production of *Finding Nemo: The Musical* (2007), youth theater show *Fancy Nancy* (2012), the first a cappella musical *In Transit* (2013), and the songs for the movie *Coco* (2017), for which she won an Academy Award for the song "Remember Me." ♪

THE SHOW GOES ON . . .

The women profiled here do not constitute an exhaustive list of women who have composed great music theater. Others not profiled include Alberta Nichols (1898–1957), Bella Spewack (1899–1990), Sylvia Fine Kaye (1913–1991), Jean Kerr (1922–2003), Helen Miller (1925–2006), Fran Landesman (1927–2011), Anne Croswell (1934–2004), Carol Hall (b. 1936), Carole Bayer Sager (b. 1947), Susan Birkenhead (b. 1950), and Polly Pen (b. 1953). "Since the turn of the twentieth century nearly two hundred American women have composed works for the stage. Women composing scores for full-length musicals, many of these reaching Broadway or Off-Broadway theaters, have numbered well over fifty."[63] Particularly in the current era, which music historian Jennifer Ashley Tepper (b. 1986) has called "the New Golden Age of Musical Theatre," it can be quite challenging for shows to get produced in the limited number of Broadway theaters. Many talented women who are waiting for their Broadway debuts have beautiful shows and substantial catalogs of music theater songs worth exploring, such as "Taylor, the Latte Boy" by Marcy Heisler (b. 1967) and Zina Goldrich (b. 1964), "Run Away with Me" with lyrics by Kait Kerrigan (b. 1981), "My Life-long Love" by Georgia Stitt (b. 1972), "Love Is Letting Go" by Jenny Giering (b. ca. 1970), "Happy" by Joy Son (b. ca. 1978), "Give Words of Love" by Zoe Sarnak (b. ca. 1988), "Huddled Masses" by Shaina Taub (b. ca. 1988), and many more.[64] Georgia Stitt recently organized nearly a hundred female composers actively writing for the stage that are listed on the MAESTRA database.[65] Chapter 12 of this book focuses on advocacy, elaborating on how we as singers, teachers, and audiences can support women writers and why it is important to seek out their work.

Figure 7.7. Georgia Stitt (photo by Matthew Murphy). *Creative Commons (CCBY-SA 2.0)*

PROFILE: GEORGIA STITT

Describe your musical background and what led you to become a composer.
The oft-told anecdote in my family is that I had a babysitter who had a piano in her house. Her name was "Truth," which I suppose is a fun detail. When my mother picked me up, the babysitter would report that I had spent the whole time at the keyboard, picking out songs, trying to figure out how that machine worked. I was seven when I asked my parents if we could have a piano of our own. We acquired what I call a church-basement spinet, and by the time I was fourteen I had totally outgrown it. My father found a baby grand in someone's attic, and he hired a piano technician to restore the sound board but took on the task of refinishing

the wooden exterior himself. The resulting instrument was a very special centerpiece in our home, and it's the piano I played until I moved out on my own. My parents weren't musicians themselves, but they valued music and creativity in a way that made pursuing a career in the arts a realistic option.

The summer after my freshman year in high school I went away to a five-week music camp at the Sewanee Summer Music Center in eastern Tennessee. I studied piano as my first instrument and clarinet as my second instrument, but for an elective I chose composing. That summer I wrote a piece for my roommate, who was a violist. At parents' weekend she and I performed it together, and it was the first time I thought, "Oh wait—I could do this!" I came home and got myself a private composition teacher who kept me writing until I had enough of a portfolio to apply for college to major in music composition.

A few summers later I got a job as a piano accompanist at a college summer stock theater at the College Light Opera Company on Cape Cod, and as I sat there playing rehearsal after rehearsal for show after show, it dawned on me that someone had written those shows. I began to realize that I'd rather be the person writing the shows than the person performing the shows, and my path became clear. I came home from summer stock and started writing for the theater.

Describe your compositional style and what it says about who you are.
I think of music in a linear way; it's very much about voice leading and forward momentum and counterpoint. I think about lines—whether the musical lines are long or short, whether or not they lead you where you're expecting to go, and how much they twist along the way. Everything about my music is connected to storytelling. If the music isn't leading you somewhere, often in partnership with a lyric, then it's not doing its job. I tend to get very frustrated when music is static, when it's not doing its part to reveal character or tension or subtext or place. Especially in the theater, I think the worst kind of composer you can be is a lazy one. And yes—that's

all extremely revealing about who I am as a person, though I can't imagine I've ever thought about it as concretely as that. The worst place for me to be is stuck in some situation where I feel bored or static or lazy. I always want to be moving ahead, hoping that the journey is both satisfying and full of surprises.

What hurdles have you encountered as a woman composer? How did you overcome them? Are there any you have yet to overcome?
It's hard to know which opportunities didn't come my way because I'm a woman and which didn't come my way just because I wasn't ready or I wasn't in the right place at the right time. I have tried very hard to make sure I'm not walking around with a chip on my shoulder, but I'll say the biggest hurdle I've observed is that men tend to get hired because of what they *might do* and women get hired because of what they *have done*. So the real trick is this: how do you get experience if no one will hire you until you have it? My secret superpower as a composer has always been the fact that I am also a music director and a very capable pianist. For years after I finished school, I couldn't get anyone to hire me as a composer, but I did get steady work on the music staff of other people's shows. I used those shows to gain experience and also to save money while I was writing my own music on the side. The first foray I made into the professional world as a composer was producing my first album, *This Ordinary Thursday*, and I paid for the whole thing myself. I sometimes say it was the world's most expensive business card, but it actually was a game changer. Instead of asking people to invest in my potential, I could hand them *an actual thing* and say, "This is what I do—I made this."

When I became a mother, I made a choice to music direct less and compose more, and as much as I hate the stereotype, the truth is that I didn't want to be away from home at my kids' bedtime six nights every week, which is what a Broadway conducting job would have asked of me. I wanted to have more control over my schedule and over the types of projects that demanded my time. Now that the kids are older, I still find myself reckoning with the work I turned down and the ways those missed opportunities might have held me back. But maybe it was the stepping away from conducting that allowed my writing to blossom. I don't know. I just know that there was about a decade there where I couldn't visualize a world that allowed me to be a composer, a conductor, and a mother. It's getting better now and I certainly have acquired more experience in each of those three areas, but if you asked me to name a female role model who was living that composer/conductor/parent life successfully, I couldn't do it.

Who are your greatest inspirations, musically and artistically?
I've always been an enormous fan of Leonard Bernstein, and it's probably for the reasons I just outlined above; even more than his music, I think I admire the way he moved through the world as such a complete musician—composer, conductor, educator, performer, academic, entertainer, and role model. In the theater, my musical heroes include Frank Loesser, Stephen Sondheim, and Gretchen Cryer and Nancy Ford, but I also continue to learn from and be inspired by a number of my colleagues, especially Michael John LaChiusa, Adam Guettel, Shaina Taub, and especially Jason Robert Brown. I love listening to John Pizzarelli, Jessica Molaskey, B. B. King, the Indigo Girls, Branford Marsalis, and the Punch Brothers. And I love complicated voices, such as Blossom Dearie, the Gipsy Kings, k. d. lang, and Rachelle Ferrell. But if I have time alone and my choice of what music gets played in the apartment, I default to very traditional dead-white-guy classical music: Bach, Stravinsky, Prokofiev, Poulenc, or Brahms. And lately I've enjoyed catching up on the entire canon of music by my fellow women composers and the wide swath of voices that got left out of my music history books.

Nearly fifty female writers are mentioned in this chapter and yet many of the women working are unaware of past successes by women. Lucy Simon incorrectly believed that she was only the third woman to have a musical produced on Broadway.[66] Lynn Ahrens joked about the number of female writers, "Oh, yeah, all two of us," with Marsha Norman adding, "And you can interview all of us in a single afternoon."[67] When we ask about female composers and lyricists, the question shouldn't be why don't women write but rather why aren't they produced and why don't we know about those that are?

FINAL THOUGHTS

The stories and examples in this chapter offer abundant reasons for singing music theater by women. These women and their songs offer inspiration to students facing the hurdles of carving out a new career, encouragement to young professionals to continue creating despite rejection and challenges, and a reminder that different perspectives can enlighten and teach us more about ourselves. The songs by these women are enlightening, beautiful, funny, and edifying, and this music has been neglected for far too long.

Perhaps more important, our world is changed by the songs we sing, and if we want a world where women are empowered to live up to their best potential, then we must illuminate the path of those who have blazed that trail. As Jeanine Tesori said, "For girls, you have to see it to be it. We stand on the shoulders of other women who have come before us."[68]

NOTES

1. Meryle Secrest, *Somewhere for Me: A Biography of Richard Rodgers* (New York: Knopf Publishers, 2001), 290.
2. Jill Halstead, *The Woman Composer: Creativity and the Gendered Politics of Musical Composition* (Aldershot, UK: Ashgate, 1997), 30.
3. Mary B. Mullett, "She Holds the Season Record for Stage Successes," *Sun*, May 6, 1917.
4. Ibid.
5. Korey R. Rothman, "Will You Remember: Female Lyricists of Operetta and Musical Comedy," *Women in American Musical Theatre: Essays on Composers, Lyricists, Librettists, Arrangers, Choreographers, Designers, Directors, Producers, and Performance Artists*, ed. Bud Coleman and Judith A. Sebesta (Jefferson, NC: McFarland, 2008), 16.

6. These songs are from the Kern's musicals *The Night Boat* (1920) and *Stepping Stones* (1923) and Youmans's musical *Oh, Please!* (1926).

7. Doug Reside, "Musical of the Month: Night Boat," January 21, 2013, www.nypl.org/blog/2013/01/31/musical-month-night-boat.

8. Bill Edwards, "Rachel Eleanora 'Dora' Nora Goldberg Bayes Gressing Norworth Clarke Gordon Friedland," ragpiano.com/perform/nbayes.shtml, accessed August 10, 2018.

9. Ibid.

10. Ibid.

11. Aaron Gandy and Katherine Webber, *Fine and Dandy: The Kay Swift Songbook* (Van Nuys, CA: Alfred Publishing, 2011), 6–9.

12. Emma Hathaway, "Tomorrow's Overture Is Always Best: The Music of Kay Swift," Yale University Library, exhibits.library.yale.edu/exhibits/show/swift, accessed August 10, 2018.

13. Kay Swift, *Who Could Ask for Anything More?* (New York: Simon and Schuster, 1943).

14. "Willow Weep for Me," nowitsthesameoldsong.blogspot.com/2012/10/willow-weep-for-me.html, accessed August 10, 2018.

15. Benjamin Sears, "Ann Ronnell," www.benandbrad.com/docs/ronell.pdf, accessed August 10, 2018.

16. Jerene Claire Cline, "Ann Ronell's Song Writing Dynamo," *Omaha Sunday World-Herald Magazine*, November 28, 1948.

17. Tighe E. Zimmers, *Tin Pan Alley Girl: A Biography of Ann Ronnell* (Jefferson, NC: McFarland, 2009), 10.

18. Uncredited, "Dana Suesse, 76 , Dies; Wrote 30's Hit Songs," *New York Times*, October, 1987. The obituary incorrectly cited the year and location of her birth.

19. Diane Telgen, *Notable Hispanic American Women, Volume 1* (Detroit: Gale Research,1993), 184–85.

20. Ibid.

21. Ibid.

22. "On the Sunny Side of the Street," "Don't Blame Me," and "I'm in the Mood for Love" are popular songs with music by Jimmy McHugh (1894–1969). "The Way You Look Tonight" is from the Hollywood film *Swing Time*.

23. Gregory Robinson, "Dorothy Fields," www.pbs.org/wnet/broadway/stars/dorothy-fields/, accessed August 10, 2018. This quotation refers to the writers John Dryden (1631–1700), George Bernard Shaw (1856–1950), and Henry David Thoreau (1817–1862).

24. This popular song is strongly associated with Frank Sinatra (1915–1998), who recorded it on his 1964 album *It Might as Well Be Swing*.

25. Of these musicals, only *Little Me* and *Wildcat* are with Cy Coleman. Leigh collaborated with Jule Styne (1905–1994) on *Peter Pan* and Elmer Bernstein (1922–2004) on *How Now, Dow Jones*.

26. Gary Konas, "Working With the Boys: Women Who Wrote Musicals in the Golden Age," *Women in American Musical Theatre*, 114–15

27. These collaborations paired Leigh with Nacio Herb Brown (1896–1964), Leonard Bernstein (1918–1990), Jule Styne, and Cy Coleman, respectively.

28. Leigh collaborated with Leonard Bernstein on *On the Town* and Jule Styne on *Do Re Mi*.

29. Robert Berkvist, "Betty Comden, Half of Lyrics Team behind Musicals of Grace and Wit, Dies at 89," *New York Times*, November 24, 2006.

30. Susan Jackson, "Mary Rodgers Guettel Feted," *Juilliard Journal* (April 2012).

31. Ibid.

32. Ibid.

33. Ibid.

34. Jennifer Jones Cavanaugh, "A Composer in Her Own Right," *Women in American Musical Theatre*, 79.

35. Ibid., 85.

36. Ibid., 85.

37. Ibid., 88.

38. The Trude Rittman archives are at the New York City Public Library.

39. Jennifer Jones Cavanaugh, "A Composer in Her Own Right," *Women in American Musical Theatre*, 89.

40. www.samuelfrench.com/p/4942/the-last-sweet-days-of-isaac, accessed August 10, 2018.

41. Judith A. Sebesta, "Social Consciousness and the 'Search for New Directions,'" *Women in American Musical Theatre*, 20.

42. Judy Klemesrud, "She's Got Her Act Together Again," *New York Times*, December 6, 1978.

43. David Sisco, "Music as Vehicle for Social Change, Part I," Contemporary Musical Theatre Blog. contemporarymusicaltheatre.wordpress.com/2013/07/02/musical-as-vehicle-for-social-change-part-i/, accessed August 10, 2018.

44. Elizabeth Swados, *Listening Out Loud: Becoming a Composer* (New York: Harper, 1988), 182.

45. Eric Grode, "A Buoyant '70s Musical about Black Lives Lands in 2018," *New York Times*, July 20, 2018.

46. Linda Armstrong, "Award-Winning Lyricist Micki Grant Talks about 'Don't Bother Me, I Can't Cope' at City Center," *New York Amsterdam News*, July 18, 2018.

47. Suzanna Bowling, *"Don't Bother Me, I Can't Cope* Opens to Standing Ovation at the York Theatre," *Times Square Chronicles*, February 29, 2016.

48. Tish Dace, "Ladies Who Write: Musicals, That Is," *Backstage*, February 21, 2001.

49. Adam Hetrick, "History-Making Women of *The Secret Garden* Reunite to Talk Breaking Ground in Musical Theatre," *Playbill*, January 7, 2016.

50. Dace, "Ladies Who Write."

51. Adam Hetrick, "For Girls, You Have to See It to Be It: The Historic and Powerful *Fun Home* Tony Acceptance Speeches You Didn't See on TV," *Playbill*, June 8, 2015.

52. Cavanaugh, "A Composer in Her Own Right," 89.

53. Charles Isherwood, "Worlds Apart in the Deep South but Forming a Bond," *New York Times*, March 22, 2005.

54. Dace, "Ladies Who Write."

55. These popular songs were performed and recorded by Brenda Russell, Joe Esposito (b. 1948), and the Rembrandts, respectively. "Piano in the Dark" was the first single from Russell's 1988 album *Get Here*.

56. Priscilla Samayoa, "Writing Processes of Musical Theater Writers: How They Create a Storyline, Compose Songs, and Connect Them to Form a Musical," writingandrhetoric.cah.ucf.edu/stylus/files/8_1/Stylus_8_1_Samayoa.pdf, accessed August 10, 2018.

57. Joanne Kaufman, "Broadway Lyrics: The Family Business," *New York Times*, December 3, 2006.

58. Chris Jones, "Cyndi Lauper Working Out the Kinks in Kinky Boots," *Chicago Tribune*, September 27, 2012.

59. Personal correspondence with Barbara Anselmi, November 8, 2012.

60. Jason Frayley, "Q&A: Sara Bareilles Shares Ingredients of 'Waitress' Tour at National Theatre," wtop.com, May 31, 2018.

61. "Broadway Musical Waitress Makes History with Its Lineup," *Associated Press*, December 1, 2015.

62. Jennifer Ashley Tepper, "Are We Living in a New Golden Age of Musical Theatre?" *Playbill*, www.playbill.com/article/are-we-living-in-a-new -golden-age-of-musical-theatre, accessed August 10, 2018.

63. Linda J. Snyder and Sarah Mantel, "Women Composers and the American Musical: The Early Years." *Journal of Singing* 69, no. 5 (2013): 527–33.

64. Matthew Hoch (b. 1975), coauthor of this book, performed under Georgia Stitt's baton in the summer of 1997 in a production of *Me and My Girl* at the College Light Opera Company on Cape Cod. He was twenty-one years old and she was twenty-five.

65. Jamie McGonigall, "Glass Ceilings and Secret Gardens: A Chat with Composer Lucy Simon," *Broadway World*, November 21, 2016.

66. Dace, "Ladies Who Write."

67. Hetrick, "For Girls, You Have to See It to Be It."

8

CCM BY WOMEN

Amanda Wansa Morgan

Carole King . . . Joan Baez . . . Memphis Minnie . . . Erykah Badu . . . Melissa Etheridge . . . Loretta Lynn.

Folk . . . rock . . . pop . . . blues . . . R&B . . . hip-hop . . . rap . . . country . . . bluegrass . . . gospel . . . jazz. When looking at the vast array of contemporary commercial music (CCM) written by women, we have several questions to answer. First, what is CCM? Second, which female performers in our contemporary American music history wrote their own music? And third, what makes popular music written by women different from that of their male counterparts?

There are entire books on the amazing accomplishments of female songwriters in popular music throughout the twentieth and twenty-first centuries, some of which are cited in this chapter. These pages will investigate the significance of this material and its origins from the experiences of musical women. This chapter is less about *what* music to examine and more about *how* to examine the female perspective on these musical works. In the following pages, we will examine how the feminist lens affects melodies, harmonies, and musical structure.

The evolution of female composers and songwriters in the American pop/rock canon directly parallels the feminist revolution of the late 1960s and advances made by women across various cultural lines, enabling music written by women to be produced and performed. As progress was made across cultural and social structures, including media and entertainment, the works of female singer-songwriters emerged in the late twentieth century onto mainstream radio, providing female listeners a canon that is both easy to connect to and accessible to sing.

Therefore, here is a brief outline of each era in American popular music of the twentieth century, highlighting the significant female songwriters in each era and examining how their music reflects the voice of their generation. The female voice and its dynamics in relation to performance of the music will also be discussed.

CCM: THE TERM AND ITS ORIGINS

In a 2008 article in the *Journal of Voice*, voice pedagogue Jeannette LoVetri (b. 1949) states:

> Contemporary commercial music (CCM) is the new term for what we used to call non-classical music. This is a generic term created to cover anything including music theater, pop, rock, gospel, R&B, soul, hip hop, rap, country, folk, experimental music, and all other styles that are not considered classical.[1]

As of the writing of this book, the term "CCM" is most widely accepted in the world of voice pedagogy. The outside world, including the commercial industry, tends to use terms like "popular" music or "pop/rock" music. There are also multiple genres and subgenres in addition to those mentioned above. The term "CCM" is further unpacked and defined in the 2018 book *So You Want to Sing CCM*, a companion to this book in the So You Want to Sing series.[2] As Sheri Sanders (b. 1972) states in her 2011 book *Rock the Audition* (in reference to selecting rock music as music theater audition material), "Listen. Rock songs were never intended to be acted. We were meant to dance to them, work out to them, make sweet love to them, and sing them in the shower or while we are wasted at a karaoke bar, but we were certainly not meant to act to them."[3] This is the music that comes out of lived experience and emotional expression, which connects to the difference between composer and songwriter. They are songs designed to express heartbreak, elation, and protest. They educate, inform, calm, ignite, and document. They provide escape, release, and a way of expression for the listener, one that they perhaps were not equipped with before.

"Composer" is a generic term for someone who writes any type of music (like an opera, symphony, song, ballet, pieces for individual instruments, musicals, etc.). Composers typically write integrated music, whether it is a single song that augments the larger story or music that is unified into a larger and overarching form. A songwriter is a composer who focuses on writing songs only (meaning a piece of music defined by having a vocal part and an accompaniment). While a collection of songs from a songwriter can be placed and woven together on an album with connectivity, their songs often stand alone as individual works of art.

Many CCM songwriters concur that—often—songs just "flow out of them," rather than the formulaic separation of music or lyrics first, as we see in more structured art forms like music theater, opera, or art song. In music theater, a song often requires edits to fit the piece into the arc of a larger story. Composers are ensuring that plot develops fully and particular pieces of information are included. But in CCM, music, lyrics, and melodic lines are so closely tied together that it would be impractical—and even inhuman—to separate them; structure is much less important, although we do see repeated structures in popular music. Therefore, the vocal range as well as the structure and content all falls within the desires of the artist in the moment. The only reconsideration would be for that artist's stamina in reproducing the work. Musical alterations can be made for live shows (such as transpositions and restructuring of verses) because most musicians are either playing by ear or from charts rather than playing the fully orchestrated music that we hear in stage productions or classical music. This flexibility allows content to take priority over structure.

WAYS TO EXAMINE CONTEXT

As we travel through the twentieth century to examine the progression and increased popularity of female singer-songwriters, it is important to identify the areas that *most* influenced the top (read: most popular) artists.

In addition to gender, factors that have surfaced when researching the women who have shaped the music industry since the early 1900s include, but are not limited to, the following: race, socioeconomic background, musical training, genre of choice, and stereotypes in American society around genres of music. A specific factor to consider is the writer's place in time to the revolution of the 1960s; there is a culture in place before the singer-songwriter emergence of the 1970s and after that is not a masculine, uphill trend. There have been periods of time in each decade where the industry supports and celebrates women as songwriters, and also times when women were in the shadows of men. The oppression of women has led to a lack of evidence throughout history of the actual amount of music written by women in popular music. "If you go to a standard rock history, you will usually find that very few female performers are listed, giving the erroneous impression that women played an insubstantial role in the creation and development of rock 'n' roll."[4] There is a constant struggle in the hearts and minds of female singer-songwriters that deserves to be celebrated independently alongside the male artists. It is this very oppression that explains the development of content for these works as well as musical style and structure. "A recurrent theme in the evolution of women's music is the need for self-identify factions of performers and consumers . . . to negotiate their collective identities based on race, ethnicity, and so on their individual subjectivities."[5] These ideas are often reflected, directly or indirectly, in the content and lyrics of CCM music.

MUSICAL STYLE AND STRUCTURE

As we reference specific songs within this genre, it is important to know how the positionality of the woman affects decisions made in the composition of the music. The lyrics are driven by content and perspective, while the music is driven by the soul and musical abilities.

The first noticeable quality of a song written by a woman is the vocal range, which affects style and how the song resonates. Often, the range in CCM songs will be limited in range for a number of reasons: the song needs be accessible by the audience—they're meant to be sung along to. The song will need to be performed over and over again—if the song contains heavy vocal athleticism and a high tessitura, a singer will need to sustain performance with lifestyle. Pop and rock songs typically fall in the lower part of the vocal range, below the passaggio, closest to the speaking range. Only the bravest of vocalists push into the passaggio or beyond.

"Vocal quality" is a term that pedagogues use to describe characteristics of tone and how it is being produced. There are specific characteristics we often hear in CCM music. Breathiness or hoarseness can represent long hours of talking/singing/shouting as well as content-based informants like having survived a hard life or feeling worn down. Twang and clarity can give the sound edge and urgency, whereas breathiness can read as defeat and fatigue (Patti Smith) or fragility and peace (Joni Mitchell). Included in vocal quality are vocal onsets and offsets, which refer, respectively, to the attack and release of the notes. Aspirate onsets are breathy and can often give peace and calm; however, a continued pattern of aspirate onsets can sacrifice clarity of tone. Conversely, glottal onsets give the phrase edge and urgency; however, there is evidence that continued use of glottal onset can be taxing on the vocal folds. And finally, growls and other guttural vocal noise are commonly present in CCM music and can also fatigue the voice over time without proper vocal hygiene and rest outside of performance.

CCM music often contains a heavy amount of belting, which is the quality associated with yelling and high emotion. Vocal quality can paint pictures of social class and education. Often, classical or more traditional styles of music can demonstrate the same quality throughout the entire piece. While the vocal tone is cleaner, and arguably healthier, this can place the quality of tone over content and emotional expression. This is the struggle of the CCM singer—creating the vocal quality desired to convey the emotion of the piece and maintaining vocal health while living what is typically a grueling lifestyle full of travel, fatigue, and heavy voice use.

Musical phrasing accompanies vocal quality, and—while these factors are not written in the music—they are often implied based on the original performances of the artists. Phrasing can include clarity of diction, or lack thereof, which represents a lot about the background of the artist and affects accessibility for the listener. Diction and pronunciation can often represent social class, which can either bring in or alienate certain audiences. Vocal agility—exhibited through riffs or melismata—can often reflect how a human being expresses emotion; they are a kind of "release." Vocal scoops can represent a plethora of intent ranging from expressing laziness to seduction. Vibrato and clarity of tone can also affect sense of authenticity. The challenge of operating with such variety highlights the importance of CCM voice training, voice science, good sound equipment, and an understanding of vocal hygiene that one needs to sustain a performance career.

A female perspective affects the structure and form of the song. Using traditional or informal methods of song analysis, we can examine the following: rhythmic choices (meter, syncopation, changes within), dissonance, use of harmonies (or omission of them), intersectionality of genre, symmetry/asymmetry (extent of improvisation), and instrumentation (acoustic versus electric arrangements).

CCM music written by women often more accurately reflects the natural arc of emotion based on content because the melodies are coming out of the soul, supported by the original artist's range and marrying lyrics and melody with the rise and fall of emotion. Often, as emotion and intensity increases, so does the pitch, resulting in the highest note toward the end of the song, creating a climax. Nonverbal voicings like "oo, ah, whoa, yeah . . ."—common syllables in pop, rock, and folk music—reflect the angst that women were finally able (or allowed) to express through their music.

The uniting factor among all of these musical elements is the prioritization of content and emotion over formal adherence to traditional musical structure. Authenticity, storytelling, and emotion inform all musical choices and drive them forward.

THE UNSUNG: 1920s–1960s

The women's movement of the 1960s provided the landscape for women who fought to get their music heard on an international scale. We have to dig into history books to find the women who operated (under the radar) prior to the 1960s as composers and songwriters. The songwriters who preceded this revolution sometimes worked alone and sometimes in partnerships. They simply didn't have the platforms to get their music heard, based on the constraints of a male-dominated music industry and market. However, women in jazz and blues found some success.

Abbey Lincoln (1930–2010) was an African American jazz artist who wrote and performed her own compositions between the 1950s and the 2000s. In regard to her writing, she states, "I've always been concerned with the story I'm telling. . . . Nobody cares whether it sounds pretty or not. . . . Can you be honest in your singing?"[6] Country singer-songwriter Wanda Jackson (b. 1937) demonstrates this in her writing, exemplified in songs such as "Cool Love" (1957) and "Mean Mean Man" (1958).

Figure 8.1.   Wanda Jackson, 1970. *Creative Commons (CCBY-SA 3.0)*

Guitarist Peggy Jones (1940–2015) wrote and produced her own material as well as earned the nickname "Lady Bo" through her association with Bo Diddley (1928–2008), playing with him on tour and on his records of the late 1950s and 1960s. Similarly, Mississippi rock 'n' roll guitarist and vocalist Cordell Jackson (1923–2004) wrote and performed her own material and started her own record label—Moon Records—in 1956.

Folk, blues, and jazz artist Odetta Holmes (1930–2008), known simply as Odetta, began recording in the 1950s and was known as the "voice of the civil rights movement." Her music and that of other brave black women gave way to the rise of the Freedom Singers as well as the DC Black Repertory Company, from which gospel/folk group Sweet Honey in the Rock grew. Odetta shared: "There was a period in my early career when I needed to learn what to say and what to leave out. . . . The civil rights movement gave me my career, it certainly made it viable for folks to see me. There was no other way a black girl singing folk songs about injustice during that time period was ever going to gain an audience."[7] What happened to Odetta and many artists like her was the phenomenon of naturally forcing them into activism simply because their music expressed experience. Black women often found themselves forced to choose between their race or gender, in terms of platform. In feminist organizations, they were often marginalized because of race, and in the Black Power movement, they were often marginalized because of gender.

To examine the effects of perspective on context and musical style, Lizzie Douglas (1897–1973), known as Memphis Minnie, provided us with a plethora of material that we can access today. With a blues career that lasted from the 1920s until the 1950s, Memphis Minnie was a gifted and strong-willed songwriter, vocalist, and guitarist. The 2014 book *Woman with Guitar: Memphis Minnie's Blues* takes an intimate look at Minnie's life, career, and lyrics.[8] Using the blues format as a vehicle, Memphis Minnie was able to report to and educate her listeners on a plethora of topics from her unique point of view. She illustrated the plight of the prostitute with "Hustlin' Woman Blues" (1935), exposed her experience with doctors and medicine through "Meningitis Blues" (1930) and "Doctor Doctor Blues" (1935), and documented her experience on the road as a black female musician with "Frisco Town" (1929), "I'm Going Don't You Know" (1937), and "Nothing in Rambling" (1940). While Minnie wrote and sang many songs about love and relationships, it was her numerous blues about lived experiences that provide documentation of her point of view regarding so many aspects of the world she had to navigate.

Blues allow for improvisation, emotional expression, and a simplicity that connects a broad swath of listeners. Living in the world of blues allows a writer and performer to sing on a number of topics as well as show technical prowess while being able to play with different groups of people. Blues music is populated by metaphor, simile, imagery, storytelling, emotional expression, and connectivity. Memphis Minnie songs, which represent blues critique, remind us that the blues is an index of oppression as well as a clarion of liberation.[9]

"Bumble Bee" (1930) is a blues in F minor and in the original recording tops out at A♭4. In fact, she doesn't go lower than a C4, making the range a mere minor sixth. It illustrates a relationship between man and woman through the metaphor of a bumble bee. It is full of direct statements of love and relationships—"Bumble bee, bumble bee, please come back to me . . . don't be gone so long . . . I don't mind you goin' / ain't going to stay so long" as well as double entendre. "Each metaphor must be judged on its own terms, and each must be sounded for depth and breadth, as well as intensity. The reduction [of the male] to the size of an insect can be seen as a way for the female singer to control and outmaneuver her oppression by the male, but too often in typical blues criticism, such metaphors, similes, and other allusions are commented upon for their intensity alone, if they are noted at all."[10] ♪

Conversely, Minnie's blues "Nothing in Rambling" shares her perspective on being a musician on the road, being a woman, and being black in America—a true representation of her positionality between these three areas of identity. The original recording was in B major and the range of the song was a mere octave from F♯3 to F♯4 with an occasional flip to B4. This is a comfortable speaking and singing range, allowing for emoting and improvisation. In five mere verses, she addresses police assumptions, celebrity life, empty promises, tragedies of homelessness and poverty, social structure, and more. ♪

Prior to the revolution of the 1960s, the American music industry was graced by popular girl groups. However, many of the girl groups of the 1950s and 1960s sang music written and produced by others, mostly men. The topic of nearly all girl group songs was love and romance, and these songs reinforced social expectations about women in other ways. At Motown Records, female singers were required to attend charm school. The girl group "look" also denied women independence or individuality. What girl groups *did* do was provide a voice for a generation of adolescents. It was their *image* that made the greatest impact with audiences, and it was this phenomenon that cultivated female audiences who would eventually turn toward purchasing the music of the female singer-songwriters of the late 1960s and early 1970s.

THE FEMALE SINGER-SONGWRITER REVOLUTION OF THE 1960s AND 1970s

The music scene during the antiwar and counterculture movement began with male-dominated rock boasting hypermasculinity. The response was led by "rock chicks" like Janis Joplin (1943–1970) who were liberated from the conventions that held back girl groups. By the mid-1960s, singer-songwriters were the first generation of women able to make it on their own in the music business because they were able to take advantage of women's liberation. These women wrote their own music, played their own songs, and spoke to a new audience of post-adolescent women who had money and freedom, giving young female singer-songwriters of the 1970s an audience of consumers. This popular music captured the complexity of the times.

The topics of these songs from the 1970s folk singer-songwriters included reflections of domesticity as well as rebellion, redefining the notion of home and what that means.

The shared experience and intimacy of their songs encouraged emotional bonds between performers and audiences, especially the female ones. Female singer-songwriters presented themselves as ordinary women, and because their songs were autobiographical and written in the first person, it was easy for fans to see similarities between their lives and their own. This era also brought development of pop, rock, folk, and soul as distinct genres that were developing simultaneously.

The early 1970s also welcomed the arrival of female disc jockeys who played women's music. Once Carole King (b. 1942) came out from behind the piano with her hit record *Tapestry* in 1971, a niche market developed for female singer-songwriters to fill medium-sized venues and sell albums, linking back to providing venues for independent female consumers to congregate. As opposed to the girl group hits of the 1960s, the folk songs of the 1970s established vocal independence, using very few—sometimes even no—backup singers. The artists explored a variety of musical styles, claimed input during the production process, wrote their own songs, and created their own arrangements. They steered away from dancing, color-coordinated outfits, and production value and focused on the lyric, authenticity, and beautiful naked vocal line.

The 1970s was also the decade when lyrics really started to matter. Female singer-songwriters sang about love and relationships but with a more assertive female voice. They communicated expectations about love but were not unrealistic. These songs spoke to 1970s women and their lived experiences. They were the only arenas where women could hear other women talk about sex and love. There was also a level of domesticity in some of these pieces, with rebellion in others, blending the traditional women's "fear sphere" with the ideals of counterculture and the women's movement. Different forms of feminism were established, and the female singer-songwriters of this era also span across other identities of sexual orientation, race, and genre of music. The shared experiences and the intimacy of their songs encouraged emotional bonds between performers and audiences. This was also reflected in the vocal stylings and instrumentation. While this music was clearly shaped by a feminist consciousness, the crusade to find the balance between traditional womanliness and feminism established a culture of confident women who love men but had lives of their own and experiences to write about. Instead of directly pushing politics or advocating feminism, many of these songwriters were simply sharing lived experience, which inherently promoted feminism and addressed the politics of females' experience in this era. The transition began with the rise of male and female songwriting teams, such as Carole King and Gerry Goffin (1939–2014), Ellie Greenwich (1940–2009) and Jeff Barry (b. 1939), and Cynthia Weil (b. 1940) and Barry Mann (b. 1939).

Carole King: Pioneer

Carole King started playing piano as a child and was writing and performing in vocal groups by her teenage years. She met Gerry Goffin in

Figure 8.2. Carole King, 2012 (photo by Michael Borkson). *Creative Commons (CCBY-SA 2.0)*

college and, together, they began working in the Brill Building, the center of the American songwriting universe. There, they wrote "hits" for other people to sing, like a modern-day hit factory. The idea of someone having a full-time job as a songwriter to pump out hits is rare today (in the 2010s); however, this was a common formula of the time, dating all the way back to Tin Pan Alley and the American standards of the early 1900s. King and Goffin wrote hits that were mostly performed by popular girl groups of the day. King would go on to sing her own music, debuting on the performer scene with *Tapestry* in 1971. This album is now a staple in the canon of American music.

The biggest hits from this album include "Beautiful," "It's Too Late," "So Far Away," and her stirring solo versions of "Natural Woman"—previously made famous by Aretha Franklin (1942–2018)—and "Will You Still Love Me Tomorrow?"—previously made famous by the Chiffons. King's ability to encapsulate the female perspective on relationships was unparalleled when *Tapestry* came out. She spoke candidly about the realities of the daily ups and downs of love, ranging from the failures exemplified in "It's Too Late" to the joys in "Natural Woman." Simple chord structures (mostly in AABA or ABAB formats) along with a standard mezzo range (most of her songs sit between G3 and C4) allowed King to focus on lyrics and emotion through phrasing. King also embraced writing in minor keys (as in "It's Too Late") or even toggling between the major and minor (as in "Natural Woman"), manipulating the listener into experiencing both the light and the darkness of love. First released on *Tapestry*, "You've Got a Friend" also became the first No. 1 hit for James Taylor (b. 1948); King says the song "wrote itself. It was written by something outside of myself through me. . . . I have found that the key to not being blocked is not to worry about it. Ever."[11]

Joni Mitchell and Laura Nyro

Joni Mitchell (b. 1943) and Laura Nyro (1947–1997) are some of the few sopranos in this motley crew of female singer-songwriters who venture above the passaggio into their head voice. Mitchell, a true soprano, has had a number of hit records in the genre of folk and some songs that even fall into the category of "art song." Mitchell's career grew out of a hobby—she set out to be a commercial visual artist, and later her albums would feature her own artwork. The Canadian-born Mitchell came up through the Toronto music scene and made her way to New York and eventually California playing folk in smaller venues from 1964 to 1969. She eventually self-produced the album *Clouds* (1969), which won a Grammy in 1970 and led to another successful album, *Blue* in 1971. Her lyrics highly poetic, Mitchell's work is also decidedly feminine. This is obviously reflected in her vocal style, which is breathy and unashamed to live in her upper register.

Blue included Mitchell's hit "California," which was originally recorded in the key of E major and features a vocal range from A3 to E5, lingering mostly in the upper octave and featuring a light vocal timbre. Similarly, "My Old Man"—also from *Blue*—is in the key of A major and soars from F♯3 to E5 and lingers within or above the female passaggio for over 75 percent of the song. It is a sharp contrast to be singing about her male lover in a breathy, bright, and feminine tone quality, floating in the upper register and evoking feelings of light and ethereal love. In "My Old Man," her musical and vocal choices paint a love that is genuine, soft, and frivolous, matching lyrics, "My old man he's a singer in the park / he's a walker in the rain / he's a dancer in the dark . . ." ♪

During her career, Nyro released a total of seven studio albums. She grew up listening to different genres of music, ranging from the Crystals to Broadway albums. In 1968, she followed the Beatles in releasing a concept album of her own entitled *Eli and the Thirteenth Confession*. In this album, each of the songs relates to the others, though the relationship between them is not a simple one. The links between the songs on this album also derive from their positions on the vinyl disk itself. The opening songs on each side—"Luckie" on side 1 and "Timer" on side 2—are drenched with joy, moving along in the same tempo, same time signature, same key, and the concluding songs on each side—"Eli's Comin'" and "The Confession"—convey a sense of predatory peril, once again in the same tempo, same time signature, and same key. Years later, Mitchell too would go on to do this with the album *Both Sides Now* (2000), which chronicles the cycle of a relationship. In addition to her poignant content, Nyro stood out due to her vocal prowess—she possessed a three-octave range, sang with confidence in all registers, and performed with great dynamic control. Nyro's writing coupled a variety of musical styles with lyrics full of poetic imagery.

Janis Joplin: The Queen of Rock

In the early 1960s, women were still encouraged to remain "feminine" in the public eye. As the revolution and counterculture began, Janis Joplin emerged from San Francisco, preceded only by Grace Slick (b. 1939). The mark of Joplin's work was the blues, her vulnerability, and her "raw" sound, throwing it in the faces of voice pedagogues who believed the "classical" way of singing was the only way. Unfortunately, the beauty of Joplin's work ultimately contributed to her demise. She fell into drug use (heroin) and died at the young age of twenty-seven. Her music reflected all of her rebellion and pain, as well as her extremist way of living, writing, and performing. Her hits included "Mercedes Benz," "Me and Bobby McGee," "Cry Baby," "Piece of My Heart," "Bye Bye Baby," "Ball and Chain," "Try (Just a Little Bit Harder)," and "Little Girl Blue." The content of her music covered love and relationships like

Figure 8.3.   Janis Joplin, 1969. *Creative Commons (CCBY-SA 3.0)*

many of her contemporaries but did so with a raw and vulnerable perspective that matched her raspy and naked vocal quality.

Joan Baez and Carly Simon

Other notable figures of the female singer-songwriter explosion of the 1960s include Joan Baez (b. 1941) and Carly Simon (b. 1945). Baez released *Joan Baez* in 1960, which was the biggest-selling album by a female folk artist at the time. Her material became more politically active as the decade progressed. Carly Simon emerged as a solo artist with her self-titled album in 1971 and proceeded to top charts with hits such as "Anticipation" (1971), "You're So Vain" (1972), "You Belong to Me" (1978), "Jesse" (1980), and "Coming Around Again" (1986).[12]

These female singer-songwriters represented a safe mainstream version of feminism. They were able to straddle the line between traditional womanliness and feminism; they were liberated but not adversarial. By establishing themselves as strong and confident women who love men but also had lives of their own, they supported feminism as an individual achievement more than as a social, political, or economic agenda. Female singer-songwriters validated the change to a more female experience. They balanced tradition and rebellion.

The Advent of Disco

Disco arose in the late 1970s but was still heavily managed, controlled, and produced by males. Therefore, the music naturally reflected a distinctly male point of view. Similarly, the late 1970s rock revival was male-dominated. The response to this from the women's movement was disco because the female voices of rock—Blondie's Debbie Harry (b. 1945), Stevie Nicks (b. 1948), and Ann (b. 1950) and Nancy Wilson (b. 1954) of Heart—took a backseat to the male ones. Disco also arose as a backlash. This ping-pong match between liberals and conservatives that grew out of the countercultural movement of the 1960s resulted in the development of an entirely new style of music and a culture that supported it. The more sexualized culture became in the late 1960s, the harder the backlash was from conservative Republicans, religious fundamentalists, and social traditionalists. As a result, voices of the youth culture became louder and louder and disappeared into nightclubs where the music was loud and driven. Disco's version of sex gave women the initiative, but men defined the terms and male composers and producers shaped the images. This directly influenced the rise of punk, as well as the content of female songwriters in 1990s rock and pop. Both movements were about trying to find the balance between these two worlds. Disco gave women power as a glamorous substitute for substantive economic and political power. This would lead to the rise of artists, like Madonna (b. 1958), who celebrated sexual independence.

PUNK, ROCK, AND POP OF THE 1980S

Coming into the 1980s, the women's liberation movement infiltrated music, movies, print media, and all different sources of culture. Sometimes the reaction was positive and encouraging, but other times it was negative. It was the backlash of conservatives that inspired female artists and creatives to push even harder into the unpredictable, both in content and delivery. Olivia Records was founded in 1973 and led the way in providing a platform for female writers and performers. The 1980s brought the development of "pop" music and expansion of women's music into many, if not all, genres of music.

Patti Smith: The Godmother of Punk

Dubbed the "godmother of punk," Patti Smith (b. 1946) was defiant from the start. Smith was characterized by her biting delivery and for being vocally eccentric—dancing around pitch, singing with hoarseness and gravel, and using glottal onsets—everything classical teachers would balk at. She often fell off pitch, going in and out of sustained pitch altogether, and used lazy diction, sounding drugged or drunk. Her songs' content did not follow form. For example, "Because the Night" (1978) is famous because of its mainstream form. This is a stark contrast to "Birdland" (1975), which becomes a poetry jam halfway through. When she recorded "Because the Night"—which was cowritten with Bruce Springsteen (b. 1949)—she was accused of selling out.[13]

Smith ended up touring in Europe as the Sex Pistols emerged, and punk took off due to class movement (as exemplified in Sex Pistols' "God Save the Queen" in 1977). Thus, she was able to take advantage of this sudden rise in punk music's popularity. Smith's music often sat in a lower register (typically between F♯3 and A4), enabling her to revel in a unique vocal quality and play with various types of sounds. Occasionally, she would pop up to a B4 or C4, for emphasis, but the majority of her music stayed in a speech-sung range. "Pissing in a River" (1976)—a tune about love and salvation through relationships—sits between A3 and E4 for 70 percent of the song.[14] Then, at the climax, the listener is met with a killer guitar solo, backup singers, and a vocal line that pops up to C4 for emphasis.

Smith's album *Horses* (1975) has been cited as one of the greatest art punk albums of all time, featuring a mixture of original songs ("Birdland," "Free Money," "Break It Up") with adaptations of other tunes, made new with Smith's poetry and original take ("Gloria" and "Land"). Smith breaks the mold of traditional song structure with her improvisational vocal work and her dive into poetry, in particular on the eccentric tune "Birdland." ♪

Madonna: The Queen of Pop

Operating in the same industry as Patti Smith were artists like Annie Lennox (b. 1954) who were benefiting off of MTV and based a lot of their brand on image. The visual medium of video offered an excellent opportunity to explore, comment upon, and question traditional gender roles. Similarly, artists like Lennox were able to take advantage of technology, which informed their writing. No artist of the 1980s exploited the visual like Madonna, who wrote a lot of her own music while also collaborating with others. While many saw Madonna's work as a regression of the progress made by her contemporaries, she is quoted claiming that she didn't set out to be a role model and this attitude was a double standard. The content of her songs indicated that she was indeed claiming control over her sexuality. Madonna perfected the art of playing with the space between women's liberation and the sexual revolution. Much of what she did in the 1980s and 1990s was about sex, yet while singing about sex and writing a 1992 book called *Sex*, Madonna believed that she had outsmarted her audience by catering to their purest interests.[15] We never quite knew if she was exploiting our interest in sex or if we were exploiting her sexuality. She did it all.

ROCK AND INDIE ROCK OF THE 1990s

The 1990s provided alternatives to the "Top 40" songs heard on the radio, with a range of louder pop-rock bands like Garbage, the Cardigans, and No Doubt juxtaposed alongside softer singers like Jewel (b. 1974), who were only backed by a folk guitar and acoustic drums while they sang more pensive lyrics. The contrast was clear both in musical style and in structure. Even the choice of electric versus acoustic guitar was a defining characteristic beginning in this period. The definitions of "rock," "pop," and "folk" started to blur, and artists began to explore having examples of all three in one album.

Another significant development was Lilith Fair, which was a touring music festival featuring only female performers. The festival began in the summer of 1997 with fifty musical artists and thirty-five performance dates. It inadvertently provided a meeting place and environment for political and feminist activists. Lilith Fair was organized by Sarah McLachlan (b. 1968). She stated that she simply wanted to do a tour with a bunch of women . . . not necessarily a reaction to Lollapalooza (a male-dominated music festival that excluded women) but to prove to everybody that there could be more than one woman on the same bill. She claimed she simply wanted a "celebration of sisterhood." She claimed the tour was not intended to be political, but it inherently promoted a vessel for women's empowerment and a meeting place for feminists to enjoy music written by women for women. The 1990s was an era where female singer-songwriters took the opportunity to explore their intersectionality—many artists emerged who identify within multiple areas of marginalized voices, and their music attempts to reflect those different points of view.

With breathy tone and lyrics laden with metaphor, McLachlan brought back the contemplative vocal sound of the 1970s folk movement, contrasting with the volume of punk and pop coming out of the 1980s. McLachlan was able to capitalize on the idea of transference and empathy in her writing, which is the idea of talking about both herself and someone else in the same song with point of view. In the 1998 book *From Lilith to Lilith Fair*, McLachlan states, "But because I'm talking in the first person it always seems like me. Half of the experiences and the song aren't mine, they're me putting myself in other people's shoes. How would I feel if . . . ?"[16] McLachlan's music is a conundrum of low range with breathy timbre—she is a mezzo and the ranges of her songs reflect that—yet her vocal quality emulates the same feminine, clear qualities of Joni Mitchell, giving her music an ethereal, "indie" quality.

Melissa Etheridge (b. 1961) burst onto the music scene in 1988 as a full-fledged rock artist but found a turning point in her career in 1993 with the release of her album *Yes I Am* and her coming out as a homosexual woman. Thus, Etheridge created a foundation for women in CCM to express their sexual identity. However, Etheridge is known not only for this identity but also for her expert guitar skills and smoky, vulnerable voice. The range of her songs mostly sit below the passaggio. In her 1992 book *She's a Rebel: The History of Women in Rock and Roll*, Gillian Gaar (b. 1959) states that "in Etheridge's songs, love became an exercise in pain, a soul-searing experience that left one either unfulfilled or forsaken by the longed-for object of desire."[17]

Another groundbreaking artist whose identity and work spans across multiple demographics is African American rock artist and activist Tracy Chapman (b. 1964), who became famous in the arena of folk as protest music. Chapman is a true alto who simultaneously plays guitar when she sings, as demonstrated in three of her biggest hits: "Fast Car" (1988), "Talkin' 'bout a Revolution" (1988), and "Give Me One Reason" (1995).[18] Another example is the guitar player and scratchy-voiced Ani DiFranco (b. 1970), who writes, sings, and plays guitar with poetic prowess and wild abandon. She is the founder of Righteous Babe Records and maintains a steady track record of entrepreneurship. Like Patti Smith, DiFranco's music is full of poetry and spoken word, interwoven with her percussive guitar and usually a backing band consisting of horns, piano, and bass playing complicated, jazz-infested chords. Her music is far from simple and often breaks with conventional song structure. Vocally, DiFranco very rarely sings above the passaggio, allowing more focus on lyrics and raw emotion.

The Indigo Girls is a folk-rock duo composed of Emily Saliers (b. 1963) and Amy Ray (b. 1964), who hit the charts in 1989 with an eponymous debut album. Since then, they have produced multiple records together and have served as role models to LGBTQ+ women internationally by being openly lesbian and sharing a canon of work that represents their individuality and claims their place in musical culture. Their strength is in the harmonization of their voices together, teaching young women that two female singers can be successful together in harmony. Of her creative process, Saliers said: "I'm usually playing some chords or picking the pattern and I start sort of channeling lyrics about stuff that I've been thinking about recently. . . . Usually it starts with the music and then it sort of all comes out together. . . . The music comes pretty easily and the lyrics are really hard."[19]

Tori Amos (b. 1963) found success as a solo artist in the early 1990s with fiery red hair and impressive piano-playing chops. She joins Joni Mitchell and Laura Nyro in the land of the sopranos, and her voice weaves below, around, and above her passaggio. On writing, she says, "The songs are alive in themselves; I always feel like I'm trying to translate. I'm only a conduit, a scribe. I could just be walking, sort of having no destination, and I'll sense this presence. Music really comes from the ethers. It's not an intellectual process."[20]

The 1990s also brought the music of k. d. lang (b. 1961), Sheryl Crow (b. 1962), Michelle Shocked (b. 1962), and many other female singer-songwriters to the mainstream music scene. The work of these women laid the groundwork for women's voices to stay in the mainstream. This is reflected in the indie rock movement of the early 2000s, which was led by Sara Bareilles (b. 1979), Ingrid Michaelson (b. 1979), and Regina Spektor (b. 1980). With the development of the Internet and music sharing online, alternative voices and new styles of music were able to circulate without the necessity of a large record company. YouTube has also allowed various music artists to create and share their work, which circulates on the underground and can eventually make its way to major labels, radio stations, and media.

HIP-HOP, R&B, AND RAP

The female writers and rappers who work within hip-hop, rap, and R&B have had to navigate the struggle between honoring a set of

oppressive conventions that prevented them from success while pursuing success within the genres. Sources have indicated that much of rap,
hip-hop, and R&B music written by women is a response to the rap and
hip-hop music written by men, which is—in itself—a response to the
world around them and the oppression of our society. Hip-hop grew
out of black artists bringing their discussions of love, sex, and identity
to the public sphere. Born out of emotional pain and autobiographical
in nature, hip-hop provides a narrative of the minority experience in
America.[21] Similarly, rap music can be viewed as dialogue between rappers, both between male rappers and female rappers as well as between
rappers and the consumer. A common topic is love and relationships
through their specific lens—the kind of love that grows in spite of oppression but holds unique characteristics because of it.[22]

The journey of women in rap and hip-hop begins with Millie Jackson
(b. 1944), known as the "mother of women rappers." Jackson got her
start in this genre by recording love raps from a female perspective in
duets with Isaac Hayes (1942–2008). She paved the way for Mary J.
Blige (b. 1971), one of the most prolific female rap and hip-hop artists,
whose career has spanned more than three decades. Blige started out
with a slew of male rappers and singers as a part of her entourage but
has since shed many of them and adopted a more pared-down approach.
She has personally dealt with drugs and mental health struggles as a result of celebrity and has worked very hard to reinvent and grow spiritu-
ally. Blige's lyrics bring attention to issues in black communities, and her
voice is authentic in its roughness. As a trailblazer in the industry, "she
pronounced her words in unashamed Black English, and she danced
her unchoreographed unladylike steps with class."[23] Another significant
voice is Chaka Khan (b. 1953), who has led a career that spans five decades and multiple music genres, from funk to R&B. Khan is not only
known for writing her own material but also for setting a precedent for
the acrobatics of the female voice in pop music, blazing a trail for many
R&B and hip-hop divas to come. Khan said about songwriting:

> To me it was just poetry. I didn't really think that I was writing a song. I
> used to write a lot of poetry in school. And it's still the same way. My songs
> start out as poems. You know, I'm mindful of things like cadence and
> which rhyme scheme I'll use, like ABAB or ACAC. Content to me is very
> important—the relevance of the content and how eloquently I can say it.[24]

The 1990s saw a resurgence of girl groups (both trios and quartets) in the R&B and hip-hop world, but unlike the groups of the 1950s and 1960s, these ladies usually wrote their own material. Led by TLC, SWV, and Salt-N-Pepa, these women spoke about their sexuality, their needs, and their empowerment, all with smooth harmonies and catchy beats. Salt-N-Pepa—composed of duo Cheryl "Salt" James (b. 1966) and Sandy "Pepa" Denton (b. 1969)—enjoyed popularity in the late 1980s and early 1990s. They used their platform to continue the tradition of reporting on the female experience, sometimes in response to their male hip-hop counterparts. Rappers, like Kimberly Denise Jones or Lil' Kim (b. 1974/1975), also came onto the radio, expressive about their sexuality and using their lyrics to educate men on how to treat women. These women combine sex and materialism in their lyrics to express their desires, and they bring light to issues that were once ignored. Other artists who wrote, performed, and produced their own work in this genre include Alicia Keys (b. 1981), Nicki Minaj (b. 1982), Lauryn Hill (b. 1975), and the incomparable Missy Elliott (b. 1971), who has also penned dozens of hits for other performers. Elliott has been a frontrunner in the phenomenon of reporting through rap and hip-hop on the female perspective, both in her own music and the music she's written for other artists. While Elliott's vocal range is extremely limited compared to her belting contemporaries of the 1990s and early 2000s, her messages are blunt and truthful. ♪

Erykah Badu (b. 1971) enjoyed popularity starting in the mid-1990s as a pioneer in the genre of "Neo-Soul." She is known for her revealing lyrics coupled with a smooth vocal quality and unique sense of style. Badu falls in line with her fellow female voices in using her music to share perspective on love and relationships as well as positionality. In her song "Window Seat" (2010), Badu shares perspective on a common theme of women's music: getting away from given circumstances but tied to relationships with men.[25] ♪

COUNTRY

Female songwriters have a long and studied history on Music Row in Nashville. There are a number of commonly accepted narratives about

Figure 8.4. Missy Elliott, 2015 (photo by Atlantic Records). *Creative Commons (CC BY SA 4.0)*

Figure 8.5. Erykah Badu, 2006 (photo by Yancho Sabev). *Creative Commons (CC BY SA 3.0)*

country music, including its perceived gender, racial, and class norms associated with southern working-class white citizens. Musical tradition ascribes vernacular qualities to these songs as the expression of an identifiable sociocultural group. Songwriters are both perpetuators of a tradition and innovators charged with continually refreshing the genres relevant to successive generations of listeners.[26]

Country music offers within itself an array of subgenres that, in turn, present varying levels of femininity and class level. There have been shifts within the country world from soft, folk-based material (almost bluegrass) to pop-infused, cosmopolitan material (Shania Twain and Martina McBride are prime examples), and back again to the honky-tonk, southern-based content of the male singers who dominated country music charts in the wake of September 11, 2001. There was a huge increase in popularity of country music after 9/11 due to the movement of patriotism in America, which identifies "country" as an American genre of music and connects patriots and conservatives through it, regardless of physical location and heritage. In the arena of pop, success has been achieved by "crossover" country artists like Martina McBride (b. 1966), Faith Hill (b. 1967), Sara Evans (b. 1971), and Shania Twain (b. 1965) who boast female-empowered, pop-influenced country music that women across socioeconomic boundaries both enjoy and want to sing along to.

Two representative icons who represent female songwriters in country music are Loretta Lynn (b. 1932) and Dolly Parton (b. 1946). Lynn and Parton stand out based on the similar way in which they present narratives about the lives and identities of working-class women. Their music, however, seems to resonate with listeners in two completely different ways, and their individual expressions of gender identity reflect elements of their personal histories and experiences with different levels of femininity. For example, Lynn has a straightforward belt singing style and the instrumentation of her music is more honky-tonk in style, representing a tough "working-class" kind of people. Parton, on the other hand, sings around and beyond the passaggio, and her songs represent rural femininity, empowering women to rise above and behave in the ways they want to behave rather than the ways that society has constructed them. This dichotomy can be best explored through comparing Lynn's hit "Fist City" (1968) and Parton's hit "Jolene" (1973).[27]

Both women came from humble, rural upbringings and had headstrong mothers who reinforced the role of the mother in hard-labor society. Their songs also present comparisons of feminine (and masculine) middle-class individuals to working-class people. This pans out musically in many ways when one examines the work of these two artists. ♪

Much of the country music sound revolves around twang and speech-sung quality, which allows the listener to relate more closely to the performer's natural sound. Each performer's voice is unique and recognizable while also sounding like a natural extension of their everyday speaking voices. They don't attempt to sound like anyone else but themselves. Their individuality as vocalists also contributes to the distinct representations of country femininity in each recording. As vocalists, Parton and Lynn have many differences—such as accents, vocal ranges, and onsets—but their abilities to write and perform songs as extensions of themselves are equally successful and significant in the country genre.

Figure 8.6.   Martha Bassett. *Courtesy of the artist*

PROFILE: MARTHA BASSETT

Describe your musical background and what led you to be a composer.

My first instruments were piano and saxophone, and I started singing publicly as a teenager. I studied voice at the University of Kentucky as an undergraduate and received an MM in vocal performance at the University of North Carolina at Greensboro. All of my performing was in the realm of classical music until my early thirties when I began fronting a swing band. At about the same time, I started learning upright bass, which I played in a rock band, an old-time string band, and backing up other singer-songwriters. Eventually I picked up guitar and formed an Americana band. It was then that I started writing songs, mainly because I thought that was what you were supposed to do.

Describe your compositional style and what it says about who you are.

My first songs were in the "jump blues" and "old time" styles that I had the most experience with. I mostly work within the adult contemporary arena—acoustic Americana. Compositionally I usually begin with lyrics, and the music reflects the rhythm of the words. I love three-part vocal harmonies. Most of my songs tell stories. As a singer, I don't like being confined to singing only my own songs, and I draw from a wide range of music for my band. I also employ other songwriters in my band.

What hurdles have you encountered as a woman composer? How did you overcome them? Are there any you have yet to overcome?

As a singer-songwriter, the hurdles have had more to do with learning the craft and having the courage to express myself than being a woman. I'm not a prolific songwriter, but I'm proud of the songs I've released. It's a lifelong process, and I hope I have a long way to go.

Who are your greatest inspirations, musically and artistically?
There are so many. As songwriters I really appreciate Gillian
Welch, Lucinda Williams, Greg Brown, Jim White, Nick Cave, and
Jeff Tweedy. I'm inspired by my colleagues here in North Carolina—it's a rich music scene with a lot of diversity. We all feed each
other's work. Really, inspirations come from everywhere. It's just a
matter of being aware.

GHOST WRITERS

"Ghost writers" are composers who write music for others to perform.
Some of the women in this area do perform their own songs, but all of
the women in this area have penned songs for others using the incredible skill of "empathetic transference." Empathetic transference is the
process that allows songwriters to write songs describing subject positions outside of their direct experience, and also the process through
which a listener will relate to and attach meaning onto a song. Empathy
provides one means for understanding across disparate experiences.

As early as the 1950s, women were actually penning hits for male
performers. Dorothy LaBostrie (1928–2007) wrote the lyrics for "Tutti
Frutti" (1955) for Little Richard (b. 1932), and Mae Boren Axton
(1914–1997) cowrote "Heartbreak Hotel" (1956) for Elvis Presley
(1935–1977). There are many books about the success of Carole King
and Gerry Goffin, but they weren't the only duo writing music for others in the mid-1900s. Cynthia Weil collaborated with Barry Mann to
write dozens of hits in the 1960s for the Ronettes, the Drifters, and the
Righteous Brothers. Ellie Greenwich collaborated with Jeff Barry in
the 1960s on hits such as "Da Doo Ron Ron" (1963) for the Crystals,
"Then He Kissed Me" (1963) for the Ronettes, and "Leader of the Pack"
(1964) for the Shangri-Las. Greenwich and Barry were seen as direct
competitors with King and Goffin.

In contemporary popular music, examples include Kandi Burruss (b.
1976), Debbie Harry (b. 1945), Linda Perry (b. 1965), Kara DioGuardi
(b. 1970), Pink (b. 1979), and Katy Perry (b. 1984). Kandi Burruss has

penned the 1999 hits "Bills Bills Bills" and "Bug-a-Boo" for Destiny's
Child and "No Scrubs" for the girl group TLC.[28] It is no surprise that
the content of Burruss's songs are female-empowering. Debbie Harry
wrote many hits for her band Blondie but also has penned successful
records for the Black Eyed Peas. Linda Perry has written many successful pop collaborations with performers such as Céline Dion (b. 1968),
Gwen Stefani (b. 1969), and Christina Aguilera (b. 1980). Beyond her
performing career, Kara DioGuardi has found success writing with Ni-
cole Scherzinger (b. 1978), Aguilera, Kelly Clarkson (b. 1982), Ashlee
Simpson (b. 1982), and Hillary Duff (b. 1987). The tough pop-rock
performer Pink has penned multiple hits for others: "If You're Gonna
Fly Away" (2002) for Faith Hill (b. 1967), "Take a Picture" (2003) for
Mya (b. 1979), "Whataya Want from Me" (2009) for Adam Lambert
(b. 1982), "I Walk Alone" (2013) for Cher (b. 1946), and "Recovering"
(2016) for Dion are a few examples.[29] Similarly, Katy Perry has written
hits for others including "Long Shot" (2009) for Clarkson.[30]

Victoria Banks (b. 1973), a Canadian songwriter who moved to Nashville in 1997, speaks at length about the experience of writing songs for
performers. Through pounding the pavement, Banks eventually ended
up in the offices of RCA and got her demo CD to the ears of Jessica
Simpson (b. 1980), who decided to record her songs. Simpson began
collaborating with Banks on songwriting, with Banks taking Simpson's
experiences and crafting them into songs. This is an example of "auratic
transference," which places the presence of the songwriter into the song
itself, regardless of the circumstances and personal involvement in later
performances, either recorded or live. There are *many* songs today that
are written by multiple writers. Perhaps this is how collaboration can
benefit a song—by combining the powers of shared experience, empathy, and crafting skill. In addition to determination, success requires
continual adjustment to the work conditions imposed by publishers and
producers who are constantly shifting their expectations.

Perhaps the most successful female songwriter in the business in the past
three decades is Diane Warren (b. 1956), who has written songs for male and
female performers, for solo artists and groups, and across multiple genres.
Her hits include "If I Could Turn Back Time" (1989) for Cher, "Un-Break
My Heart" (1996) for Toni Braxton (b. 1967), "Because You Loved Me"
(1996) for Dion, "How Do I Live" (1997) for LeAnn Rimes (b. 1982), and

"I Was Here" (2011) for Beyoncé (b. 1981).[31] There are multiple wonderful interviews with Warren one can listen to that give insight into her process and her experience with various artists and working in different environments. ♪

BREAKING GROUND: INTERNATIONAL CROSSOVER

Due to the confines of space—and since "CCM" is an American-based pedagogic term and field of study—this chapter has focused on American artists, although there is (literally) a world of female songwriters who deserve to be lauded and studied. A few representative international artists should be mentioned, however, including Selena (1971–1995), Chrissy Amphlett (1959–2013), Björk (b. 1965), Adele (b. 1988), Celia Cruz (1925–2003), Joan Armatrading (b. 1950), and Gloria Estefan (b. 1957). Armatrading is one of Britain's most highly acclaimed singer-songwriters. She has struggled to find success in America, however, mostly based on her music living across genres and illustrating the difficulties a black performer has crossing into a white-dominated genre of the industry. Armatrading revealed:

> When I play and when I write and arrange, to me it is often multiple voices and they have to all fit. That's why I write and arrange myself, because it's not just the melody and the lyric, it's the whole thing, and although when I write and write on the guitar or the piano, I have to make sure that the song stands up just on that solo instrument, too. . . . It has to complement the song and, as you say, it should relate to the story being told.[32]

The Cuban American artist Gloria Estefan is one of the most successful international stars to cross over into the pop charts from another type of music genre. Her band, Miami Sound Machine, was established in 1974 under the name Miami Latin Boys. Gloria (then Fajardo) joined in 1977, and she and the leader of the band, Emilio (b. 1953), married in 1978. Miami Sound Machine initially found great success through their Latin dance tunes but started using Gloria's sentimental power ballads beginning in the 1980s. As Estefan gained experience, she continued to write her own songs as well as songs for others. In 2018, Emilio and Gloria Estefan received the Library of

Figure 8.7. Joan Armatrading, early 1980s (photo by Eddie Mallin). *Creative Commons (CC BY SA 2.0)*

Congress Gershwin Prize for Popular Song. While Carole King was the award's first and only previous female recipient (in 2013), Estefan is the first woman of Hispanic heritage to win this award. ♪

FINAL THOUGHTS

"Whenever women speak their own truths, either in the speaking itself or in the content during both, they challenge the norms that constrain them, and they give voice to the experiences, concerns, enjoys of other women who are constructing their own voices."[33] Most women writing CCM songs are focused on content above vocal production. However, the two seem to remain naturally intertwined with one another. In the 2007 book *I Got Thunder*, Odetta (1930–2008) says the following: "If we consider a song a recipe, let's call what the singer brings to the song the spices they use. When I went to that bowl to make the recipe, I pulled a little of that spice from here and a little of that spice from there. So it was a matter of choosing what affected me, allowing that to inform me and reaching as far as I could go with it."[34]

If you are interested in learning more about CCM, you must ask yourself why you are seeking to study and sing CCM music in the first place. What is your purpose? Is it for a music theater audition?[35] Are you interested in singing it as an independent artist, like a cover? Are you simply collecting experience with CCM singing to be able to perform and write your own material? Again, what is your purpose?

Since the canon of CCM music is so vast, it serves many purposes. It is the music we dance around in our kitchen to, make love to, protest with, or songs we used to tell our parents a secret that they didn't know about us. We use CCM songs as therapy, workout jams, motivational moments, and as ways to escape from reality or face it head on. This is where lived experience and connection to material is paramount. Content and emotional connection takes precedence over clarity of tone quality; however, it is beautiful when they coexist together—using melodic line as an expressive language.

There are so many songs written by men and women alike, especially with other overlapping experiences such as gender identity, sexuality, class, place of origin, and oppressed experience. If a singer wishes to sing a song originally written by and performed by a person of a different background, it is up to the artist in the moment to discern her connection to the music she is singing and—if authenticity is at the forefront of the performance experience—the material should be fair game. However, research and understanding of the background of the song is key. Singing a song written by a woman will most likely connect the singer to that writer's experience as well as provide a musical landscape that a mezzo or soprano voice can navigate.

NOTES

1. Jeannette LoVetri, "Editorial: Contemporary Commercial Music," *Journal of Voice* 22, no. 3 (2008): 260.

2. Matthew Hoch, ed. *So You Want to Sing CCM* (Lanham, MD: Rowman & Littlefield, 2018).

3. Sheri Sanders, *Rock the Audition—How to Prepare for and Get Cast in Rock Musicals* (New York: Hal Leonard Corporation, 2011), 1.

4. Gillian Gaar, *She's a Rebel: The History of Women in Rock and Roll* (Seattle, WA: Seal Press, 1992), 142.

5. Eileen M. Hayes and Linda F. Williams, *Black Women and Music: More Than the Blues* (Urbana: University of Illinois Press: 2007), 153.

6. LaShonda Barnett, *I Got Thunder: Black Women Songwriters on Their Craft* (Cambridge, MA: Da Capo Press, 2007), 118.

7. Ibid., 179.

8. Paul Garon and Beth Garon, *Woman with Guitar: Memphis Minnie's Blues*, revised and expanded edition (San Francisco: City Lights Publishers, 2014).

9. Ibid., 169.

10. Ibid., 161–62.

11. Mina Carson, Tisa Lewis, and Susan M. Shaw, *Girls Rock! Fifty Years of Women Making Music* (Lexington: University of Kentucky Press, 2004), 51.

12. These songs are from the albums *Anticipation* (1971), *No Secrets* (1972), *Boys in the Trees* (1978), *Come Upstairs* (1980), and *Coming Around Again* (1987), respectively. The single "Coming Around Again" was originally released in 1986 as part of the soundtrack for the film *Heartburn*.

13. "Birdland" is from the album *Horses* (1975) and "Because the Night" is from the album *Easter* (1978).

14. "Pissing in a River" is from the 1976 album *Radio Ethiopia*. It was also featured in both the 1980 movie *Times Square* and the 1997 independent film *All Over Me*.

15. Madonna, *Sex* (Barcelona and Madrid: Ediciones B, 1992).

16. Buffy Childerhose, *From Lilith to Lilith Fair* (New York: St. Martin's Press, 1998), 211.

17. Gaar, *She's a Rebel*, 372.

18. These songs are from the albums *Tracy Chapman* (1988) and *New Beginning* (1995), respectively.

19. Carson, Lewis, and Shaw, *Girls Rock!*, 371.

20. Susan Cheever and Brigitte Lacombe, "Tori Amos," *Rolling Stone*, November 13, 1997, 104.

21. Ron Stallworth, *Gangster Rap Music: An Informal Study of Its Message and Correlation to the Gang Environment* (Salt Lake City: Utah Division of Investigation Salt Lake Area Gang Project, 1993).

22. Eileen M. Hayes and Linda F. Williams, eds., *Black Women and Music: More Than the Blues* (Urbana: University of Illinois Press: 2007), 27–28.

23. Sister Souljah, "Mary's World: A Former Public Enemy Follows the Career of the Queen of Hip Hop Soul," *New Yorker*, October 4, 1999, 58.

24. Barnett, *I Got Thunder*, 65.

25. "Window Seat" is from the 2010 album *New Amerykah Part Two (Return of the Ankh)*.

26. Diane Pecknold and Kristine M. McCusker, *Country Boys and Redneck Women: New Essays in Gender and Country Music* (Jackson: University Press of Mississippi, 2016), 102–124.

27. Ibid., 166–84. Both of these songs are the title tracks for their respective albums.

28. These songs are from the albums *The Writing's on the Wall* (1999) and *FanMail* (1999), respectively.

29. These songs are from the albums *Cry* (2002), *Moodring* (2003), *For Your Entertainment* (2009), and *Closer to the Truth* (2013), respectively. "Recovering" was released as a single.

30. "Long Shot" is from the Album *All I Ever Wanted* (2009).

31. These songs are from the albums *Heart of Stone* (1989), *Secrets* (1996), *Falling into You* (1996), *You Light Up My Life: Inspirational Songs* (1997), and *4* (2011).

32. Barnett, *I Got Thunder*, 111.

33. Carson, Lewis, and Shaw, *Girls Rock!*, 53.

34. Barnett, *I Got Thunder*, 182.

35. If you are preparing a music theater audition, I strongly recommend that you consult Sheri Sanders and her materials because singing a pop-rock song for a music theater audition is an entirely different experience and has a different purpose then simply singing a CCM song for one's own artistic fulfillment.

9

SINGING AND VOICE SCIENCE

Scott McCoy

This chapter presents a concise overview of how the voice functions as a biomechanical, acoustic instrument. We will be dealing with elements of anatomy, physiology, acoustics, and resonance. But don't panic: the things you need to know are easily accessible, even if it has been many years since you last set foot in a science or math class!

All musical instruments, including the human voice, have at least four things in common, consisting of a power source, sound source (vibrator), resonator, and a system for articulation. In most cases, the person who plays the instrument provides power by pressing a key, plucking a string, or blowing into a horn. This power is used to set the sound source in motion, which creates vibrations in the air that we perceive as sound. Musical vibrators come in many forms, including strings, reeds, and human lips. The sound produced by the vibrator, however, needs a lot of help before it becomes beautiful music—we might think of it as raw material, like a lump of clay that a potter turns into a vase. Musical instruments use resonance to enhance and strengthen the sound of the vibrator, transforming it into sounds we identify as a piano, trumpet, or guitar. Finally, instruments must have a means of articulation to create the nuanced sounds of music. Let's see how these four elements are used to create the sounds of singing.

PULMONARY SYSTEM: THE POWER
SOURCE OF YOUR VOICE

The human voice has a lot in common with a trumpet: both use flaps of tissue as a sound source, both use hollow tubes as resonators, and both rely on the respiratory (pulmonary) system for power. If you stop to think about it, you quickly realize why breathing is so important for singing. First and foremost, it keeps us alive through the exchange of blood gases—oxygen in, carbon dioxide out. But it also serves as the storage depot for the air we use to produce sound. Most singers rarely encounter situations in which these two functions are in conflict, but if you are required to sustain an extremely long phrase, you could find yourself in need of fresh oxygen before your lungs are totally empty.

Misconceptions about breathing for singing are rampant. Fortunately, most are easily dispelled. We must start with a brief foray into the world of physics in the guise of Boyle's Law. Some of you no doubt remember this principle: the pressure of a gas within a container changes inversely with changes of volume. If the quantity of a gas is constant and its container is made smaller, pressure rises. But if we make the container get bigger, pressure goes down. Boyle's law explains everything that happens when we breathe, especially when we combine it with another physical law: nature abhors a vacuum. If one location has reduced pressure, air flows from an area of higher pressure to equalize the two, and vice versa. So if we can create a zone of reduced air pressure by expanding our lungs, air automatically flows in to restore balance. When air pressure in the lungs is increased, it has no choice but to flow outward.

As we all know, the air we breathe goes in and out of our lungs. Each lung contains millions and millions of tiny air sacs called alveoli, where gases are exchanged. The alveoli also function like ultra-miniature versions of the bladder for a bag pipe, storing the air that will be used to set the vocal folds into vibration. To get the air in and out of them, all we need to do is make the lungs larger for inhalation and smaller for exhalation. Always remember this relationship between cause and effect during breathing: we inhale because we make ourselves large; we exhale because we make ourselves smaller. Unfortunately, the lungs are organs, not muscles, and have no ability on their own to accomplish this feat. For this reason, your bodies came from the factory with special muscles designed to enlarge and compress your entire thorax (rib cage), while simultaneously moving your lungs. We can classify these muscles in two main categories: any muscle that has the ability to increase the volume capacity of the thorax serves an inspiratory function; any muscle that has the ability to decrease the volume capacity of the thorax serves an expiratory function.

Your largest muscle of inspiration is called the diaphragm (figure 9.1). This dome-shaped muscle originates from the bottom of your sternum (breastbone) and completely fills the area from that point around your ribs to your spine. It's the second-largest muscle in your body, but you probably have no conscious awareness of it or ability to directly control it. When we take a deep breath, the diaphragm contracts and the cen-

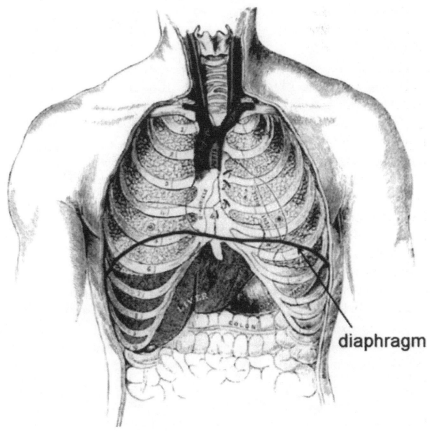

diaphragm

Figure 9.1. Location of Diaphragm. *Courtesy of Scott McCoy*

tral portion flattens out and drops downward a couple inches into your abdomen, pressing against all of your internal organs. If you release tension from your abdominal muscles as you inhale, you will feel a gentle bulge in your upper or lower belly, or perhaps in your back, resulting from the displacement of your innards by the diaphragm. This is a good thing and can be used to let you know you have taken a good inhalation.

The diaphragm is important, but we must remember that it cannot function in isolation. After you inhale, it relaxes and gently returns to its resting position through an action called elastic recoil. This movement, however, is entirely passive and makes no significant contribution to generating the pressure required to sustain phonation. Therefore, it makes no sense at all to try to "sing from your diaphragm"—unless you intend to sing while you inhale, not exhale!

Eleven pairs of muscles assist the diaphragm in its inhalatory efforts, which are called the external intercostal muscles (figure 9.2). These muscles start from ribs one through eleven and connect at a slight angle downward to ribs two through twelve. When they contract, the entire thorax moves up and out, somewhat like moving a bucket handle. With the diaphragm and intercostals working together, you are able to increase the capacity of your lungs by about three to six liters, depending on your gender and overall physical stature; thus, we have quite a lot of air available to power our voices.

Eleven additional pairs of muscles are located directly under the external intercostals, which, not surprisingly, are called the internal intercostals (figure 9.2). These muscles start from ribs two through twelve and connect upward to ribs one through eleven. When they contract, they induce the opposite action of their external partners: the thorax is made smaller, inducing exhalation. Four additional pairs of expiratory muscles are located in the abdomen, beginning with the rectus (figure 9.2). The two rectus abdominis muscles run from your pubic bone to your sternum and are divided into four separate portions, called bellies of the muscle (lots of muscles have multiple bellies; it is coincidental that the bellies of the rectus are found in the location we colloquially refer to as our belly). Definition of these bellies results in the so-called ripped abdomen or six-pack of body builders and others who are especially fit.

The largest muscles of the abdomen are called the external obliques (figure 9.3), which run at a downward angle from the sides of the rec-

internal intercostal muscles

external intercostal muscles

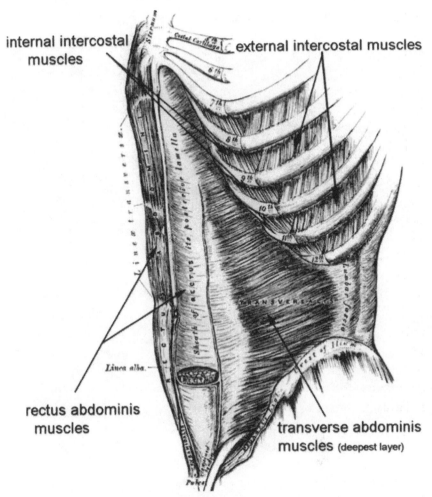

rectus abdominis muscles

transverse abdominis muscles (deepest layer)

Figure 9.2. Intercostal and Abdominal Muscles. *Courtesy of Scott McCoy*

tus, covering the lower portion of the thorax, and extend all the way to the spine. The internal obliques lie immediately below, oriented at an angle that crisscrosses the external muscles. They are slightly smaller, beginning at the bottom of the thorax, rather than extending over it. The deepest muscle layer is the transverse abdominis (figure 9.2), which is oriented with fibers that run horizontally. These four muscle pairs completely encase the abdominal region, holding your organs and digestive system in place while simultaneously helping you breathe.

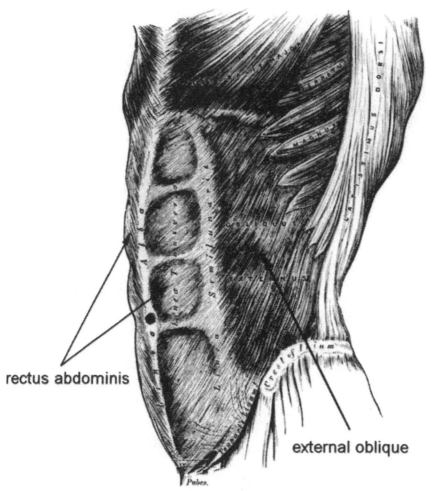

rectus abdominis

external oblique

Figure 9.3. External Oblique and Rectus Abdominis Muscles. *Courtesy of Scott McCoy*

Your expiratory muscles are quite large and can produce a great deal of pulmonary or air pressure. In fact, they easily can overpower the larynx. Healthy adults generally can generate more than twice the pressure that is required to produce even the loudest sounds; therefore, singers must develop a system for moderating and controlling airflow and breath pressure. This practice goes by many names, including breath support, breath control, and breath management, all of which rely on the principle of muscular antagonism. Muscles are said to have an antagonistic relationship when they work in opposing directions, usually pulling on a common point of attachment, for the sake of increasing stability or motor control. You can see a clear example of muscular antagonism in the relationship between your biceps (flexors) and triceps (extensors) when you hold out your arm. In breathing for singing, we activate inspiratory muscles (e.g., diaphragm and external intercostals) during exhalation to help control respiratory pressure and the rate at which air is expelled from the lungs.

One of the things you will notice when watching a variety of singers is that they tend to breathe in many different ways. You might think that voice teachers and scientists, who have been teaching and studying singing for hundreds, if not thousands, of years, would have come to agreement on the best possible breathing technique. But for many reasons, this is not the case. For one, different musical and vocal styles place varying demands on breathing. For another, humans have a huge variety of body types, sizes, and morphologies. A breathing strategy that is successful for a tall, slender woman might be completely ineffective in a short, robust man. Our bodies actually contain a large number of muscles beyond those we've already discussed that are capable of assisting with respiration. For an example, consider your latissimi dorsi muscles. These large muscles of the arm enable us to do pull-ups (or pull-downs, depending on which exercise you perform) at the fitness center. But because they wrap around a large portion of the thorax, they also exert an expiratory force. We have at least two dozen such muscles that have secondary respiratory functions, some for exhalation and some for inhalation. When we consider all these possibilities, it is no surprise at all that there are many ways to breathe that can produce beautiful singing. Just remember to practice some muscular antagonism—maintaining a degree of inhalation posture during exhalation—and you should do well.

LARYNX: THE VIBRATOR OF YOUR VOICE

The larynx, sometimes known as the voice box or Adam's apple, is a complex physiologic structure made of cartilage, muscle, and tissue. Biologically, it serves as a sphincter valve, closing off the airway to prevent foreign objects from entering the lungs. When firmly closed, it also is used to increase abdominal pressure to assist with lifting heavy objects, childbirth, and defecation. But if we gently close this valve while we exhale, tissue in the larynx begins to vibrate and produce the sounds that become speech and singing.

The human larynx is a remarkably small instrument, typically ranging from the size of a pecan to a walnut for women and men, respectively. Sound is produced at a location called the glottis, which is formed by two flaps of tissue called the vocal folds (aka vocal cords). In women, the glottis is about the size of a dime; in men, it can approach the diameter of a quarter. The two folds are always attached together at their front point but open in the shape of the letter V during normal breathing, an action called abduction. To phonate, we must close the V while we exhale, an action called adduction (just like the machines you use at the fitness center to exercise your thigh and chest muscles).

Phonation only is possible because of the unique multilayer structure of the vocal folds (figure 9.4). The core of each fold is formed by muscle, which is surrounded by a layer of gelatinous material called the lamina propria. The vocal ligament also runs through the lamina propria, which helps to prevent injury by limiting how far the folds can be stretched for

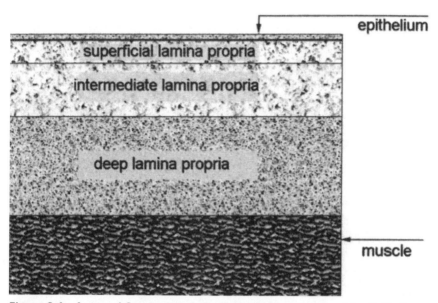

Figure 9.4.   Layered Structure of the Vocal Fold. *Courtesy of Scott McCoy*

high pitches. A thin, hairless epithelial layer that is constantly kept moist with mucus secreted by the throat, larynx, and trachea surrounds all of this. During phonation, the outer layer of the fold glides independently over the inner layer in a wavelike motion, without which phonation is impossible.

We can use a simple demonstration to better understand the independence of the inner and outer portions of the folds. Explore the palm of your hand with your other index finger. Note that the skin is attached quite firmly to the flesh beneath it. If you poke at your palm, that flesh acts as padding, protecting the underlying bone. Now explore the back of your hand. You will observe that the skin is attached quite loosely—you easily can move it around with your finger. And if you poke at the back of your hand, it is likely to hurt; there is very little padding between the skin and your bones. Your vocal folds combine the best attributes of both sides of your hand. They provide sufficient padding to help reduce impact stress, while permitting the outer layer to slip like the skin on the back of your hand, enabling phonation to occur. When you are sick with laryngitis and lose your voice (a condition called aphonia), inflammation in the vocal folds couples the layers of the folds tightly together. The outer layer no longer can move independently over the inner, and phonation becomes difficult or impossible.

The vocal folds are located within the five cartilaginous structures of the larynx (figure 9.5). The largest is called the thyroid cartilage, which is shaped like a small shield. The thyroid connects to the cricoid cartilage below it, which is shaped like a signet ring—broad in the back and narrow in the front. Two cartilages that are shaped like squashed pyramids sit atop the cricoid, called the arytenoids. Each vocal fold runs from the thyroid cartilage in front to one of the arytenoids at the back. Finally, the epiglottis is located at the top of the larynx, flipping backward each time we swallow to prevent food and liquid from entering our lungs. Muscles connect between the various cartilages to open and close the glottis and to lengthen and shorten the vocal folds for ascending and descending pitch, respectively. Because they sometimes are used to identify vocal function, it is a good idea to know the names of the muscles that control the length of the folds. We've already mentioned that a muscle forms the core of each fold. Because it runs between the thyroid cartilage and an arytenoid, it is named the thyroarytenoid muscle

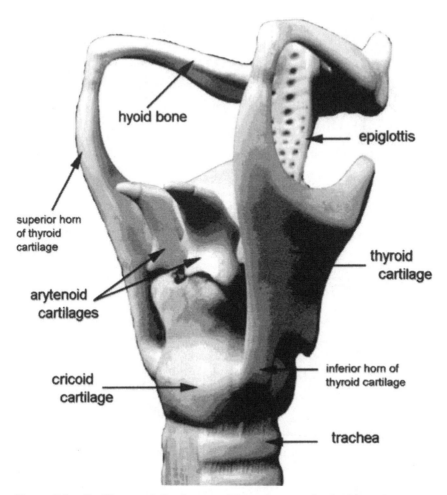

Figure 9.5. Cartilages of the Larynx, Viewed at an Angle from the Back.
Courtesy of Scott McCoy

(formerly known as the vocalis muscle). When the thyroarytenoid, or TA muscle, contracts, the fold is shortened and pitch goes down. The folds are elongated through the action of the cricothyroid, or CT muscles, which run from the thyroid to cricoid cartilage.

Vocal color (timbre) is created by the combined effects of the sound produced by the vocal folds and the resonance provided by the vocal tract. While these elements can never be completely separated, it is useful to consider the two primary modes of vocal fold vibration and their resulting sound qualities. The main differences are related to the relative thickness of the folds and their cross-sectional shape (figure 9.6). The first option depends on short, thick folds that come together with nearly square-shaped edges. Vibration in this configuration is given a variety of names, including mode 1, thyroarytenoid (TA) dominant, chest mode, or modal voice. The alternate configuration uses longer, thinner folds that only make contact at their upper margins. Common names include mode 2, cricothyroid (CT) dominant, falsetto mode, or loft voice. Singers vary the vibrational mode of the folds according to the quality of sound they wish to produce.

Before we move on to a discussion of resonance, we must consider the quality of the sound that is produced by the larynx. At the level of the glottis, we create a sound not unlike the annoying buzz of a duck call. That buzz, however, contains all the raw material we need to create speech and singing. Vocal or glottal sound is considered to be complex, meaning it consists of many simultaneously sounding frequencies (pitches). The lowest frequency within any tone is called the fundamental, which corresponds to its named pitch in the musical scale. Orchestras tune to a pitch called A-440, which means it has a frequency of 440 vibrations per second, or 440 Hertz (abbreviated Hz). Additional frequencies are included above the fundamental, which are called overtones. Overtones in the glottal sound are quieter than the fundamental. In voices, the overtones usually are whole number multiples of the fundamental, creating a pattern called the harmonic series (e.g., 100 Hz, 200 Hz, 300 Hz, 400 Hz, 500 Hz, etc. or G2, G3, D4, G4, B4—note that pitches are named by the international system in which the lowest C of the piano keyboard is C1; middle-C therefore becomes C4, the fourth C of the keyboard) (figure 9.7).

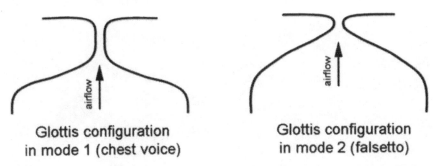

Glottis configuration in mode 1 (chest voice)

Glottis configuration in mode 2 (falsetto)

Figure 9.6. Primary Modes of Vocal Fold Vibration. *Courtesy of Scott McCoy*

Singers who choose to make coarse or rough sounds as might be appropriate for rock or blues often add overtones that are inharmonic, or not part of the standard numerical sequence. Inharmonic overtones also are common in singers with damaged or pathological voices.

Under most circumstances, we are completely unaware of the presence of overtones—they simply contribute to the overall timbre of a voice. In some vocal styles, however, harmonics become a dominant feature. This is especially true in throat singing or overtone singing, as is found in places like Tuva. Throat singers tune their vocal tracts so precisely that single harmonics are highlighted within the harmonic spectrum as a separate, whistle-like tone. These singers sustain a low-pitched drone and then create a melody by moving from tone to tone within the natural harmonic series. You can learn to do this too. Sustain a comfortable pitch in your range and slowly morph between the vowels /i/ and /u/. If you listen carefully, you will hear individual harmonics pop out of your sound.

The mode of vocal fold vibration has a strong impact on the overtones that are produced. In mode 1, high-frequency harmonics are relatively strong; in mode 2, they are much weaker. As a result, mode 1 tends to yield a much brighter, brassier sound.

VOCAL TRACT: YOUR SOURCE OF RESONANCE

Resonance typically is defined as the amplification and enhancement (or enrichment) of musical sound through supplemental vibration. What does this really mean? In layman's terms, we could say that resonance makes instruments louder and more beautiful by reinforcing the original vibrations of the sound source. This enhancement occurs in two primary ways, which are known as forced and free resonance (there is nothing pejorative in these terms: free resonance is not superior to forced resonance). Any object that is physically connected to a vibrator can serve as a forced resonator. For a piano, the resonator is the soundboard (on the underside of a grand or on the back of an upright); the vibrations of the strings are transmitted directly to the soundboard through a structure known as the bridge, which also is found on violins and guitars. Forced resonance also plays a role in voice production. Place your hand on your chest and say /a/ at a low pitch. You almost certainly felt the vibrations of forced resonance. In singing, this might best be considered your private resonance; you can feel it and it might impact your self-perception of sound, but nobody else can hear it. To understand why this is true, imagine what a violin would sound like if it were encased in a thick layer of foam rubber. The vibrations of the string would be damped out, muting the instrument. Your skin, muscles, and other tissues do the same thing to the vibrations of your vocal folds.

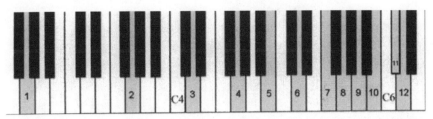

Figure 9.7. Natural Harmonic Series, Beginning at G2. *Courtesy of Scott McCoy*

By contrast, free resonance occurs when sound travels through a hollow space, such as the inside of a trumpet, an organ pipe, or your vocal tract, which consists of the pharynx (throat), oral cavity (mouth), and nasal cavity (nose). As sound travels through these regions, a complex pattern of echoes is created; every time sound encounters a change in the shape of the vocal tract, some of its energy is reflected backward, much like an echo in a canyon. If these echoes arrive back at the glottis at the precise moment a new pulse of sound is created, the two elements synchronize, resulting in a significant increase in intensity. All of this happens very quickly—remember that sound is traveling through your vocal tract at more than seven hundred miles per hour.

Whenever this synchronization of the vocal tract and sound source occurs, we say that the system is in resonance. The phenomenon occurs at specific frequencies (pitches), which can be varied by changing the position of the tongue, lips, jaw, palate, and larynx. These resonant frequencies, or areas in which strong amplification occurs, are called formants. Formants provide the specific amplification that changes the raw, buzzing sound produced by your vocal folds into speech and singing. The vocal tract is capable of producing many formants, which are labeled sequentially by ascending pitch. The first two, F1 and F2, are used to create vowels; higher formants contribute to the overall timbre and individual characteristics of a voice. In some singers, especially those who train to sing in opera, formants three through five are clustered together to form a super formant, eponymously called the singer's formant, which creates a ringing sound and enables a voice to be heard in a large theater without electronic amplification.

Formants are vitally important in singing, but they can be a bit intimidating to understand. An analogy that works really well for me is to think of formants like the wind. You cannot see the wind, but you know it is present when you see leaves rustling in a tree or feel a breeze on your face. Formants work in the same manner. They are completely invisible and directly inaudible. But just as we see the rustling leaf, we can hear, and perhaps even feel, the action of formants through how they change our sound. Try a little experiment. Sing an ascending scale beginning at B♭3, sustaining the vowel /i/. As you approach the D♯ or E♭ of the scale, you likely will feel (and hear) that your sound becomes a bit stronger and easier to produce. This occurs because the scale tone and formant are on the same pitch, providing additional amplification. If you change to an /u/ vowel, you will feel the same thing at about the same place in the scale. If you sing to an /o/ or /e/ and continue up the scale, you'll feel a bloom in the sound somewhere around C5 (an octave above middle C); /a/ is likely to come into its best focus at about G5.

To remember the approximate pitches of the first formants for the main vowels, /i–e–a–o–u/, just think of a C-major triad in first inversion, open position, starting at E4: /i/ = E4, /e/ = C5, /a/ = G5, /o/ = C5, and /u/ = E4 (figure 9.8). If your music theory isn't strong, you could use the mnemonic "every child gets candy eagerly." These pitches might vary by as much as a minor third higher and lower but no farther: once a formant changes by more than that interval, the vowel that is produced must change.

Formants have absolutely no preference for what they amplify—they are indiscriminate lovers, just as happy to bond with the first harmonic as the fifth. When men or women sing low pitches, there almost always will be at least one harmonic that comes close enough to a formant to produce a clear vowel sound. The same is not true for women with high voices, especially sopranos, who routinely must sing pitches that have a

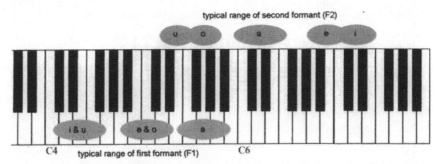

Figure 9.8. Typical Range of First and Second Formants for Primary Vowels. *Courtesy of Scott McCoy*

fundamental frequency higher than the first formant of many vowels. Imagine what happens if she must sing the phrase "and I'll leave you forever," with the word "leave" set on a very high, climactic note. The audience won't be able to tell if she is singing "leave" or "love"; the two will sound identical. This happens because the formant that is required to identify the vowel /i/ is too far below the pitch being sung. Even if she tries to sing "leave," the sound that comes out of her mouth will be heard as some variation of /a/.

Fortunately, this kind of mismatch between formants and musical pitches rarely causes problems for anyone but opera singers, choir sopranos, and perhaps ingenues in classic music theater shows. Almost everyone else generally sings low enough in their respective voice ranges to produce easily identifiable vowels.

Second formants also can be important, but more so for opera singers than everyone else. They are much higher in pitch, tracking the pattern /u/ = E5, /o/ = G5, /a/ = D6, /e/ = B6, /i/ = D7 (you can use the mnemonic "every good dad buys diapers" to remember these pitches) (figure 9.8). Because they can extend so high, into the top octave of the piano keyboard for /i/, they interact primarily with higher tones in the natural harmonic series. Unless you are striving to produce the loudest unamplified sound possible, you probably never need to worry about the second formant; it will steadfastly do its job of helping to produce vowel sounds without any conscious thought or manipulation on your part.

If you are interested in discovering more about resonance and how it impacts your voice, you might want to install a spectrum analyzer on your computer. Free (or inexpensive) programs are readily available for download over the Internet that will work with either a PC or Mac computer. You don't need any specialized hardware—if you can use Skype or FaceTime, you already have everything you need. Once you've installed something, simply start playing with it. Experiment with your voice to see exactly how the analysis signal changes when you change the way your voice sounds. You'll be able to see how harmonics change in intensity as they interact with your formants. If you sing with vibrato, you'll see how consistently you produce your variations in pitch and amplitude. You'll even be able to see if your tone is excessively nasal for the kind of singing you want to do. Other programs are available that will help you improve your intonation (how well you sing in tune) or enhance your basic musicianship skills. Technology truly has advanced sufficiently to help us sing more beautifully.

MOUTH, LIPS, AND TONGUE: YOUR ARTICULATORS

The articulatory life of a singer is not easy, especially when compared to the demands placed on other musicians. Like a pianist or brass player, we must be able to produce the entire spectrum of musical articulation, including dynamic levels from hushed pianissimos to thunderous fortes, short notes, long notes, accents, crescendos, diminuendos, and so on. We produce most of these articulations the same way instrumentalists do, which is by varying our power supply. But singers have another layer of articulation that makes everything much more complicated; we must produce these musical gestures while simultaneously singing words.

As we learned in our brief examination of formants, altering the resonance characteristics of the vocal tract creates the vowel sounds of language. We do this by changing the position of our tongue, jaw, lips, and sometimes palate. Slowly say the vowel pattern /i–e–a–o–u/. Can you feel how your tongue moves in your mouth? For /i/, it is high in the front and low in the back, but it takes the opposite position for /u/. Now slowly say the word "Tuesday," noting all the places your tongue comes into contact with your teeth and palate and how it changes shape as you produce the vowels and diphthongs. There is a lot going on in there—no wonder it takes so long for babies to learn to speak!

Our articulatory anatomy is extraordinarily complex, in large part because our bodies use the same passageway for food, water, air, and sound. As a result, our tongue, larynx, throat, jaw, and palate are all interconnected with common physical and neurologic points of attachment. Our anatomical Union Station in this regard is a small structure called the hyoid bone. The hyoid is one of only three bones in your entire body that do not connect to other bones via a joint (the other two are your patellae, or kneecaps). This little bone is suspended below your jaw, freely floating up and down every time you swallow. It is a busy place, serving as the upper suspension point for the larynx, the connection for the root of the tongue, and the primary location of the muscles that open your mouth by dropping your jaw.

Good singing—in any genre—requires a high degree of independence in all these articulatory structures. Unfortunately, nature conspires against us to make this difficult to accomplish. From the time we were born, our bodies have relied on a reflex reaction to elevate the palate and raise the larynx each time we swallow. This action becomes habitual: palate goes up, larynx also lifts. But depending on the style of music we are singing, we might need to keep the larynx down while the palate goes up (opera and classical) or palate down with the larynx up (country and bluegrass). As we all know, habits can be very hard to change, which is one of the reasons that it can take a lot of study and practice to become an excellent singer. Understanding your body's natural reflexive habits can make some of this work a bit easier.

There is one more significant pitfall to the close proximity of all these articulators: tension in one area is easily passed along to another. If your jaw muscles are too tight while you sing, that hyperactivity will likely be transferred to the larynx and tongue—remember, they all are interconnected through the hyoid bone. It can be tricky to determine the primary offender in this kind of chain reaction of tension. A tight tongue could just as easily be making your jaw stiff, or an elevated, rigid larynx could make both tongue and jaw suffer.

Neurology complicates matters even further. You have sixteen muscles in your tongue, fourteen in your larynx, twenty-two in your throat and palate, and another sixteen that control your jaw. Many of these are very small and lie directly adjacent to each other, and you often are required to contract one quite strongly while its next-door neighbor must remain totally relaxed. Our brains need to develop laser-like control, sending signals at the right moment with the right intensity to the precise spot where they are needed. When we first start singing, these brain signals come more like a blast from a shotgun, spreading the neurologic impulse over a broad area to multiple muscles, not all of which are the intended target. Again, with practice and training, we learn to refine our control, enabling us to use only those muscles that will help, while disengaging those that would get in the way of our best singing.

FINAL THOUGHTS

This brief chapter has only scratched the surface of the huge field of voice science. To learn more, you might visit the websites of the National Association of Teachers of Singing (NATS), the Voice Foundation (TVF), or the National Center for Voice and Speech (NCVS). You can easily locate the appropriate addresses through any Internet search engine. Remember: knowledge is power. Occasionally, people are afraid that if they know more about the science of how they sing, they will become so analytical that all spontaneity will be lost or they will become paralyzed by too much information and thought. In my forty-plus years as a singer and teacher, I've never encountered somebody who actually suffered this fate. To the contrary, the more we know, the easier—and more joyful—singing becomes. ♪

10

VOCAL HEALTH FOR SINGERS

Wendy LeBorgne

GENERAL PHYSICAL WELL-BEING

All singers, regardless of genre, should consider themselves as "vocal athletes." The physical, emotional, and performance demands necessary for optimal output require that the artist consider training and maintaining their instrument as an athlete trains for an event. With increased vocal and performance demands, it is unlikely that a vocal athlete will have an entire performing career completely injury free. This may not be the fault of the singer, as many injuries occur due to circumstances beyond the singer's control such as singing through an illness or being on a new medication seemingly unrelated to the voice. ♪

Vocal injury has often been considered taboo to talk about in the performing world as it has been considered to be the result of faulty technique or poor vocal habits. In actuality, the majority of vocal injuries presenting in the elite performing population tend to be overuse and/or acute injury. From a clinical perspective over the past seventeen years, younger, less experienced singers with fewer years of training (who tend to be quite talented) generally are the ones who present with issues related to technique or phonotrauma (nodules, edema, contact ulcers), while more mature singers with professional performing careers tend to present with acute injuries (hemorrhage) or overuse and misuse injuries (muscle tension dysphonia, edema, GERD) or injuries following an illness. There are no current studies documenting use and training in correlation to laryngeal pathologies. However, there are studies that document that somewhere between 35 percent and 100 percent of professional vocal athletes have abnormal vocal fold findings on stroboscopic evaluation. Many times these "abnormalities" are in singers who have no vocal complaints or symptoms of vocal problems. From a performance perspective, uniqueness in vocal quality often gets hired and perhaps a slight aberration in the way a given larynx functions may become quite marketable. Regardless of what the vocal folds may look like, the most integral part of performance is that the singer must maintain agility, flexibility, stamina, power, and inherent beauty (genre appropriate) for their current level of performance taking into account physical, vocal, and emotional demands.

Unlike sports medicine and the exercise physiology literature where much is known about the types and nature of given sports injuries, there is no common parallel for the vocal athlete model. However, because the vocal athlete utilizes the body systems of alignment, respiration, phonation, and resonance with some similarities to physical athletes, a parallel protocol for vocal wellness may be implemented/considered for vocal athletes to maximize injury prevention knowledge for both the singer and teacher. This chapter aims to provide information on vocal wellness and injury prevention for the vocal athlete.

CONSIDERATIONS FOR WHOLE BODY WELLNESS

Nutrition

You have no doubt heard the saying "You are what you eat." Eating is a social and psychological event. For many people, food associations and eating have an emotional basis resulting in either overeating or being malnourished. Eating disorders in performers and body image issues may have major implications and consequences for the performer on both ends of the spectrum (obesity and anorexia). Singers should be encouraged to reprogram the brain and body to consider food as fuel. You want to use high-octane gas in your engine, as pouring water in your car's gas tank won't get you very far. Eating a poor diet or a diet that lacks appropriate nutritional value will have negative physical and vocal effects on the singer. Effects of poor dietary choices for the vocal athlete may result in physical and vocal effects ranging from fatigue to life-threatening disease over the course of a lifetime. Encouraging and engaging in healthy eating habits from a young age will potentially prevent long-term negative effects from poor nutritional choices. It is beyond the scope of this chapter to provide a complete overview of all the dietary guidelines for pediatrics, adolescents, adults, and the mature adult; however, a listing of additional references to help guide your food and beverage choices for making good nutritional choices can be found online at websites such as Dietary Guidelines for Americans, Nutrition .gov Guidelines for Tweens and Teens, and Fruits and Veggies Matter. See the online companion web page on the NATS website for links to these and other resources. ♪

Hydration

"Sing wet, pee pale." This phrase was echoed in the studio of Van Lawrence regarding how his students would know if they were well hydrated. Generally, this rule of pale urine during your waking hours is a good indicator that you are well hydrated. Medications, vitamins, and certain foods may alter urine color despite adequate hydration. Due to the varying levels of physical and vocal activity of many performers, in order to maintain adequate oral hydration, the use of a hydration calculator based on activity level may be a better choice. These hydration calculators are easily accessible online and take into account the amount and level of activity the performer engages in on a daily basis. In a recent study of the vocal habits of musical theater performers, one of the findings indicated a significantly underhydrated group of performers.[1]

Laryngeal and pharyngeal dryness as well as "thick, sticky mucus" are often complaints of singers. Combating these concerns and maintaining an adequate viscosity of mucus for performance has resulted in some research. As a reminder of laryngeal and swallowing anatomy, nothing that is swallowed (or gargled) goes over or touches the vocal folds directly (or one would choke). Therefore, nothing that a singer eats or drinks ever touches the vocal folds, and in order to adequately hydrate the mucous membranes of the vocal folds, one must consume enough fluids for the body to produce a thin mucus. Therefore, any "vocal" effects from swallowed products are limited to potential pharyngeal and oral changes, not the vocal folds themselves.

The effects of systemic hydration are well documented in the literature. There is evidence to suggest that adequate hydration will provide some protection of the laryngeal mucosal membranes when they are placed under increased collision forces as well as reducing the amount of effort (phonation threshold pressure) to produce voice. This is important for the singer because it means that with adequate hydration and consistency of mucus, the effort to produce voice is less and your vocal folds are better protected from injury. Imagine the friction and heat produced when two dry hands rub together and then what happens if you put lotion on your hands. The mechanisms in the larynx to provide appropriate mucus production are not fully understood, but there is enough evidence at this time to support oral hydration as a vital component of every singer's vocal health regime to maintain appropriate mucosal viscosity.

Although very rare, overhydration (hyperhidrosis) can result in dehydration and even illness or death. An overindulgence of fluids essentially makes the kidneys work "overtime" and flushes too much water out of the body. This excessive fluid loss in a rapid manner can be detrimental to the body.

In addition to drinking water to systemically monitor hydration, there are many nonregulated products on the market for performers that lay claim to improving the laryngeal environment (e.g., Entertainer's Secret, Throat Coat Tea, Greathers Pastilles, Slippery Elm, etc.). Although there may be little detriment in using these products, quantitative research documenting change in laryngeal mucosa is sparse. One study suggests that the use of Throat Coat when compared to a placebo treatment for pharyngitis did show a significant difference in decreasing the perception of sore throat.[2] Another study compared the use of Entertainer's Secret to two other nebulized agents and its effect on phonation threshold pressure (PTP).[3] There was no positive benefit in decreasing PTP with Entertainer's Secret.

Many singers use personal steam inhalers and/or room humidification to supplement oral hydration and aid in combating laryngeal dryness.

There are several considerations for singers who choose to use external means of adding moisture to the air they breathe. Personal steam inhalers are portable and can often be used backstage or in the hotel room for the traveling performer. Typically, water is placed in the steamer and the face is placed over the steam for inhalation. Because the mucous membranes of the larynx are composed of a saltwater solution, one study looked at the use of nebulized saline in comparison to plain water and its potential effects on effort or ease to sound production in classically trained sopranos.[4] Data suggested that perceived effort to produce voice was less in the saline group than the plain water group. This indicated that the singers who used the saltwater solution reported less effort to sing after breathing in the saltwater than singers who used plain water. The researchers hypothesized that because the body's mucus is not plain water (rather it is a saltwater—think about your tears), when you use plain water for steam inhalation, it may actually draw the salt from your own saliva, resulting in a dehydrating effect.

In addition to personal steamers, other options for air humidification come in varying sizes of humidifiers from room size to whole house humidifiers. When choosing between a warm air or cool mist humidifier, considerations include both personal preference and needs. One of the primary reasons warm mist humidifiers are not recommended for young children is due to the risk of burns from the heating element. Both the warm mist and cool air humidifiers act similarly in adding moisture to the environmental air. External air humidification may be beneficial and provide a level of comfort for many singers. Regular cleaning of the humidifier is vital to prevent bacteria and mold buildup. Also, depending on the hardness of the water, it is important to avoid mineral buildup on the device and distilled water may be recommended for some humidifiers.

For traveling performers who often stay in hotels, fly on airplanes, or are generally exposed to other dry-air environments, there are products on the market designed to help minimize drying effects. One such device is called a Humidflyer, which is a face mask designed with a filter to recycle the moisture of a person's own breath and replenish moisture on each breath cycle.

For dry nasal passages or to clear sinuses, many singers use Neti pots. Many singers use this homeopathic flushing of the nasal passages regularly. Research supports the use of a Neti pot as a part of allergy relief and chronic rhinosinusitis control when utilized properly, sometimes in combination with medical management.[5] Conversely, long-term use of nasal irrigation (without taking intermittent breaks from daily use) may result in washing out the "good" mucus of the nasal passages, which naturally helps to rid the nose of infections. A study presented at the 2009 American College of Allergy, Asthma, and Immunology (ACAAI) annual scientific meeting reported that when a group of individuals who were using twice-daily nasal irrigation for one year discontinued using it, they had an increase in acute rhinosinusitis.[6]

Tea, Honey, and Gargle to Keep the Throat Healthy

Regarding the use of general teas (which many singers combine with honey or lemon), there is likely no harm in the use of decaffeinated tea (caffeine may cause systemic dryness). The warmth of the tea may provide a soothing sensation to the pharynx and the act of swallowing can be relaxing for the muscles of the throat. Honey has shown promising results as an effective cough suppressant in the pediatric population.[7] The dose of honey given to the children in the study was two teaspoons. Gargling with salt or apple cider vinegar and water are also popular home remedies for many singers with the uses being from soothing the throat to curing reflux. Gargling plain water has been shown to be efficacious in reducing the risk of contracting upper respiratory infections. I suggest that when gargling, the singer only "bubble" the water with air and avoid engaging the vocal folds in sound production. Saltwater as a gargle has long been touted as a sore throat remedy and can be traced back to 2700 BCE in China for treating gum disease. The science behind a saltwater rinse for everything from oral hygiene to sore throat is that salt (sodium chloride) may act as a natural analgesic (pain killer) and may also kill bacteria. Similar to the effects that not enough salt in the water may have on drawing the salt out of the tissue in steam inhalation, if you oversaturate the water solution with excess salt and gargle it, it may act to draw water out of the oral mucosa, thus reducing inflammation.

Another popular home remedy reported by singers is the use of apple cider vinegar to help with everything from acid reflux to sore throats. Dating back to 3300 BCE, apple cider vinegar was reported as a medicinal remedy, and it became popular in the 1970s as a weight loss diet cocktail. Popular media reports apple cider vinegar can improve conditions from acne and arthritis to nosebleeds and varicose veins. Specific efficacy data regarding the beneficial nature of apple cider vinegar for the purpose of sore throat, pharyngeal inflammation, and/or reflux have not been reported in the literature at this time. Of the peer-reviewed studies found in the literature, one discussed possible esophageal erosion and inconsistency of actual product in tablet form.[8] Therefore, at this time, strong evidence supporting the use of apple cider vinegar is not published.

Medications and the Voice

Medications (over the counter, prescription, and herbal) may have resultant drying effects on the body and often the laryngeal mucosa. General classes of drugs with potential drying effects include: antidepressants, antihypertensives, diuretics, ADD/ADHD medications, some oral acne medications, hormones, allergy drugs, and vitamin C in high doses. The National Center for Voice and Speech (NCVS) provides a listing of some common medications with potential voice side effects including laryngeal dryness. This listing does not take into account all medications, so singers should always ask their pharmacist of the potential side effects of a given medication. Due to the significant number of drugs on the market, it is safe to say that most pharmacists will not be acutely aware of "vocal side effects," but if dryness is listed as a potential side effect of the drug, you may assume that all body systems could be affected. Under no circumstances should you stop taking a prescribed medication without consulting your physician first. As every person has a different body chemistry and reaction to medication, just because a medication lists dryness as a potential side effect, it does not necessarily mean you will experience that side effect. Conversely, if you begin a new medication and notice physical or vocal changes that are unexpected, you should consult with your physician. Ultimately, the goal of medical management for any condition is to achieve the most benefits with the least side effects. Please see the companion page on the NATS website for a list of possible resources for the singer regarding prescription drugs and herbs. ♪

In contrast to medications that tend to dry, there are medications formulated to increase saliva production or alter the viscosity of mucus. Medically, these drugs are often used to treat patients who have had a loss of saliva production due to surgery or radiation. Mucolytic agents are used to thin secretions as needed. As a singer, if you feel that you need to use a mucolytic agent on a consistent basis, it may be worth considering getting to the root of the laryngeal dryness symptom and seeking a professional opinion from an otolaryngologist.

Reflux and the Voice

Gastroesophageal reflux (GERD) and/or laryngopharyngeal reflux (LPR) can have a devastating impact on the singer if not recognized and treated appropriately. Although GERD and LPR are related, they are considered as slightly different diseases. GERD (Latin root meaning "flowing back") is the reflux of digestive enzymes, acids, and other stomach contents into the esophagus (food pipe). If this backflow is propelled through the upper esophagus and into the throat (larynx and pharynx), it is referred to as LPR. It is not uncommon to have both GERD and LPR, but they can occur independently.

More frequently, people with GERD have decreased esophageal clearing. Esophagitis, or inflammation of the esophagus, is also associated with GERD. People with GERD often feel heartburn. LPR symptoms are often "silent" and do not include heartburn. Specific symptoms of LPR may include some or all of the following: lump in the throat sensation, feeling of constant need to clear the throat/postnasal drip, longer vocal warm-up time, quicker vocal fatigue, loss of high frequency range, worse voice in the morning, sore throat, and bitter/raw/brackish taste in the mouth. If you experience these symptoms on a regular basis, it is advised that you consider a medical consultation for your symptoms. Prolonged, untreated GERD or LPR can lead to permanent changes in both the esophagus and/or larynx. Untreated LPR also provides a laryngeal environment that is conducive for vocal fold lesions to occur as it inhibits normal healing mechanisms.

Treatments of LPR and GERD generally include both dietary and lifestyle modifications in addition to medical management. Some of the dietary recommendations include: elimination of caffeinated and carbonated beverages, smoking cessation, no alcohol use, and limiting tomatoes, acidic foods and drinks, and raw onions or peppers, to name a few. Also, avoidance of high-fat foods is recommended. From a lifestyle perspective, suggested changes include not eating within three hours of lying down, eating small meals frequently (instead of large meals), elevating the head of your bed, avoiding tight clothing around the belly, and not bending over or exercising too soon after you eat.

Reflux medications fall in three general categories: antacids, H2 blockers, and proton pump inhibitors (PPI). There are now combination drugs that include both an H2 blocker and proton pump inhibitor. Every medication has both associated risks and benefits, and singers should be aware of the possible benefits and side effects of the medications they take. In general terms, antacids (e.g., Tums, Mylanta, Gaviscon) neutralize stomach acid. H2 (histamine) blockers, such as Axid (nizatidine),Tagamet (cimetidine), Pepcid (famotidine), and Zantac (ranitidine), work to decrease acid production in the stomach by preventing histamine from triggering the H2 receptors to produce more acid. Then there are the PPIs: Nexium (esomeprazole), Prevacid (lansoprazole), Protonix (pantoprazole), AcipHex (rabeprazole), Prilosec (omeprazole), and Dexilant (dexlansoprazole). PPIs act as a last line of defense to decrease acid production by blocking the last step in gastric juice secretion. Some of the most recent drugs to combat GERD/LPR are combination drugs (e.g., Zegrid [sodium bicarbonate plus omeprazole]), which provide a short-acting response (sodium bicarbonate) and a long release (omeprazole). Because some singers prefer a holistic approach to reflux management, strict dietary and lifestyle compliance is recommended and consultation with both your primary care physician and naturopath are warranted in that situation. Efficacy data on non-regulated herbs, vitamins, and supplements are limited, but some data do exist.

Physical Exercise

Vocal athletes, like other physical athletes, should consider how and what they do to maintain both cardiovascular fitness and muscular strength. In today's performance culture, it is rare that a performer stands still and sings, unless in a recital or choral setting. The range of physical activity can vary from light movement to high-intensity choreography with acrobatics. As performers are being required to increase their on-stage physical activity level from the operatic stage to the pop-star arena, overall physical fitness is imperative to avoid compromise in the vocal system. Breathlessness will result in compensation by the larynx, which is now attempting to regulate the air. Compensatory vocal behaviors over time may result in a change in vocal performance. The health benefits of both cardiovascular training and strength training are well documented for physical athletes but relatively rare in the literature for vocal performers.

Mental Wellness

Vocal performers must maintain a mental focus during performance and a mental toughness during auditioning and training. Rarely during vocal performance training programs is this important aspect of performance addressed, and it is often left to the individual performer to develop their own strategy or coping mechanism. Yet, many performers are on antianxiety or antidepressant drugs (which may be the direct result of performance-related issues). If the sports world is again used as a parallel for mental toughness, there are no elite-level athletes (and few junior-level athletes) who don't utilize the services of a performance/sports psychologist to maximize focus and performance. I recommend that performers consider the potential benefits of a performance psychologist to help maximize vocal performance. Several references that may be of interest to the singer include: the audio recording of *Visualization for Singers* (1992) and the classic voice pedagogy book *Power Performance for Singers: Transcending the Barriers* (1998).[9] ♪

Unlike instrumentalists, whose performance is dependent on accurate playing of an external musical instrument, the singer's instrument is uniquely intact and subject to the emotional confines of the brain and body in which it is housed. Musical performance anxiety (MPA) can be career threatening for all musicians, but perhaps the vocal athlete is more severely impacted. The majority of literature on MPA is dedicated to instrumentalists, but the basis of definition, performance effects, and treatment options can be considered for vocal athletes. Fear is a natural reaction to a stressful situation, and there is a fine line between emotional excitation and perceived threat (real or imagined). The job of a performer is to convey to an audience through vocal production, physical gestures, and facial expression a most heightened state of emotion. Otherwise, why would audience members pay top dollar to sit for two or three hours for a mundane experience? Not only is there the emotional conveyance of the performance but also the internal turmoil often experienced by the singers themselves in preparation for elite performance. It is well documented in the literature that even the most elite performers have experienced debilitating performance anxiety. MPA is defined on a continuum with anxiety levels ranging from low to high and has been reported to comprise four distinct components: affect, cognition, behavior, and physiology. Affect comprises feelings (e.g., doom, panic, anxiety). Affected cognition will result in altered levels of concentration, while the behavior component results in postural shifts, quivering, and trembling. Finally physiologically the body's autonomic nervous system (ANS) will activate, resulting in the "fight or flight" response.

In recent years, researchers have been able to define two distinct neurological pathways for MPA. The first pathway happens quickly and without conscious input (ANS), resulting in the same fear stimulus as if a person were put into an emergent, life-threatening situation. In those situations, the brain releases adrenaline, resulting in physical changes of increased heart rate, increased respiration, shaking, pale skin, dilated pupils, slowed digestion, bladder relaxation, dry mouth, and dry eyes, all of which severely affect vocal performance. The second pathway that has been identified results in a conscious identification of the fear/threat and a much slower physiologic response. With the second neuromotor response, the performer has a chance to recognize the fear, process how to deal with the fear, and respond accordingly.

Treatment modalities to address MPA include psycho-behavioral therapy (including biofeedback) and drug therapies. Elite physical performance athletes have been shown to benefit from visualization techniques and psychological readiness training, yet within the performing arts community, stage fright may be considered a weakness or character flaw precluding readiness for professional performance. On the contrary, vocal athletes, like physical athletes, should mentally prepare themselves for optimal competition (auditions) and performance. Learning to convey emotion without eliciting an internal emotional response by the vocal athlete may take the skill of an experienced psychologist to help change ingrained neural pathways. Ultimately, control and understanding of MPA will enhance performance and prepare the vocal athlete for the most intense performance demands without vocal compromise.

VOCAL WELLNESS: INJURY PREVENTION

In order to prevent vocal injury and understand vocal wellness in the singer, general knowledge of common causes of voice disorders is imperative. One common cause of voice disorders is vocally abusive behaviors or misuse of the voice to include phonotraumatic behaviors such as yelling, screaming, loud talking, talking over noise, throat clearing, coughing, harsh sneezing, and boisterous laughing. Chronic or less than optimal vocal properties such as poor breathing techniques, inappropriate phonatory habits during conversational speech (glottal fry, hard glottal attacks), inapt pitch, loudness, rate of speech, and/or hyperfunctional laryngeal-area muscle tone may also negatively impact vocal function. Medically related etiologies, which also have the potential to impact vocal function, range from untreated chronic allergies and sinusitis to endocrine dysfunction and hormonal imbalance. Direct trauma, such as a blow to the neck or the risk of vocal fold damage during intubation, can impact optimal performance in vocal athletes depending on the nature and extent of the trauma. Finally, external irritants ranging from cigarette smoke to reflux directly impact the laryngeal mucosa and ultimately can lead to laryngeal pathology.

Vocal hygiene education and compliance may be one of the primary essential components for maintaining the voice throughout a career. This section will provide the singer with information on prevention of vocal injury. However, just like a professional sports athlete, it is unlikely that a professional vocal athlete will go through an entire career without some compromise in vocal function. This may be a common upper respiratory infection that creates vocal fold swelling for a short time, or it may be a "vocal accident" that is career threatening. Regardless, the knowledge of how to take care of your voice is essential for any vocal athlete.

Train Like an Athlete for Vocal Longevity

Performers seek instant gratification in performance sometimes at the cost of gradual vocal building for a lifetime of healthy singing. Historically, voice pedagogues required their students to perform vocalises exclusively for up to two years before beginning any song literature. Singers gradually built their voices by ingraining appropriate muscle memory and neuromotor patterns through development of aesthetically pleasing tones, onsets, breath management, and support. There was an intensive master-apprentice relationship and rigorous vocal guidelines to maintain a place within a given studio. Time off was taken if a vocal injury ensued or careers potentially were ended, and students were asked to leave a given singing studio if their voices were unable to withstand the rigors of training. Training vocal athletes today has evolved and appears driven to create a "product" quickly, perhaps at the expense of the longevity of the singer. Pop stars emerging well before puberty are doing international concert tours, yet many young artist programs in the classical arena do not consider singers for their programs until they are in their mid- to late twenties.

Each vocal genre presents with different standards and vocal demands. Therefore, the amount and degree of vocal training are varied. Some would argue that performing extensively without adequate vocal training and development is ill-advised, yet singers today are thrust onto the stage at very young ages. Dancers, instrumentalists, and physical athletes all spend many hours per day developing muscle strength, memory, and proper technique for their craft. The more advanced the artist or athlete, generally the more specific the training protocol becomes. Consideration of training vocal athletes in this same fashion is recommended. One would generally not begin a young, inexperienced singer on a Wagner aria without previous vocal training. Similarly, in nonclassical vocal music, there are easy, moderate, and difficult pieces to consider pending level of vocal development and training.

Basic pedagogical training of alignment, breathing, voice production, and resonance are essential building blocks for development of good voice production. Muscle memory and development of appropriate muscle patterns happen slowly over time with appropriate repetitive practice. Doing too much, too soon for any athlete (physical or vocal) will result in an increased risk for injury. When the singer is being asked to do "vocal gymnastics," they must be sure to have a solid basis of strength and stamina in the appropriate muscle groups to perform consistently with minimal risk of injury.

Vocal Fitness Program

One generally does not get out of bed first thing in the morning and try to do a split. Yet many singers go directly into a practice session or audition without proper warm-up. Think of your larynx like your knee, made up of cartilages, ligaments, and muscles. Vocal health is dependent upon appropriate warm-ups (to get things moving), drills for technique, and then cooldowns (at the end of your day). Consider vocal warm-ups a "gentle stretch." Depending on the needs of the singer, warm-ups should include physical stretching; postural alignment self-checks; breathing exercises to promote rib cage, abdominal, and back expansion; vocal stretches (glides up to stretch the vocal folds and glides down to contract the vocal folds); articulatory stretches (yawning, facial stretches); and mental warm-ups (to provide focus for the task at hand). Vocalises, in my opinion, are designed as exercises to go beyond warm-ups and prepare the body and voice for the technical and vocal challenges of the music they sing. They are varied and address the technical level and genre of the singer to maximize performance and vocal growth. Cooldowns are a part of most athletes' workouts. However, singers often do not use cooldowns (physical, mental, and vocal) at the end of a performance. A recent study looked specifically at the benefits of vocal cooldowns in singers and found that singers who used a vocal cooldown had decreased effort to produce voice the next day.[10]

Systemic hydration as a means to keep the vocal folds adequately lubricated for the amount of impact and friction that they will undergo has been previously discussed in this chapter. Compliance with adequate oral hydration recommendations is important and subsequently so is the minimization of agents that could potentially dry the membranes (e.g., caffeine, medications, dry air). The body produces approximately two quarts of mucus per day. If not adequately hydrated, the mucus tends to be thick and sticky. Poor hydration is similar to not putting enough oil in the car engine. Frankly, if the gears do not work as well, there is increased friction and heat, and the engine is not efficient.

Speak Well, Sing Well

Optimize the speaking voice utilizing ideal frequency range, breath, intensity, rate, and resonance. Singers generally are vocally enthusiastic individuals who talk a lot and often talk loudly. During typical conversation, the average fundamental speaking frequency (times per second the vocal folds are impacting) for a male varies from 100 to 150 Hz and 180 to 230 Hz for women. Because of the delicate structure of the vocal folds and the importance of the layered microstructure vibrating efficiently and effectively to produce voice, vocal behaviors or outside factors that compromise the integrity of the vibration patterns of the vocal folds may be considered phonotrauma.

Phonotraumatic behaviors can include yelling, screaming, loud talking, harsh sneezing, and harsh laughing. Elimination of phonotraumatic behaviors is essential for good vocal health. The louder one speaks, the farther apart the vocal folds move from midline, the harder they impact, and the longer they stay closed. A tangible example would be to take your hands, move them only six inches apart, and clap as hard and as loudly as you can for ten seconds. Now, move your hands two feet apart and clap as hard, loudly, and quickly as possible for ten seconds. The farther apart your hands are, the more air you move and the louder the clap, and the skin on the hands becomes red and ultimately swollen (if you do it long enough and hard enough). This is what happens to the vocal folds with repeated impact at increased vocal intensities. The vocal folds are approximately 17 mm in length and vibrate at 220 times per second on A3, 440 on A4, 880 on A5, and more than 1,000 per second when singing a high C. That is a lot of impact for little muscles. Consider this fact when singing loudly or in a high tessitura for prolonged periods of time. It becomes easy to see why women are more prone than men to laryngeal impact injuries due to the frequency range of the voice alone.

In addition to the amount of cycles per second (cps) the vocal folds are impacting, singers need to be aware of their vocal intensity (volume). One should be aware of the volume of the speaking and singing voice and consider using a distance of three to five feet (about an arm's-length distance) as a gauge for how loud to be in general conversation. Using cell phones and speaking on a Bluetooth device in a car generally results in greater vocal intensity than normal, and singers are advised to minimize unnecessary use of these devices.

Singers should be encouraged to take "vocal naps" during their day. A vocal nap would be a short period of time (five minutes to an hour) of complete silence. Although the vocal folds are rarely completely still (because they move when you swallow and breathe), a vocal nap minimizes impact and vibration for a short window of time. A physical nap can also be refreshing for the singer mentally and physically.

Avoid Environmental Irritants: Alcohol, Smoking, Drugs

Arming singers with information on the actual effects of environmental irritants so that they can make informed choices on engaging in exposure to these potential toxins is essential. The glamour that continues to be associated with smoking, drinking, and drugs can be tempered with the deaths of popular stars such as Amy Winehouse and Cory Monteith who engaged in life-ending choices. There is extensive documentation about the long-term effects of toxic and carcinogenic substances, but here are a few key facts to consider when choosing whether to partake.

Alcohol, although it does not go over the vocal folds directly, does have a systemic drying effect. Due to the acidity in alcohol, it may increase the likelihood of reflux, resulting in hoarseness and other laryngeal pathologies. Consuming alcohol generally decreases one's inhibitions, and therefore you are more likely to sing and do things that you would not typically do under the influence of alcohol.

Beyond the carcinogens in nicotine and tobacco, the heat at which a cigarette burns is well above the boiling temperature of water (water boils at 212 degrees F; cigarettes burn at over 1400 degrees F). No one would consider pouring a pot of boiling water on their hand, and yet the burning temperature for a cigarette results in significant heat over the oral mucosa and vocal folds. The heat alone can create a deterioration in the lining, resulting in polypoid degeneration. Obviously, cigarette smoking has been well documented as a cause for laryngeal cancer.

Marijuana and other street drugs are not only addictive but can cause permanent mucosal lining changes depending on the drug used and the method of delivery. If you or one of your singer colleagues is experiencing a drug or alcohol problem, research or provide information and support on getting appropriate counseling and help.

SMART PRACTICE STRATEGIES FOR SKILL
DEVELOPMENT AND VOICE CONSERVATION

Daily practice and drills for skill acquisition are an important part of any singer's training. However, overpracticing or inefficient practicing may be detrimental to the voice. Consider practice sessions of athletes: they may practice four to eight hours per day broken into one- to two-hour training sessions with a period of rest and recovery in between sessions. Although we cannot parallel the sports model without adequate evidence in the vocal athlete, the premise of short, intense, focused practice sessions is logical for the singer. Similar to physical exercise, it is suggested that practice sessions do not have to be all "singing." Rather, structuring sessions so that one-third of the session is spent on warm-up; one-third on vocalises, text work, rhythms, character development, and so on; and one-third on repertoire will allow the singer to function in a more efficient vocal manner. Building the amount of time per practice session—increasing duration by five minutes per week, building to sixty to ninety minutes—may be effective (e.g., Week 1: twenty minutes three times per day; Week 2: twenty-five minutes three times per day, etc.).

Vary the "vocal workout" during your week. For example, if you do the same physical exercise in the same way day after day with the same intensity and pattern, you will likely experience repetitive strain–type injuries. However, cross-training or varying the type and level of exercise aids in injury prevention. So when planning your practice sessions for a given week (or rehearsal process for a given role), consider varying your vocal intensity, tessitura, and exercises to maximize your training sessions, building stamina, muscle memory, and skill acquisition. For example, one day you may spend more time on learning rhythms and translation and the next day you spend thirty minutes performing coloratura exercises to prepare for a specific role. Take one day a week off from vocal training and give your voice a break. This does not mean complete vocal rest (although some singers find this beneficial), but rather a day without singing and limited talking.

Practice Your Mental Focus

Mental wellness and stress management are equally as important as vocal training for vocal athletes. Addressing any mental health issues is paramount to developing the vocal artist. This may include anything from daily mental exercises/meditation/focus to overcoming performance anxiety to more serious mental health issues/illness. Every person can benefit from improved focus and mental acuity.

ADDITIONAL VOCAL WELLNESS TIPS

When working with singers across all genres, the most common presentation in my voice clinic relates to vocal fatigue, acute vocal injury, and loss of high frequency range. Vocal fatigue complaints are generally related to the duration of their rehearsals, recording sessions, "meet and greets," performances, vocal gymnastics, general lack of sleep, and the vocal requirements to traverse their entire range (and occasionally outside of physiological comfort range). Depending on the genre performed, singing includes a high vocal load with the associated risk of repetitive strain and increased collision force injuries. Acute vocal injuries within this population include phonotraumatic lesions (hemorrhages, vocal fold polyps, vocal fold nodules, reflux, and general vocal fold edema/erythema). Often these are not injuries related to problematic vocal technique but rather due to "vocal accidents" and/or overuse (due to required performance/contract demands). Virtually all singers are required to connect with the audience from a vocal and emotional standpoint. Physical performance demands may be extreme and at times highly cardiovascular and/or acrobatic. Both physical and vocal fitness should be foremost in the minds of any vocal performer, and these singers should be physically and vocally in shape to meet the necessary performance demands.

The advanced and professional singer must possess a flexible, agile, and dynamic instrument and have appropriate stamina. Singers must have a good command of their instrument as well as exceptional underlying intention to what they are singing as it is about relaying a message, characteristic sound, and connecting with the audience. Singers must reflect the mood and intent of the composer requiring dynamic control, vocal control/power, and an emotional connection to the text.

Commercial music singers use microphones and personal amplification to their maximal capacity. If used correctly, amplification can be used to maximize vocal health by allowing the singer to produce voice in an efficient manner while the sound engineer is effectively able to mix, amplify, and add effects to the voice. Understanding both the utility and limits of a given microphone and sound system is essential for the singer both for live and studio performances. Using an appropriate microphone can not only enhance the singer's performance but can also reduce vocal load. Emotional extremes (intimacy and exultation) can be enhanced by appropriate microphone choice, placement, and acoustical mixing, thus saving the singer's voice.

Not everything a singer does is "vocally healthy," sometimes because the emotional expression may be so intense it results in vocal collision forces that are extreme. Even if the singer does not have formal vocal training, the concept of "vocal cross-training"—which can mean singing in both high and low registers with varying intensities and resonance options—before and after practice sessions and services is likely a vital component to minimizing vocal injury.

FINAL THOUGHTS

Ultimately, the singer must learn to provide the most output with the least "cost" to the system. Taking care of the physical instrument through daily physical exercise, adequate nutrition and hydration, and focused attention on performance will provide a necessary basis for vocal health during performance. Small doses of high-intensity singing (or speaking) will limit impact stress on the vocal folds. Finally, attention to the mind, body, and voice will provide the singer with an awareness when something is wrong. This awareness and knowledge of when to rest or seek help will promote vocal well-being for the singer throughout his or her career.

NOTES

1. Wendy LeBorgne et al., "Prevalence of Vocal Pathology in Incoming Freshman Musical Theatre Majors: A 10-year Retrospective Study," Fall Voice Conference, New York, 2012.

2. Josef Brinckmann et al., "Safety and Efficacy of a Traditional Herbal Medicine (Throat Coat) in Symptomatic Temporary Relief of Pain in Patients with Acute Pharyngitis: A Multicenter, Prospective, Randomized, Double-Blinded, Placebo-Controlled Study," *Journal of Alternative and Complementary Medicine* 9, no. 2 (2003): 285–298.

3. Nelson Roy et al., "An Evaluation of the Effects of Three Laryngeal Lubricants on Phonation Threshold Pressure (PTP)," *Journal of Voice* 17, no. 3 (2003): 331–342.

4. Kristine Tanner et al., "Nebulized Isotonic Saline versus Water Following a Laryngeal Desiccation Challenge in Classically Trained Sopranos," *Journal of Speech Language and Hearing Research* 53, no. 6 (2010): 1555–1566.

5. Christopher L. Brown and Scott M. Graham, "Nasal Irrigations: Good or Bad?" *Current Opinion in Otolaryngology, Head and Neck Surgery* 12, no. 1 (2004): 9–13.

6. Talal N. Nsouli, "Long-Term Use of Nasal Saline Irrigation: Harmful or Helpful?" American College of Allergy, Asthma and Immunology Annual Scientific Meeting, Abstract 32, 2009.

7. Mahmood Noori Shadkam et al. "A Comparison of the Effect of Honey, Dextromethorphan, and Diphenhydramine on Nightly Cough and Sleep Quality in Children and Their Parents," *Journal of Alternative and Complementary Medicine* 16, no. 7 (2010): 787–793.

8. Laura L. Hill et al., "Esophageal Injury by Apple Cider Vinegar Tablets and Subsequent Evaluation of Products," *Journal of the American Dietetic Association* 105, no. 7 (2005): 1141–1144.

9. Joanna Cazden, *Visualizations for Singers* (Burbank, CA: Voice of Your Life, 1992); Shirlee Emmons and Alma Thomas, *Power Performance for Singers: Transcending the Barriers* (New York: Oxford University Press, 1998).

10. Renee O. Gottliebson, "The Efficacy of Cool-Down Exercises in the Practice Regimen of Elite Singers," PhD dissertation, University of Cincinnati, 2011.

USING AUDIO
ENHANCEMENT TECHNOLOGY

Matthew Edwards

In the early days of popular music, musicians performed without electronic amplification. Singers learned to project their voices in the tradition of vaudeville performers with a technique similar to operatic and operetta performers who had been singing unamplified for centuries. When microphones began appearing on stage in the 1930s, vocal performance changed forever since the loudness of a voice was no longer a factor in the success of a performer. In order to be successful, all a singer needed was an interesting vocal quality and an emotional connection to what he or she was singing. The microphone would take care of projection.[1]

Vocal qualities that may sound weak without a microphone can sound strong and projected when sung with one. At the same time, a singer with a voice that is acoustically beautiful and powerful can sound harsh and pushed if he or she lacks microphone technique. Understanding how to use audio equipment to get the sounds a singer desires without harming the voice is crucial. The information in this chapter will help the reader gain a basic knowledge of terminology and equipment commonly used when amplifying or recording a vocalist as well as providing tips for singing with a microphone.

THE FUNDAMENTALS OF SOUND

In order to understand how to manipulate an audio signal, you must first understand a few basics of sound including frequency, amplitude, harmonics, and resonance.

Frequency

Sound travels in waves of compression and rarefaction within a medium, which for our purposes is air (see figure 11.1). These waves travel through the air and into our inner ears via the ear canal. There they are converted via the eardrums into nerve impulses that are transmitted to the brain and interpreted as sound. The number of waves per second is measured in Hertz (Hz), which gives us the frequency of the sound that we have learned to perceive as pitch. For example, we hear 440 Hz (440 cycles of compression and rarefaction per second) as A4, the pitch A above middle C.

Amplitude

The magnitude of the waves of compression and rarefaction determines the amplitude of the sound, which we call its "volume." The larger the waves of compression and rarefaction, the louder we perceive the sound to be. Measured in decibels (dB), amplitude represents changes in air pressure from the baseline. Decibel measurements range from zero decibels (0 dB), the threshold of human hearing, to 130 dB, the upper edge of the threshold of pain.

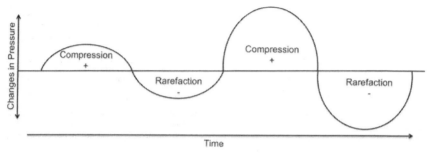

Figure 11.1. **Compression and Rarefaction.** *Creative Commons*

Harmonics

The vibrating mechanism of an instrument produces the vibrations necessary to establish pitch (the fundamental frequency). The vibrating mechanism for a singer is the vocal folds. If an acoustic instrument, such as the voice, were to produce a note with the fundamental frequency alone, the sound would be strident and mechanical like the emergency alert signal used on television. Pitches played on acoustic instruments consist of multiple frequencies, called overtones, which are emitted from the vibrator along with the fundamental frequency. For the purposes of this chapter, the overtones that we are interested in are called harmonics. Harmonics are whole number multiples of the fundamental frequency. For example, if the fundamental frequency is 220 Hz (A3), the harmonic overtone series would be 220 Hz, 440 Hz (fundamental frequency times two), 660 Hz (fundamental frequency times three), 880 Hz (fundamental frequency times four), and so on. Every musical note contains both the fundamental frequency and a predictable series of harmonics, each of which can be measured and identified as a specific frequency. This series of frequencies then travels through a hollow cavity (the vocal tract) where they are attenuated or amplified by the resonating frequencies of the cavity, which is how resonance occurs.

Resonance

The complex waveform created by the vocal folds travels through the vocal tract, where it is enhanced by the tract's unique resonance characteristics. Depending on the resonator's shape, some harmonics are amplified and some are attenuated. Each singer has a unique vocal tract shape with unique resonance characteristics. This is why two singers of the same voice type can sing the same pitch and yet sound very different. We can analyze these changes with a tool called a spectral analyzer as seen in figure 11.2. The slope from left to right is called the spectral slope. The peaks and valleys along the slope indicate amplitude variations of the corresponding overtones. The difference in spectral slope between instruments (or voices) is what enables a listener to aurally distinguish the difference between two instruments playing or singing the same note.

Because the throat and mouth act as the resonating tube in acoustic singing, changing their size and shape is the only option for making adjustments to timbre for those who perform without microphones. In electronically amplified singing, the sound engineer can make adjustments to boost or attenuate specific frequency ranges, thus changing the singer's timbre. For this and many other reasons discussed in this chapter, it is vitally important for singers to know how audio technology can affect the quality of their voice.

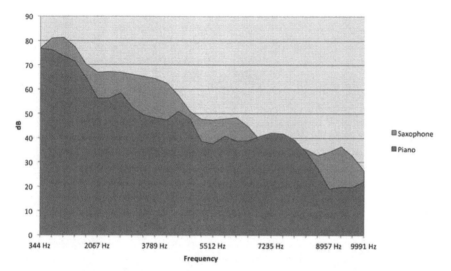

Figure 11.2. The figure above shows two instruments playing the same pitch. The peak at the far left is the fundamental frequency and the peaks to the right are harmonics that have been amplified and attenuated by the instrument's resonator resulting in a specific timbre. *Courtesy of Matthew Edwards*

SIGNAL CHAIN

The signal chain is the path an audio signal travels from the input to the output of a sound system. A voice enters the signal chain through a microphone, which transforms acoustic energy into electrical impulses. The electrical pulses generated by the microphone are transmitted through a series of components that modify the signal before the speakers transform it back into acoustic energy. Audio engineers and producers understand the intricacies of these systems and are able to make an infinite variety of alterations to the vocal signal. While some engineers strive to replicate the original sound source as accurately as possible, others use the capabilities of the system to alter the sound for artistic effect. Since more components and variations exist than can be discussed in just a few pages, this chapter will discuss only basic components and variations found in most systems.

Microphones

Microphones transform the acoustic sound waves of the voice into electrical impulses. The component of the microphone that is responsible for receiving the acoustic information is the diaphragm. The two most common diaphragm types that singers will encounter are dynamic and condenser. Each offers advantages and disadvantages depending on how the microphone is to be used.

Dynamic Dynamic microphones consist of a dome-shaped Mylar diaphragm attached to a free-moving copper wire coil that is positioned between the two poles of a magnet. The Mylar diaphragm moves in response to air pressure changes caused by sound waves. When the diaphragm moves, the magnetic coil that is attached to it also moves. As

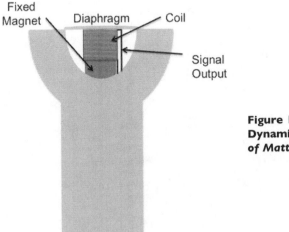

Figure 11.3. Basic Design of a Dynamic Microphone. *Courtesy of Matthew Edwards*

the magnetic coil moves up and down between the magnetic poles, it produces an electrical current that corresponds to the sound waves produced by the singer's voice. That signal is then sent to the soundboard via the microphone cable.

The Shure SM58 dynamic microphone is the industry standard for live performance because it is affordable, nearly indestructible, and easy to use. Dynamic microphones such as the Shure SM58 have a lower sensitivity than condenser microphones, which makes them more successful at avoiding feedback. Because of their reduced tendency to feedback, dynamic microphones are the best choice for artists who use handheld microphones when performing. ♪

Condenser   Condenser microphones are constructed with two parallel plates: a rigid posterior plate and a thin, flexible anterior plate. The anterior plate is constructed of either a thin sheet of metal or a piece of Mylar that is coated with a conductive metal. The plates are separated by air, which acts as a layer of insulation. In order to use a condenser microphone, it must be connected to a soundboard that supplies "phantom power." A component of the soundboard, phantom power sends a 48-volt power supply through the microphone cable to the microphone's plates. When the plates are charged by phantom power, they form a capacitor. As acoustic vibrations send the anterior plate into motion, the distance between the two plates varies, which causes the capacitor to release a small electric current. This current, which corresponds with the acoustic signal of the voice, travels through the microphone cable to the soundboard where it can be enhanced and amplified.

Electret condenser microphones are similar to condenser microphones, but they are designed to work without phantom power. The anterior plate of an electret microphone is made of a plastic film coated with a conductive metal that is electrically charged before being set into place opposite the posterior plate. The charge applied to the anterior plate will last for ten or more years and therefore eliminates the need for an exterior power source. Electret condenser microphones are often used in head-mounted and lapel microphones, laptop computers, and smartphones.

Recording engineers prefer condenser microphones for recording applications due to their high level of sensitivity. Using a condenser microphone, performers can sing at nearly inaudible acoustic levels and

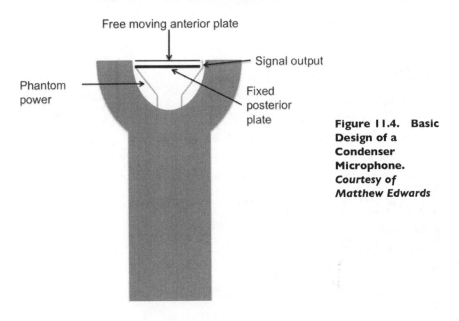

Free moving anterior plate

Signal output

Phantom power

Fixed posterior plate

Figure 11.4. Basic Design of a Condenser Microphone. Courtesy of Matthew Edwards

obtain a final recording that is intimate and earthy. While the same vocal effects can be recorded with a dynamic microphone, they will not have the same clarity as those produced with a condenser microphone.

Frequency Response   Frequency response is a term used to define how accurately a microphone captures the tone quality of the signal. A "flat response" microphone captures the original signal with little to no signal alteration. Microphones that are not designated as "flat" have some type of amplification or attenuation of specific frequencies, also known as cut or boost, within the audio spectrum. For instance, the Shure SM58 microphone drastically attenuates the signal below 300 Hz and amplifies the signal in the 3 kHz range by 6 dB, the 5 kHz range by nearly 8 dB, and the 10 kHz range by approximately 6 dB. The Oktava 319 microphone cuts the frequencies below 200 Hz while boosting everything above 300 Hz with nearly 5 dB between 7 kHz and 10 kHz (see figure 11.5). In practical terms, recording a bass singer with the Shure SM58 would drastically reduce the amplitude of the fundamental frequency while the Oktava 319 would produce a slightly more consistent boost in the range of the singer's formant. Either of these options could be acceptable depending on the situation, but the frequency response must be considered before making a recording or performing live.

252

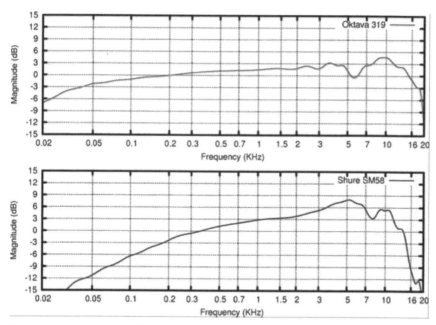

Figure 11.5. Example Frequency Response Graphs for the Oktava 319 and the Shure SM58. *Wikimedia Commons*

Amplitude Response   The amplitude response of a microphone varies depending on the angle at which the singer is positioned in relation to the axis of the microphone. In order to visualize the amplitude response of a microphone at various angles, microphone manufacturers publish polar pattern diagrams (also sometimes called a directional pattern or a pickup pattern). Polar pattern diagrams usually consist of six concentric circles divided into twelve equal sections. The center point of the microphone's diaphragm is labeled 0° and is referred to as "on-axis" while the opposite side of the diagram is labeled 180° and is described as "off-axis."

Although polar pattern diagrams appear in two dimensions, they actually represent a three-dimensional response to acoustic energy. You can use a round balloon as a physical example to help you visualize a three-dimensional polar pattern diagram. Position the tied end of the balloon away from your mouth and the inflated end directly in front of your lips. In this position, you are singing on-axis at 0° with the tied end of the balloon being 180°, or off-axis. If you were to split the balloon in half vertically and horizontally (in relationship to your lips), the point at which those lines intersect would be the center point of the balloon. That imaginary center represents the diaphragm of the microphone. If you were to extend a 45° angle in any direction from the imaginary center and then drew a circle around the inside of the balloon following that angle, you would have a visualization of the three-dimensional application of the two-dimensional polar pattern drawing.

The outermost circle of the diagram indicates that the sound pressure level (SPL) of the signal is transferred without any amplitude reduction, indicated in decibels (dB). Each of the inner circles represents a -5 dB reduction in the amplitude of the signal up to -25 dB. Figure 11.7 below is an example.

Figures 11.8, 11.9, and 11.10 show the most commonly encountered polar patterns.

When you are using a microphone with a polar pattern other than omnidirectional (a pattern that responds to sound equally from all

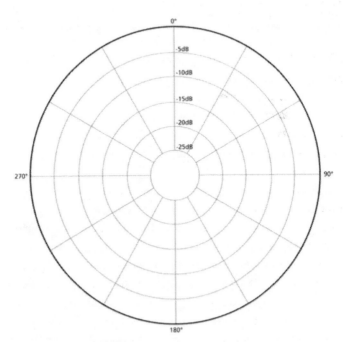

Figure 11.6. Example of a Microphone Polar Pattern.
Wikimedia Commons

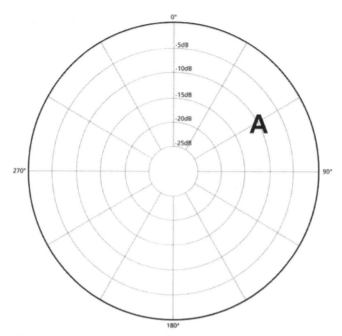

Figure 11.7. If the amplitude response curve intersected with point A, there would be a –10 dB reduction in the amplitude of frequencies received by the microphone's diaphragm at that angle. *Wikimedia Commons*

directions), you may encounter frequency response fluctuations in addition to amplitude fluctuations. Cardioid microphones in particular are known for their tendency to boost lower frequencies at close proximity to the sound source while attenuating those same frequencies as the distance between the sound source and the microphone increases. This is known as the "proximity effect." Some manufacturers will notate these frequency response changes on their polar pattern diagrams by using a combination of various lines and dashes alongside the amplitude response curve.

Sensitivity   While sensitivity can be difficult to explain in technical terms without going into an in-depth discussion of electricity and electrical terminology, a simplified explanation should suffice for most readers. Manufacturers test microphones with a standardized 1 kHz tone at 94 dB in order to determine how sensitive the microphone's diaphragm will be to acoustic energy. Microphones with greater sensitivity can be placed farther from the sound source without adding excessive noise to the signal. Microphones with lower sensitivity will need to be placed closer to the sound source in order to keep excess noise at a minimum. When shopping for a microphone, the performer should audition several next to each other, plugged into the same soundboard, with the same volume level for each. When singing on each microphone, at the same distance, the performer will notice that some models replicate the voice louder than others. This change in output level is due to differences in each microphone's sensitivity. If a performer has a loud voice, they may prefer a microphone with lower sensitivity (one that requires more acoustic energy to respond). If a performer has a lighter voice, they may prefer a microphone with higher sensitivity (one that responds well to softer signals).

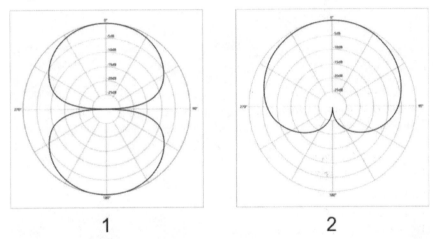

Figure 11.8. Diagram 1 represents a bidirectional pattern; diagram 2 represents a cardioid pattern. *Creative Commons*

Equalization (EQ)

Equalizers enable the audio engineer to alter the audio spectrum of the sound source and make tone adjustments with a simple electronic interface. Equalizers come in three main types: shelf, parametric, and graphic.

256256256

256

256296256296

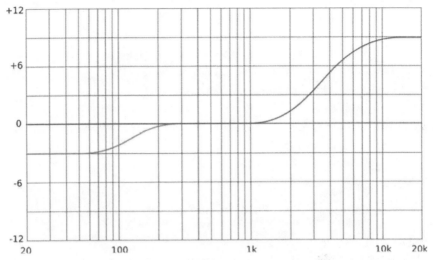

Figure II.II. The frequency amplitude curves above show the effect of applying a shelf EQ to an audio signal. *Wikimedia Commons*

frequencies below 65 Hz and effectively removes the hum from the microphone signal.

Parametric   Parametric units simultaneously adjust multiple frequencies of the audio spectrum that fall within a defined parameter. The engineer selects a center frequency and adjusts the width of the bell curve surrounding that frequency by adjusting the "Q" (see figure 11.12). He or she then boosts or cuts the frequencies within the bell curve to alter the audio spectrum. Parametric controls take up minimal space on a soundboard and offer sufficient control for most situations. Therefore, most live performance soundboards have parametric EQs on each individual channel. With the advent of digital workstations, engineers can now use computer software to fine-tune the audio quality of each individual channel using a more complex graphic equalizer in both live and recording studio settings without taking up any additional physical space on the board. However, many engineers still prefer to use parametric controls during a live performance since they are usually sufficient and are easier to adjust mid-performance.

Parametric adjustments on a soundboard are made with rotary knobs similar to those in figure 11.13 below. In some cases, you will find a button labeled "low cut" or "high pass" that will automatically apply a shelf

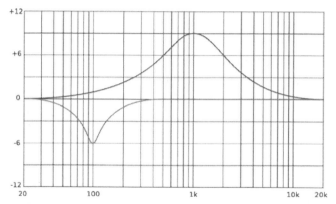

Figure 11.12. The frequency amplitude curves above display two parametric EQ settings. The top curve represents a boost of +8 dB set at 1 kHz with a relatively large bell curve—a low Q. The lower curve represents a high Q set at 100 Hz with a cut of –6 dB. *Wikimedia Commons*

Figure 11.13. This is an example of a parametric EQ interface. The "LO CUT" button applies a shelf EQ at 80 Hz when depressed. *Courtesy of Matthew Edwards*

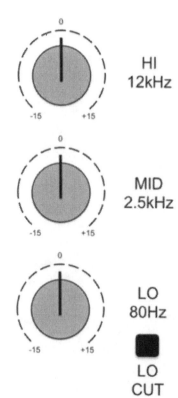

filter to the bottom of the audio spectrum at a specified frequency. On higher-end boards, you may also find a knob that enables you to select the high pass frequency.

Graphic   Graphic equalizers enable engineers to identify a specific frequency for boost or cut with a fixed frequency bandwidth. For example, a ten-band equalizer enables the audio engineer to adjust ten specific frequencies (in Hz): 31, 63, 125, 250, 500, 1K, 2K, 4K, 8K, and 16K. Graphic equalizers are often one of the final elements of the signal chain, preceding only the amplifier and speakers. In this position, they can be used to adjust the overall tonal quality of the entire mix.

Utilizing Equalization   Opinions on the usage of equalization vary among engineers. Some prefer to only use equalization to remove or reduce frequencies that were not a part of the original sound signal. Others will use EQ if adjusting microphone placement fails to yield acceptable results. Some engineers prefer a more processed sound and may use equalization liberally to intentionally change the vocal quality of the singer. For instance, if the singer's voice sounds dull, the engineer could add "ring" or "presence" to the voice by boosting the equalizer in the 2–10 kHz range.

Compression

Many singers are capable of producing vocal extremes in both frequency and amplitude levels that can prove problematic for the sound team. To help solve this problem, engineers often use compression.

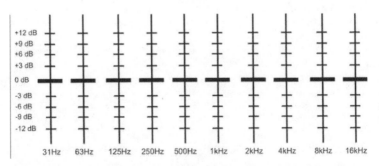

Figure 11.14.   Example of a Graphic Equalizer Interface. *Courtesy of Matthew Edwards*

Compressors limit the output of a sound source by a specified ratio. The user sets the maximum acceptable amplitude level for the output, called the "threshold," and then sets a ratio to reduce the output once it surpasses the threshold. The typical ratio for a singer is usually between 3:1 and 5:1. A 4:1 ratio indicates that for every 4 dB beyond the threshold level, the output will only increase by 1 dB. For example, if the singer went 24 dB beyond the threshold with a 4:1 ratio, the output would only be 6 dB beyond the threshold level (see figure 11.15).

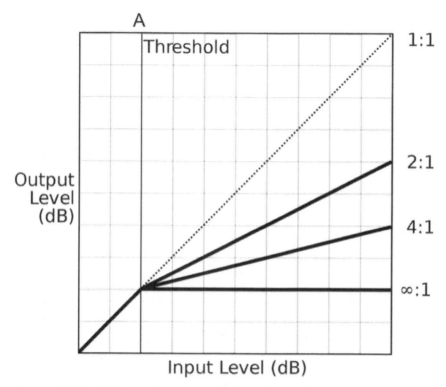

Figure 11.15. This graph represents the effects of various compression ratios applied to a signal. The 1:1 angle represents no compression. The other ratios represent the effect of compression on an input signal with the threshold set at line A. *Wikimedia Commons*

Adjusting the sound via microphone technique can provide some of the same results as compression and is preferable for the experienced artist. However, compression tends to be more consistent and also gives the singer freedom to focus on performing and telling a story. The additional artistic freedom provided by compression is especially beneficial to singers who use head-mounted microphones, performers who switch between vocal extremes such as falsetto and chest voice, and those who are new to performing with a microphone. Compression can also be helpful for classical singers whose dynamic abilities, while impressive live, are often difficult to record in a manner that allows for consistent listening levels through a stereo system.

If a standard compressor causes unacceptable alterations to the tone quality, engineers can turn to a multiband compressor. Rather than affecting the entire spectrum of sound, multiband compressors allow the engineer to isolate a specific frequency range within the audio signal and then set an individual compression setting for that frequency range. For example, if a singer creates a dramatic boost in the 4-kHz range every time they sing above an A4, a multiband compressor can be used to limit the amplitude of the signal in only that part of the voice. By setting a 3:1 ratio in the 4-kHz range at a threshold that corresponds to the amplitude peaks that appear when the performer sings above A4, the engineer can eliminate vocal "ring" from the sound on only the offending notes while leaving the rest of the signal untouched. These units are available for both live and studio use and can be a great alternative to compressing the entire signal.

Reverb

Reverb is one of the easier effects for singers to identify; it is the effect you experience when singing in a cathedral. An audience experiences natural reverberation when they hear the direct signal from the singer and then, milliseconds later, they hear multiple reflections as the acoustical waves of the voice bounce off the side walls, floor, and ceiling of the performance hall.

Many performance venues and recording studios are designed to inhibit natural reverb. Without at least a little reverb added to the sound, even the best singer can sound harsh and even amateurish. Early reverb units transmitted the audio signal through a metal spring, which added supplementary vibrations to the signal. While some engineers still use spring reverb to obtain a specific effect, most now use digital units. Common settings on digital reverb units include wet/dry, bright/dark, and options for delay time. The wet/dry control adjusts the amount of direct signal (dry) and the amount of reverberated signal (wet). The bright/dark control helps simulate the effects of various surfaces within a natural space. For instance, harder surfaces such as stone reflect high frequencies and create a brighter tone quality while softer surfaces such as wood reflect lower frequencies and create a darker tone quality. The delay time, which is usually adjustable from milliseconds to seconds, adjusts the amount of time between when the dry signal and wet signals reach the ear. Engineers can transform almost any room into a chamber music hall or concert stadium simply by adjusting these settings.

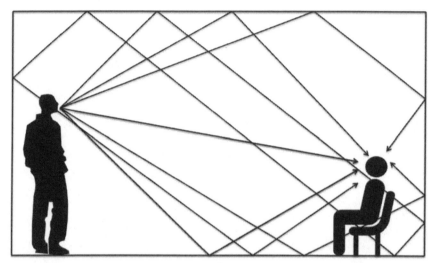

Figure 11.16. This diagram illustrates the multiple lines of reflection that create reverb. *Courtesy of Matthew Edwards*

Delay

Whereas reverb blends multiple wet signals with the dry signal to replicate a natural space, delay purposefully separates a single wet signal from the dry signal to create repetitions of the voice. With delay, you will hear the original note first and then a digitally produced repeat of the note several milliseconds to seconds later. The delayed note may be heard one time or multiple times and the timing of those repeats can be adjusted to match the tempo of the song.

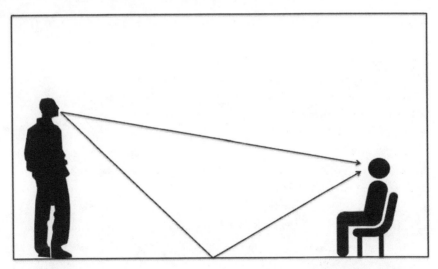

Figure 11.17. This diagram illustrates how a direct line of sound followed by a reflected line of sound creates delay. *Courtesy of Matthew Edwards*

Auto-Tune

Auto-Tune was first used in studios as a useful way to clean up minor imperfections in otherwise perfect performances. Auto-Tune is now an industry standard that many artists use, even if they are not willing to admit it. Auto-Tune has gained a bad reputation in the past few years, and whether or not you agree with its use, it is a reality in today's market. If you do not understand how to use it properly, you could end up sounding like T-Pain.[2]

Both Antares and Melodyne have developed Auto-Tune technology in both "auto" and "graphical" formats. "Auto" Auto-Tune allows the engineer to set specific parameters for pitch correction that are then computer controlled. "Graphical" Auto-Tune tracks the pitch in the selected area of a recording and plots the fundamental frequency on a linear graph. The engineer can then select specific notes for pitch correction. They can also drag selected pitches to a different frequency, add or reduce vibrato, and change formant frequencies above the fundamental. To simplify, the "auto" function makes general corrections while the "graphic" function makes specific corrections. The "auto" setting is usually used to achieve a specific effect (for instance "Believe" by

Cher), while the "graphic" setting is used to correct small imperfections in a recorded performance.

Digital Voice Processors

Digital voice processors are still relatively new to the market and have yet to gain widespread usage among singers. While there are several brands of vocal effects processors available, the industry leader as of this printing is a company called TC-Helicon. TC-Helicon manufactures several different units that span from consumer to professional grade. TC-Helicon's premier performer-controlled unit is called the VoiceLive 3. The VoiceLive 3 incorporates more than twelve vocal effects, eleven guitar effects, and a multi-track looper with 250 factory presets and 250 memory slots for user presets. The VoiceLive 3 puts the effects at the singer's feet in a programmable stomp box that also includes phantom power, MIDI in/out, a USB connection, guitar input, and monitor out. Onboard vocal effects include equalization, compression, reverb, and "auto" Auto-Tune. The unit also offers μMod (an adjustable voice modulator), a doubler (for thickening the lead vocal), echo, delay, reverb, and several other specialized effects.[3] ♪

One of the most impressive features of digital voice processors is the ability to add computer-generated harmonies to the lead vocal. After the user sets the musical key, the processor identifies the fundamental frequency of each sung note. The computer then adds digitized voices at designated intervals above and below the lead singer. The unit also offers the option to program each individual song, with multiple settings for every verse, chorus, and bridge.

THE BASICS OF LIVE SOUND SYSTEMS

Live sound systems come in a variety of sizes from small practice units to state-of-the-art stadium rigs. Most singers only need a basic knowledge of the components commonly found in systems that have one to eight inputs. Units beyond that size usually require an independent sound engineer and are beyond the scope of this chapter.

Following the microphone, the first element in the live signal chain is usually the mixer. Basic portable mixers provide controls for equalization, volume level, auxiliary (usually used for effects such as reverb and compression), and, on some units, controls for built-in digital effects processors. Powered mixers combine an amplifier with a basic mixer, providing a compact solution for those who do not need a complex system. Since unpowered mixers do not provide amplification, you will need to add a separate amplifier to power this system.

The powered mixer or amplifier connects to speaker cabinets, which contain a "woofer" and a "tweeter." The woofer is a large round speaker that handles the bass frequencies while the tweeter is a horn-shaped speaker that handles the treble frequencies. The crossover, a component built into the speaker cabinet, separates high and low frequencies and sends them to the appropriate speaker (woofer or tweeter). Speaker cabinets can be either active or passive. Passive cabinets require a powered mixer or an amplifier in order to operate. Active cabinets have an amplifier built-in and do not require an external amplifier.

If you do not already own a microphone and amplification system, you can purchase a simple setup at relatively low cost through online vendors such as Sweetwater.com and MusiciansFriend.com. A dynamic microphone and a powered monitor are enough to get started. If you would like to add a digital voice processor, Digitech and TC-Helicon both sell entry-level models that will significantly improve the tonal quality of a sound system.

Monitors are arguably the most important element in a live sound system. The monitor is a speaker that faces the performers and allows them to hear themselves and/or the other instruments on stage. On-stage volume levels can vary considerably, with drummers often producing sound levels as high as 120 dB. Those volume levels make it nearly impossible for singers to receive natural acoustic feedback while performing. Monitors can improve aural feedback and help reduce the temptation to oversing. Powered monitors offer the same advantages as powered speaker cabinets and can be a great option for amplification when practicing. They are also good to have around as a backup plan in case you arrive at a venue and discover they do not supply monitors. In-ear monitors offer another option for performers and are especially useful for those who frequently move around the stage.

MICROPHONE TECHNIQUE

The microphone is an inseparable part of the contemporary commercial music singer's instrument. Just as there are techniques that improve singing, there are also techniques that will improve microphone use. Understanding what a microphone does is only the first step to using it successfully. Once you understand how a microphone works, you need hands-on experience.

The best way to learn microphone technique is to experiment. Try the following exercises to gain a better understanding of how to use a microphone when singing:

- Hold a dynamic microphone with a cardioid pattern directly in front of your mouth, no farther than one centimeter away. Sustain a comfortable pitch and slowly move the microphone away from your lips. Listen to how the vocal quality changes. When the microphone is close to the lips, you should notice that the sound is louder and has more bass response. As you move the microphone away from your mouth, there will be a noticeable loss in volume and the tone will become brighter.
- Next, sustain a pitch while rotating the handle down. The sound quality will change in a similar fashion as when you moved the microphone away from your lips.
- Now try singing breathy with the microphone close to your lips. How little effort can you get away with while producing a marketable sound?
- Try singing bright vowels and dark vowels and notice how the microphone affects the tone quality.
- Also experiment with adapting your diction to the microphone. Because the microphone amplifies everything, you may need to underpronounce certain consonants when singing. You will especially want to reduce the power of the consonants /t/, /s/, /p/, and /b/.

FINAL THOUGHTS

Since this is primarily an overview, you can greatly improve your comprehension of the material by seeking other resources to deepen your knowledge. There are many great resources available that may help clarify some of these difficult concepts. Most important, you must experiment. The more you play around with sound equipment on your own, the better you will understand it and the more comfortable you will feel when performing or recording with audio technology.

NOTES

1. Paula Lockheart, "A History of Early Microphone Singing, 1925–1939: American Mainstream Popular Singing at the Advent of Electronic Amplification," *Popular Music and Society* 26, no. 3 (2003): 367–385.

2. For example, listen to T-Pain's track "Buy You a Drank (Shawty Snappin')."

3. "VoiceLive 3," TC-Helicon, www.tc-helicon.com/products/voicelive-3/, accessed May 2, 2016.

12

ADVOCACY FOR WOMEN COMPOSERS

Erin Guinup

Female lyricist Rachel Crothers (1878–1958) gave a speech in 1912 that posed the question: "Drama is drama. What difference does it make whether women or men are working on it?"[1] More than one hundred years ago, she raised the question as to whether art suffers when women are not contributing. She followed that statement with, "If you want to see the sign of the times . . . watch women. Their evolution is the most important thing in modern life." She recognized that gender inequality would make an impact on future generations and society as a whole.

Gender inequality in music—as well as racial inequality—persists in modern times, and it begs the following questions: Why does inequality matter, and what can we do to change it? Why does it matter to embrace the music of women and other marginalized groups? What is the remedy to improve gender parity and what can we do as singers, directors, audiences, and music lovers to expand the variety of repertoire heard?

IS MUSIC BY WOMEN NOT BEING PERFORMED?

Anecdotally, we all know that compositions by women are not performed as frequently as works by male composers, but how significant is this imbalance? Are women not as talented, are they not writing, or is there a deeper reason? Why aren't the concerts we attend balanced, with men and women equally represented on programs? As mentioned in chapter 2, a study by the Baltimore Symphony Orchestra during the 2014–2015 season found that only 1.8 percent of works programmed by twenty-two major orchestras were written by women. When looking at works from living composers, women still only account for 14.3 percent.[2]

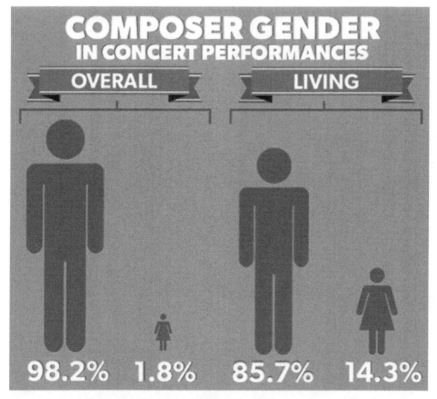

Figure 12.1. Composer Gender Disparity, Baltimore Symphony Orchestra Study (infographic by Rachel Upton and Ricky O'Bannon).

The Count, a study by the Lilly Awards and Dramatists Guild of America tracking gender equity in American theater productions, found similar numbers. Inspired by a 2001 study by the New York State Council of the Arts (NYSCA) that found just 17 percent of writers on shows written in the past fifty years were female, the 2015 study of the Count showed a slight uptick to 22 percent, and those women were primarily lyricists, bookwriters, and playwrights.[3] Julia Jordan (b. ca. 1969), lead researcher for the Count, points out that female music theater composers are a very small minority of those produced and those productions are almost exclusively in New York.[4] Tony-nominated lyricists Lisa Kron (b. 1961) and Madeleine George (b. ca. 1972) write, "Without numbers [statistics], there are only whining playwrights and their personal feelings. And the fact is, every single playwright has at some point believed that they wrote a better play than someone else who got produced. . . . Unless we believe that white men are inherently better playwrights than everyone else, we have to accept that the numbers are the result of an implicit, systemic bias on the part of producing organizations."[5]

As discussed in chapter 2, the 2018 Grammy Awards recognized just one female artist in the major award categories and sparked the hashtag #GrammysSoMale, causing Recording Academy president Neil Portnow (b. 1948) to respond, "Women need to step it up," to which women responded with exasperation that they could not break through and be heard.[6] Is the problem, as the Grammy president suggested, that women are not "stepping up"? This doesn't seem to be true. There isn't a problem with women lacking training, as 62 percent of American bachelor's degrees in the arts and humanities are awarded to women. Nor is there an issue with women pursuing careers in stage writing, as 43 percent of the members of the Dramatists Guild of America are women.[7] Marsha Norman (b. 1947) ponders this question when she writes the following:

The list of top American novelists, poets, and short story writers is easily half women and reflects all races and creeds. The only American to win the Nobel Prize in Literature in the past fifty years was a woman, the great Toni Morrison. The richest writer in the world is a woman, J.K. Rowling, and the longest-running play in England was written by a woman, Agatha Christie. The problem is not that women can't write. And it's not the audiences, either—they like plays by women. . . . Broadway plays written by women earn on average 18 percent more than those written by men, even controlled for the type of play, size of theatre, and corrected for whopping successes like *Wicked*, whose book was written by a woman, the great Winnie Holzman.[8]

The Count points out that 20 percent seems to be the accepted threshold for inclusion of women in most arts except orchestras, which have achieved gender parity due to blind auditions. Their report offers this conclusion on why women are not more represented: "Why are we missing the voices of women in the theatre? There is one simple answer: artistic directors and producers choose not to present their [work]."[9] Jordan adds, "The idea that women aren't writing is dead wrong. They just aren't getting through the pipeline to be produced."[10] Composer Elizabeth Swados (1951–2016) wrote the following:

> With regard to composing, I think one reason why it lags so far behind other fields in its opportunities for women is that it is essentially a behind-the-scenes endeavor. From a historical point of view, we know that Clara Schumann used her husband's name to get her works performed. Fanny Mendelssohn published under the name of her brother Felix. The nineteenth-century audience was unwilling to accept the notion of a woman's musical intellect. Modern audiences may be ready for a woman's music, but certainly the male-dominated inner sanctum of conductors, musical directors, and producers is not. Musical politics, by its nature, is not something that people see. It happens off-camera. And because of that, there is no pressure for men to behave in a "liberated" fashion for appearance's sake. . . . When an activity is not visible, such change is bound to happen more slowly.[11]

While artistic directors today are likely not intentionally excluding female composers, an unconscious bias often occurs due to a tendency to program works one already knows or is connected to in some way. Historically, white male composers have been far better known than their marginalized contemporaries, and their work has more frequently been curated and canonized for broad audiences. Artistic directors must exercise awareness and conscious decision making to feature those creators who are worthy of, but often denied, inclusion on programs. If we hope to attain true inclusion, it is imperative that we toss out the assumption that women, people of color, and other marginalized artists do not see their work performed simply because they do not exist.

WHY DOES GENDER PARITY MATTER?

Why does singing music by women matter? There are many reasons, but one is simply that we miss out on a vast horizon of perspectives if we solely perform music by dead white men. Just as travel expands one's view of the world, songs from a variety of viewpoints lead us to a broader range of experiences that can allow us to understand ourselves more completely and to see new possibilities and potential. Music theater composer Georgia Stitt (b. 1972) responded to Rachel Crothers's quotation above with the following:

The point is that women make up about half of the world's population, and to have a culture of theater that does not represent the voices of those women is to overlook the stories that they alone can tell and the perspectives through which they see the world. Saying "drama is drama" is like saying "people are people." We say it, but it doesn't actually mean anything. People are these completely individual, unique creatures who are defined by where we live, how we live, what we know and what we believe. We look for similarities among people but we also revel in our differences. Drama springs forth in unique ways from unique people. It reflects the point of view of its author, and those authors come from vastly different places, cultures, religions, races and, yes, genders. Our stories are not the same because we are not the same; we are different, and our work is us.

That's all very idealistic, though. The practicality of the situation is that even if the women are telling the stories, they are not being produced nearly as often. The *New York Times* in 2009 suggested that women are not writing as many plays as their male counterpoints. That's probably true. We're not conducting as many orchestras, either, or holding as many political offices because we're catching up. My ninety-year-old grandmother told me that as a young woman in the 1930s she thought that she might like to be a Presbyterian minister, but she was told that that was not an appropriate job for a woman. My mother, twenty-five years later, told her father that she wanted to be a doctor. He said, "You mean a nurse. Doctors are men." It was only my generation, the children of the 1960s and 1970s, that started to offer up female role models in greater supply. Of course there have been female writers and composers since the beginning of time. It's not that they didn't exist. But you can't argue that they were mainstream.

Finally, an anecdote. I had a student in a musical theater class at USC (where I taught in the 2012–2013 academic year). I gave her a song to learn and she was struggling with it. She said, "I usually just play the prostitute or the girlfriend or the maid—unless I'm in the chorus, where I'm tap dancing in a bikini." If we want our daughters to have female role models, first we have to be them, and then we have to write them.[12]

By recognizing women who have composed in the past, we send a clear signal that the voices of women are valued, even if they were not celebrated in their time. While women's contributions in the past may have been ignored, it is unethical to continue with the false narrative that women cannot write at the same level as men. By failing to include their voices in the classes we teach and the programs we perform, we continue to reinforce the wrongs of the past and risk repeating history and silencing voices again.

WHAT IS THE REMEDY, AND WHAT CAN I DO ABOUT IT?

We all bear responsibility for restoring the legacies of those who have been forgotten and improving prospects for the composers of tomorrow. While decision makers of large organizations can have great influence, our power as singers, listeners, and teachers should not be diminished. Change happens not with one person or action but with the cumulative actions of many. We can all take small but impactful steps to rebalance the scales of gender parity and create a more diverse future of music. Here are ten ways you might consider applying to advocate and raise awareness for women composers.

Seek Out Their Work and Sing Their Songs

This simple step should come first and foremost. We have to look for music by women and include it on our programs. When we can't find our car keys, we don't assume they don't exist; we keep looking until we find them. The same is true of finding music written by women that covers a wide range of themes and styles. If you look beyond the first page of a Google search, you will find treasures that are waiting to be discovered. Rob Deemer (b. 1970), founder of the Composer Diversity Database, said, "It's not that this music is not good; it's just that it's not known. Choosing music by women is such an easy thing but has vast ramifications versus the many monumental challenges in the world. Simply choosing a song can create a huge footprint and ripple that reflects the changes we want to see in the world."[13] There are thousands of songs by women available if we take a little effort to find them. The Composer Diversity Database is a great place to start, with more than 3,700 searchable composers at the time of this writing. Additional ways to discover music by women include talking with other performers and composers, networking, online message boards, YouTube or Spotify playlists, and composer websites.[14] ♪

Attend Performances of Works by Women Composers

If we say we want music by women, we need to go when it is programmed. Pay attention to groups and artists that are performing work by women and support those concerts with your wallet. The law of supply and demand dictates that more work will be performed if performances are profitable and popular. Support the inclusion of women on programs with your attendance and take time to thank or recognize organizations for programming works by women.

Call Out Organizations That Fail to Include Women in Their Programming

If you notice that your favorite theater, symphony, or recitalist has programmed an all-white-male season, consider contacting their management and tell them that you hope they will do a better job in the future. Lyricist Marsha Norman writes, "We all have to be on 'team mode.' This means going to see plays by women, telling artistic directors that you want to see more plays by women, saying 'I'll be on your board but only if . . .' We really have to get in a demand situation and we have to do it ourselves."[15]

Create Opportunities for Female Composers to Be Seen and Heard

This may be as simple as including songs by women on a recital, writing program notes that inform and highlight their work, including music by women and people of color in music history survey classes, and using listening examples by women for music theory classes. One voice teacher recently posted online that she planned to have every student in her studio sing at least one song by a female composer this year. A choral teacher recently ordered a set of posters featuring female composers and composers of color for her classroom. Visibility equals normalcy, and it sends the message that the glass ceilings of the past are no longer impenetrable. ♪

Include Others in Decision Making

Consider including students and members of ensembles you work with in discovering and selecting repertoire. By setting parameters and fostering individual ownership versus top-down decision making, we can solidify our objectives and increase engagement in the messages conveyed as an ensemble. Composer Kieren MacMillan (b. 1969) said, "Based on my experience, asking every member to recommend pieces by female-identifying composers of color, and then programming from that selection, will have a very different impact and effect than having only those 'at the top' program pieces by female-identifying composers of color—even if exactly the same pieces ultimately get programmed. The more it's in the DNA of *everyone* in the organization, the easier it is to achieve parity in the future."[16]

Be Intentional in Your Listening Habits

Choose to include women in your recreational listening. There are many Spotify and YouTube playlists focused on female composers, and it is easy to curate your own from your discoveries. When I write or read, I tend to listen to film scores, so I created a YouTube playlist of female film composers, which I played while writing this chapter. With the vast array of listening technology available to us, music by women is more easily accessible than ever, and it is our collective responsibility to avail ourselves of this opportunity. An intentional search for women composers does not take long, but it will yield fascinating and transformative results. ♪

Connect with Living Women Composers

Consider notifying living composers when you perform their work by sending a message through their website or social media, especially if they are not well known. An acknowledgment that their work is appreciated can be encouraging and may lead to further dialogue that can enhance your experience of performing their songs. These contacts also sometimes offer opportunities for cross-promotion of performances. Schools might even consider seeking out workshops or event panels with female composers.

Legally Buy Their Music and Commission New Works

A composer will struggle to create new works if she can't pay her bills. Encourage students and colleagues to legally purchase sheet music and recordings. Also consider commissioning new work from composers when resources allow. As teachers, we set the precedent that supporting living composers enhances both our own growth as singers and the development of representation in the art form. Eileen Strempel (b. 1967) writes, "With the memorable illustration of a performance, teachers can inspire others to discover the unique thrill of a premiere of a work especially composed for their voice and personality."[17] Increasingly, scores by women past and present are more widely available online. Resources for finding such works include websites such as New Musical Theatre, Foundry Music's library of sheet music by women composers, and composer websites. ♪

Educate and Raise Awareness

Talking about gender inequity helps us overcome our unconscious biases and normalizes expectations of equity. Include opportunities for audiences to discuss these issues in postperformance dialogues or for students to explore these issues in vocal repertoire classes. Challenge audiences and students to take action and offer tiny steps they can easily enact to do their part in improving equity.

Go Beyond Gender Diversity

To achieve a true representation of the human experience in music and theater, we cannot focus on gender diversity as the sole prominent issue. As historical power structures have sought to erase the accomplishments of women, they have often to an even greater degree excluded work by people (and especially women) of color, LGBTQ+ creators, people with disabilities, and countless others who now find themselves shamefully underrepresented. If the goal of art is to reflect and shape life, we must pursue an artistic future that represents as many stories and perspectives as possible. Similarly, if we care about performing work by women, we must extend that support to all who encounter the same struggle against exclusive artistic and societal power structures.

HOW ARE OTHERS ADVOCATING?

The suggestions above are easy steps by which to do our part in evening out the imbalance that has historically hampered female composers. In the past decade, a new surge of feminism, called the "fourth wave of feminism"[18] by author Kira Cochrane (b. 1977) and marked by the Me Too era, has launched countless initiatives aimed at addressing gender parity. The following are examples of efforts that may inspire you to action.

Opera composer Missy Mazzoli (b. 1980) is working to inspire young women to compose through the Luna Composition Lab. The project includes one-on-one mentoring and lessons with an established female composer, networking, performances, and recording opportunities. "There's so much work to do," Mazzoli said. "But also it's really easy to program women: you just do it. There's no longer any excuse for not doing it. A lot of orchestras will say, 'Our programming focuses on works that are from the eighteenth and nineteenth century, when, like it or not, women were not encouraged to compose.' My question then is, that's fine: what are you doing to make sure that doesn't happen in the twenty-first century? And our response to that is Luna Lab. We're going to make sure that the next generation, hopefully, does not have the same kind of problem."[19]

Brian Lauritzen (b. ca. 1982) recognized that he had a megaphone as a classical radio disc jockey for KUSC in Los Angeles and has used his position and privilege as a white male to call attention to organizations that fail to program women and composers of color. His efforts have gained national attention as he has raised awareness and encouraged orchestras and choirs to be more diverse in their programming. He says that people are hungry to listen to music they have not heard before and that listeners miss out on music that is beautiful and interesting when broadcasters and conductors fail to discover and program music beyond the well-known classics. "You think you are learning the history of music, but in reality you are only learning part of the history of classical music if you don't go beyond the classical canon into lesser-known works."[20]

Simply raising awareness of the problem makes a difference. A prominent lyricist and composer took results of the Count directly to the decision makers at theaters, talked to them about why gender parity matters, and challenged them to be part of the solution. The Count and the conversations associated with it have been credited with a significant rise in female writers involved with productions in recent years. Women have risen from just 20 percent in 2015 to more than 30 percent in New York City in 2018.[21]

In addition to creating the Count, the Lilly Awards honor the work of women in American theater and strengthen connections within the community. The people behind this event recognized that awards equal attention and attention opens doors. Disney's *Frozen* (2013) composer Kristen Anderson-Lopez (b. 1972) said, "It really is my favorite award because it's a coming together of the sisterhood of women doing their best to make a living and have a voice in a profession where the odds are still stacked against us."[22] The Lillys also award grants, commissions, and paid apprenticeships to midcareer and emerging artists in all disciplines; advocate for resources to help music theater composers create and advance their work, including family writing residencies and child care support to overcome the barriers women face in their child-bearing years; and made strong statements about sexual harassment.

The Kronos Quartet launched an initiative called Fifty for the Future: The Kronos Learning Repertoire. This project consists of commissioning a library of fifty works, with half being written by women, "designed to guide young amateur and early-career professional string quartets in developing and honing the skills required for the performance of twenty-first-century repertoire." The inclusion of a diverse and balanced group of composers sends a subtly powerful message to young musicians that they can create the music of the future. Wouldn't it be wonderful to have a similar library of art songs or music theater selections for young musicians?

Composer Georgia Stitt founded MAESTRA in 2016 after two encounters with young composers who sought advice from her because they didn't know any other female composers. Stitt determined that female composers needed a networking community and organized an initial gathering of twenty-four female music theater composers. There are now nearly one hundred women in this group and an additional list of 330 women in a Facebook group for music directors called Maestra MDs. The group offers a sense of community and visibility, as well as opportunities for advancement. Stitt writes, "We named ourselves MAESTRA because any time I type 'maestra' into my computer, it autocorrects to 'maestro.' Even technology seems to have been programmed to assume that women do not conduct or take musical leadership."

Stitt recounted that a turning point for her occurred around that same time during the 2016 revival of *Sweet Charity*. The director had asked for an all-female band and they really struggled to find a guitarist. Everyone they asked kept referring them to one player who was not available. "It can't be that there's only one player in all of New York." Orchestrator Mary-Mitchell Campbell (b. ca. 1972) said it was challenging "because a lot of times you go for the easy answers and those are typically male. Just because they are the people who do it all the time."[23] They recognized that we have to be working together to help each other be seen.

Stitt says she was deeply influenced by the book *Listening Out Loud* (1988) by Elizabeth Swados (1951–2016), in which the author writes: "If you become known as a 'women's composer,' you'll be met by the prejudice that makes people feel you don't have what it takes to write for most 'professional' situations. At the same time, don't abandon your fellow females, as women are apt to do in the theater, for instance, the moment they get a nod from a male producer or theater owner. Should you find yourself in a position of power, use it to secure work for other women. This is the way to make and solidify changes."[24]

Helping lift up other women seems to be key. Hollywood's Plus One initiative encourages women to bring another woman when invited to a career-advancing opportunity. A number of theaters are reaching out to women and celebrating their work, including Firebrand Theatre in Chicago and the Raise Your Voice program from Seattle's 5th Avenue Theatre. Stitt said, "There's just something about the more women there are in the business, the more you see the other women. Once you get to the female musicians, they know other female musicians."[25]

The National Association of Teachers of Singing (NATS) has created an advocacy committee—and books like this volume—to raise awareness. Past president Linda J. Snyder (b. 1948) writes, "Setting repertoire goals for ourselves and for our students, to include diversity of gender and ethnicity in composers represented in classes and recital, is vital to our mission of excellence in teaching."[26] Committee chair Loraine Sims (b. 1956) adds, "We want to encourage teachers to make it a personal goal to use this repertoire in competition and programming recitals for our students and ourselves."[27]

The Women Composers Festival of Hartford provides an educational and entertainment platform for the promotion of and discovery of music by women. Artistic director Penny Brandt (b. 1978) said, "It's possible to include a woman in every music history class in every genre if you do the research." Started twenty years ago with an emphasis on both historical and living female composers, festival organizers hope to change the narrative to include women who were not recognized in their lifetimes but would have been if not for biases that excluded them.

Several of the people I interviewed noted the importance of not relegating women and composers of color to a single event in the season and inadvertently creating an isolating effect that detracts from these creators' visibility as legitimate contributors to the art. Brandt acknowledged this as a fair criticism and said, "We are focusing on women because they haven't been part of the conversation for so long. They deserve to be the center of attention for a time."[28] To reconcile these two ideas, perhaps the solution is to highlight underrepresented composers as often as possible, but also to include them in programs throughout the season to ensure that diversity in programming is normalized for future generations.

INTERSECTIONALITY IN ARTISTIC REPRESENTATION

It is important to emphasize that advocacy cannot end with heterosexual, cisgender white women. One of the important discoveries of the Count was how much of the disparity between men and women is due to women of color not being represented. Jordan noted that women of color are vastly underrepresented and that improving visibility of composers of color will boost the representation of women as a whole. Composer Elizabeth A. Baker (b. 1988) writes, "As a black woman who composes and performs, I am faced with hard barriers to pursue a career in a field that I love, a field that has saved my life in difficult times, a field that has given my life meaning and purpose, space and tones that

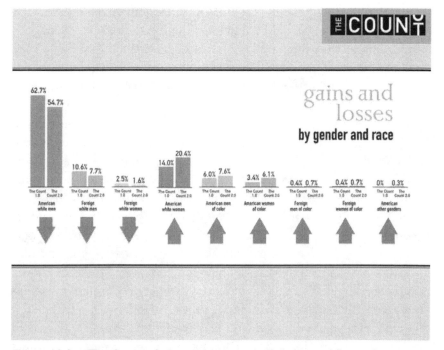

Figure 12.2.   The Count: Gains and Losses by Gender and Race. *Courtesy of Julia Jordan and the Lilly Awards*

have been my blanket as I cried myself to sleep wishing that I could wake up and be a pretty white girl with all the promise and possibilities in the world in front of her."[29] Iranian composer Niloufar Nourbakhsh (b. 1992) adds that "the power structure within classical music not only did not reach out to these communities, but made it even more difficult for them to participate. The absence of the unprivileged is a loss for the classical music scene as a whole. The inclusion of these voices will not only give pathway to stories that previously didn't have a chance to shine, but it will also give capital to the classical music scene by including communities of the unprivileged; thus, we hope to find ourselves in a growing prosperous classical music scene that is colorful and powerful in the stories that it can share with the world through music."[30] A world in which true gender parity in creative fields is the norm cannot exist without the same equality being normalized for all underrepresented communities. As we build the future of music together, we have an opportunity to ensure that composers like Baker and Nourbakhsh see themselves represented artistically from a young age and, in doing so, experience consistent affirmation of their intrinsic worth as creators and storytellers.

ADVOCACY FOR WOMEN: THE BIG PICTURE

Singing music by women allows us as singers to participate in the broader conversation about women, their contributions in the world, and the issues they care about. Historically, music has played a key role in social and political movements, and the perspective of women can offer insights on how we can address social issues and work toward solutions. Stitt writes, "In order to build a vibrant community of artists and citizens, I believe you have to be an active participant. Build roots in the communities you want to support and the organizations you want to see thrive. Give time, give money, give mentorship, give visibility . . . but you must give. As an artist, as a citizen, as a human . . . it's what we are here to do."[31]

Laura Hynes (b. 1977) is a soprano who has combined her gifts to create a musical performance in support of Sexual Assault Awareness Month called *Raise Your Voice* (2013). Using songs by women including

Germaine Taillefaire (1892–1982)—one of the composers of Les Six who was herself a survivor of domestic abuse—Libby Larsen (b. 1950), and Marya Hart (b. 1957), she created a dramatic work incorporating poetry, letters, instrumentalists, and a dancer that profoundly impacted audiences and herself. Hynes shares: "Prior to this recital, I had been feeling less drawn to the opera business, having left a rigorous performing career in Europe in part due to my disappointment with its inherent misogyny and what I often felt was a myopic view of creativity. The positive response to *Raise Your Voice* changed me forever. A young woman said to me afterwards, 'I felt like you told my story.'"[32]

Composer Jenny Giering (b. ca. 1970) has written compelling musicals and art songs that often focus on how we redefine ourselves after loss, with topics including the aftermath of 9/11, children growing up, and being misunderstood and unaccepted by society.[33] However, when she was diagnosed with breast cancer in 2014 and permanently debilitated by complications, she thought her career was over and wrote a letter to Senator Elizabeth Warren (b. 1949) that has become a powerful piece of advocacy for health care. Her most recent work, *What We Leave Behind* (2018), is a compelling autobiographical one-woman musical that declares that "the ill cannot be reduced to their illness" and "that life can still be alive with wonder and hope, provided we are brave enough to embrace it."[34] Her career and her songs are a powerful testament that art can be healing and transformative and have an impact on the dialogue surrounding health issues. ♪

Kristo Kondakçi (b. ca. 1991) is the founder of the Sheltering Voices project with Eureka Ensemble. This choir made up of homeless women from the Boston area has garnered national media attention and been "transformational for everyone involved."[35] Commissioning a new work from composer Stephanie Ann Boyd (b. 1990) and poet and women's rights advocate Jessica Lynn Suchon (b. ca. 1991) strengthened the message and allowed the women in the choir to "see themselves in the story and take their story upon them as they memorized their parts over the two and a half month process." Kondakçi adds, "Musicians by nature are social innovators and powerful for offering commentary and working that message with other people." This beautiful blend of incorporating women composers for a project for women has brought a depth to the experience for these women and to those who witnessed their performance. ♪

FINAL THOUGHTS

In the past decade, momentum has gathered for addressing inequity in all segments of our society. Especially in light of the Me Too movement, the time is ripe to redress many of the issues that have perpetuated centuries of hurdles for women and other marginalized artists to create and contribute their voices through their music.

So many of the women covered in this book had exceptional talent and promising starts to their careers. However, many of them had to give up their passions because they couldn't find support, and many were not credited as they should have been. The success stories happened largely because others, especially other women, supported them and recognized their talents.

As performers, decision makers, composers, and audience members, we all have a responsibility to improve awareness of music that has been suppressed for far too long. There remains a lot of conscious and unconscious fighting to keep women down in the creative industries, and if we hope to succeed, we must do everything possible to build each other up. Those who don't understand the past are doomed to repeat it. What a wonderful opportunity we have, then, to halt that repetition by beginning to write the future.

NOTES

1. Barbara Sicherman, *Notable American Women: A Biographical Dictionary, Volume 4: The Modern Period*, ed. Carol Hurd Green (Cambridge, MA: Belknap Press, 1986), 175.

2. Ricky O'Bannon, "By the Numbers: Female Composers," www.bsomusic .org/stories/by-the-numbers-female-composers/, accessed September 1, 2018.

3. Susan Jonas and Suzanne Bennett, "Report on the Status of Women: A Limited Engagement?" New York State Council on the Arts Report, January 2002; Marsha Norman, *Why the Count Matters*, Lilly Awards and the Dramatists Guild of America, www.thelillyawards.org/media/2016/06/The-Count-by -The-Lilly-Awards-Dramatists-Guild.pdf, accessed September 1, 2018.

4. Personal correspondence with Julia Jordan, September 5, 2018.

5. Lisa Kron and Madeleine George, "Why Parity?" *Why the Count Matters*, Lilly Awards and the Dramatists Guild of America, www.thelillyawards.org/

media/2016/06/The-Count-by-The-Lilly-Awards-Dramatists-Guild.pdf, accessed September 1, 2018.

6. Michelle Amabile Angermiller, "Grammys So Male? 'Women Need to Step Up,' Says Recording Academy President," *Variety*, January 28, 2018.

7. Statistic according to the Count. Norman, *Why the Count Matters*.

8. Marsha Norman, "Not There Yet. What Will It Take to Achieve Equality for Women in Theatre?" *American Theater Magazine*, November 2009.

9. Norman, *Why the Count Matters*.

10. Personal correspondence with Julia Jordan, August 22, 2018.

11. Elizabeth Swados, *Listening Out Loud: Becoming a Composer* (New York: Harper, 1988), 180.

12. Georgia Stitt, "Drama Is Drama: Women's Voices in Theater," newmusicaltheatre.com/blogs/green-room/drama-is-drama-women-s-voices-in-theater, accessed October 11, 2013.

13. Personal correspondence with Rob Deemer, August 22, 2018.

14. Additional resources for finding music by women can be found in the appendix of this book.

15. Norman, *Why the Count Matters*.

16. Personal correspondence with Kieren MacMillan, September 4, 2018.

17. Eileen Strempel, "The Women Composer Question in the Twenty-First Century," *Journal of Singing* 65, no. 2 (November/December 2008): 171.

18. Kira Cochrane, *All the Rebel Women: The Rise of the Fourth Wave of Feminism* (London: Guardian Books, 2014).

19. Brian Lauritzen, "Composers: The Future Is Female," brianlauritzen.com/2017/10/24/composers-the-future-is-female/, October 24, 2017.

20. Personal correspondence with Brian Lauritzen, August 8, 2018.

21. Personal correspondence with Julia Jordan, August 22, 2018.

22. www.thelillyawards.org/about-the-lilly-awards/, accessed September 1, 2018.

23. Bethany Rickwald, "An All-Female Band Lets *Sweet Charity* Grab Destiny by the Bass," www.theatermania.com/off-broadway/news/georgia-stitt-mary-mitchell-campbell-interview_79204.html, November 27, 2016.

24. Swados, *Listening Out Loud*, 184.

25. Personal correspondence with Georgia Stitt, July 30, 2018.

26. Personal correspondence with Linda Snyder, August 24, 2018.

27. Personal correspondence with Loraine Sims, September 5, 2018.

28. Personal correspondence with Penny Brandt, August 27, 2018.

29. Elizabeth A. Baker, "Ain't I a Woman Too," nmbx.newmusicusa.org/aint-i-a-woman-too/, August 8, 2018.

30. Personal correspondence with Niloufar Nourbakhsh, September 8, 2018.

31. georgiastitt.com/activism/, accessed September 1, 2018.

32. Personal correspondence with Laura Hynes, August 23, 2018.

33. *The Mistress Cycle*, a musical about mistresses from around the world, was the winner of the 1996 NATS Art Song Composition Competition. The book and lyrics are by Beth Blatt (b. 1957).

34. www.jennygiering.com/what-we-leave-behind/, accessed September 1, 2018.

35. Personal correspondence with Kristo Kondakçi, August 13, 2018.

13

MUSIC BY WOMEN

The Future

The future of women in music shows promise in the emergence of new opportunities, the increasing acceptance of gender diversity, and the budding talent of young female composers. Although the environment is improving, it is still necessary to take a proactive approach. In the words of Pauline Oliveros (1932–2016): "If a performer is playing a program, they need to play music by women as well as by men. And if an audience goes to a concert and there's no music by women, they have to confront the management about it. If that doesn't happen, the change is not going to take place."[1]

NEW OPPORTUNITIES: WOMEN'S MUSIC FESTIVALS

Music by women continues to be underrepresented on concert programs, and people are starting to notice. As mentioned previously in chapters 2 and 12, the Baltimore Symphony Orchestra completed a survey of twenty-one American orchestras that revealed that works by women composers made up only 1.8 percent of the 2014–2015 concert season.[2] Prominent female conductor and Baltimore Symphony Orchestra music director Marin Alsop (b. 1956) commented: "I thought it was

changing, and then it didn't change."[3] In June 2018, NPR reported that
the Philadelphia Orchestra had no works by women programmed for
its 2018–2019 season; but by August, public outcry led the orchestra to
announce it was adding compositions by two women: Stacey Brown (b.
1976) and Anna Clyne (b. 1980).[4]

Because symphonies and concert halls weren't programming music
by women, some decided to make their own performance opportunities. The twentieth-first century has seen a proliferation of music festivals spotlighting female composers.[5] Many of these festivals have been
scheduled in the month of March to recognize Women's History Month.
Congress originally designated Women's History Week as March 7–14
in 1982, but in 1987 it was expanded to Women's History Month.
Typically taking place in late March, the Women Composers Festival
of Hartford began in 2001; it has had an annual call for score submissions for women, applications for performers of music by women, and
applications for the festival's Women Composers Forum. From 2005 to
2014, pianist Sylvie Beaudette (b. 1965) served as artistic director for
the Women in Music Festival at the Eastman School of Music, which
was also held in March in honor of Women's History Month. Assistant
professor of chamber music and accompanying, Beaudette shared her
thoughts on the development of the festival:

> During the ten years of the Women in Music Festival, I have witnessed a
> major shift, from trying to recruit five short noontime concerts to having
> waiting lists for twice the number of performances in a week; from speak-
> ing far and wide about the importance of featuring women composers in
> concert programs to students contacting me to ask if they could perform
> a piece. Engaging music that is well written . . . is what musicians crave
> and are enthusiastic about. They want to share good music, regardless of
> the composer's gender.[6]

Although the festival no longer exists, Beaudette still is an advocate
for female composers. In 2017 she collaborated with the Susan B. Anthony Center for Women's Leadership on Women's Voices, a concert
celebrating the women's suffrage movement and the centennial of
women gaining the right to vote in New York State.

Associate professor of music and department chair at the Mississippi
University for Women, pianist Julia Mortyakova (b. 1982) describes

Figure 13.1. Julia Mortyakova (center) with Coauthors Matthew Hoch and Linda Lister at the 2018 Music by Women Festival. *Courtesy of the authors*

what led her to create the Music by Women Festival, which was launched in March 2017. ♪

> Since Mississippi University for Women was the first public higher educa-
> tion for women in the country, I thought it would be the perfect setting
> for a festival highlighting the works by women. The idea of the festival
> was first proposed by me during my interview at MUW in spring 2012. I
> was very happy for the project to come to fruition after I received official
> institutional support in the fall of 2016.[7]

In the spirit of Lilith Fair, there are also new music festivals for women in CCM genres. The historic Women's March—held on January 21, 2017, across the country—inspired Lani Ramos (b. 1969) to create the Rock and Rogue Women's Music and Food Festival in New Orleans. Ramos, leader of the band Big Pearl and the Fugitives of Funk, started the festival that June. Besides traditional main stage performances of

"Women Who Rock," the 2018 festival included a variety of features: women's empowerment panel discussions, food stands featuring female chefs, and a "Tomboy Tent" for girls ages eight to fifteen. The tent had a stage for bands led by young girls and STEAM workshops led by Electric Girls.[8] Music festivals for women are doing more than just providing opportunities to hear and perform the work of female composers; they are also empowering women of all ages to find and follow their true calling. ♪

FEMININE ENDINGS

While second-wave feminism gained a voice in the 1960s, it wasn't until the 1990s that feminist music criticism gained notoriety. In 1991, musicologist Susan McClary (b. 1946) published *Feminine Endings: Music, Gender, and Sexuality,* and reaction was strong.[9] She drew a lot of attention for likening the first movement of *Symphony No. 9* (1824) by Ludwig van Beethoven (1770–1827) to "the throttling murderous rage of a rapist incapable of attaining release."[10] The title of McClary's book refers to a long-standing term used to describe "weak" cadences as "feminine," whereas a "strong" cadence was labeled "masculine." Addressing this misogynistic projection onto analysis of harmonic progressions, she wrote that music by women was demeaned by the patriarchal tradition and "condemned as pretty yet trivial."[11] Twenty years later, McClary shared that other than one rave in *The Village Voice,* the book received "not only negative reviews, but outraged, vitriolic reactions— and more than a few death threats."[12]

McClary's scholarship was part of the "new musicology" movement that emerged during the late 1980s, and *Feminine Endings* is regarded as one of new musicology's earliest and most important works. In addition to feminism, new musicology examined music from a variety of cultural perspectives, including gender studies, queer theory, and racial considerations, among others. The term itself is a double-edged sword: "new musicology" has a positive or negative connotation depending on whether the scholar who uses it is conservative or progressive. While championed by some, traditional musicologists were skeptical and viewed these critical studies as less legitimate (at best) or outrageous (at worst). Needless to say, the new musicology movement was quite

Figure 13.2. Susan McClary (photo by Mike Sands). *Creative Commons (CC BY-SA 2.0)*

controversial when first introduced. The discipline has advanced considerably over the past thirty years.

In 1993, composer Rhian Samuel (b. 1944) wrote: "The music of women composers, then, need not be divisive and alienating. May it pave the way for feminist criticism."[13] Two years later, she—along with Julie Anne Sadie (b. 1948)—released *The Norton/Grove Dictionary of Women Composers*, the first concise reference work of its kind.[14] Also in 1993, feminist musicologist Marcia Citron (b. 1945) published *Gender and the Musical Canon*, another groundbreaking piece of scholarship that challenged long-held notions about the museum-like nature of the Western musical canon.[15] Examining the social context and politics surrounding the musical works that were canonized and preserved shined a spotlight on the male dominance of European musical culture over the course of the previous centuries.

Since 2000, feminist musicology has continued to thrive. While research in the 1980s concentrated primarily on the musical accomplishments of white women, more recent work explores women in music from diverse ethnic and racial backgrounds. In 2000, Pirkko Moisala (1953) and Beverley Diamond (b. 1948) published *Music and Gender*, which reflected their experiences working with women musicians in Africa, Europe, the Middle East, and North America.[16] Naomi André (b. ca. 1971) has advocated for an intersectional approach to feminist musicology, particularly focusing on black representation in opera.[17] Queer musicology has also exploded; *Songs in Black and Lavender: Race, Sexual Politics, and Women's Music* (2010) by Eileen M. Hayes (b. ca. 1960) is considered to be a pivotal work.[18] And as musicology—and ethnomusicology—continues to expand its boundaries to encompass nonclassical genres such as jazz, country, and hip-hop, gender studies related to these musical art forms are emerging as well.[19]

DIVERSITY AND ACCEPTANCE

While they have helped shed light on female composers of past centuries, books such as *Sounds and Sweet Airs: The Forgotten Women of Classical Music* by Anna Beer (b. 1964) focus on the work of white female composers.[20] Fanny Hensel (1805–1847) and Clara Schumann

(1819–1896) typify the Caucasian Victorian depiction of the female composer. But in the twenty-first century, women composers are emerging from diverse backgrounds and experiences. And some are forming organizations to bring awareness of this diversity and to support their fellow female composers.

Korean-born Jin Hee Han (b. ca. 1980) founded the Asian Women Composers' Association of New York City in 2015 to serve young Asian female composers in the city. And in 2017, Niloufar Nourbakhsh (b. 1992) established the Iranian Female Composers Association.[21] Formerly a student of Laura Kaminsky (b. 1956), Nourbakhsh garnered attention for her vocal work "An Aria for the Executive Order" (2017), a response to the Trump administration Muslim ban that was commissioned by the Women Composers Festival of Hartford. When asked about the first steps needed to remove obstacles for women composers, especially in her native Iran, Nourbakhsh says: "I believe the first step is to create a safe space that allows people to be themselves. The second

Figure 13.3. Niloufar Nourbakhsh. *Creative Commons (CC BY-SA 3.0)*

step is to provide tools that are necessary for these composers to elevate to their next goal, whatever it would be for them as an artist."[22] ♪

Other female composers come from a background combining diverse traditions. Gabriela Lena Frank (b. 1972) was born in Berkeley, California, to a father of Lithuanian Jewish descent and a Peruvian mother of Spanish, Chinese, and Quechua heritage; thus, Frank "identifies herself as an American mestiza, a woman of mixed European and Native American ancestry." As a composer, she explores the concept of *mestizaje* ("mestizo-ism") in music because, as she notes, "we're all living in a mestizo society now."[23] Her song cycle *New Andean Songs* (2007) for soprano, mezzo-soprano, two percussionists, and two pianists explores poetry collected by Peruvian folklorist José María Arguedas (1911–1969), who cultivated a multilingual and multicultural ethos.

Another diverse group gaining awareness and acceptance is the transgender community. Many of the new female composer associations and music festivals invite women and women-identifying composers to participate. Despite lingering cultural backlash in some parts of the country, transgender musicians and composers are speaking out, sharing their work, and finding a platform. Alex Temple (b. 1983) mused about her experiences as a composer on the trans-female spectrum in a 2013 blog post entitled "I'm a Trans Composer. What the Hell Does That Mean?"

> While I don't think of my work as specifically female, I *do* think of it as specifically genderqueer. Just as I often feel like I'm standing outside the world of gendered meanings, aware of them but never seeing them as inevitable natural facts like so many humans seem to do. . . . The four songs of *Behind the Wallpaper* go one step further. In that piece, I tried to convey an outsider's view not just of music, but of the experience of living in the world.[24]

The unique experience and outlook of trans composers like Temple and Mari Esbael Valverde (b. 1987) can bring an innovative creativity to the repertory. With numerous choral commissions, Valverde has had her works performed by the San Diego Women's Chorus, the Seattle Men's Chorus, and the San Francisco Gay Men's Chorus. She set her own text in the aptly named anthem "United in Song: An Anthem for Our Time" (2017).

MEN SUPPORTING WOMEN

It is encouraging to see examples of men actively supporting music by women. For instance, in 2017 Olga Vocal Ensemble, a male a cappella group in the Netherlands, announced their feminist a cappella project *It's a Woman's World* (2018) featuring Hildegard von Bingen (1098–1179), Suor Leonora d'Este (1515–1575), Nina Simone (1933–2003), Beyoncé (b. 1981), modern composers, Hindu saints, and mansplaining. On their Kickstarter page, Olga says, "People ask us: 'Why feminism? You're men!' We're doing this project because people often don't expect men to care, and we want to reverse that expectation. We're artists, and music is our platform, so we'll use that platform to support feminism and inspire both women and men. #HeForShe"[25] ♪

While the scholarship of women in music is understandably dominated by women—most notably with the pioneering scholarship of Carol Neuls-Bates (b. 1939), Jane Bowers (b. 1936), Judith Tick (b. 1943), Karin Pendle (b. 1939), and Christine Battersby (b. 1946), in addition to McClary, Citron, and Samuel mentioned above—men have a crucial role to play in the academy as well, where most musicians receive their training.[26] James Briscoe (b. 1949) was an early example of a male musicologist who made an enormous contribution to the academic world with the publication of the *Historical Anthology of Music by Women* (HAMW) in 1987. This anthology became a widely used textbook and paved the way for the first university courses devoted to the study of women in music. Briscoe expanded his efforts in 1997 with the publication of a sequel, the *Contemporary Anthology of Music by Women*, and he updated HAMW in 2004 with a revised and expanded version entitled the *New Historical Anthology of Music by Women*.[27] At universities, male professors are teaching women in music courses with greater frequency, and male musicologists and theorists are increasingly embracing music by women. Stephen Rodgers (b. 1974) at the University of Oregon is one example. Over the past decade, he has emerged as the world's leading scholar on the lieder of Fanny Hensel.

In 2017, I (Matthew) founded the first-ever Women in Music course at Auburn University, and one thing that struck me immediately was the number of men who enrolled in the course. There were almost as many as the women, which was astonishing in light of the fact that the music department is female heavy by a ratio of almost 2:1. These young men were genuinely excited about the material covered and topics discussed throughout the course, and their enthusiasm was infectious. As a performer and presenter at the first two installations of the Music by Women Festival at Mississippi University for Women (MUW) in Columbus, Mississippi, I was also impressed at the number of men who attended as performers and presenters. These trends represent positive changes that are occurring and point to a bright future for women composers.

Perhaps most important, men need to be proactive about programming and singing music composed by women. Women don't only write for women's voices—there is a wealth of repertoire out there for tenors, baritones, basses, and even countertenors. Male conductors of choral ensembles also need to be mindful about including women composers on their programs. If everyone—female and male—gets on board with this mission, the musical landscape of America and the world could change overnight.[28]

FEMININE BEGINNINGS: THE NEXT GENERATION

Music by women has yet to gain equal footing, so we are still at the beginning of a long journey toward parity in our profession. But the future looks encouraging, thanks to growing support movements and the burgeoning talent of the next generation of female composers. In 2017, Missy Mazzoli (b. 1980) and Ellen Reid (b. 1966) founded a mentorship program for young female composers. Sponsored by the Kaufman Music Center, the Luna Composition Lab is "open to any composer eighth grade to rising college freshman who identifies as female or gender non-conforming." Participants receive performance and recording opportunities for their work, but the most important element is private compositions lessons and one-on-one mentorship from a professional female composer. Composer and conductor Maya Miro Johnson (b. 2001) was a 2018 Luna Composition Lab Fellow. Before the Luna Lab, she was part of the Utah Young Composers Project as well as an apprentice conductor under Marin Alsop with the National Youth Orchestra of the United States of America (NYO-USA). Johnson revealed: "My hope is that one day we can simply call ourselves 'composers/conductors (who happen to be female),' rather than 'women composers/conductors,' and that we no longer feel treated like some special subgroup but simply like equal artists, thinkers, and professionals."[29] Talented young women like Johnson secure a promising future for female composers who hopefully won't need to be labeled as female composers. ♪

Figure 13.4. Maya Miro Johnson. *Creative Commons (CC BY-SA 3.0)*

Female composers rejoiced on social media when composer Nia Franklin (b. 1993) was crowned Miss America 2019. Franklin has an undergraduate degree in music composition from East Carolina University and a master's degree in composition from the University of North Carolina School of the Arts. Franklin premiered her first opera, *King Solomon*, in 2015 and hopes to pursue a doctorate in composition at either the Juilliard School or Princeton University. The morning after Franklin won the title, the Composer Diversity Database celebrated her win on Twitter, as did Missy Mazzoli who tweeted: "Miss America is a composer yes YES!!!"[30]

FINAL THOUGHTS

So You Want to Sing Music by Women is an advocacy book: an effort to encourage and champion women composers and creators of music across all genres. NATS's enthusiastic support for this project as one of the final books in the So You Want to Sing series is evidence that the efforts of women are being recognized, and progress—however slow—is being made. While women composers still face formidable challenges in the male-dominated music world, the mountains look a bit more surmountable than they used to.

The feminist movement has come a long way since the 1960s. I suspect that Simone de Beauvoir (1908–1986) would be heartened by the Me Too movement that took place almost exactly fifty years after American women began reading an English translation of her book *The Second Sex* (1949, trans. 1953), which many credit as the start of the modern feminist movement. The musical world is no exception to progress. How pleased Nadia Boulanger (1887–1979) would be if she were alive to see the music being composed by women today. As Bob Dylan (b. 1941) once famously sang, "The times they are a-changing."

NOTES

1. Pauline Oliveros, interview with Tara Rodgers, *Pink Noises: Women on Electronic Music and Sound* (Durham, NC: Duke University Press, 2010), 31.
2. www.bsomusic.org/stories/by-the-numbers-female-composers/, accessed August 15, 2018.
3. Ibid.
4. Tom Huizenga, "After Criticism, Philadelphia Orchestra Adds Female Composers to Its New Season," *NPR*, www.npr.org/sections/deceptivecadence/2018/08/02/634864751/after-criticism-philadelphia-orchestra-adds-female-composers-to-its-new-season, accessed August 13, 2018.
5. For a list of women's music festivals, see the appendix.
6. Personal correspondence with Sylvie Beaudette, August 13, 2018.
7. *IAWM Journal*, cpb-us-e1.wpmucdn.com/blogs.massart.edu/dist/a/1711/files/2017/06/IAWM-Journal-Spring-2017-3-2kc6ej9.pdf, accessed August 13, 2018.
8. STEAM is an acronym that adds the "Arts" to the traditional STEM acronym for "Science, Technology, Engineering, and Mathematics." The Electric

Girls is an organization devoted to helping young girls excel at science, technology, engineering, and math and increasing their confidence and proficiency in STEM.

9. Although the academic discipline of women in music began in the 1980s, these efforts were more topical and anthologizing in nature and did not have the feminist angle that McClary introduced to musicological circles.

10. Susan McClary, *Feminine Endings: Music, Gender, and Sexuality* (Minneapolis: University of Minnesota Press, 1991), 130.

11. Ibid., 18–19.

12. Susan McClary, "Feminine Endings at Twenty," *Transcultural Music Review* 15 (2011), www.sibetrans.com/trans/public/docs/trans_15_02 _McClary.pdf, accessed August 3, 2018.

13. Rhian Samuel, "Feminist Musicology: Endings or Beginnings?" *Women: A Cultural Review* 3, no. 1 (1993): 69.

14. Works referenced in this passage are the following: Aaron I. Cohen, *International Encyclopedia of Women Composers* (New York: Bowker, 1981); Julie Anne Sadie and Rhian Samuel, eds., *The Norton/Grove Dictionary of Women Composers* (New York: W.W. Norton, 1995). Cohen's work predates Sadie and Samuel's, but its open-door policy meant that it was not entirely trustworthy; it was therefore superseded by *The Norton/Grove Dictionary of Women Composers*, which is both critical and selective.

15. Marcia J. Citron, *Gender and the Musical Canon* (New York: Cambridge University Press, 1993).

16. Pirkko Moisala and Beverley Diamond, eds., *Music and Gender* (Champaign: University of Illinois Press, 2000).

17. Naomi André, *Blackness in Opera* (Champaign, IL: University of Chicago Press, 2012); Naomi André, *Black Opera: History, Power, Engagement* (Champaign, IL: University of Chicago Press, 2018).

18. Eileen M. Hayes, *Songs in Black and Lavender: Race, Sexual Politics, and Women's Music* (Champaign: University of Illinois Press, 2010).

19. Works referenced in this passage include the following: Tricia Rose, *Rap Music and Black Culture in Contemporary America* (Middletown, CT: Wesleyan University Press, 2004); Sheila Whiteley et al., *Music, Space, and Place: Popular Music and Cultural Identity* (Farnham, UK: Ashgate Publishing, 2005); Nichole T. Rustin and Sherrie Tucker, *Big Ears: Listening for Gender in Jazz Studies* (Durham, NC: Duke University Press, 2008); Pamela Fox, *Natural Acts: Gender, Race, and Rusticity in Country Music* (Ann Arbor: University of Michigan Press, 2009).

20. Anna Beer, *Sounds and Sweet Airs: The Forgotten Women of Classical Music* (London: OneWorld Publications, 2016).

21. For a list of women composers organizations, see the appendix.

22. Niloufar Nourbakhsh, interview with Rebecca Lentjes, *If You Care to Listen*, www.icareifyoulisten.com/2018/06/5-questions-niloufar-nourbakhsh -founder-iranian-female-composers-association/, accessed August 13, 2018.

23. Deborah Hayes, *Women of Influence in Contemporary Music*, ed. Michael K. Slayton (Lanham, MD: Scarecrow Press, 2011), 85–86.

24. www.alextemplemusic.com/2013/07/trans/, accessed August 12, 2018.

25. www.kickstarter.com/projects/olgavocalensemble/olga-vocal-ensembles -feminist-a-cappella-album/description, accessed August 13, 2018.

26. The seminal musicological works referenced in this passage are the following: Carol Neuls-Bates, *Women in Music: An Anthology of Source Readings* (New York: Harper & Row, 1982); Jane Bowers and Judith Tick, eds., *Women Making Music: The Western Art Tradition: 1150–1950* (Champaign: University of Illinois Press, 1987); Karin Pendle, *Women and Music: A History* (Bloomington: Indiana University Press, 1991) and *Gender and Genius* (Bloomington: Indiana University Press, 1989). Both Neuls-Bates's and Pendle's books are now available in revised editions (1995 and 2001, respectively).

27. James Briscoe, *Historical Anthology of Music by Women* (Bloomington: Indiana University Press, 1987) and *Contemporary Anthology of Music by Women* (Bloomington: Indiana University Press, 1987). Briscoe released a second edition of the original work entitled the *New Historical Anthology of Music by Women* in 2004, also published by Indiana University Press.

28. Please see the appendix and the online resources for a wealth of information about repertoire collections, indexes and databases, and distribution companies devoted to publishing music by women.

29. www.kaufmanmusiccenter.org/kc/article/qa-with-2018-luna-compos ition-lab-fellow-maya-miro-johnson/, accessed August 12, 2018.

30. Missy Mazzoli, Twitter post, September 10, 2018, 8:48 p.m., twitter .com/missymazzoli/status/1039133500681674753.

APPENDIX

Additional Resources

This book is merely a starting point as you begin your journey discovering and performing the magnificent music that has been created by women. Fortunately, there are many resources available for the performer or singing teacher interested in exploring this repertoire. This appendix categorizes and annotates areas for further exploration. Websites for all of these resources can be accessed on the designated page on the NATS website.[1] ♪

REPERTOIRE DATABASES AND CATALOGS

In the Internet age, print-based repertoire lists are limiting and out-of-date the second they are printed. The following websites are up-to-date archives for exploring music created by women, with different sites devoted to different genres. These resources serve as excellent starting points for exploring this music and discovering new repertoire.

Audible Women

As described on its website, Audible Women is "an online directory for female-identifying, trans, and nonbinary artists who make sound,

sound art, noise, and music (acoustic or electronic) with a bit of an experimental and exploratory bent." Artists are welcomed to submit listings and join the resource, which was started by Sydney-based sound artist and writer Gail Priest.

Choral Music by Women Composers Database

This database, established by the Orange County Women's Chorus in Laguna Hills, California, lists more than four hundred choral works by women composers. The database can be sorted by composer name, birth date, nationality, title, voicing, duration, difficulty, and publisher. Personal websites of living composers are also listed.

ClarNan Editions: Historic Music by Women Composers

Founder, editor, and publisher Barbara Garvey Jackson established ClarNan Editions in 1984. ClarNan is an abbreviated amalgam of the names of Clara Schumann (1819–1896), Nannerl Mozart (1751–1829), and Nannette Streicher (1769–1833), the piano builder of Ludwig van Beethoven (1770–1827). The company publishes the works of forty-one historic female composers.

Composer Diversity Database

What began as an Excel spreadsheet where composers could enter their own information has now spawned the Composer Diversity Database. On the database website, you can search for composers by gender (including female and nonbinary) and/or demographic and genre, as well as location (inside or outside United States) and life status (living or deceased). The database was founded by composer Rob Deemer (b. 1970), head of composition at the State University of New York (SUNY) at Fredonia.

The Kapralova Society

The Kapralova Society is a Canadian nonprofit organization created by Karla Hartl in 1998 to honor Czech composer Vitezslava Kapralova (1915–1940) and other female composers of classical music. The society also has a separate database for women composers of electroacoustic music, experimental music and sound art, film music, and jazz.

LiederNet Archive

The LiederNet Archive, created in 1995 and still curated by Emily Ezust, has been a core resource for singers for more than two decades. Many users don't realize that the art song database features the ability to filter composer (and poet) surnames by gender, making it a useful resource for exploring art songs by women composers.

Many Many Women

This database is a master index of more than one thousand female composers, improvisers, and sonic artists. Founded by Steve Peters and now managed by Megan Mitchell, the index focuses on women composers of experimental and avant-garde music as opposed to mainstream CCM styles. Mitchell says they welcome trans composers "as long as they are not cis men."

Music Theory Examples by Women

Supervised by Eastman PhD candidate Molly Murdock, this database provides a multitude of musical examples by women for use in music theory classes. Instead of using Johann Sebastian Bach (1685–1750) or Ludwig van Beethoven (1770–1827), instructors can find useful examples by composers such as Amy Beach (1867–1944) and Margaret Bonds (1913–1972). Users can search for literature according to the following parameters: meter and rhythm, scales and tonalities, chords and harmonies, cadences, embellishing tones, form, texture, twentieth and twenty-first century, and score reading.

Musik und Gender im Internet

This German-language website explores the confluence of music history and women's studies. The project lists its goal as the development of "the methodical aspects of women and gender studies and to integrate it into musicology studies in universities and conservatoriums." Its archive contains many articles devoted to various topics related to feminist musicology.

OTHER DIGITAL RESOURCES

The Internet also offers many other digital resources supporting music by women and both historic and contemporary female composers. These resources range from blogs and websites to online journals and publishing companies. The following is a list of some of the most well-known of these resources.

Compos(h)er

This cleverly named Tumblr blog highlights 165 historic female composers. It contains numerous embedded YouTube links to recordings and performances of music by women. The anonymous blogger lists some of her more obscure favorites as Maria Agata Szymanowska (1789–1831), Mel Bonis (1858–1937), Henriette Renié (1875–1956), Dora Pejačević (1885–1923), Henriëtte Hilda Bosmans (1895–1952), and Elisabet Hermodsson (1927–2017).

Donne: Women in Music

Curator Gabriella Di Laccio invites visitors to Donne to "spread the word and join us in recognizing that women are musical geniuses too." The website features "The Big List," ten pages of women composers from Sappho (ca. 610 BCE–570 BCE) to Alma Deutscher (b. 2005). The website also has an extensive video archive of interviews with living women composers.

Hildegard Publishing Company

This publishing company was founded in 1988 by Sylvia Glickman. The mission of Hildegard is "to publish compositions by women composers which display the highest level of excellence and musical merit" and which "have been historically overlooked and undervalued." As expected, their publications include Hildegard von Bingen (1098–1179) but also feature composers as contemporary as Karen E. Christianson (b. 1995).

The Margaret Zach International Women Composers Library

Directed by pianist, organist, and harpsichordist Miriam S. Zach, this library began as a noncirculating research collection in Gainesville, Florida. Now it also fosters collaborative and Internet resources. The library functions as a resource to draw musicologists, performers, and music educators to conferences, workshops, and courses. Local community musical organizations have ready access to the collection to expand their performance repertoires.

Women and Music: A Journal of Gender and Culture

This journal is published yearly for the International Alliance for Women in Music (IAWM) by the University of Nebraska Press. It is especially "interested in work that provides a critical perspective on music and/or sound, and in work that considers the role of gender, sexuality, race, citizenship, class, or other cultural and social factors in the production, circulation, historicisation, or consumption of music."

Women in Music Timeline

Oxford Music Online created this timeline of women in music. It begins in 810 with Kassia (ca. 810–865), a composer of Byzantine chant, and continues through 2000 with Jessye Norman's premiere performance at Carnegie Hall of *woman.life.song* by Judith Weir (b. 1954). The timeline is a helpful resource for students and newcomers to women's studies in music.

PRINT RESOURCES

Many new music history books continue to provide a growing body of research on woman composers, often blending musicology with gender studies. While hundreds of specific studies exist on various composers and issues within feminist musicology, this list will focus primarily on classic musicological works, surveys, and anthologies. There are also a variety of song anthologies available, which serve as valuable resources for performers who wish to program more music by women.

Beer: *Sounds and Sweet Airs: The Forgotten Women of Classical Music*

With an emphasis that is more historical than musicological, Anna Beer's book discusses eight of the most famous and interesting figures in the history of Western art music: Francesca Caccini (1587–after 1641), Barbara Strozzi, (1619–1677), Élisabeth Jacquet de la Guerre (1665–1729), Marianna Martines (1744–1812), Fanny Mendelssohn Hensel (1805–1847), Clara Schumann (1819–1896), Lili Boulanger (1893–1918), and Elizabeth Maconchy (1907–1994). Although the selections are somewhat arbitrary and the omissions curious, the book has a populist angle and is an engaging read. An overarching theme of the book is the unique struggles that women faced at various points in history and within specific cultures.

Bowers and Tick: *Women Making Music: The Western Art Tradition, 1050–1950*

In this classic work of musicology—one of the first of its kind devoted to women's studies—editors Jane Bowers and Judith Tick present biographies of outstanding performers and composers, as well as analyses of women musicians as a class, and provide examples of music from all periods, including medieval chant, Renaissance song, baroque opera, German lieder, and twentieth-century compositional practice. Unlike most standard historical surveys, the book not only sheds light upon the musical achievements of women, it also illuminates the historical contexts that shaped and defined those achievements. Figures highlighted include Barbara Strozzi (1619–1677), Clara Schumann (1819–1896), Luise Adolpha le Beau (1850–1927), Ethel Smyth (1858–1944), and Ruth Crawford Seeger (1901–1953). The phenomenon of women's orchestras is also covered.

Briscoe: *Contemporary Anthology of Music by Women*

James Briscoe's contemporary anthology highlights thirty composers across a wide variety of genres, among them Emma Lou Diemer (b. 1927), Joan La Barbara (b. 1947), Libby Larsen (b. 1950), Nicola Le-Fanu (b. 1947), Tania León (b. 1943), Elisabeth Lutyens (1906–1983), Joni Mitchell (b. 1943), Meredith Monk (b. 1942), Undine Smith Moore (1904–1989), Dolly Parton (b. 1946), Lucy Simon (b. 1943), and Judith Lang Zaimont (b. 1945). The score anthology is accompanied by a listening anthology.

Briscoe: *New Historical Anthology of Music by Women*

First released in 1987, Briscoe's anthology was the first college textbook of its kind and helped to establish university courses devoted to women in music. The *New Historical Anthology of Music by Women* is a revised edition released in 2004. The anthology covers forty-three composers from Sappho (ca. 610 BCE–570 BCE), Kassia (ca. 810–865), and Hildegard von Bingen (1098–1179) through living composers such as Thea Musgrave (b. 1928), Ellen Taaffe Zwilich (b. 1939), and Augusta Read Thomas (b. 1964). The score anthology is accompanied by a listening anthology.

Citron: *Gender and the Musical Canon*

Winner of the Pauline Alderman Prize from the International Alliance of Women in Music, Marcia J. Citron's book has become a classic text in musicological gender studies. At the time of publication, *Gender and the Musical Canon* was a groundbreaking piece of scholarship that challenged long-held notions about the museum-like nature of the Western musical canon. Examining the social context and politics surrounding the musical works that were canonized and preserved in the standard music history books studied in universities, it shone a spotlight on the male dominance of European musical culture over the course of the previous centuries.

Dunbar: *Music, Women, Culture: An Introduction*

The second edition of Julie C. Dunbar's undergraduate textbook boasts a companion website of listening examples as streaming audio tracks. While many college-level textbooks focus on Western art traditions, Dunbar is cross-cultural, examining the contributions of women in popular music and the commercial music industry. The textbook has many useful online resources, making it an ideal learning tool for millennials.

Friedberg: *Art Songs by American Women Composers*

This fifteen-volume series, published by Southern Music and edited by Ruth C. Friedberg, is exclusively devoted to publishing art songs written by American women. Composers featured include Amy Beach (1867–1944), Florence Price (1887–1953), Ruth Schonthal (1924–2006), Claire Brook (1925–2012), Edith Boroff (b. 1925), Emma Lou Diemer (b. 1927), Flicka Rahn (b. 1944), Elizabeth Raum (b. 1945), and Elisenda Fabregas (b. 1955).

Gray: *The World of Women in Classical Music*

This large volume by Anne C. Gray provides a comprehensive overview as well as "information on women behind the scenes in orchestras, opera companies, publishing, recording, and as pioneering impresarios and agents." Gray places a special emphasis on the philanthropic efforts of women and how they had a profound influence on music over the generations.

Kimball: *Women Composers: A Heritage of Song*

With volumes for both high and low voice, Carol Kimball's collection in the Hal Leonard Vocal Library series contains songs by twenty-two female composers including Anna Amalia (1739–1807), Amy Beach (1867–1944), Lili Boulanger (1893–1918), Nadia Boulanger (1887–1979), Francesca Caccini (1587–after 1641), Cécile Chaminade (1857–1944), Isabella Colbran (1785–1845), Fanny Hensel (1805–1847), Augusta Holmès (1847–1903), Mary Howe (1882–1964), Josephine Lang (1815–1880), Liza Lehmann (1862–1918), Alma Mahler (1879–1964), Maria Malibran (1808–1836), Lady Poldowski (1880–1932), Louise Reichardt (1779–1826), Corona Schröter (1751–1802), Clara Schumann (1819–1896), Barbara Strozzi (1619–1677), Pauline Viardot (1821–1910), Jane Vieu (1871–1955), and Bettine von Arnim (1785–1859).

Mabry: *Journal of Singing* Articles

The *Journal of Singing* is the official publication of the National Association of Teachers of Singing (NATS), offering peer-reviewed articles on a wide variety of topics from voice pedagogy and performance to vocal literature. The New Directions column—written by Sharon Mabry from 1985 to 2009—is a particularly fruitful resource for learning more about women as composers of vocal music. Mabry is a staunch advocate for music by women with a particular interest in collaborating with living composers and programming new music.

Marrazzo: *The First Solos: Songs by Women Composers*

Edited by Randi Marrazzo, this Hildegard Publishing release is available in three volumes for high, medium, and low voice. Composers featured in the collection include Frances Allitsen (1848–1912), Rosa Giacinta Badella (1660–1715), Marion Bauer (1882–1955), Amy Beach (1867–1944), Lili Boulanger (1893–1918), Settimia Caccini (1591–1661), Cécile Chaminade (1857–1944), Isabella Colbran (1785–1845), Charlotte Duchambge (1778–1858), Margaret Essex (1775–1807), Agatha Backer Grøndahl (1847–1907), Mary Harvey (1629–1704), Carrie Jacobs-Bond (1862–1946), Johanna Kinkel (1810–1858), Margaret Ruthven Lang (1867–1972), Liza Lehmann (1862–1918), Sophie Mercken (1776–1821), Loïsa Puget (1810–1889), Louise Reichardt (1779–1826), Corona Elisabeth Schröter (1751–1802), Clara Schumann (1819–1896), Lily Strickland (1884–1958), Maria Szymanowska (1789–1831), Alba Trissina (fl. ca. 1622), Pauline Viardot (1821–1910), Bettine von Arnim (1785–1859), Ingeborg von Bronsart (1840–1913), and Maude Valérie White (1855–1937).

McClary: *Feminine Endings: Music, Gender, and Sexuality*

Susan McClary's famous essays on feminist music criticism were cutting-edge and controversial when they were published in 1991, warranting a second edition that was released a decade later in 2002. The title of McClary's book refers to a long-standing term used to describe "weak" cadences as "feminine," whereas a "strong" cadence was labeled "masculine." Addressing this misogynistic projection onto analysis of harmonic progressions, she wrote that music by women was demeaned by the patriarchal tradition and "condemned as pretty yet trivial." McClary's scholarship was part of the "new musicology" movement that emerged during the late 1980s, and *Feminine Endings* is regarded as one of new musicology's earliest and most important works. In addition to feminism, new musicology examined music from a variety of cultural perspectives, including gender studies, queer theory, and racial considerations, among others.

Neuls-Bates: *Women in Music: An Anthology of Source Readings*

Carol Neuls-Bates edits this anthology containing "letters, diaries, poems, novels, and reviews that reveal women's achievements not only as patrons and educators but also as composers and performers." After broad sections devoted to the first four epochs of music—the Middle Ages, Renaissance, baroque, and classical eras—considerably more attention is paid to the nineteenth and twentieth centuries. The primary sources collected by Neuls-Bates offer a fascinating insight into women music makers of the past millennium.

Pendle: *Women and Music: A History*

This book, first published in 1991 and edited by Karin Pendle, explores female composers across many eras, geographical areas, and genres. In addition to a chronological history, there are also essays on feminist aesthetics in music and women's support and encouragement of musicians. Perhaps the most comprehensive study devoted to surveying the entire history of women in music, it has become a standard textbook in many universities. The book is divided into seven broad sections: (i) Feminist Aesthetics, (ii) Ancient and Medieval Music, (iii) the Fifteenth through the Eighteenth Centuries, (iv) the Nineteenth Century and the Great War, (v) Modern Music around the Globe, (vi) Women in the World of Music, and (vii) the Special Roles of Women. A second, definitive edition was released in 2001.

Sadie and Samuel: *The Norton-Grove Dictionary of Women Composers*

Edited by Julie Anne Sadie and composer Rhian Samuel (b.1944), this dictionary is a substantial resource of more than six hundred pages. The dictionary's entries chronicle the lives and works of 875 women composers of Western classical music. When first published in 1995, *The Norton-Grove Dictionary of Women Composers* was revolutionary and quickly became the most important one-volume reference work for anyone interested in studying the subject of women in music.

Taylor: *Art Songs and Spirituals by African-American Women Composers*

Also by Hildegard Publishing, this collection edited by Vivian Taylor spotlights songs and spiritual arrangements by Margaret Bonds (1913–1972), Betty Jackson King (1928–1994), Dorothy Rudd Moore (b. 1940), Undine Smith Moore (1904–1989), Julia Perry (1924–1979), Zenobia Powell Perry (1908–2004), and Florence Price (1887–1953). The anthology is a celebration of those women who successfully overcame two barriers as composers: gender and race.

FESTIVALS AND WORKSHOPS

In the past few years, music festivals for women have exploded. On both sides of the Atlantic, these events are rapidly increasing in number, scope, and attendance. There are growing festival opportunities for both classical and CCM composers and performers. In addition, there are new projects, networks, and camps geared to helping the professional development of women composers.

3Rivers Womyn's Music Festival

This music festival was developed to empower "womyn of Asian/ Pacific Islander, Arab/Middle Eastern, Black/African American/Caribbean/West Indies, Native/Indigenous, and Hispanic/Latin descent." Besides live music, the festival has included yoga classes and workshops to the "wo-manifest" community on "651 fern filled acres in Michigan."

Balancing the Score: Supporting Female Composers

Starting in 2018, this new development scheme by Glyndebourne Opera offers four UK-based, post-graduate women a two-year, part-time residency with the company. They are introduced to "commissioning opportunities at Glyndebourne" and will "investigate different approaches to the creation of new opera."

Canadian Women Composers Project

Hoping to create more awareness of vocal compositions by Canadian women, this project presents recitals featuring female composers across Canada. The 2017–2018 season also involved Canadian female designer Carly Cumpson, who created a dress for every recital in "a celebration of the women of Canada!"

Festival Présences Féminines

Under the direction of Claire Bodin, this French festival "opens up a world that has long been marginal, hidden, forgotten, sometimes denied, often despised and underestimated, a world yet rich and real: that of the musical creation of women." The festival takes place in late March each year and features many internationally renowned women musicians and composers.

Frauenkomponiert

This nonprofit association promotes female composers through its concert series, which focuses on orchestral works. Under director Jessica Horsley, the 2018 festival featured works by Agnes Tyrrell (1846–

1883), Amy Beach (1867–1944), Heidi Baader-Nobs (b. 1940), and
Alma Deutscher (b. 2005). Although the title is German, the festival's
title appears in all lowercase in its branding: "frauenkomponiert."

International Festival of Women Composers

Founded by Miriam Zach in 1996, this festival started in Gainesville,
Florida, but since 2017 has taken place on the campus of Iowa State
University. It is held in March in honor of Women's History Month.
The 2018 program featured Alma Mahler (1879–1964), Florence Price
(1887–1953), Libby Larsen (b. 1950), Lori Laitman (b. 1955), Meg
Bowles (b. 1957), and Jodi Goble (b. ca. 1975).

Just Fearless Women Rising Music Festival

Founded by Kisha Mays, this festival in Miami, Florida, celebrates
women in CCM genres. DJ Citizen Jane was the headliner of the 2018
festival, which was held at the culmination of the Just Fearless Women
Rising Economic Empowerment Summit. The festival provides business development strategies and partnership opportunities for women
entrepreneurs around the world.

LunArt Festival

LunArt was founded by flutist Iva Ugrčić. The 2018 festival was held
in Madison, Wisconsin, "celebrating works created by women: past and
present, from revered to forgotten, from rap to rhapsody!" It included
emerging composers' concerts and master classes, lectures on women's
musical history, and panel discussions. The driving idea of this festival
is "to create a vibrant, safe space for women where creativity is the
queen!"

Music by Women Festival
(Mississippi University for Women)

Held on the campus of the Mississippi University for Women
(MUW), the Music by Women Festival was created by pianist Julia

Mortyakova in 2017. The three-day festival includes concerts, lecture recitals, papers, and presentations solely spotlighting female composers. The festival events take place in historic Poindexter Hall on MUW's beautiful campus, which is set against the backdrop of the antebellum architecture of Columbus, Mississippi. We have had the honor of performing at the Music by Women Festival, which draws its performing artists and composers from all over North America.

National Women's Music Festival (NWMF)

Sponsored by the nonprofit organization Women in the Arts, the NWMF began in 1974. Now a four-day festival, it displays female musicians from a wide variety of CCM genres besides an orchestral program led by a female conductor. It also sponsors an Emerging Artist Contest and the NWMF Drum Chorus. It is the longest-running women's music festival in America.

The Summers Night Project

The Australian organization Tura New Music invited submissions for this project aiming "to provide support and mentoring for women composers to create new compositions for performances in Perth, Adelaide, and Melbourne, with the aim of growing the gender diversity of composers in music programs Australia-wide." The project was inspired by Anne Summers (b. 1945), author of "The Women's Manifesto: A Blueprint for How to Get Equality for Women in Australia" (2017).

Women Composers Festival of Hartford

Composer and pianist Heather Seaton started this festival in 2001. Now under the direction of musicologist Penny Brandt, this two-day event includes a music marathon and a keynote speaker as well as composer forums and concerts. For the 2019 festival, Jennifer Jolley (b. 1981) was named composer-in-residence and the Nouveau Classical Project was named ensemble-in-residence.

Women's Redrock Music Festival

Since 2006, this two-day festival held near Capitol Reef National Park has been providing performing opportunities to female CCM artists and "empowering independent women and gender diverse musicians from Utah and around the world." Among the performers at the 2018 festival were Flor de Toloache, the first all-female mariachi group; hip-hop duo the Blu Janes; and the blues band Sister Wives.

Young Women Composers Camp

Temple University sponsors this twelve-day summer program for young women composers between the ages of fourteen and nineteen. There is no application fee for the camp. Classes include composition workshop, theory and ear training, chorale, orchestration, private composition lessons, electronic music, songwriting, and jazz improvisation. The Young Women Composers Camp "aims to amplify the voices of young women, to allow them access to a high level of musical training, and to close the gender gap in the music composition field and create a more equitable music sector."

GRANTS AND AWARDS

Recognizing the gender gap that has long impeded the success of women composers, a number of awards, grants, scholarships, and competitions have emerged to help support gender parity. These awards come primarily from professional organizations and foundations but seem to embrace female composers in numerous genres.

Billie Burke Ziegfeld Award

The Ziegfeld Club, Inc. in New York City grants this $10,000 award to "an emerging female composer or composer-lyricist who compellingly demonstrates outstanding artistic promise in musical theater composing, and who can clearly show how the grant money and mentorship will further her artistic career."

IAWM Competitions

The International Alliance for Women in Music offers a number of competitions for female composers including the Miriam Gideon Prize ($500) to a composer of at least fifty years of age for a work for solo voice and one to five instruments, the Libby Larsen Prize ($300) to a composer who is currently enrolled in school for a work in any medium, and the PatsyLu Prize ($500) for classical art music in any form by black women and/or lesbians.

The Lilly Awards

Created in 2010 to honor women's achievement in American theater, the Lilly Awards were founded by Julia Jordan (b. ca. 1967), Marsha Norman (b. 1947), and Theresa Rebeck (b. 1958). Named in honor of playwright Lillian Hellman (1905–1984), the Lillys have unique names such as the "You've Changed the World Award" and the "Go Write a Musical Award."

Listen Up! Music by Women Artist Grants (Allied Arts Foundation)

The Allied Arts Foundation awards more than $15,000 in this "cross-genre competition for new works by women composers and songwriters in the state of Washington." Works entered must be new and unpublished, but they may be contemporary classical, electroacoustic, blues, R&B, jazz, multimedia, or sound installations.

National Sawdust Hildegard Competition

In 2017, National Sawdust began this competition for emerging female and nonbinary composers. Winners receive a $7,000 prize along with mentoring by prominent female composers. Sponsored by the Virginia B. Toulmin Foundation, the 2018 mentors were National Sawdust creative director Paola Prestini (b. 1975), Du Yun (b. 1977), and Angélica Negrón (b. 1981).

New York Women Composers Seed Grants

New York Women Composers, Inc. sponsors this seed grant program that awards $750 grants "for concert projects that include a substantial commitment to the performance of music by NYWC members." Concert projects should feature more than one composer and need not be constituted solely of music by women. Applications are open to soloists, ensembles, and producing organizations.

Opera America Grants for Female Composers

The Virginia B. Toulmin Foundation sponsors these Opera America Discovery Grants of up to $15,000 to individual female composers to support new opera compositions. The commissioning grants program assists Opera America Professional Company members to "commission works by talented women who compose for the opera stage," covering half of the composer's fee "for a full production of a commissioned work, with awards up to $50,000."

Roberta Stephen Composition Award (ACWC)

Established by Calgary composer Roberta Stephen (b. 1931), the Association of Canadian Women Composers (ACWC) oversees this annual award for a Canadian woman composer "aged thirty-six or older for professional development such as further studies, conferences, or workshops, or composers' festivals." It offers two $500 awards annually.

Sirens Funding: Association of British Orchestras

In 2016, Diana Ambache financed a ten-year fund, Sirens, "which aims to raise awareness and appreciation of the music written by historical women from around the world." The fund has helped present orchestral performances of works by Maria Grimani (ca. 1680–ca. 1720), Maria Antonia Walpurgis (1724–1780), Louise Farrenc (1804–1875), Cécile Chaminade (1857–1944), Germaine Tailleferre (1892–1983), Lili Boulanger (1893–1918), Dorothy Howell (1898–1982), and Grace Williams (1906–1977).

Women Make Music (PRS Foundation)

This program strives to support and develop female songwriters and composers in a multitude of genres to spotlight new music being written by women in the United Kingdom. It also attempts to create awareness of the gender gap in the music industry to "break down assumptions and stereotypes" and encourage "role models for future generations."

Women's Philharmonic Advocacy Performance Grants

The WPA awards grants from $500 to $1000 to "encourage orchestras to perform music composed by historic and contemporary women composers." Their website even provides a listing of repertoire suggestions, noting: "We are particularly promoting historic works, since composers who are no longer living are at a disadvantage in promoting their own music!"

PROFESSIONAL ORGANIZATIONS

Associations of like-minded female composers are an obvious support for women in the industry. Such associations exist at the city, state, national, and international level. Furthermore, there are also initiatives, centers, and creative laboratories where women composers can connect, find encouragement and funding, and share their work.

Archiv Frau und Musik

This international music archive in Frankfurt, Germany, hosts the world's most significant digital archive (DDF) of female composers. Founded in Cologne in 1979, it moved to Frankfurt in 2001. They sponsor a composer-in-residence program every three years. Former composer scholars of the program include Manuela Kerer (b. 1980) and Belma Bešlić-Gál (b. 1978).

Asian Women Composers Association
New York City (AWCANYC)

AWCANYC is a cooperative serving "young Asian women composers from all over the world to share their story through music" and helping them turn "their music into sellable products." The association was founded by composer Jin Hee Han (b. ca. 1980). It presents monthly concerts and publishes a newsletter called "In the Loop."

Association of Canadian Women Composers (ACWC)

Also known as Association des femmes compositeurs canadiennes (AFCC), this organization supports music written by Canadian women and women-identified composers. ACWC/AFCC publishes a biannual journal. Founded in 1981 by Carolyn Lomax, the association also sponsors the ACWC Choral Collective, which is designed to encourage interaction between female composers and choral conductors looking for new works to program.

The Boulanger Initiative

This initiative was founded by violinist Laura Colgate and organist Joy-Leilani Garbutt. Inspired by Nadia Boulanger (1887–1979) and Lili Boulanger (1893–1918), its mission involves mounting a concert series devoted to women composers as well as creating educational opportunities and commissions for new music.

Chinese Woman Composers' Association (CWCA)

Founded in 2002, this Hong Kong–based organization "encourages and promotes not only Chinese woman composers but Chinese woman performers at all stages of their careers throughout the world. It is committed to enhance the profile of Chinese woman musicians." The association has opened its membership to people in the general public who support their mission.

Clara Schumann Society (CSS)

Tenor David Kenneth Smith is the founder and editor of CSS. One can become a Performance Member of the society by performing her work and submitting a program of the event, while Research Members need to submit detailed information (title page, abstract, table of contents) so their research can be added to the society website.

International Alliance for Women in Music (IAWM)

IAWM is an international organization for "women and men dedicated to fostering and encouraging the activities of women in music, particularly in the areas of musical activity such as composing, performing, and research in which gender discrimination is an historic and ongoing concern." They advocate for more representation of women composers on concert programs and in university textbooks. In addition, they publish a biannual journal and hold an annual competition called the Search for New Music by Women Composers (SNM).

Iranian Female Composers Association (IFCA)

The Iranian Female Composers Association was founded in 2017 by members Niloufar Nourbakhsh (b. 1992), Anahita Abbasi (b. 1985), and Aida Shirazi (b. ca. 1987). Their goal is to discover and mentor young Iranian female composers between the ages of eighteen and twenty-two "who face profound cultural and educational roadblocks in music." IFCA's launch concert was held on April 1, 2018, at National Sawdust in Brooklyn.

Luna Composition Lab

In partnership with Face the Music, the Kaufman Music Center's Luna Composition Lab began in 2017. It pairs "any composer eighth grade to rising college freshman who identifies as female or gender nonconforming" for bimonthly lessons with a professional female composer and mentor. Previous mentors have been Tamar Muskal (b. 1965), Ellen Reid (b. 1966), Kristin Kuster (b. 1973), Missy Mazzoli (b. 1980), Reena Esmail (b. 1983), and Gity Razaz (b. 1986).

Nadia and Lili Boulanger International Centre

Nadia Boulanger (1887–1979) started a memorial fund in honor of her sister Lili Boulanger (1893–1918), granting awards to composers from 1942 to 1965, after which the Friends of Lili Boulanger took over the scholarship program. After Nadia's death in 1979, the Nadia and Lili Boulanger International Foundation was formed, but it was dissolved in 2009 and renamed the Boulanger International Centre. Located in Bagnolet, France, the center still sponsors scholarships and a voice-piano competition, in line with the tradition of Nadia as a prominent teacher and mentor to other musicians.

New York Women Composers, Inc. (NYWC)

Founded in 1984, this organization serves New York state and New York City metropolitan area residents who are women composers of classical music or their supporters. Its mission is "to create performing, recording, networking, and mentoring opportunities for its members." Notable board members have included Victoria Bond (b. 1945) and Alice Shields (b. 1943).

The Rebecca Clarke Society

Celebrating the life and work of Rebecca Clarke (1886–1979), this society began in 2000. Its current president is musicologist Liane Curtis. The society tracks new research on Clarke in addition to recordings and concert performances of her compositions. The society website also contains a detailed listing of fifty-two vocal works and twelve choral works by Clarke.

The Sorel Organization

The Elizabeth and Michel Sorel Charitable Organization, Inc. "intends to create opportunities for women in composition, conducting, piano, voice and film scoring" and "help expand the boundaries for women in music." It collaborates on a number of composition contests, commissions, scholarships, and youth programs.

Women in Music (WiM)—UK

This is an organization for women musicians in the United Kingdom. The organization's website contains helpful links to other organizations, competitions, and resources. WiM does an annual survey of female musicians included on the BBC Proms concerts. In the 2018 Proms season, 14 percent of the composers were female, but 40 percent of the living composers programmed were female.

Women in Music (WIM)—USA

Based in New York, Women in Music (WIM) is an international organization for "women at all stages in their careers——from students to seasoned veterans—and men who support our cause." Members are not just songwriters but also music industry professionals such as agents, publishers, publicists, recording engineers, and record label executives. There are WIM chapters in Atlanta, Barbados, Boston, Brazil, Canada, Chicago, Great Britain, Los Angeles, Miami, Nashville, New York, Northern Ireland, and Washington, D.C.

Women's Opera Network (WON)

Open to any current female member of Opera America, this network aims to "promote the advancement of talented women." The year-long WON Mentorship Program pairs an opera professional with a protégé to assist in career development of women in leadership roles in opera. Composer Laura Kaminsky (b. 1956) serves on the WON Steering Committee.

NOTE

1. In this appendix, dates of composers are listed but not dates of authors, organizers, administrators, or performers. Also, unlike the chapters of the book, birth and death dates of historical figures are repeated if they reappear in a new section. We recognize that readers will likely approach the appendix differently than chapters, referencing specific sections as needed as opposed to reading it straight through from top to bottom. Within entries, composers are listed in chronological birth order with the exception of anthologies, where complete contents are listed alphabetically by last name.

GLOSSARY

Academy Awards: The annual awards ceremony of the Academy of
Motion Picture Arts and Sciences. Also called the "Oscars," the event
is Hollywood's biggest night of the year. There are two categories
in which the Oscars honor composers: Best Original Score and Best
Original Song. The first Academy Awards ceremony was held on May
16, 1929, and the Oscars for these two categories were first awarded
in 1935. Since that time, only three women have won in the scoring
categories—two of them for music and one for lyrics. Composers
Rachel Portman (b. 1960) and Anne Dudley (b. 1956) won Oscars
for *Emma* (1996) and *The Full Monty* (1997), respectively, and lyricist
Marilyn Bergman (b. 1929) won an Oscar in the Best Original Score
category for *Yentl* (1983). In the Best Original Song category, ten
women have won twelve Academy Awards since 1936.

A Cappella: Italian for "in the church style," but over time the phrase
has come to mean to sing without instrumental accompaniment.
Many choral works are sung a cappella.

ACDA: Acronym for the American Choral Directors Association.

Agnus Dei: The fifth and final part of the mass ordinary. The Agnus
Dei is sung during communion.

AGO: Acronym for the American Guild of Organists.

American Choral Directors Association: Founded in 1959, the American Choral Directors Association (ACDA) is a nonprofit music education organization whose central purpose is to promote excellence in choral music through performance, composition, publication, research, and teaching. In addition, ACDA strives through arts advocacy to elevate choral music's position in American society. ACDA is particularly known for its national and regional conferences, as well as for its monthly publication, the *Choral Journal*.

American Guild of Organists: An organization whose mission is to promote the organ in its historic and evolving roles, to encourage excellence in the performance of organ and choral music, and to provide a forum for mutual support, inspiration, education, and certification of guild members. Membership is not limited to professional organists but is open to anybody with an interest in the organ, organ literature, or sacred choral music.

Anthem: A piece of choral music that sets a biblical text that supplements the liturgy. Anthems are generally sung at the offertory or during communion. Ethel Smyth (1858–1944), Amy Beach (1867–1944), Natalie Sleeth (1930–1992), and Judith Bingham (b. 1952) are notable women composers of anthems.

Antiphon: A liturgical chant that precedes and follows a psalm or canticle during a service of worship.

Aspirate Onset: A breathy, ripple-like closing of the vocal folds. Aspirate onset occurs when singers inhale and then start to exhale while leaving the glottis open. Shortly thereafter, they close the glottis just enough to bring the vocal folds into vibration.

Auratic Transference: A songwriting process that places the presence of the songwriter into the song itself, regardless of the circumstances and personal involvement in later performances, either recorded or live.

Basso Continuo: A feature of ensemble music in the seventeenth and eighteenth centuries, consisting of a bass line played on a melodic instrument, together with a chord-playing instrument (usually either a harpsichord or organ).

Belt: A loud vocal quality in a modal or chest register that resembles yelling. A belt quality is the modal or chest register quality carried above approximately E/F/G4, at a loud volume or with increased intensity, and without vowel modification. Belting is using that sound quality. A belter is someone who can easily make this sound and is comfortable in material written to be sung in this quality. This is the only term that can be used multiple ways to describe vocal output. "I am a belter, belting out a belt song." Belting is often found in styles of CCM as well as most contemporary music theater.

Benedictus: See Sanctus.

Bollywood: The Hindi-language film industry in India. Bollywood is the largest motion picture industry in the world, turning out more than two thousand films every year. Asha Bhosle (b. 1933) has sung as a playback singer in more than one thousand Bollywood films.

Bookwriter: A member of a musical writing team that creates the plot, dramatic structure, and character development. The bookwriter works closely with the lyricist and composer in writing the dialogue and shaping the arc of the show. Many people credit the bookwriter with the success or failure of a Broadway show. Prominent female bookwriters include Marsha Norman (b. 1947) for *The Secret Garden* (1991) and *The Color Purple* (2005) and Lisa Kron (b. 1961) for *Fun Home* (2013).

Bossa: A Brazilian musical style in the bossa nova tradition implying a fusion of samba and jazz.

Bossa Nova: Brazilian genre of popular music. Literally translating as the "new thing," bossa nova emerged in the mid-1950s and built on the tradition established by samba. Bossa nova fused together elements of samba with the harmonic and melodic complexity of jazz, particularly the "cool jazz" movement that had emerged in the United States. Elis Regina (1945–1982) is perhaps the world's most famous female exponent of bossa nova.

Boston Six: Another name for the Second New England School.

Buccal Speech: An alternative way of speaking that does not utilize the lungs or larynx. In buccal speech, air is stored in the oral cavity (usually the cheek), which acts as an alternate lung. The air is then sent into the mouth, where speech is created without the engagement of the vocal folds. Buccal speech is also widely known as "Donald Duck talk," as the famous Disney character is the quintessential example of buccal speech in the mass media. Buccal speech is sometimes used as an extended vocal technique in avant-garde music.

Cabaret: A genre in the music theater style that is usually performed in small cabarets, or nightclubs, by singing entertainers. Cabaret casts are often small, and there is usually no narrative or other production elements (costumes, sets, scenery, etc.) generally associated with music theater productions. Cabaret songs are perhaps best thought of as music theater songs that stand alone and are not from musicals.

Cantata: A genre of sacred choral music. Eighteenth-century cantatas were usually choral-orchestral works based on Lutheran chorale tunes, which also provide some of the melodic and contrapuntal material for the opening choral movement. The full homophonic chorale is then presented at the end of the cantata. Soloists offer recitatives and arias between these two movements, which bookend the work. In later eras, the term is used more broadly and can be applied to any sacred work composed for soloists, choirs, and orchestra (or organ). These cantatas are still in several movements but are usually shorter than a full-length oratorio. Fanny Hensel (1805–1847) wrote two cantatas—*Hiob* (*Job*) and *Lobgesang*—both in 1831. Anna Thorvaldsdottir (b. 1977) and Caroline Shaw (b. 1982) have written contemporary cantatas as two of the *Seven Responses* (2016), a major work commissioned by the Crossing that reimagines *Membra Jesu nostri* (1680) by Dietrich Buxtehude (1737/1739–1797).

Canticle: A poetic biblical or religious text that is sung during a service of worship. Some of the most frequently sung canticles include the Magnificat (Luke 1:46–55) and Nunc Dimittis (Luke 2:29–32)—both commonly sung at an evening service—and the Te Deum (an early Christian hymn) and Jubilate (Psalm 100), which are both morning service canticles. Composers have also set these texts as large choral-orchestral works. *Canticle of the Sun* (1924) by Amy Beach (1867–1944) sets a poetic text by St. Francis of Assisi (1181/1182–1226).

CCM: Abbreviation for contemporary commercial music.

Cembalo: Another name for a harpsichord.

Chanson: A French popular song, usually sung in a cabaret atmosphere or dance hall. Édith Piaf (1915–1963) is the most well-known singer of chansons.

Circular Singing: The vocal equivalent of the circular breathing practiced by instrumentalists. The term was coined by Joan La Barbara (b. 1947), who utilized the technique in her 1974 work *Circular Singing*.

Cisgender: Describing one who identifies with their gender assigned at birth. Cisgendered individuals have a sense of personal identity that corresponds with their sex and gender. Cis is sometimes defined as an abbreviation for "comfortable in skin."

Commission: An order for a new composition in which a person or organization agrees to pay a composer for the creation of a new work. Commissions are how composers make a living. They can come from individuals, symphonies, opera companies, music festivals, or universities. In the twenty-first century, "crowd commissions" have become more common, with groups of people banding together to commission and perform new compositions.

Communion: The sharing of bread and wine in remembrance of the crucifixion of Christ in a Christian worship service. Communion occurs at the end of mass.

Contemporary Commercial Music (CCM): An umbrella term for all styles and genres that fall outside of classical singing. The term CCM was coined by Jeannette LoVetri (b. 1949) as a more positive alternative to its pejorative predecessor, "nonclassical."

Counterculture: A way of life and set of attitudes opposed to or at variance with the prevailing social norm. The counterculture of the 1960s was a movement that erupted in the Western world and aimed to dismantle conservative ideas and norms as well as injustices toward marginalized groups of people.

Credo: The third and central part of the mass ordinary. The Credo is the Latin version of the Nicene Creed, a statement of belief widely used in Christian liturgy.

Dance Arranger: A composer that works with a show's composer and choreographer to create dance numbers in musicals. The dance arranger expands ideas and shapes them to fit the choreography. Dance arrangers sometimes also serve as vocal arrangers and orchestrators.

Deep Listening: A sonic awareness practice developed by composer Pauline Oliveros (1932–2016), who described it as "listening in every way possible to everything possible to hear no matter what everyone else is doing."

Dissonance: Intervals or moments in music that cause tension and desire to be resolved to consonant intervals. Dissonant chords are often caused by close intervals, like a minor second (m2) or major seventh (M7).

Downtempo: See Trip-Hop.

Electronica: The use of electronic-based sounds and styles, which became a common musical practice during the twentieth and twenty-first centuries. Examples of operas utilizing electronica include *Angel's Bone* (2016) by Du Yun (b. 1977) and *No Guarantees* (still a work-in-progress) by Cynthia Lee Wong (b. 1982).

Empathetic Transference: The process that allows songwriters to write songs describing subject positions outside of their direct experience, and also the process through which a listener will relate to and attach meaning to a song. Empathy provides one means for understanding across disparate experiences.

Eucharist: Another name for communion or—in the Anglican tradition—the entire mass.

Evening Service: Canticles sung at evening prayer, usually the Magnificat and Nunc Dimittis.

Fado: A Portuguese song genre. The songs are usually strophic in form, with lyrics laden with longing and regret. Fado is usually accompanied by a twelve-stringed guitar—called a *guitarra portuguesa*—a *violao* (a smaller guitar), or an accordion. Fado has its roots in the African and Moorish culture that has historically dominated the Iberian Peninsula. Amália Rodrigues (1920–1999) is the quintessential exponent of the genre.

Feminism: The advocacy of women's rights based on the equality of the sexes. Feminism is a movement associated with feminist theory and contains many branches of ideologies on how equality can be achieved.

Flamenco: A repertory of both music and dance that evolved in Andalusia, in southern Spain. Although its specific origins are unclear, flamenco may have developed as a result of Arab-speaking peoples and their influence in the region. In addition to singing, dancing, snapping, and foot-stamping are also essential features of flamenco. Concha Buika (b. 1982) is a famous example of a flamenco singer.

Florentine Camerata: An academy of scholars, poets, musicians, and scientists who met at the home of count Giovanni de' Bardi (1534–1612) in Florence during the final decades of the sixteenth century.

Their discussions about Greek artistic ideals—and music and drama specifically—led to the earliest experiments in opera during the final years of the century. Known members of the Florentine Camerata included the composers Emilio de' Cavalieri (ca. 1550–1602), Jacopo Peri (1561–1633), and Giulio Caccini (ca. 1551–1618); the poet Ottavio Rinuccini (1562–1621); and Vincenzo Galilei (ca. 1520–after 1591), father of the astronomer Galileo Galilei (1564–1642). Giulio Caccini was the father of the composer Francesca Caccini (1587–after 1641).

Gender Nonconforming: A term denoting people whose appearance or demeanor may not conform to societal expectations of their biological sex or gender assignment. Gender nonconformists may be transgender, gay, lesbian, bisexual, or nonbinary, or they may not identify with any of these designations.

Gender Parity: The state of being equal. Gender parity measures inequality, particularly relating to status or pay.

German Romanticism: A German poetic movement that arose immediately after the French Revolution in the German cities of Berlin and Jena. The movement soon spread to Heidelberg, Dresden, Vienna, and Munich. Important German Romantic poets included Novalis (1772–1801), Friedrich Schlegel (1772–1829), Ludwig Tieck (1773–1853), Clemens Brentano (1778–1842), and Joseph von Eichendorff (1778–1857). These poets developed in the shadow of Johann Wolfgang von Goethe (1749–1832), whose poems—while rooted in the classical tradition—featured many elements of German Romanticism. German Romantic themes and imagery include heightened individuality, the evocative world of nature, the seductiveness of mystery, and spiritual salvation. Fanny Hensel (1805–1847) and Clara Schumann (1819–1896) wrote their lieder during the height of German Romanticism.

Gloria: The second part of the mass ordinary. The Gloria is a Christian hymn of praise sung during the first part of the mass.

Glottal Fry: Phonation at the lowest pitches of the voice, either male or female. Produces an imprecise phonation reminiscent of "clicking." Minimal airflow is needed to produce glottal fry. Glottal fry is sometimes used as an extended vocal technique in avant-garde music.

Glottal Onset: Hard closing of the vocal folds. Sometimes called a hard attack, a glottal onset involves inhaling, closing the vocal folds, and then beginning to sing, creating a percussive beginning to vowels, like saying "uh-oh."

Grammy Awards: Originally called the Gramophone Awards, the Grammys are annual awards given by the National Academy of Recording Arts and Sciences to recognize outstanding recordings in the music industry. The 2018 Grammy Awards recognized just one female artist in the major award categories and sparked the hashtag #GrammysSoMale.

Grawemeyer Awards: Five awards that are given annually by the University of Louisville. One of these prizes is the Grawemeyer Award for Music Composition. The award is one of the most substantial in the composition world, ranging from $100,000 to $150,000 over the course of the award's history. Unlike the Pulitzer Prize, which only honors American citizens, the Grawemeyer Foundation accepts nominations from all over the world. Since 1985—the prize's inaugural year—only two women have won the Grawemeyer Award for music composition: Finnish composer Kaija Saariaho (b. 1952) in 2003 for her opera *L'amour de loin* (2000) and South Korean composer Unsuk Chin (b. 1961) in 2004 for her *Concerto for Violin and Orchestra* (2002).

Great White Way: Another name for Broadway. The name comes from the brilliant lights and signs that line the street where most Broadway theaters are situated.

Growling: A low, guttural vocalization. In addition to being used as an extended vocal technique in new music, growling is also applied in some types of heavy metal music. Growling is sometimes used as an extended vocal technique in avant-garde music.

Harlem Renaissance: An artistic movement that flourished in Harlem, New York, throughout the 1920s. This rich cultural development of African American artists encompassed literature, poetry, and music. It was epitomized by poets such as Langston Hughes (1902–1967) and Countee Cullen (1903–1946), as well as jazz musician Duke Ellington (1899–1974). The movement had a profound effect on female composers such as Florence Price (1887–1953) and Margaret Bonds (1913–1972).

Homophony: One of the three principal textures of music, homophony describes multiple voices that move together in more or less the same rhythm. It is different from monophony in that each voice has its own distinct pitch, thus creating harmony.

IAWM: Acronym for the International Alliance for Women in Music.

IFCM: Acronym for International Federation for Choral Music.

Inhaled Singing: A technique that involves singing while inhaling as opposed to exhaling. The result is a sound rooted in glottal fry. While some pitch variation is possible, the technique is limited in scope compared to traditional singing. Inhaled singing is sometimes used as an extended vocal technique in avant-garde music.

International Alliance for Women in Music: An organization that was formed in 1995 from the merger of three organizations that "arose during the women's rights movements of the 1970s to combat inequitable treatment of women in music": the International League of Women Composers (ILWC), the International Congress on Women in Music (ICWM), and American Women Composers (AWC), Inc. According to the IAWM website, the organization consists of "women and men dedicated to fostering and encouraging the activities of women in music, particularly in the areas of musical activity such as composing, performing, and research in which gender discrimination is an historic and ongoing concern." The IAWM hosts international congresses and annual competitions and publishes two journals: *Women and Music: A Journal of Gender and Culture* and the *Journal of the International Alliance for Women in Music*.

International Federation for Choral Music: The International Federation for Choral Music (IFCM) was founded in 1982 for the purpose of facilitating communication and exchange between choral musicians throughout the world. IFCM is perhaps best known for its triennial World Symposium on Choral Music, which brings together choral musicians from every corner of the globe.

Intersectionality: An analytic framework that explores the overlapping of oppressive institutional power systems—such as sexism, racism, classism, ableism, sizeism, homophobia, and transphobia—and how these interlocking systems of power impact those who are most marginalized in society. Intersectional theory was first introduced into feminist theory in 1989 by scholar and civil rights advocate Kimberlé Williams Crenshaw (b. 1959).

Jeu-parti: A type of troubadour or trouvère poetry cast in the form of a dialogue. The topic of a *jeu-parti* is usually love. Dame Maroie de

Diergnau and Dame Margot (both fl. ca. 1250) wrote a *jeu-parti* that has been preserved in two manuscripts.

Jubilate: A setting of Psalm 100. The Jubilate is usually sung during a morning service. Amy Beach (1867–1944) composed her *Festival Jubilate* in 1893.

Jukebox Musical: A music theater work comprised of songs by a pop music artist or rock band that were not originally written for the musical. Often the preexisting songs are strung together with a newly contrived dramatic plot or a biographical portrayal of the artist's life. Examples include *Head over Heels* (2018), an Elizabethan love story told with songs by the Go-Go's, and *Beautiful: The Carole King Musical* (2014).

Kyrie: The first part of the mass ordinary. The Kyrie occurs at the beginning of the mass.

Legit: A style of music theater singing heavily influenced by Western classical technique. Although the term is short for "legitimate," this does not imply that other styles are illegitimate.

Les Six: A group of six French composers in the first half of the twentieth century who modeled their art after the aesthetic and artistic principles of Erik Satie (1866–1925) and Jean Cocteau (1889–1963). Members of Les Six included Louis Durey (1888–1979), Arthur Honegger (1892–1955), Darius Milhaud (1892–1974), Francis Poulenc (1899–1963), Georges Auric (1899–1973), and Germaine Taillefaire (1892–1983), the only woman in the group. The name Les Six was given to them in 1920 by the French music critic Henri Collet (1885–1951).

Librettist: The author of a libretto.

Libretto: The script of an opera. The libretto is generally written first and then set to music by the composer.

Liederabend: An evening of art song in an intimate venue, usually the living room or parlor of a private home. While the name *Liederabend* implies that only German art songs (lieder) are performed, contemporary *Liederabends*—or *Liederabende* (plural)—often program art songs in multiple languages.

Liederjahr: A German term meaning "year of song" used to describe 1840, the year in which Robert Schumann (1810–1856) wrote close to 140 lieder. Major song cycles from this prolific year include *Liederkreis*, Op. 24; *Myrthen*, Op. 25; *Kerner-Lieder*, Op. 35; *Liederkreis*, Op. 39; *Frauenliebe und -leben*, Op. 42; and *Dichterliebe*, Op. 48. 1840 was also the year he married Clara Wieck (1819–1896).

Lilly Awards: A foundation started in the spring of 2010 as an outlet to honor the work of women in American theater. The founders of the Lilly Awards are Marsha Norman (b. 1947), Theresa Rebeck (b. 1958), and Julia Jordan (b. ca. 1969). The awards are named for playwright Lillian Hellman (1905–1984), who famously said, "You need to write like the devil and act like one when necessary." In partnership with the Dramatists Guild, the Lilly Awards conduct a national survey simply called "the Count" that accurately showcases which theaters are producing works by women and which are not. Analyzing three years of data from productions in regional theaters in America, a study published in 2015 found that only 22 percent of these productions were written by women.

Litany: A prayer consisting of a series of invocations and supplications by the leader with alternate responses by the congregation. Litanies are often set to music. Isabella Leonarda (1620–1704) composed several litanies.

Lyricist: The writer of the words to a song. A lyricist often works closely with a music theater composer to create songs. Notable female lyricists on Broadway include Rida Johnson Young (1875–1926), Betty Comden (1917–2006), and Lynn Ahrens (b. 1948).

Madrigal: A Renaissance genre of vocal music that consists of secular texts set in a polyphonic style. The two schools of madrigal composition included the Italian madrigal, which came first, and the English madrigal, which appropriated many of the conventions of the Italian school. Although the French also dabbled in the madrigal genre, these polyphonic secular songs are usually called chansons. Maddalena Casulana (ca. 1544–ca. 1590) is the most notable woman composer of madrigals.

Magnificat: The canticle of the Virgin Mary in Luke 1:46–55. Also called the Song of Mary, the Magnificat is usually sung during an evening service or as a large orchestral-choral work. Chiara Margarita Cozzolani (1602–1678) wrote two Magnificat settings in 1650.

Mansplaining: A term used to describe a man explaining something to a woman in a condescending and sexist manner. The word was added to the *Oxford New English Dictionary* in 2018.

Marian Antiphon: An antiphon in praise of the Virgin Mary. The four Marian antiphons are *Alma redemptoris mater* ("Nourishing Mother of the Redeemer"), *Ave regina coelorum* ("Hail, Queen of Heaven"),

Regina coeli ("Rejoice, Queen of Heaven"), and *Salve regina* ("Hail, Holy Queen"). Isabella Leonarda (1620–1704) composed settings of Marian antiphons.

Mass: The liturgy of the Eucharist. As a musical genre, a setting of the five parts of the mass ordinary: the Kyrie, Gloria, Credo, Sanctus, and Agnus Dei. The *Mass in D* by Ethel Smyth (1858–1944) is perhaps the most famous example of a mass by a woman composer.

Me Too: A women's empowerment movement against sexual harassment and assault. It gained national attention in 2017 with the viral spread of the hashtag #MeToo and the *Time* magazine cover naming the founder of the movement Tarana Burke (b. 1973), along with singer-songwriter Taylor Swift (b. 1989) and other "Silence Breakers," as Person of the Year. After numerous actresses came forward with abuse allegations against film producer Harvey Weinstein (b. 1952), the movement encouraged victims to go public with their experiences. It has resulted in the resignations of many high-profile men in film, television, and government who have been accused of harassing or assaulting women.

Mestizo: A Spanish word used in Latin America to describe someone of mixed race, especially someone of Spanish and Native American descent.

Monodrama: An operatic work with a single performer, who may play one or multiple characters. Examples include *Aunt Helen* (2012) by Monica Pearce (b. 1984) and *Beethoven's Slippers* (2016) by Judith Cloud (b. 1954).

Monody: A particular style of accompanied vocal solo that developed in Italy at the beginning of the baroque era (ca. 1600). In monody, a recitative-like solo vocal line is accompanied by a basso continuo. Monody is closely associated with the beginnings of opera.

Monophony: One of the three principal textures of music, monophony describes a single unaccompanied melodic line.

Morning Service: Canticles sung at morning prayer, usually the Jubilate and Te Deum.

Motet: A polyphonic piece of choral music. The term "motet" has meant different things at different times in music history. Thirteenth-century motets could be either sacred or secular and were in Latin or French, often multi-textual (with several texts occurring simultaneously in different voices), and almost always based on a cantus firmus derived from Gregorian chant. In the fourteenth century, many motets were isorhythmic. From the fifteenth century onward, any polyphonic setting of a sacred Latin text that is not part of a mass was considered to be a motet. Beginning in the sixteenth century, the term "motet" could apply to polyphonic sacred compositions in any language. Vittoria Aleotti (ca. 1573–1620) and Isabella Leonarda (1620–1704) were both composers of baroque motets.

MTV: A television station that exclusively aired music videos—miniature movies that serve as a visual accompaniment to a popular song. Launched in 1981, MTV was a pivotal marketing tool as well as a form of artistic expression in the music business. The channel enormously influenced the youth culture of the 1980s and 1990s. MTV is an abbreviation for "Music Television." Although the channel originally focused on music videos, MTV now is mostly known for its reality shows.

Multimedia: A term used to describe the use of multiple forms of media in artistic or communicative expression. The media elements could include prerecorded audio tracks, projections of text, images, animation, and/or video. Multimedia elements are becoming increasingly common in song recital settings and especially in operatic productions. Operas by women that specify the need for a multimedia approach include *Frankenstein, or the Modern Prometheus* (1990) by Libby Larsen (b. 1950) and *Oceanic Verses* (2009) by Paola Prestini (b. 1975).

Multiphonics: More than one pitch produced at the same time. While usually an instrumental technique, vocalists can also produce multiphonics, typically in one of two ways: throat singing or whistling while phonating. Multiphonics are sometimes used as an extended vocal technique in avant-garde music.

Music Director: The person responsible for executing the musical aspects of a production. The music director works with the actors, chorus, and orchestra and often conducts performances while playing the keyboard. On Broadway, female music directors have included Trude Rittman (1908–2005) and Tania León (b. 1943).

New Musicology: A movement in musicology beginning in the late 1980s that examined music from a variety of cultural perspectives, including gender and race. With an emphasis on criticism, feminism, and queer theory, it was a reaction to the research-based "old" musicology of the earlier part of the twentieth century. *Feminine Endings: Music, Gender, and Sexuality* (1991) by Susan McClary (b. 1946) is considered to be a seminal book in new musicology.

Nunc Dimittis: The canticle of the Simeon in Luke 2:29–32. Also called the Song of Simeon, the Nunc Dimittis is usually sung during an evening service.

Octavo: The name for a short, published choral composition. Historically, the term derives its name from the folding of a large sheet of paper into eight sections, resulting in sixteen printed pages (front and back). Hence, the term also came to mean a particular size: about eight to ten inches tall.

Off-Broadway: New York theaters that are located outside of the Broadway theater district. Off-Broadway productions tend to be smaller and less expensive and thus can be a breeding ground for innovation. The seating capacity is often less as well. Off-Broadway productions are not eligible for Tony Award consideration but can be considered for Obie Awards—a separate set of awards for Off-Broadway theater.

Oratorio: A musical genre for chorus, orchestra, and soloists. Oratorios generally have a biblical or religious narrative but are written for the concert hall as opposed to a liturgical worship service. Unlike opera, oratorios are generally not staged and do not feature sets and costumes, although the soloists do usually play specific characters in the narrative. The oratorio proper is always set in the vernacular, although the earliest examples were in Latin. *Oratorium nach den Bildern der Bibel* (1831) by Fanny Hensel (1805–1847) is an example of an oratorio that fits the traditional definition. *Anthracite Fields* by Julia Wolfe (b. 1958) is a modern secular oratorio about Pennsylvania coal miners that won the Pulitzer Prize in 2015.

Orchestrator: The arranger of the orchestral parts of a show's musical score. The orchestrator takes the composer's music and makes choices regarding which instruments will play what music. Sarah Travis (fl. ca. 2005) is the only woman to win the Tony Award for Best Orchestration, which she won for the 2005 Broadway revival of *Sweeney Todd* by Stephen Sondheim (b. 1930).

Oscars: See Academy Awards.

Partsong: A song (or lied) for more than one voice. In nineteenth-century Germany and Austria, partsongs were usually four-part lieder

(SATB or TTBB) that set German Romantic poetry. Fanny Hensel (1805–1847) wrote six partsongs on texts by Joseph Freiherr von Eichendorff (1788–1857), Ludwig Uhland (1787–1862), Emanuel von Geibel (1815–1884), and her husband, Wilhelm Hensel (1794–1861).

Passaggio: A transition between vocal registers. Literally means "passage" in Italian.

Plantation Songs: Songs sung by African slaves held on American plantations in the eighteenth and nineteenth centuries. Plantation songs were often rhythmic and repetitive as both work songs and dance songs.

Playback Singer: A singer whose singing is prerecorded for use in movies. Marni Nixon (1930–2016) and Asha Bhosle (b. 1933) are famous examples.

Polyphony: One of the three principal textures of music, polyphony describes two or more voices moving simultaneously, each with its own pitch and rhythmic identity.

Prima Prattica: The Renaissance style of composition employing imitative species counterpoint. Prima prattica works were almost always a cappella polyphonic choral works. Maddalena Casulana (ca. 1540–ca. 1590) composed in the prima prattica style.

Prix de Rome: A French prize for student artists created by Louis XIV (1638–1715) in 1663. Originally for painters and sculptors, it was expanded to include composers in 1803. In 1913, Lili Boulanger (1893–1918) was the first woman to win the composition prize. Since then these women composers have also won: Marguerite Canal (1890–1978) in 1920, Jeanne Leleu (1898–1979) in 1923, Elsa Barraine (1910–1999) in 1929, Yvonne Desportes (1907–1993) in 1932, Odette Gartenlaub (1922–2014) in 1948, Adrienne Clostre (1921–2006) in 1949, Éveline Plicque-Andreani (fl. ca. 1960) in 1950, Thérèse Brenet (b. 1935) in 1965, and Monic Cecconi-Botella (b. 1936) in 1966. The prize was discontinued after 1968.

Psalm: One of the 150 Psalms of David found in the Bible. Psalms are almost always a sung portion of the liturgy, and many composers have set psalm texts as choral works. Lili Boulanger (1893–1918) composed three famous psalm settings.

Pulitzer Prize: An annual award given by Columbia University to honor significant American achievements in journalism, letters, drama, and music. The Pulitzer Prize in Music has been awarded annually since 1943. At the time of the writing of this book, only seven women have won the Pulitzer Prize for Music: Ellen Taaffe Zwilich (b. 1939) for *Three Movements for Orchestra* in 1983; Shulamit Ran (b. 1949) for her *Symphony* in 1991; Melinda Wagner (b. 1956) for her *Concerto for Flute, Strings, and Percussion* in 1999; Jennifer Higdon (b. 1962) for her *Violin Concerto* in 2010; Caroline Shaw (b. 1982) for her choral work *Partita for 8 Voices* in 2013; Julia Wolfe (b. 1958) for her oratorio *Anthracite Fields* in 2015; and Du Yun (b. 1977) for her opera *Angel's Bone* in 2017.

Punk: A subgenre of rock music that emerged in England during the 1970s. Punk was a form of social protest, and the lyrics of punk were usually intensely political in nature. Punk music is usually loud in volume, with an intense and harsh vocal quality. The music and lyrics—as well as the dress and behavior of the performers—were deliberately provocative. The Sex Pistols are credited as the originators of punk.

Ranchera: A blues-influenced folk music of Mexico, usually scored for voice and guitar. Like the blues, the lyrics of *ranchera* music are often about hard times and fond reminiscence. Chavela Vargas (1919–2012) gained international recognition as a performer of *rancheras*.

Requiem: A funeral mass to honor the dead. Many composers have written choral-orchestral settings of the requiem mass, which offers a different collection of texts than the standard five-part mass. The best-known settings by women composers are the requiems of Carol Barnett (b. 1949) and Eleanor Daley (b. 1955), composed in 1981 and 1994, respectively. Elisabeth Lutyens (1906–1983) also wrote a secular work entitled *Requiem for the Living* in 1949.

Rococo: An eighteenth-century reaction to the formal and grandiose structure of baroque music. Rococo music—most often associated with the keyboard works of François Couperin (1668–1733)—is characterized as graceful and free flowing and often features ornaments or embellishments called *agréments*. Rococo is one of the signals of a late-baroque shift toward the dawning classical era. Marianna von Martines (1744–1812) wrote keyboard works in the rococo style.

SAB: Abbreviation that describes a three-part choral work for mixed voices: soprano-alto-bass.

Samba: An Afro-Brazilian dance established in Brazil at the beginning of the twentieth century. Sambas featured a vocal soloist and choral refrains over a distinctive syncopated rhythmic pattern. Samba songs are usually in 2/4 meter, and the genre has its roots in the West African slave trade to South America. Samba is an important forerunner of bossa nova.

Sanctus: The fourth part of the mass ordinary. The Sanctus is sung at the beginning of communion. Sometimes called the Sanctus-Benedictus, referring to the second part of the text.

SATB: Abbreviation that describes a four-part choral work for mixed voices: soprano-alto-tenor-bass.

Screaming: A vocal technique that is self-explanatory. However, there is a technique to screaming in a non-damaging way. Consultation with a knowledgeable acting voice teacher is highly recommended.

Second New England School: A group of six composers active in Boston at the turn of the twentieth century. The members of the "Boston Six" were John Knowles Paine (1839–1906), Arthur Foote (1853–1937), George Chadwick (1854–1931), Edward MacDowell (1861–1908), Horatio Parker (1863–1919), and Amy Beach (1867–1944), the only woman in the group. The "Second New England School" contrasts with the "First New England School" of the previous century, a designation for the style of William Billings (1746–1800) and his contemporaries. The name is also a spinoff of the "Second Viennese School" represented by Arnold Schoenberg (1874–1951), Alban Berg (1885–1935), and Anton Webern (1883–1945).

Seconda Prattica: The baroque style of composition employing monody with basso continuo accompaniment. The earliest operas associated with the Florentine Camerata are all composed in the seconda prattica style. *La liberazione di Ruggiero dall'isola d'Alcina* (1625) by Francesca Caccini (1587–after 1641) is an example of a seconda prattica work.

Service: A group of texts used in a religious ceremony. The Anglican tradition has two services: morning and evening, each with their own distinct canticles and litanies. Amy Beach (1867–1944) wrote a complete *Service in A* (1905), which sets both the morning and evening canticles.

Song Cycle: A group of art songs designed to be performed in sequence due to an overlying narrative or theme, often with texts by the same poet. Examples of song cycles by women composers include *From the Dark Tower* (1972) by Dorothy Rudd Moore (b. 1940) and *Try Me, Good King* (2000) by Libby Larsen (b. 1950).

Sonic Awareness: See Deep Listening.

Spiritual: African American religious folk song cultivated during the nineteenth and early twentieth centuries. Traditional spirituals usually employ a call-and-response format and refrains. Spiritual themes depict the struggles of a hard life combined with deep faith and a sense of determined optimism. Undine Smith Moore (1904–1989) composed choral works that are influenced by the spiritual tradition.

Sprechstimme: A vocal quality or style that lies somewhere in between speech and singing. Although exact pitches are notated—with an *x* over each note stem—and are expected to be performed with accuracy, it is also incumbent on the performer to give the vocal line a speech-like quality. Sprechstimme is considered to be an extended vocal technique in avant-garde music.

STEAM: An acronym that adds the "Arts" to the traditional STEM acronym for "Science, Technology, Engineering, and Mathematics."

Stile recitativo: A type of vocal monody with an emphasis on natural declamation. Invented by the Florentine Camerata, the vocal style developed concurrently with the genesis of opera in the late sixteenth and early seventeenth century.

Sturm und Drang: A movement in theatrical writing that took place in Germany between the late 1760s and the mid-1780s. Literally meaning "storm and stress," proponents of the movement rebelled against neoclassical dictums and eighteenth-century rationalism with a drama that emphasized passion, inspiration, and individualism. Gotthold Ephraim Lessing (1729–1781) and Johann Gottfried Herder (1744–1803) are considered to be central figures. The lieder of Maria Theresia von Paradis (1759–1824) exemplify characteristics of Sturm und Drang.

Suffragette: A term used to describe a woman in the late nineteenth and early twentieth century who fought for women's right to vote. The women's suffrage movement was led in England by Emmeline

Pankhurst (1858–1928) and in the United States by Susan B. Anthony (1820–1906). The Nineteenth Amendment granted American women the right to vote in 1920. Composer Ethel Smyth (1858–1944) was a suffragette, writing the anthem "The March of the Women" in 1910.

Symbolism: A French literary movement from the second half of the nineteenth century closely associated with the poets Charles Baudelaire (1821–1867), Stéphane Mallarmé (1842–1898), and Paul Verlaine (1844–1896). Although symbolism did not manifest itself as a musical movement per se, a basic understanding of symbolism is essential to the performer of French *mélodies*, many of which are settings of symbolist poems. Lili Boulanger (1893–1918) was strongly attracted to symbolist poets, as evidenced in her choice of song texts.

Te Deum: An early Christian hymn. The Te Deum is usually sung during a morning service or as a large orchestral-choral work.

Throat Singing: An eccentric singing technique that involves specific manipulation of the singer's jaw, lips, mouth, and sinuses to produce several overtones simultaneously. The fundamental note that produces these overtones is always a specific pitch in the TA/mode 1 register. Throat singing is considered to be an extended vocal technique in avant-garde music.

Time's Up: A women's empowerment movement against sexual assault, harassment, and inequality in the workplace. In response to Harvey Weinstein and in support of the Me Too movement, it was announced in an open letter online and a full-page advertisement in the *New York Times* on January 1, 2018. The three hundred supporters who were the original signatories were primarily Hollywood actresses such as Reese Witherspoon (b. 1976), Ashley Judd (b. 1968), Eva Longoria (b. 1975), Kerry Washington (b. 1977), and Meryl Streep (b. 1949). Singer-songwriters who signed the original letter were Taylor Swift (b. 1989) and Mariah Carey (b. 1970). It established the Time's Up Legal Defense Fund, housed and administered by the National Women's Law Center, to provide legal and public relations assistance for women whose careers have been affected by harassment and/or retaliation.

Tin Pan Alley: Music publishers and songwriters that dominated the music scene in the late nineteenth and early twentieth century. Although it eventually came to refer to the sheet music industry as a whole, it initially denoted a specific area of West 28th Street in Manhattan where the majority of songwriters were located.

Tony Awards: More formally known as the Antoinette Perry Awards for Excellence in Broadway Theatre, these annual awards are sponsored by the American Theatre Wing and the Broadway League. The Tony Awards have been given each season since 1947, and one of the awards is for Best Original Score. In spite of this long history, only three women have won the Tony for Best Original Score without male writing partners and for only two musicals: Cyndi Lauper (b. 1953) won her Tony for the music and lyrics to *Kinky Boots* in 2013, and Jeanine Tesori (b. 1961) and Lisa Kron (b. 1961) each took home a Tony for the music and lyrics (respectively) for *Fun Home* in 2015. Ironically, the American Theatre Wing was started by a group of female playwrights, directors, and actresses—including Rachel Crothers (1878–1958) and Dorothy Donnelly (1880–1928)—and the awards were shortened to the masculine "Tony" rather than Antoinette Perry's spelling of "Toni," despite the fact that she donated the money that initially funded these awards.

Tragédie en musique: A type of French opera in the late seventeenth and early eighteenth centuries that combined conventions from classical French theater with ballet traditions. Jean-Baptiste Lully (1632–1687) is credited as the inventor of the *tragédie en musique*. Later in his career, Lully began using a new label for this genre—the *tragédie lyrique*—which is virtually identical in style to its predecessor.

Tragédie lyrique: See *Tragédie en musique*.

Transgender: A term used to describe people whose gender identity does not correspond to the gender they were assigned at birth. The T in LGBTQ+ represents transgender individuals, and sometimes the abbreviation "trans" is utilized. *As One* (2014) by Laura Kaminsky (b. 1956) is the first opera with a transgender leading character. Trans opera singers of note include Lucia Lucas (b. ca. 1981) and Holden Madagame (b. 1990).

Trip-Hop: A musical style fusing hip-hop and electronica that emerged in the 1990s. Sometimes called downtempo, it is associated with British bands such as Massive Attack.

Trobairitz: A female troubadour. Beatriz de Dia (ca. 1160–1212)—also called "La Comtessa de Dia"—is a famous example of a *trobairitz*.

Troubadour: One of a class of lyric poets and poet-musicians often of knightly rank who flourished from the eleventh century to the end of the thirteenth century. Troubadours were found in the south of France and the north of Italy. A major theme of their poetry was courtly love.

Trouvère: One of a school of poets who flourished from the eleventh to the fourteenth centuries and who composed mostly narrative works. Trouvères were found in the north of France. Dame Maroie de Diergnau and Dame Margot (both fl. ca. 1250) were female trouvères from Arras.

TTBB: Abbreviation that describes a four-part choral work for male voices: tenor-tenor-bass-bass.

Ululation: A long, wavering, high-pitched vocal sound produced by the deliberate and rapid manipulation of the tongue. Ululation is a distinct and idiomatic sound heard in certain types of world music. Ululations are sometimes used as an extended vocal technique in avant-garde music.

Visual Album: An album in which every song has an accompanying music video, with the videos telling an overarching story or serving a specific unified concept. Examples of visual albums by female artists include *Lemonade* (2016) by Beyoncé (b. 1981) and Florence and the Machine's *The Odyssey* (2016).

Vocal Agility: The ability to move the voice with speed and control across multiple pitches. Vocal agility is often demonstrated through riffs or melismas.

Vocal Hygiene: The care and upkeep of the voice. Good vocal hygiene typically includes a regimen to prevent injury as well as treatment for a range of conditions from natural fatigue to injury. This regimen can include proper warm-up techniques, medicine, therapy, and lifestyle choices that support vocal health rather than harm it.

Vocal Range: The total span of notes a singer can sing. A singer's vocal range comprises the highest and lowest notes they can produce and all the notes in between, regardless of quality. Sometimes a singer's vocal range is stated in terms of actual—meaning, the actual collection of notes the voice can make—or concert, meaning the collection of notes that can be consistently produced at a strong enough quality to perform multiple times in a row.

Women's Liberation Movement: A political alignment of feminism and the counterculture that emerged in the late 1960s in the Western world and that effected great change—politically, intellectually, and culturally—throughout the world. Women of culturally diverse backgrounds proposed that economic, psychological, and social freedom were necessary for women to progress from their status as second-class citizens in their societies.

Women's March: A women's rights protest that took place on January 21, 2017, in response to the previous day's presidential inauguration. It is estimated that half a million people attended the march in Washington, D.C., the largest protest there since the Vietnam War era. Approximately five million marched nationwide.

Year of the Woman: A term used to describe 2018, in which a record number of women ran for political office in the midterm elections. It is considered a response to the 2016 election loss of Hillary Clinton (b. 1947). Previously, 1992 was labeled the Year of the Woman when a record number of female senators were elected, considered by many to be a response to the treatment of Anita Hill (b. 1956) in Senate confirmation hearings for Supreme Court Justice Clarence Thomas (b. 1948).

Yodeling: A style of singing often associated with folk music of the Swiss Alps. Yodeling features the singing of leaps and a rapid alternation between the two principal vocal registers (TA and CT). A "yodel" can also be a short section of yodeling, sung on a single breath. Derived from the (middle-high) German verb "jôlen," meaning "to call," yodeling is thought to have originated as a call between mountain peoples. Whether there was a practical use for yodeling is unclear, but its popularity as an interesting and engaging folk music endures. Due to the use of both registers, yodelers often have an extensive range of three octaves or more. A singer who practices yodeling is called a yodeler.

INDEX

Brahms, Johannes, 121, 167
Brandt, Penny, 281, 316
Braxton, Toni, 201
Bray, Stephen, 161
"Break It Up," 190
Breaking the Waves, 85
breath control, 212
breath management, 212, 237
breath support, 212
Bregenzer Festspiele, 80
Brenet, Thérèse, 14, 339
Brentano, Clemens, 331
Bresson, Robert, 135
Brice, Fanny, 148
Brickell, Edie, 38, 160
Bridges of the Madison County, The, 158
Brigadoon, 152
"Bright Rails," 63
Bright Star, 38, 160
Brighton Early Music Festival, 75
Bring in 'da Noise, Bring in 'da Funk, 37
Bring It On: The Musical, 161
Briscoe, James, 20, 297, 309
Britten, Benjamin, 32
"Broken Hearted Romeo," 148
Bronsart, Ingeborg von, 311
Brontë sisters, xx, 69, 348
Brook, Claire, 310
Brooklyn College, 109
Brown, Greg, 200
Brown, Jason Robert, 28, 158, 167
Brown, Stacy, 290
Brown of Harvard, 141
Brown University, 109
Browning, Elizabeth Barrett, 63, 66
Bryn-Julson, Phyllis, 125–126, 132
buccal speech, 128–129, 327
Buffalo Philharmonic, 59

"Bug-a-Boo," 200
Buika, Concha, 12, 330
"Bumble Bee," 181
Burke, Tarana, 336
Burleigh, H. T., 115
Burnett, Carol, 37
Burruss, Kandi, 200–201
Bush, Kate, 69
Bussotti, Sylvano, 123
Buxtehude, Dietrich, 117, 128, 328
"Bye Bye Baby," 186
Byron, Lord, 62
Byzantine chant, 3, 307

cabaret, 11, 328
Cabildo, 76
Caccini, Francesca, 6, 34, 75–76, 94, 308, 310, 331, 341
Caccini, Giulio, 75, 331
Caccini, Settimia, 311
Caesar, Sid, 150
caffeine, 230, 238
Cage, John, 122–124
Caillat, Colbie, 41
Caldwell, Anne, 143–144
"California," 185
Callas, Maria, 77
Campbell, Mary-Mitchell, 280
Cambridge University, 25, 106
Camelot, 152
Campana, Francesca, 6
Canadian Opera Company, 74–75
Canadian Women Composers Project, 314
Canal, Margarite, 14, 339
Candeille, Amélie-Julie, 76
Candide, 91
"Can't We Be Friends?" 144
Cantet, Laurent, 135
Canticle of the Sun, 102, 328

Villard de Beaumesnil, Henriette
  Adélaïde, 8
Violet, 158
Virginia Opera, 79
Virginia State University, 58, 111
Virginia Tech, 81
Visage, 123
Visione 97, 109
visual album, 29, 345
Visuddhimagga, 103
Viva O'Brien, 148
vocal agility, 178, 345
vocal athletes, 225–226, 233–237,
  242
vocal cross–training, 241, 243
vocal fatigue, 232, 242
vocal fitness, 238, 242
vocal folds, 129, 177, 208, 214–216,
  219, 226–228, 230, 238–240, 243,
  247, 326, 327, 331
vocal health, 177, 225, 228, 238–239,
  243, 345
vocal injury, 225, 236–237, 242, 243
vocal ligament, 214
vocal longevity, 237
vocal naps, 240
vocal timbre, 185
vocal tract, 216, 218–219, 222, 247
vocal wellness, 242
vocalises, 237–238, 241
voice box, 213
Voice–Box (opera), 86
Voice Foundation, The (TVF), 224
Voice of Ariadne, The, 79
Voice Secrets, xx
Voices of Earth, 107

Wagner, Lauren, 65
Wagner, Melinda, 15, 340
Wagner, Richard, 31, 55, 73, 237

Waitress, 38, 162
Walker, Alice, 161
Walker, Gwyneth, 109
Walpurgis, Maria Antonia, 319
Walt Disney Hall, 92
Warburg, John, 146
Ward, Robert, 77
Warlock, Peter, 103
warm-ups, 238
Warren, Diane, 201–202
Warren, Elizabeth, 284
Warsaw Chamber Opera, 75
Washington, Dinah, 148
Washington, Kerry, 343
Washington University, St. Louis,
  105
Water Lilies, 106
Webern, Anton, 341
Weil, Cynthia, 183, 200
Weir, Judith, 79–80, 307
Weisgall, Hugo, 62
Wellesley College, 108
Wells, Brad, 126
Wells, Kitty, 11
Wen–chung, Chou, 110
Werfel, Franz, 53
Welch, Gillian, 200
Wesleyan University, 67
West Edge Opera, 80
Westminster Cathedral Choir,
  106–107
Westminster Choir College, 111
"What a Difference a Day Makes,"
  148
What We Leave Behind, 284
"Whataya Want from Me," 201
"When Love Is Young," 141
"Whistling in the Dark," 148
White, Jim, 200
White, Maude Valérie, 10, 311

ABOUT THE AUTHORS AND CONTRIBUTORS

Matthew Hoch is associate professor of voice at Auburn University. He is the author of several books, including *A Dictionary for the Modern Singer*, *Welcome to Church Music and the Hymnal 1982*, and *Voice Secrets: 100 Performance Strategies for the Advanced Singer*, coauthored with Linda Lister. He is also the editor of *So You Want to Sing Sacred Music* and *So You Want to Sing CCM*. His articles have appeared in the *Journal of Voice*, *Journal of Singing*, *Voice and Speech Review*, *Opera Journal*, *Choral Journal*, *The Chorister*, *American Music Teacher*, *Classical Singer*, *College Music Symposium*, *Kodály Envoy*, *Journal of the Association of Anglican Musicians*, and the *Journal of the International Alliance for Women in Music*. Hoch is president of the New York Singing Teachers Association (NYSTA) and is the 2016 winner of the Van L. Lawrence Fellowship, awarded jointly by the Voice Foundation and the National Association of Teachers of Singing (NATS). He holds the BM from Ithaca College, MM from the Hartt School, DMA from the New England Conservatory, and the Certificate in Vocology from the National Center for Voice and Speech (NCVS). Hoch is affiliate faculty in women's studies at Auburn University, where he developed the institution's first-ever Women in Music course, offered at both undergraduate and graduate levels and in live and online formats.

Linda Lister is associate professor of voice and director of opera at the University of Nevada, Las Vegas. She is author of *Yoga for Singers: Freeing Your Voice and Spirit through Yoga, So You Want to Sing Light Opera,* and coauthor of *Voice Secrets: 100 Performance Strategies for the Advanced Singer* (with Matthew Hoch) and *Red Rock Mantras* (with Gianni Becker). Her writings have appeared in the *Opera Journal, Journal of Singing, Classical Singer, American Music Teacher, Popular Music and Society, The Brontës in the World of the Arts,* and *Music in American Life: An Encyclopedia of the Songs, Styles, Stars, and Stories That Shaped Our Culture.* A Phi Beta Kappa graduate of Vassar College, she received her MM from the Eastman School of Music and her DMA from the University of North Carolina at Greensboro. She won the 2014 American Prize in Directing as well as two first place directing awards from the National Opera Association. As a soprano soloist, she appears on the albums *The American Soloist, Midnight Tolls,* and *Moments of Arrival.* Also a composer, she sings her own art songs on the Albany Records release *Pleas to Famous Fairies.* Lister has composed two operas: *How Clear She Shines!* (about the Brontë sisters) and *State of Grace* (about a yoga teacher who faces cancer).

✿ ✿ ✿

Matthew Edwards is associate professor of voice and voice pedagogy at Shenandoah Conservatory and artistic director of the CCM Voice Pedagogy Institute. His current and former students have performed on and off Broadway as well as on national and international tours and major motion picture soundtracks and have appeared on Billboard music charts. Edwards is the author of *So You Want to Sing Rock 'n' Roll* and has contributed chapters to *Manual of Singing Voice Rehabilitation, The Vocal Athlete, Get the Callback,* and *A Dictionary for the Modern Singer.* He has authored articles for the *Journal of Singing, Journal of Voice, American Music Teacher, VOICEPrints,* and *Southern Theatre.* Edwards regularly presents workshops on functional training for the CCM singer at conferences and universities throughout the United States.

Erin Guinup is an active concert performer, conductor, voice teacher, and public speaker. A classically trained soprano, Guinup has performed a wide range of operatic and music theater repertoire with ensembles including Northwest Repertory Singers, Ensign Symphony, and Tacoma Concert Band. Her internationally performed one-woman show *The Ladies of Lyric and Song: Female Composers and Lyricists of the American Musical Theatre* has been praised as "an amazing tour-de-force." She is an acclaimed voice teacher whose students have appeared on Broadway, regional theater, and operatic stages, as well as television's *The Voice, American Idol,* and *America's Got Talent.* Guinup is the conductor of the Tacoma Refugee Choir and is a frequent clinician and international speaker on musical topics and hosts the "Why We Sing" podcast. Her "Musically Spoken" workshops guide teams and Fortune 100 companies to encourage healthy communication and teamwork as individuals find their voice figuratively and physically, and she has worked with speakers for TEDx talks and presentations for major corporations. She is a proud member of the National Association of Teachers of Singing (NATS) and currently serves as the Western Washington district governor.

Wendy LeBorgne is a voice pathologist, speaker, author, and master class clinician. She actively presents nationally and internationally on the professional voice and is the clinical director of two successful private practice voice centers: the ProVoice Center in Cincinnati and BBIVAR in Dayton. LeBorgne holds an adjunct professorship at University of Cincinnati College-Conservatory of Music as a voice consultant, where she also teaches voice pedagogy and wellness courses. She completed a BFA in musical theater from Shenandoah Conservatory and her graduate and doctoral degrees from the University of Cincinnati. Original peer-reviewed research has been published in multiple journals, and she is a contributing author to several voice textbooks. Most recently, she coauthored *The Vocal Athlete* textbook and workbook with Marci Rosenberg. Her patients and private students currently can be found on radio, television, film, cruise ships, Broadway, Off-Broadway, national tours, commercial music tours, and opera stages around the world.

Scott McCoy is a noted author, singer, conductor, and pianist with extensive performance experience in concert and opera. He is professor of voice and pedagogy, director of the Swank Voice Laboratory, and director of the interdisciplinary program in singing health at Ohio State

University. His voice science and pedagogy textbook, *Your Voice: An Inside View*, is used extensively by colleges and universities throughout the United States and abroad. McCoy is the associate editor of the *Journal of Singing* for voice pedagogy and is a past president of the National Association of Teachers of Singing (NATS). He also served NATS as vice president for workshops, program chair for the 2006 and 2008 national conferences, chair of the voice science advisory committee, and a master teacher for the intern program. Deeply committed to teacher education, McCoy is a founding faculty member in the NYSTA Professional Development Program (PDP), teaching classes in voice anatomy, physiology, acoustics, and voice analysis. He is a member of the distinguished American Academy of Teachers of Singing (AATS).

Amanda Wansa Morgan serves as assistant professor and coordinator of musical theatre at Kennesaw State University. At KSU, she teaches classes in music theater performance, voice, acting, and music theater history and literature. Morgan served on the faculty at the University of Mississippi for three years and also held the position of director of music education at Charleston Stage, serving as music director, director, sound designer, dialect coach, music arranger, and/or composer. Additionally, she has musically directed at the Alliance Theatre, Six Flags over Georgia, Atlanta Lyric Theatre, Actor's Express, Playhouse on the Square, Post Playhouse, and the Osceola Center for the Arts. As a composer, Morgan's original musicals have been produced at Orlando Shakespeare Theatre and Charleston Stage. She holds an MFA in acting from the University of Central Florida and undergraduate degrees in music and theater from Florida State University. She has also worked as a professional actor throughout the Southeast since 2001. Additionally, Morgan holds a Certificate of Figure Proficiency from Estill Voice Systems. She is an active member of the Musical Theatre Educators Alliance (MTEA), Southeastern Theatre Conference (SETC), National Association of Teachers of Singing (NATS), Dramatist's Guild, and ASCAP.